CAMBRIDGE URBAN AND ARCHITECTURAL STUDIES

5   THE EVOLUTION OF DESIGNS
Biological analogy in architecture and the applied arts

# CAMBRIDGE URBAN AND ARCHITECTURAL STUDIES

GENERAL EDITORS:

LESLIE MARTIN
*Emeritus Professor of Architecture, University of Cambridge*
LIONEL MARCH
*Professor of Design, The Open University*

VOLUMES IN THIS SERIES:

# The evolution of designs

Biological analogy in architecture and the applied arts

## PHILIP STEADMAN

Lecturer in Design
The Open University

CAMBRIDGE UNIVERSITY PRESS

CAMBRIDGE
LONDON · NEW YORK · MELBOURNE

Published by the Syndics of the Cambridge University Press
The Pitt Building, Trumpington Street, Cambridge CB2 1RP
Bentley House, 200 Euston Road, London NW1 2DB
32 East 57th Street, New York, NY 10022, U.S.A.
296 Beaconsfield Parade, Middle Park, Melbourne 3206, Australia

First published 1979

Photoset and printed in Malta
by Interprint Limited

*Library of Congress Cataloguing in Publication Data*
Steadman, Philip, 1942—
The evolution of designs.
(Cambridge urban and architectural studies; 5)
Includes bibliographical references and index.
1. Architecture —Philosophy. 2. Architectural
design. 3. Nature (Aesthetics). I. Title.
II. Series.
NA2500.S74    720'.1    78-18255
ISBN  0  521  22302  4

The most expert Artists among the Ancients ... were of [the] Opinion that an Edifice was like an Animal, so that in the Formation of it we ought to imitate Nature.

L. B. Alberti, Ten Books on Architecture,<br>trans. J. Leoni (London, 1955), book 9, p. 194.

# CONTENTS

# ILLUSTRATIONS

# ACKNOWLEDGEMENTS

The explorations involved in this study have taken me into areas which I am, formally speaking, quite unqualified to enter: into art history, archaeology, anthropology, the history of science, biology, philosophy and cybernetics. I am painfully aware of the dangers of 'a little knowledge' in any of these subjects; and particularly that the drawing of analogies between one subject and another is a potentially even more dangerous exercise. For these reasons the customary expressions of thanks to colleagues and friends who have given me help are all the more deeply felt; and the equally customary dissociation of their names from responsibility for any of the opinions advanced here are probably all the more necessary.

In particular I am grateful to Nick Bullock for help with German architectural theory, and with translation; and to Tony Vidler for his ideas on the theory of type-forms. Nick Humphrey made some valuable suggestions on psychological and biological points. Carrie Humphrey directed me to some of the anthropological literature. Barrie Wilson presented me with a copy of the Rev. J. G. Wood's *Nature's Teachings*. With Bill Hillier and Adrian Leaman I have discussed several topics, but have found especially valuable their ideas relating to Karl Popper's 'World Three' of objective knowledge and its implications for architectural and design theory, as touched on below.

Earlier versions of parts of the argument of the book were incorporated into a thesis submitted to the Faculty of Architecture and Fine Arts at Cambridge — a thesis which has undergone many vicissitudes, and whose history must be about the most tortuous of any ever presented anywhere. I received the most helpful criticisms and comments along that long route from three men distinguished in very different fields and all now dead: Bill Howell, Lancelot Law Whyte and David Clarke. I also received help from Robin Middleton, who provided several items of information about French architectural history; and from Joseph Rykwert. Finally I have profited most from many conversations over the years, both on the subject of this book and about design theory in general, with Lionel March.

The manuscript was typed by Barbara Jones.

# 1

# Introduction

When I was no more than a boy and beginning to show some interest in living creatures I can remember being sternly warned by my elders to beware of the dangers of analogies. It was said in the same tone one might tell someone not to eat a certain kind of mushroom.[1]
J. T. Bonner

Underlying [the doctrines of the modern movement in architecture] was an implied belief in biotechnical determinism. And it is from this theory that the current belief in the supreme importance of scientific methods of analysis and classification is derived. . . . Form was merely the result of a logical process by which the operational needs and the operational techniques were brought together. Ultimately these would fuse in a kind of biological extension of life, and function and technology would become totally transparent. . . . The relation of this notion to Spencerian evolutionary theory is very striking.[2]
A. Colquoun

In this work I have tried to set out and subject to critical analysis the many analogies which have been made, by a great variety of writers, between biology and the applied arts, in particular architecture. My purpose in doing this is twofold: it is to show what I believe to be useful and valuable in such analogies, and to show what I believe to be dangerous and pernicious. Thus the work is written with a theoretical and polemical purpose first of all — although some small contributions are offered to the history of ideas and to art history along the way.

I have come to the study through an interest in the theory of design, especially architectural design, and a concern with what contribution, if any, systematic or scientific research can make to design. In the last twenty years or so there has been increasing activity in design research, 'environmental studies' ('environment' in the sense of 'built environment') and research in architecture — this last in its turn coming out of a somewhat longer tradition of the study of engineering and materials problems, in what has conventionally been distinguished as 'building science'.

Such research has been enormously wide in its scope, and varied in its methods and aims. It is nevertheless possible to see many of the (often undeclared) theoretical premises of these studies as having their origin in the ideological dogmas of the 'modern movement' in architecture, or perhaps to trace them further back, to the artistic philosophies of the nineteenth century. I will argue later that a great misconception in design research, in particular in the so-called 'design methods movement' and in recent attempts to employ the computer in design, has been the prevalent notion that *to apply scientific or rational thinking in design must in some sense involve making the design process itself 'scientific'.* I regard this idea not only as non-sensical, but ultimately highly dangerous.

On the other hand I believe most strongly — and would emphasise, while there is now such a mood of irrationalism and anti-scientific prejudice abroad in the design professions and in the architectural press — that this does not mean that rational thought applied in research to the problems of design and architecture can make no contribution to improving either design processes or their final results. Quite the opposite: there is today a great need, perhaps greater than ever before, for some hard thinking about the fundamental questions of design. And in particular, as it will be argued here, these questions can be illuminated not by any attempt to make the process of designing 'scientific', but rather by subjecting the *products* of design — material artefacts, especially buildings — to scientific study.

Such a programme of empirical investigation and theoretical analysis would bring the material products of architecture and the applied arts within the scope of what Herbert Simon has termed 'the sciences of the artificial' — sciences devoted to the study of all kinds of man-made objects and structures, material or otherwise.[3] Such a science of material, utilitarian artefacts is, of course, well-established, inasmuch as it already forms part of archaeology (and the present study will touch on the history of archaeological theory, focussing on the applications of biological analogy in that subject). The tradition of 'building science' previously mentioned also constitutes as it stands an 'artificial science' devoted to the study of architecture. But the subject matter of building science has until recently been made up from separate topics in the study of building materials, building elements, engineering structure, and the environmental behaviour of enclosures in terms of heat, light and sound. There is the opportunity, in my view, to extend — or perhaps better, to integrate — the fields of interest of building science so as to cover *some* of those features of building design which are more usually regarded as 'architectural': the geometrical organisation of their parts and structures, the topological relations of rooms one to another, the structure of circulation routes, and so on. The programme and promise of such an architectural science will be treated at greater length below.

Meanwhile, the whole conception of devoting buildings and other utilitarian artefacts — tools, domestic implements and the like — to scientific analysis raises the vexed question of how far such a project might feasibly and desirably extend. That is to say, given that such artefacts both serve practical everyday purposes, and may at the same time be works of art in a more elevated sense, how is the demarcation to be drawn between what is amenable to scientific treatment and what is in the realm of cultural, aesthetic and moral factors and values?

The ambition of the 'design methods movement' and of certain extreme figures in the modern movement in architecture was, in aiming to comprehend the entire process of design within a supposedly scientific methodology, to claim in effect the *complete* range of considerations or factors in design for scientific treatment. By contrast, the subject matter of an 'architectural science' as advanced here is conceived as covering only a restricted range of factors, principally those which relate to buildings as physical, three-dimensional, space-enclosing objects. It is possible, though more contentious, that some of the social functions of architecture in accommodating patterns of activity might be also brought within its scope.

The way in which such studies are applicable and useful to the design of new buildings is in providing increased knowledge and greater understanding of the particular aspects of building geometry or behaviour in question. Such knowledge would serve to *inform* the designer, by adding to the wider and more general body of experience and knowledge with which he is equipped by his education and by his professional life. It would, perhaps, contribute more to *critical assessment* of designs once produced than to stimulation of hypothesis and invention — though there are possibilities here, too. The knowledge could be built up in a piecemeal and gradual fashion, as in present-day building science, without any necessity of being immediately all-inclusive or complete.

However, the question of demarcation — if this is the correct term — remains. There is a parallel concern in anthropological theory, some reference to which will be helpful in this context, with the distinction between the study of what features of human society, institutions and artefacts can be regarded as utilitarian and practical, and what features are to be seen as cultural or symbolic. The reason that the word 'demarcation' is possibly not the right one is that the generally held modern anthropological view is not of a simple two-part division into 'practical' and 'cultural', but rather of culture being *overlaid* onto the practical functions of life, transforming them and giving them meaning.

The problem is more complicated yet, however. When we are talking of *design*, it is not simply a matter of distinguishing, as in anthropology, between the scientific study of what is to be explained by reference to practical or 'biological' considerations, and the scientific study or historical description of what is to be attributed to cultural factors. We make a conceptual distinction, certainly, between the activity of an architectural or an artificial *science*, on the one hand, and the activity of architectural, industrial or craft *design* on the other. But clearly, in the end, the practical interest of the scientific activity is in the *application* of its findings to the design activity. Thus the issue is raised of the further distinction between the objective and analytical character of science, and the value-laden, subjective and synthetic character of design. There follows yet another question; which features of the behaviour of buildings or material artefacts are the subject in principle of scientific *predictions*, and which are not?

These points must await the fuller discussion of later chapters. To return to the main purpose: in what follows I have tried to trace, as mentioned, the origin of certain biological ideas which have been influential in the design theory of the modern movement and subsequently in the 'design methods movement'. The immediate question which arises is 'Why *biological* ideas?'. What is the particular relevance of examining the invocation of specifically biological analogies to these more general questions of the role of science in design?

I shall hope to answer this in some detail, but in summary there are characteristics of designed objects such as buildings, and characteristics of the ways designs are produced, viewed both at an individual and at a cultural level, which lend themselves peculiarly well to description and communication via biological metaphor. The ideas of 'wholeness', 'coherence', 'correlation' and 'integration', used to express the organised relationship between the parts of the biological organism, can be applied to describe similar qualities in the well-designed artefact. The adaptation of the organism to its environment, its fitness, can be compared to the harmonious relation of a building to its surroundings, and, more abstractly, to the appropriateness of any designed object for the various purposes for which it is intended. Perhaps most significantly it is biology, of all sciences, which first confronted the central problem of teleology, of *design* in nature; and it is very natural that of all sciences it should for this reason attract the special interest of designers.

A second point is that as a matter of historical fact, it *has* been biology out of all the sciences to which architectural and design theorists have most frequently turned. Indeed it is surprising, in view of the ubiquity of biological references and ideas in the writings of the architectural theorists of the last hundred years, that no work of book length has so far been devoted to the history and theory of biological analogy. The history is certainly a fragmented one, leading into many remote corners and backwaters of the architectural literature. Nevertheless analogy with biology is a constant and recurring theme – to be found most prominently in Wright, Sullivan and Le Corbusier, but very widely elsewhere too, as I will demonstrate.

The only historical coverage of any general kind which I have been able to discover is Peter Collins's article on 'Biological Analogy',[4] the main substance of which was subsequently included as a chapter in his book *Changing Ideals in Modern Architecture 1750–1950*.[5] I have made repeated use of Professor Collins's paper, as my references will show. Three of the main themes which he develops — the relationship of organisms to their environment, Cuvier's principle of the correlation of organs, and the relationship of form to function — are central to the discussion here. But despite the broad coverage of the different aspects which Collins provides, he seems to have no particular theoretical stance of his own, and his treatment is disjointed. Different authors and instances are held out more for their curiosity value, one senses, than because Collins is committed — on the one side or the other — on the question of the validity or continuing usefulness of such analogies.

While the history of the subject is certainly itself fragmented — further complicated by the fact that the time taken for biological thinking to make an impact on architectural or design theory is often as much as fifty years, or more — the fact is, I believe, that if all the various separate analogies are once set together, then the picture as a whole is a relatively coherent one.

With the analogies laid out in organised form, it is possible to proceed to the critical task of sorting out what is useful and illuminating from what is trivial, what is misleading, and what is downright dangerous. I believe — and it is for this reason I have thought it of value to reconstruct their history — that some of these biological ideas have been the root cause of certain theoretical shortcomings in recent design theory, and that in particular they have contributed significantly to the idea described above that architectural design could be made a wholly scientific procedure.

There *is* one central fallacy, I believe, at the heart of most of the historical analogies made between architecture and biology — of which Geoffrey Scott's 'Biological Fallacy' is just one aspect — and which arises principally out of an improper equation of the Darwinian mechanisms of organic evolution with the 'Lamarckian' characteristics of the transmission of culture and the inheritance of material property. Alan Colquoun is one of the few architectural commentators to relate the 'biotechnical determinism' of the modern movement explicitly to nineteenth-century cultural evolutionism and in particular to the philosophy of Herbert Spencer — as the quotation at the head of this chapter indicates. A demonstration of the nature of this biological fallacy goes a long way to explain other related failings in the philosophy of the modern movement in architecture, as Colquoun emphasises. I have tried to amplify some of these points here, particularly in relation to Christopher Alexander's work, which is I suggest based largely on an extended biological analogy coming through cybernetics and the theories of W. Ross Ashby.

I most definitely do not think, however, that the fact of certain kinds of biological analogy made in the past being fallacious ones has meant that all such analogies between biology and architecture are useless or entirely misleading and should be immediately abandoned. The fact that the biological theme is such a constant one in past architectural theory in itself suggests its importance. And, so long as the central fallacy which has confused previous theory is avoided, some of the principal concepts of modern biological philosophy — of evolution, of morphology, of classification, of the behaviour of dynamic systems, of the transmission of information through hereditary processes — all these have, at the abstract, formal level, a great deal to offer those infant sciences which are devoted to the study of man-made objects and their design.

There are techniques or mathematical approaches which several authors have already applied to the study of architectural phenomena — numerical classification methods, or various branches of systems theory, for example — which have ultimately biological origins. An architectural science conceived of as a 'science of the artificial' could, in short, borrow a lot of conceptual and methodological apparatus from biology.

Of course there are other sciences which would contribute, perhaps more — both social sciences and physical sciences. And when all is said and done, the fact is that buildings, machines and implements are inert physical objects and not organisms; and the relevance of biological ideas to their study can only remain in the end of an analogical and metaphorical nature. In a mature science the use of intellectual props of this kind can be dispensed with. But at an early stage they have their value (if also their dangers).

There is some advantage to be gained here from the fact that other disciplines, in particular anthropology and archaeology, have gone through and emerged from periods of intense adherence to and subsequent revulsion from biological analogy, in the wild evolutionary enthusiasm of late-nineteenth-century thought and the counter-reaction which this brought in the early part of this century. This experience and the debate which it generated — and continues to generate — can perhaps help show the way to a newly developing architectural research, while keeping it from falling into old and demonstrated errors.

The trouble with biological analogy in architecture in the past is that much of it has been of a superficial picture-book sort: 'artistic' photos of the wonders of nature through a microscope, juxtaposed with buildings or the products of industrial design. But analogy at a deeper level can be a most fundamental source of understanding and of scientific insight, as many writers on that subject have pointed out. The conclusion of J. T. Bonner's essay on 'Analogies in Biology', from which the terrible warning at the beginning of this chapter is drawn, is that though analogies are certainly hazardous — they are the stock-in-trade of quacks and crackpots — at the same time, if made with sufficient care, watching always for where the analogy breaks down, they can be a most fertile source of new ideas and knowledge. At least some philosophers of science would argue that analogy is absolutely central not only to the psychological genesis of scientific theory, but to its continuing extension, development and intelligibility as well.

A word should be said about the detailed format of the exposition of biological analogies with architecture and artefacts which follows. This study combines a primary theoretical purpose with a certain amount of history, and hence the retailing of the ideas of particular historical individuals. This has posed the problem of whether to give the history first and then to draw out the theoretical points, or whether rather to present first the theoretical arguments, and illustrate these by reference to the works of individual writers. Since the principal intention is a theoretical one, I have chosen to do the latter. The penalty is paid, however, of a certain amount of chronological dislocation, and the discussion of the same authors or architects under a number of heads.

It is perhaps unnecessary to say this, but to avoid any possible misunderstanding (particularly in the art-historical fraternity), I would point out that by making reference to biological ideas in the writings of some theorist I do not intend to imply that such ideas provide the key to the whole of that individual's architectural or design philosophy. In many cases these references are merely incidental asides, illustrations, small parts of much larger arguments. (On the other hand there are several writers cited – Greenough, Sullivan, Alexander – for whom biological analogy is central and crucial.) In effect a unified theoretical overview of the range and interconnected structure of the variety of biological analogies, or aspects of a single large analogy, is assembled eclectically for the present purposes out of the ideas of a number of theorists; and could not be attributed as such to any single writer.

It is not suggested, either, that biological analogy and its pitfalls can be blamed for *all* the theoretical failures or misconceptions which are here exposed. There are other factors involved, to which some attention will be drawn as the argument proceeds. It *is*, however, suggested that metaphors from biology can be blamed for much of the trouble. All history must be selective, must have a point of view, must take a particular route through the phenomena and ideas of which it treats; and I have chosen here to take the biological route.

Finally, attention should be drawn to the use, in the subtitle of this book, of the specific phrase 'biological analogy'. This is chosen deliberately in preference to the term 'organic analogy', which is older, has wider connotations, and is a subject to which much critical and historical discussion has been devoted elsewhere, in the context of literature and the fine arts perhaps more than in architecture and the applied arts. The interest here is in recent design theory, and in what biological science can offer to an 'architectural science'. Therefore the historical treatment goes back in the main only to the beginnings of biology as a scientific subject around the start of the nineteenth century.

Despite the fact that the 'organic analogy' involves a much looser metaphorical comparison of works of art with the phenomena of nature, and is concerned with aesthetic qualities rather than with strictly scientific parallels, there is clearly a large area of overlap between what has been traditionally denoted by the two terms. The next chapter accordingly begins with a brief account of some of the ideas of 'organic analogy' in architecture, of their historical origins, and of their continuity with the more properly biological aspects of analogy to be developed later.

# 2
# The organic analogy

## The relation of the parts to the whole in the organism and in the work of art

Critics and philosophers since ancient Greece have looked to natural organisms as offering perfect models of that harmonious balance and proportion between the parts of a design which is synonymous with the classical ideal of beauty. The qualities of wholeness, of integrity, of a unity in structure such that the parts all contribute to the effect or purpose of the whole, and no part may be removed without some damage to the whole — these are central concepts in the aesthetics and in the natural history of Aristotle, and are characteristics in the Aristotelian view both of living beings and of the best works of art. J. A. Stewart summarises Aristotle's view of the analogy in this way:

> Living organisms, and works of art, are schemata, definite after their kinds, which Nature and Man respectively form by qualifying matter. The quantity of matter used in any case is determined by the form subserved; the size of a particular organ, or part, is determined by its form, which again is determined by the form (limiting the size) of the whole organism, or work. Thus animals and plants grow to sizes determined by their particular structures, habitats, and conditions of life, and each separate organ observes the proportion of the whole to which it belongs. The painter or sculptor considers the symmetry of the whole composition in every detail of his work.[1]

The analogy has two distinct kinds of interpretation, the one to do with visual appearance or composition, the other functional — although the two are interrelated. In the first case it is the 'organic' wholeness of the work of art — in which a balanced and proportional relation of the parts to the whole and of the whole to its parts is achieved — which is seen to be the source of beauty in that work. This wholeness or coherence provides the basis for the same kind of satisfaction as is derived from the contemplation of the beauties of nature; the two sources of aesthetic pleasure are one.

Both Plato, in the *Phaedrus*, and Aristotle, in the *Poetics*, require that the literary work, as for example the tragedy, have this 'organic' form. It should be not just a mere aggregation of parts, from which some might be omitted or to which others could be added, but well-shaped overall, with a clear beginning, middle and end. The same organic principle in poetic composition and critical analysis is advocated in the early nineteenth century by the German Romantics, by Goethe, Schlegel and Schelling — whose influence we can follow on the American architects of the end of the century — and most prominently by Coleridge, as in his critical writings on Shakespeare, where the idea of organic form is seen not so much in terms of static balance, but more as something which grows and develops out of the material. The form is integral or 'innate' to the work, rather than being preconceived and 'impressed' onto it.[2]

## Functional beauty in art and nature

The second interpretation of the organic analogy, the functional view, is in some ways a development from or further explanation of the first. Here the analogy comes to form one part of the more general aesthetics of *functionalism*, the equation of the beautiful with the useful or with the expression of usefulness, the idea that an artefact which is well-designed and adapted for its purpose will be seen to be beautiful through a recognition of this fitness for use. Again the idea is a very ancient one, and can be traced back to Aristotle, for whom our perception of the beauty of animals arises through a rational appreciation of the structure of their parts and the functions of their organs. In Aristotle's natural history not only is each limb or separate structure seen as serving some definite purpose, some particular function; but each of these functions of the parts is subservient to, contributes to, the greater purpose of the whole.

The part only has a functional meaning in relation to the whole: the legs serve the purpose of support and locomotion for the body, and without the body they, and it, are useless. The heart has 'sinews' which spread throughout the body and transmit motion to its parts. The whole body relies for its continued functioning and existence on each and all of the various organs working together. Aristotle's statement of his functional approach to anatomical investigation is expressed, in *The Parts of Animals*, thus:

> Now, as each of the parts of the body, like every other instrument, is for the sake of some purpose, viz., some action, it is evident that the body as a whole must exist for the sake of sawing and not sawing for the sake of the saw, because sawing is the using of the instrument, so in some way the body exists for the sake of the soul, and the parts of the body for the sake of those functions to which they are naturally adapted.[3]

For functionalist aesthetics, then, it is this necessary functional role of every limb and organ in the working of the whole body which is the reason for our deriving aesthetic pleasure from the forms of creatures and plants (and, as a corollary, for our horror at bodily deformity).[4] It is not the contribution of the parts to the surface appearance of the whole in some kind of balanced visual arrangement which is as important as our recognition, through their appearance, of their functional significance – even though this be only a vague apprehension of their purposes, rather than any complete scientific biological understanding. And so our pleasure or satisfaction has more the character of intellectual appreciation of an end or meaning than of simple sensual impression.

Since it is the integration of the various functioning parts into a balanced and organised *functional* whole which is held to be the source of beauty, it follows that in the artistic context this would be most particularly evident in the applied arts, the design of tools and useful objects, and in architecture, where each work has clear, ordinary, practical functions as well as any symbolic, decorative or expressive aspects over and above this everyday usefulness.

The distinction was made, by Francis Hutcheson and by Lord Kames in the eighteenth century, between free or intrinsic beauty, which derived from 'uniformity amidst variety' and was unconnected with function, and dependent or relative beauty, which was the kind of functional beauty arising from adaptation to use, the concept of which we are examining here.[5] Hutcheson looked more to the beauty of machines – their ingenuity, economy and efficiency – than he did to natural examples. The same interest in machine design as a model for the work of art can be found among Hutcheson's contemporaries, Berkeley and Hume, turning as they did to the examples provided by the beginnings of the English Industrial Revolution.

The mechanical theme in functionalism was taken up extensively amongst architectural and design theorists in the nineteenth century. It is perhaps the most frequent leitmotif of the theoretical writings of the modern movement also: an enthusiastic appreciation of the products of the new engineering, in which 'rationalists' and functionalists saw the results of adherence to the same principles of economy and simple directness of adaptation to practical purposes which they had been praising in the designs of nature.

Thus we find two parallel traditions of analogy in functionalist aesthetics – and later in the aesthetic philosophies of the modern movement – looking in one direction to the works of nature, and in the other to the works of mechanical and civil engineering. Peter Collins has distinguished these as the 'biological analogy' and the 'mechanical analogy';[6] and his terms were perhaps suggested in turn by Geoffrey Scott's 'Biological and Mechanical Fallacies'.[7] It would be neither possible nor appropriate to our subject to try to cover here the complex history of the 'machine aesthetic' – which would account, in any case, for much of the history of modern architectural theory. It is worth noting, however, in relation to the biological analogy in architecture and design in the nineteenth century, that a great part of contemporary biology itself took the view that the natural organism also might be considered as a mechanism, albeit a highly complicated and elaborate one.

Philosophically the setting of animal and human physiology within a wholly mechanical world view can be credited to Descartes.[8] By denying physical extension to the human soul, and withdrawing it from the body (whatever problems this later created in explaining the relation between the two entities), Descartes opened the way for a theory of the workings of organs and bodily systems according to purely mechanical principles. For Descartes himself the machine most directly comparable to the animal body was the church organ. He greatly admired the demonstration by Harvey of the hydraulic pump-and-valve character of the circulation system of the blood. His own theory of the nervous control of muscular movements imagined the nerves operating in a similar way, as hollow tubes along which flowed a 'subtle fluid' — the 'animal spirits' — to operate valves actuating the muscles at their extremities.

By the end of the seventeenth century a number of 'iatromechanical' systems had been proposed for the explanation of physiological phenomena, in particular muscular movement; as for instance that of Borelli.[9] In the early eighteenth century, the mechanical models most frequently invoked were the celebrated animal automata of Vaucanson — his flute-player and duck — which were indubitably highly ingenious, though can hardly be said to have simulated organic function in anything but superficial movement and appearance.

The most polemical statement of the mechanical viewpoint, taking Descartes's line of argument to its logical conclusion, was La Mettrie's *L'Homme Machine* of 1748.[10] (*His* model for the brain was not a pipe organ, but a harpsichord.) It should be understood, however, that La Mettrie was not concerned particularly to defend a metaphysical position, but rather to propose a scientific programme and a heuristic method for physiology and psychology.[11] To study the body and brain *as if* they were machines was the intellectual strategy which offered the greatest promise of results; the machine was a model or analogy which would guide investigation. Both La Mettrie's and *a fortiori* Descartes's calls for a mechanical biology were, however, wholly premature. Most seriously, they conspicuously lacked any account of chemical processes going on in the body. It required the basic developments in chemistry of the eighteenth century before any approach at all could be made to the phenomena, say, of respiration or of digestion.[12]

The work of the great French anatomist Georges Cuvier in the early 1800s may be taken as representative of the more general way in which, with the rise of a properly scientific biology, the mechanical philosophy was carried into laboratory and investigative technique. C. C. Gillispie has described Cuvier's approach to the study of the animal body as like that of an engineering student approaching some machine to be analysed. 'He teaches about it as a master-sergeant teaches some recruit the functioning and nomenclature of the rifle.'[13] Again Henri Milne-Edwards, a disciple of Cuvier, said that he had tried 'to grasp the manner in which organic forms might have been invented by comparing and studying living things as if they were machines created by the industry of man'.[14]

Von Bertalanffy has coined the term 'machine-theoretical' to describe this general line of biological thinking.[15] His examples of the analogy of bodies with mechanisms include Weismann's theory of embryonic development, advanced in the 1890s, which imagined the organism in embryo as composed of a number of 'developmental machines', *anlagen* or 'determinants', each of which would develop into a fully grown organ or part of the body in the adult; and the classic nineteenth-century neurology of centres and reflexes, which tried to resolve the nervous system into 'a sum of apparatuses for definite functions, and similarly animal behaviour into separable processes occurring in those structures'.[16] As von Bertalanffy says, according to this idea the organism was seen somewhat like a robot or coin-in-the-slot machine, which responded to stimuli from the outside environment in a quite automatic, deterministic way.

In the twentieth century the animated dolls of Vaucanson have their more serious counterparts in the 'self-regulating' and adaptive automata built by such exponents of biological cybernetics as Grey Walter and W. Ross Ashby;[17] while the analogy of human and animal intelligence with the operation of computers has informed many areas of modern psychology.

It is not unexpected that for architects and structural or civil engineers, because they deal with statical problems and the distribution of weight and strength, the area of biology of most direct interest should be anatomy. And of all biological works it is perhaps D'Arcy Thompson's classic essay *On Growth and Form* which has most directly stimulated architects — well-thumbed copies are still to be found in most architecture school libraries.[18] We shall come shortly to the analogies which have been drawn *from* anatomy and applied *to* building construction. With D'Arcy Thompson the process is the other way about. He makes a whole series of comparisons of mechanical structures with plant stems and with animal skeletons; he draws parallels between, for example, the structure of bones and their artificial man-made counterparts in girders and columns; he shows how the hollow bones of the vulture's wings are stiffened 'after the manner of a Warren's truss', and how the human femur matches the design of heavy cranes (figure 1).[19]

We shall find that the Forth Bridge is one of the great works of Victorian engineering to which architects point as exemplifying the functional beauty which comes from the application of rational, mechanical design principles. The same bridge is taken by D'Arcy Thompson as an illustration of several points in *Growth and Form*, notably in discussion of plant stems and bones.

1    Metacarpal bone from vulture's wing; stiffened after the manner of a Warren's truss.

The anatomist may learn many a lesson from the Forth Bridge, he says[20] (so turning the design theorist's organic analogy neatly around). The tubes from which the bridge is built correspond even in detail to the structure of cylindrical plant stalks, and their strengthening rings to the joints in the bamboo stem, one of the strongest of vegetable structures. Again, the quadruped skeleton, such as that of the horse or ox, may for the purposes of mechanical analysis be considered as a kind of double cantilever system, somewhat like the Forth Bridge — where the legs correspond to the bridge's piers, and the backbone, neck and tail are cantilevered out from these supports (figure 2).[21]*

These subjects will be taken up again in later chapters: both the particular analogy of anatomical structures with engineering structures, and the more general and central issue of whether organisms *can* legitimately be treated, for the purposes of scientific study, as machines, or whether on the contrary the special properties of life in some sense elude the engineering viewpoint — that is, the long-lasting opposition of 'vitalism' and 'mechanism'. This controversy takes on great importance in the evolutionary battles raging from the 1860s onwards.

Meanwhile, we return to the theoretical question of the dual aspect of functionalist aesthetics, involved as it is with overlapping metaphors or analogies between organism, machine, and building or work of art, which can perhaps be simplified by means of the scheme set out in figure 3. The diagram illustrates the organic analogy — the organism as a model for design — and the mechanical analogy — the machine as a model for the work of art. At the same time we have a mechanistic biology — the organism as machine — which would cover the tradition of Descartes and La Mettrie. And

---

*R. J. Mainstone, however, has pointed to the mild structural deceit in the design of the bridge, in the way in which the outer span of each end cantilever has to be tied down to large quantities of ballast concealed in the piers of the approach, in order to prevent the cantilever tipping when loaded, for example, with a train on the opposite side of the point of support. *Developments in Structural Form* (London, 1975), p. 248.

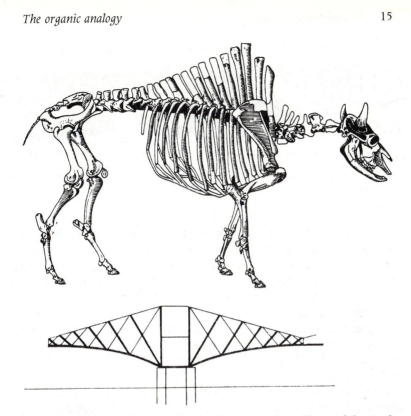

2   Skeleton of fossil bison (above) and two-armed cantilever of the Forth
Bridge (below).

to complete the symmetry of this plan we can find examples of comparisons
made the other way around — the machine as organism — though this is
perhaps more common now in the days of servomechanisms and electronic
brains than it was in the nineteenth century. Then the analogy was made
with reference to boats, carriages or musical instruments; and particularly in
the application of evolutionary theory in ethnology to the progressive development of primitive tools and artefacts (as we shall see in later chapters).

It should be remarked that there is frequently a moral attitude underlying the
functionalist view as a whole. No part of the work should be dispensable,
unnecessary to the general aim. Every part should have a meaning, it should
'play its part'. Thus an approval of economy of means, a kind of artistic
thriftiness, is implied. Since there is an intellectual and aesthetic satisfaction
in knowing how the work is made, how it is constructed, how it functions
and what it is for, it is important that there should be no deception.
   Indeed functionalism in architecture in the modern movement has
made a virtue out of the positive emphasis of the means of construction, of

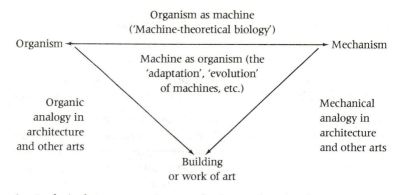

Organism as machine
('Machine-theoretical biology')

Organism ←———————————————————————→ Mechanism

Machine as organism (the
'adaptation', 'evolution'
of machines, etc.)

Organic
analogy in
architecture
and other arts

Mechanical
analogy in
architecture
and other arts

Building
or work of art

3   Analogies between organisms, mechanisms and works of art.

the material, and of the purpose of each part. The structural functions of the various supporting members of the building are made clear, they are laid bare; and the various internal spaces are allowed to protrude their characteristic shapes through to the outside form, they are 'ex-pressed' — as though the organs of the body could be seen bulging through the skin. It is not enough that each part should have a definite function: it must be seen to have a function, and that function should be made evident. Edward de Zurko in his history of functionalism refers to these ideas in terms of a 'moral or ethical analogy' — although it is difficult to see why the word 'analogy' is warranted — and traces them back, amongst other roots, to the ideal of *claritas pulchri* in Thomist aesthetics, a concept with complex connotations but amongst which is that of clarity of organisation and expression.[22]

As a final point about functionalist aesthetics, we may note that despite the emphasis on utility and practical reason in design, and despite the pairing of the analogy with organisms and the analogy with machines, there is no exclusive historical correlation of functionalism in architecture with a materialistic and overly technological modernism.

For the mid-nineteenth-century sculptor and writer Horatio Greenough, the lessons of the organic and mechanical analogies were to supply correctives to the crass commercial architecture of his time. For Louis Sullivan, the leading prophet of American architectural functionalism, the same was true — nor did he believe that ornament was inimical to a functional architecture, but rather that it could articulate structure and develop the symbolic expression of function. In English architectural thought of the nineteenth century, the moral functionalism of Pugin is associated with a backward-looking historical reverence for the 'true principles' of Gothic building and a horror of the depredations of industrialism. For many of the architects of the English Arts and Crafts movement — Lethaby, Baillie Scott — and for several figures generally regarded as modernists — Loos, Breuer — functional principles were

exemplified in vernacular building and in the unselfconsciousness and directness of traditional construction.

## Geometrical systems of proportion, derived from nature and applied in art

We now leave functionalism for the moment and return, if briefly, to the first
and more strictly compositional aspect of the organic analogy, the analogy
made in terms of balanced and proportioned appearance. Strictly speaking
this is something of a sidetrack from the main argument, and a dead end
at that; but the topic is so much a part of what has generally been thought of
as biological analogy in architecture and design that some mention could
hardly be omitted. I refer to the subject of geometrical methods for deriving
the proportions of the work of art. Here the analogy of artwork with organism
in the compositional aspect found its expression in the attempted codification
in numerical and geometrical systems of mathematical laws of harmony.
These laws were held to apply not just to pictorial, architectural or musical
composition, but were common also to the realm of natural creation, and
derived from the underlying order of the entire cosmos.

Rudolf Wittkower has written of the influence of this neo-Pythagorean
and neo-Platonic tradition of ideas in Renaissance systems of architectural
proportion.[23] Here the parallel was drawn especially between the harmonic
interrelationship of the parts of the human body and the proportional
harmony which ought to be achieved in architectural design. The idea is to
be found first in Vitruvius, and is taken over by several of the Renaissance
commentators.

The analogies made are more or less naive. At one level, it is urged that
the layout of the building match the body part for part. Vasari, for example, in
his recommendations for the design of an ideal palace, compares the facade
with the face, the central door with the mouth, the symmetrically placed
windows with eyes, the courtyard with the body, staircases with legs and
arms.[24] More abstractly, the general bilateral symmetry of the body is to be
matched in an equivalent mirror symmetry of the parts of the building about
its central axis, without any such one-to-one correspondence of parts. And
more generally still, the typical proportional ratios to be detected in the
measurements of the human figure and limbs are to be employed for sizing
the elements of the building, without any sense at all of the plan or facade
corresponding to the body in general disposition.

Typically these aims were expressed symbolically in diagrams in which
the human figure — which had such significance as the paradigm of the ideal
relationship of the parts to the whole in Renaissance art — might be inscribed
in the plan of a church (figure 4).[25] As Wittkower emphasises, this is not
evidence of an anthropocentric world view. Since man was made in the

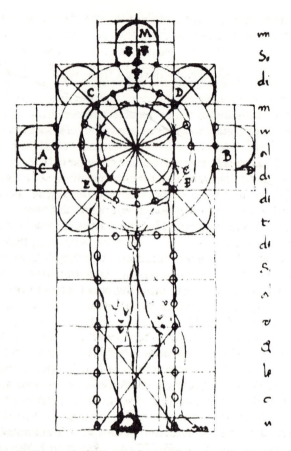

4    Francesco di Giorgio, human figure inscribed in church plan.

image of God, so it was believed the proportions exemplified in the human form would reflect a divine and cosmic order.

The supposed affinity between the beauty of organic, natural forms and artistic, artificial forms, dependent on their sharing certain fundamental mathematical (particularly geometrical) principles of design, persisted as an idea with diminishing support through the seventeenth and eighteenth centuries. The tradition was preserved in progressively debased and garbled form, in the inherited secret wisdom of the masons; while in aesthetics and criticism there was decreased enthusiasm for the particular detailed analogy between visual and musical harmony which the Renaissance theorists, following Pythagoras, had made — and subsequently for any mathematical basis for proportion at all.[26]

In the middle nineteenth century, however, with the detailed archaeological study of the monuments of antiquity and the growth of art-historical scholarship, an interest was revived in systems of classical proportion as a key to both man-made and natural design. As just one example out of several possibilities, we might take the work of D. R. Hay, who revived Pythagorean geometrical and proportional principles in his *The Science of Beauty, as Developed in Nature and Applied in Art.*[27] Hay was friendly with the zoologist and anatomist John Goodsir, professor of anatomy at Edinburgh, who was interested in aesthetics and an enthusiast for Goethe's writings on morphology.[28] They both belonged to a club devoted to the discussion of questions of natural and artistic form, set up in Edinburgh in 1851.

Meanwhile German scholars had rediscovered and were polishing up that 'gem' of ancient geometry, the golden section.[29] The original work of Zeising was very influential; as Herbert Read says, Zeising 'tried to prove that the Golden Section is the key to all morphology, both in nature and in art',[30] and he inspired others such as Moessel in Germany, and — through the psychological work of G. T. Fechner — Cook and Schooling in England.[31] Much of the evidence for the supposed importance of the golden number system in relation to natural form came from exact botanical observations of the arrangement of leaves and stems in plants, and of the patterns of petals in flowers — the subject of phyllotaxis.[32]

There is no question that mathematically a process of incremental growth by the addition of progressively larger units in series can result in types of pattern whose dimensions lie in Fibonacci series and, in the special case, in golden section proportions.[33] Regular growth processes of this kind result often in spiral forms, of which the patterns of seeds on the sunflower head, the pine-cone and the arrangement of segments around the skin of the pineapple are the most impressive and admired examples. The example from zoology which is most frequently offered in this connection is the spiral molluscan shell such as that of the snail (whose exact mathematical form was first appreciated by that distinguished geometer Sir Christopher Wren); while the helico-spiral shapes of many animal horns and tusks reveal the same growth principles. Much of the biological work in this area is brought together in D'Arcy Thompson's *On Growth and Form,*[34] which gives mathematical description to many of the geometrically more regular natural forms and gives straightforward scientific explanations of the processes of growth by which they are produced.

Unfortunately the discovery of the golden section and related logarithmic spiral patterns in natural form was invested with a wholly exaggerated significance by the later aesthetic commentators and the proportional theorists. One such was Sir Theodore Cook, who tackled the subject of *Spirals in Nature and Art*[35] in a book published in 1903, and went on to call his second work on the same topic *Curves of Life* (1914),[36] indicating by these titles his conviction that the spiral had profound significance as a universal natural principle of vitality and beauty. So we find him attempting, for example, golden section analyses of Botticelli's *Venus*.[37] It is hardly necessary to point out that analyses of this kind, either of paintings or of buildings, cannot be claimed to explain any simple growth principle either in the form of the human body depicted or in the architectural form; nor indeed the 'growth' of the pictorial or architectural composition under the artist's hand. It is only what D'Arcy Thompson calls dismissively a series of 'mystical conceptions' about the golden section which allow its overenthusiastic application in ways which in the end become quite meaningless.

Not only golden section patterns, logarithmic spirals and Fibonacci series were appropriated from their biological context by this school of writers on proportion. These authors also illustrated the radial or rotational symmetries of flower petals and of seed pods; and they were impressed by the symmetries of the extraordinarily elegant skeletons of the Radiolaria, minute sea organisms, thousands of types of which were discovered by Haeckel and depicted in a series of exquisite colour plates in his *Kunst-Formen der Natur*.[38] All these, as well as the symmetries of crystals, were adduced as evidence of a pervading geometric order in nature, an order which is 'Heaven's First Law' and if understood could be applied in art. Typical of this genre are such works as Samuel Colman's *Nature's Harmonic Unity*,[39] and, to a lesser degree, the writings of Jay Hambidge and Matila Ghyka.[40]

Hambidge makes a distinction of terminology between what he calls 'static' symmetry (the radial symmetry of certain crystal forms, flowers or Radiolaria) and the kind of symmetry found, say, in spiral phyllotaxis and the growth of shells, which he calls 'dynamic' or 'active'.[41] But the patterns of repeated rectangles of increasing size which his 'dynamic' systems of symmetry generate derive their (quite real) aesthetic significance simply from the repetition of similar shapes; and as applied in design, their connection with vitality, with the processes of growth in natural form extended over time, which the name 'dynamic' is meant to connote, is rather tenuous.

While their declared aim at a general level might have been quite admirable, the interpretation that these writers actually made of the geometrical principles which might be abstracted from nature and applied in design is mostly confused and superficial, and has numerological or almost astrological overtones. In some respects their enterprise is admittedly a reasonable one. It is certainly true that there are many examples to be found in plant structures and small sea creatures — even more so in crystal forms — of regular patterns of symmetrical organisation which might provide models for design. On the other hand these patterns arise out of the intrinsic geometrical constraints which operate on the close-packing of repeated spatial elements in two or three dimensions — constraints which would apply, evidently, in the formation of patterns of any kind, whether organic or inorganic, man-made or natural. Once the common underlying mathematical laws of symmetry have been formulated, then the specific analogy of artwork with organism becomes irrelevant, perhaps, and might better be dropped. (Of course a similar criticism can be made of other kinds of biological analogies with artefacts, the difference being that the laws of symmetry have been mathematically determined, whereas the underlying basis for analogy in other respects is possibly not so clear.)

One might remark here, parenthetically but for the sake of completeness, on one further aspect of biological inspiration for architecture and design — which can hardly be termed 'analogy' — which is the use of organic forms, those of vegetation in particular, as models for sculptured decoration on buildings and for architectural and graphical ornament. The employment of plant and animal designs in decoration is practically universal throughout the history of architecture and the applied arts, of course; but in the latter half of the nineteenth century there was special interest in plant form for the abstract ornamental features which it embodies, of symmetry, pattern and curved line. Foremost amongst the works of the period which attempted to codify such principles was Owen Jones's magnificent *Grammar of Ornament* of 1856.[42] Later came, amongst others, Christopher Dresser with his *Art of Decorative Design* and *Principles of Decorative Design*,[43] urging 'the young ornamentist to study the principles on which Nature works',[44] and containing lengthy discussions of plant adaptations and growth habits; also Lewis Day's *Nature in Ornament* (1892), from which connection may perhaps be made to Victor Horta and the artists of the Art Nouveau.[45] Finally mention should be made of Louis Sullivan's *System of Architectural Ornament* with its explicit source in seed and petal forms.[46]

But to return to proportional theory, difficulties arise here when the attempt is made to derive key dimensions, shapes or proportions for the building or work of art as a whole from the inspection of natural form. The implication is that a certain fixity or absolute character is to be found in the forms and sizes of plants and animals; but this fixity is attributed neither to the geometrical constraints of symmetry, nor to the adaptation of biological form to purpose and way of life, that is to functional explanations. Indeed there would be a certain basic contradiction between the idea on the one hand that organic forms are fixed and absolute, and the acknowledgement on the other of the plasticity of form by which the organism is adapted to circumstances. One does not find the proportional theorists following the example of such investigators of the functional origins of organic form as D'Arcy Thompson, in whose work shape, size and pattern are attributed to the operation of mechanical forces, geometrical constraints, principles of growth and the like.

When it comes to the analysis of existing works, as opposed to the act of composition, then there is a further failing in the work of the proportional theorists, which is no doubt to be attributed to their excessive enthusiasm in seeking to demonstrate the occurrence of the ratios and sizes which they have found in nature. This is that there are so many lines superimposed on the reproductions of paintings or the photographs of vases or buildings to which the methods are often applied, there are so many possible points of emphasis or significant features — whose exact position cannot be determined more closely than within a few per cent — that the proportional analyst is almost bound to find *some* places where the sought-for proportions occur; he is bound to score a hit somewhere. But this coincidence is of course nothing more than coincidence. It is a way of working which is quite opposite to the biological approach, where such significant dimensions of the organism as can be unambiguously identified are measured, with some specific mathematical pattern and associated functional explanation already in mind.

But if in this form the biological analogy between the natural organism and the work of art, interpreted narrowly in terms of geometrical systems of proportion, degenerated in the end into pedantic mysticism and mumbo-jumbo, this was by no means its only interpretation. The original metaphor, which had emphasised the *wholeness* of the artwork and the organism, the somehow necessary relation of all the parts in their contribution to the whole, could lead and did lead in quite other directions.

# 3

# The classificatory analogy: building types and natural species

Much of eighteenth-century natural history, leading up to and culminating in the great work of Buffon and Linnaeus, was devoted to the question of classification, or systematics. There were two different kinds of approach taken to this task, distinguished as *systems* — outstanding amongst which was the system of Linnaeus — and *methods*, or rather method, since there was essentially only one. In both cases it was imagined that a more or less perfect continuity existed between species, so that they might in principle all be laid out across a two-dimensional surface or table. Every space in this grid would ultimately be filled, or if there were gaps, these would signify the places of species which were not yet found, or alternatively which had disappeared in some historical catastrophe.

The layout of the table of classification differed with different authors. Most typically it took the form of an imagined 'ladder of creation' on the rungs of which all organisms could be placed in a graded progression from the simplest to the most complex, the lowest to the highest. This idea has a long history going back well before Buffon and Linnaeus; a history which has been extensively explored by Arthur Lovejoy in his classic monograph *The Great Chain of Being*.[1] The image found its most extreme expression in the French eighteenth-century naturalist Bonnet's *Echelle des Etres*,[2] which he extended to include inorganic 'beings' such as rocks and crystals at the bottom end, through plants and animals, right up to man at the summit.

Other writers saw the network of relations which linked the species in other forms, sometimes branching, sometimes even polyhedral in shape. Philip Ritterbush has traced the tree metaphor for the classification of organisms to the German naturalist Pallas, who first placed plants and animals on two separate branches.[3] By the beginning of the nineteenth century the tree scheme had become a commonplace. It is important to emphasise that both the linear series or ladder and the branching tree system were classificatory schemes only, and were not intended to signify any progress in the evolutionary sense. In so far as any temporal dimension was introduced, it was in the concept, as with Bonnet, that the whole ladder of species might move forwards or upwards together — like some great cosmic escalator — towards states of higher perfection. The whole taxonomic order was fixed from the start, and the species merely traversed in procession this predetermined route.

Both the *systems* and the *method* turned on the identification of visible elements or characters of the plant or animal, their number, size, shape and spatial configuration. Indeed it is no accident that greater attention was paid to the classification of plants than to that of animals, not just because plant specimens were more readily available and easier to handle, but because by contrast with animals their special structures were all on the exterior, and displayed to the eye.

The technique of classification was to determine the visible differences and similarities of form between species, and thus group them into families, and grade them into the continuous scale of the classificatory table. The *systems* worked by isolating just a few elements from the whole form of the plant, and using the variations and resemblances in these chosen elements for the basis of the analysis. Thus Linnaeus built his system on a characterisation of the organs of reproduction of the plant, their fruits and flowers. Other systems were possible using other elements. The *method* worked by taking the first species to be examined, and making a complete description of *all* features. The process was repeated with successive species, but marking only the differences from species already described, and not repeating any similarities. Thus whatever order the species might be examined in, the same overall distinctions and resemblances would in the end emerge.

For the purposes of analysing the analogy with contemporary architectural classification — the description and enumeration of types or 'species' of building — we should notice a number of general points. First, the methods of classification used in eighteenth-century natural history turned on visible and formal properties of plant or animal species; and although organs corresponding to certain biological functions might be singled out to provide the basis of a system, the principle of classification was nevertheless not at bottom a functional one.

Second, the idea that the classification would come to order *all* species into a continuous series, with minute gradations marking the differences of species at all points, carried with it a series of implications. It implied the possible existence of a transformational or combinatorial principle, whereby the classification might be extended, beyond the known species, either to indicate the positions of species still undiscovered or lost in the past, or else, even more exciting, to generate theoretical species of kinds unknown to nature.[4]

This transformation — again not to be confused with an evolution in time, since it is conceived of as effecting a movement across the theoretical space of classification of all species, not as constituting a historical process of change in a single species — might consist in a systematic permutation or combination of parts or elements. We can once more, as in so many areas of natural history, find this idea first formulated by Aristotle, who saw the variety of animal species as deriving from an exhaustive recombination of a limited number of different kinds of component organs: 'different kinds of mouths, and stomachs, and perceptive and locomotive organs. . . . When all the combinations are exhausted there will be as many sorts of animal as there are combinations of the necessary organs.'[5]

Alternatively, the demonstration of general and overall similarities between whole groups of species suggested the concept of animal or plant archetypes, theoretical plans, of which the actual cases to be found in nature were different transformations or variously distorted modifications.

It will be clear that the idea of recombination of organs in all possible permutations is really incompatible with the idea of the harmonious and coherent relation of all the parts to each other and to the whole of the organism — despite Aristotle's simultaneous adoption of both views. The consistent permutation of all conjunctions of organs would produce many monstrosities — like those comic or fabulous beasts made up from the head of one species, the body of another, and the legs of a third. For some eighteenth-century natural historians, such as Maupertuis, such monsters were necessary all the same, in order to complete the whole permutational plan — and had disappeared through their inability to survive.[6]

By comparison the idea of archetypes recognises a certain coherence in organic form, by means of a structure which is transformed, but never beyond a certain limit of distortion. The theory of archetypes was elaborated principally by the late-eighteenth- and early-nineteenth-century German school of transcendental zoology, or *Naturphilosophie*. This group, of which the best-known figure is Goethe — botanist as well as poet and man of letters — and which also included Meckel and Oken, had been impressed more by the underlying structural similarities between species than by their differences. If basic plans could be found for whole groups of species, might it not be possible to go further and find a single basic plan common to *all* creatures, or to all plants?

Goethe thought this; that behind the varied appearances of plants there might be discoverable an essential primordial plant-type, the *Urpflanze* as he called it, a kind of idealised model, of which the plants found in nature were different manifestations, and represented a variety of the possible realisations of this fundamental type. The idea had been forming in his mind for some years when Goethe left for Italy in 1786, and a visit to the botanical garden at Padua focussed his thoughts on the problem again. Later on in his journey, in Sicily, he wrote in his diary:

> Seeing so much new and burgeoning growth, I came back to my old notion and wondered whether I might not chance upon my archetypal plant.

There must be such a plant, after all. If all plants were not moulded on one pattern, how could I recognise that they *are* plants?[7]

At this stage it seems that Goethe was actually expecting to come across and recognise the *Urpflanze* on his travels. Later on the notion became more abstract. Goethe developed a theoretical model of plant structure with the stems as geometrical axes of growth, along which were arranged differently modified forms of a primordial leaf able, through various transformations, to be manifested either in different geometrical leaf shapes or else in petals or seed pods (figure 5). This permutational system of representing plant types suggested to Goethe the same possibility of generating new theoretical plants as had occurred to others. The invented plants, Goethe says, 'will be imbued with inner truth and necessity. And the same law will be applicable to all that lives.'[8]

Goethe's followers in the *Naturphilosophie* school developed his morphological studies further, and applied them to animal as well as plant species. They pursued the idea of a similarity in structural plan, not only between one phylum and another, and between species in the same phylum, but even to a similarity of different parts in the same body. Thus the skull in vertebrates was regarded as a modified form of a group of vertebrae – a discovery claimed by both Goethe and Oken. In England the tradition was carried into the mid nineteenth century by the anatomist Richard Owen, who abstracted an archetypal skeleton from all vertebrates — mammals, birds, fish and reptiles — which was itself composed of a longitudinal series of variously transformed versions of a single archetypal vertebra.[9] Owen even speculated that life on other planets might manifest other possible modifications of the same archetype, similar in basic plan but unlike in detail those on earth. Of the supposed relationships which *Naturphilosophie* saw between the archetypes of the phyla, G. S. Carter says: 'Their comparisons were often very far-fetched and indeed fantastic.' Nevertheless,

However fantastic these ideas may seem to us, it is important to realise that they were prevalent, and in Germany dominant, in zoology at a time shortly before that in which Darwin did his work on evolution. It was in these ideas, not always in their most extreme forms, that the minds of many of the elder zoologists of the latter part of the century were formed.[10]

Goethe was one of the first to use, in an essay *Zur Naturwissenschaft uberhaupt, besonders zur Morphologie* (1817), the term 'morphology', which had the significance of a study of form and structure in inorganic as well as organic nature, and of the geometrical factors which govern form.[11] It was thus, as applied to animal form, a kind of 'non-functional' anatomy. There was a strong analogy drawn between organic or skeletal structure and crystal structure, whose laws of axial and symmetrical growth had been announced

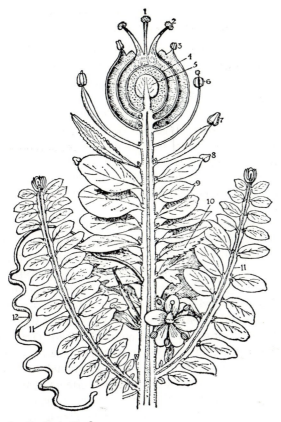

5    Goethe's *Urpflanze*.

by R. J. Haüy, the 'father of crystallography', in his *Traité de Mineralogie* of 1801.[12]

As Ritterbush points out, 'For over a century, branching crystals had been grown in solutions and had been exhibited as "stone plants" as evidence confirming mechanical explanations of plant growth.'[13] Now, in the view of *Naturphilosophie*, an abstract geometrical science might be forthcoming which would unify the phenomena of crystal and plant form and show them to be based on identical fundamental principles. Goethe was an enthusiastic amateur mineralogist as well as botanist. An entry in his diary to the effect of 'architecture ... being like mineralogy, botany and zoology' indicates his conviction that all these subjects were governed by general and universal laws of spatial structure.

From this brief survey of eighteenth-century natural history, its methods of classification, and its consequences for a transformational constructive theory of types developed from archetypes, we can now turn to parallel developments in architectural history and theory, and so discover the basis of analogy. The emergence of archaeology as an organised scholarly enterprise in the eighteenth century, as well as accumulated evidence from travellers' accounts and foreign expeditions, had provided architectural writers with an increasing mass of quite disorganised material on the variety of historical and national or local styles in building. Any comprehensive theory of architecture would have to set this material in order, organise it into some classificatory scheme, and draw some lessons which would be useful for a modern 'style', for future architecture.

Many of the treatises of the time, such as those of J.-F. Blondel, Le Roy, and later Durand, are devoted to this task; to classification and analysis of types of building, as well as of successive architectural periods and geographical variations in building styles.[14] There was a greater and more catholic historical awareness than at any previous time of the whole panorama of the architecture of the past. This was a contributing factor no doubt in the stylistic confusion of nineteenth-century architecture, its chaotic eclecticism, as the various historical styles were revived and adopted in turn.

The parallel here in biology would be with the great increase in the number of natural species known to science through the eighteenth century, again as the result of travellers' discoveries and naval or colonial expeditions whose express purpose was to make collections; and the corresponding efforts at the classification of species, as already described. In a very loose and metaphorical way, the geographical variety in styles of contemporary architecture could be seen to correspond to the variety of living species, while the historical styles reconstructed from archaeological evidence would be the counterparts of fossil species.

There was a further problem for the eighteenth- and nineteenth- century architects, and that was the emergence, with the industrial and social revolutions, of demands for quite new types of building with functions which were largely unprecedented. Up to that time it was almost possible for the whole variety of human activities to be accommodated comfortably in the few traditional forms which had been inherited from the Romans — the villa, the tenement, the basilica, the theatre, the temple. The education of the architect had been centred on Classical models, and the assumption was that the limited range of forms of Classical buildings, as transmitted through Vitruvius and the Renaissance commentators, would suffice for all eventualities.

Not only did mechanical invention and industrial progress create the requirement for structures appropriate for the accommodation of factories of all kinds, mills, warehouses, docks and, for example, in the nineteenth century, the whole variety of buildings associated with the railways; but more immediately — since these industrial structures were widely regarded as being outside the scope of the architectural profession, and were left to builders and engineers — there were the buildings required by the new and ever more complicated organisation of society, such as the hospitals, commercial exchanges, barracks, town halls, prisons, slaughter-houses and markets, consideration of which J.-F. Blondel introduced for the first time into the curriculum of architectural education in the 1760s.[15] The secular programme of the *Encyclopédie*, with its elaborate and detailed descriptions and classifications of the variety of manufactures and industrial processes, was influential on this change of attitude. And the revolutionary French architects, such as Ledoux, had been attempting to develop a vocabulary of suitably revolutionary forms intended to respond to these emerging practical, as well as some more Utopian, social demands.

Now it would be wrong to try to force the argument that any very strong or deliberate analogy of classification is to be found from natural history in architectural theory at this period. (Later on, in the nineteenth century, we shall find biological taxonomy invoked explicitly as a model for classifying building and artefact types and styles.) After all, the task of classification is one which faced many emerging disciplines at the same time.

Nevertheless there is one important aspect in which, I believe, a parallelism or line of connection is to be found, and this concerns the concept of the creation of theoretical new species, which for natural history was perhaps a slightly whimsical and incidental conceit but for architecture is clearly the absolute centre of interest. The practical purpose of classification in architecture, beyond historical description and scientific analysis, lies in the hope that out of an ordering of the variety of buildings of the past will come theoretical principles, which may be applied in designing new buildings, of new forms, to answer new programmes and new circumstances.

Thus we find J. N. L. Durand's revolutionary synthetic method of architectural composition, as expounded in his *Leçons d'Architecture* of 1819, being developed out of his previous work on classificatory analysis of building types and their history.[16] The plans of large numbers of historical buildings, grouped according to their general functions — theatres, stadia, markets and so on — are set out in the plates of Durand's *Recueil et Parallèle des Edifices* of 1801, all drawn to common scales, arranged like nothing so much as the specimens for some work of natural history or geology (figure 6).[17]

Durand's system of composition involves the setting up of principal and subsidiary axes for a building, around which pre-designed elements — the basic molecules or cells of the structure — are then disposed in symmetrical arrangement. The method bears close affinities with Haüy's rules for crystal formation; or with Goethe's transformational system for the generation of all plants from the archetypal plant. It was Durand's intention that the students of his *Leçons* should, by studying types and their underlying prin-

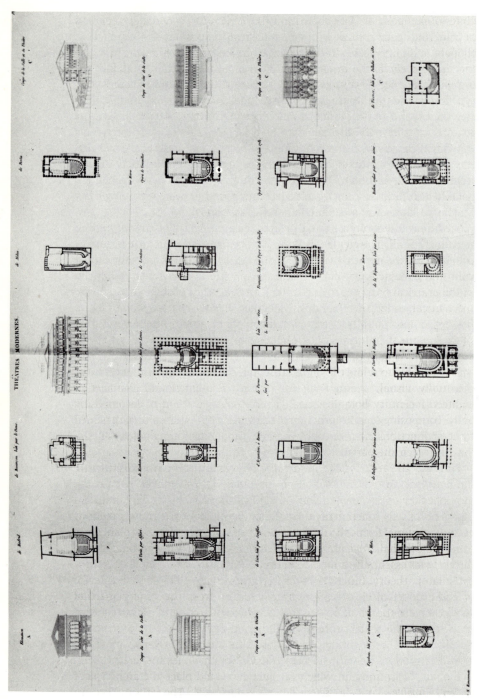

6   J. N. L. Durand, modern theatres drawn to a common scale.

ciples of composition, be enabled to cope with what would otherwise be a bewildering and endless variety of individual, unrelated problems. He thought it 'an impossible thing to wish to understand Architecture by study-ing successively all the species of buildings in all the circumstances that can modify them'; but if the student were to devote himself to mastering general type-forms, then he would be in a position to modify these types appropria-tely, to respond to the particular exigencies of function, site, budget and the requirements of individual clients.[18]

What is paradoxical about Durand's system is that, despite the fact that the original classification of historical buildings is a functional one, at least at the level of the building's function as a whole, and despite the necessity for new building types being occasioned by the appearance of new functional demands — industrial, social and so on — his compositional procedure is essentially a formal, geometrical one, and not in a certain sense functional at all. The elements of composition are discrete structural units — columns, arches, domes — which are set together according to combinatorial rules and governed overall by geometrical constraints of symmetry. In so far as the practical purposes of the building are taken care of, it is by a somewhat mechanical assignment of various functions to the separate rooms created by the compositional process. Circulation routes joining these rooms are mapped onto the abstract armature of symmetrical axes around which the composition is built up.

Is it possible to relate the *formal* character of this method of Durand's to the essentially visual, geometrical, in a word, non-functional, character of eighteenth-century botanical classification; to its method of decomposing and recomposing organic form in separated elements, which although named by their functions, are not conceived in terms of functioning *systems* or rela-tions between the parts?

Certainly the archetypes of *Naturphilosophie* came under powerful criticism, not only for their remoteness from observed natural reality, but for the fact that they offered no explanation of what the causes of variety in species might be, of why functionally the different permutations or transformations of the archetypal forms should occur. Goethe's system for deriving plant types from the original *Urpflanze*, although an extremely fertile and imaginative insight, was essentially a method of description only, and offered no kind of explanatory theory. Indeed the archetype was finally no more than a device or end-product of classification, an abstraction from the variety of actual species, and so the whole process was largely circular. Goethe did not concern himself with the actual processes of plant growth, with the detailed structure of tissues or with the mechanisms of plant physiology.

Ritterbush makes an important distinction which is relevant here, between a scientific *illustration*, in which category he would place the archetype of *Naturphilosophie*, and a scientific *representation*.[19] The illustration, in

Ritterbush's terms, is an image of nature which may be highly abstracted, like the *Urpflanze*, but is still only a means by which the external world and its appearances are organised and recognised. In a representation, on the other hand, there enters some degree of scientific explanation in terms of 'cause and effect, disposition in space and time, or observed sequences of operations. Such representations arise through a process of abstraction which generalises them in these respects. Thus, the models employed by scientists represent principles of construction or operation.'[20]

In the chapters which follow we will see how the comparative anatomy of the first half of the nineteenth century, as exemplified above all in the work of Georges Cuvier, transforms the classificatory and 'illustrative' natural history of the eighteenth century, by founding its investigations on just those 'principles of construction or operation' to which Ritterbush alludes. This in turn gives rise to new criteria for the classification of species, by reference to organic function. So we will return in due course to the analogy with biological taxonomy in architecture.

Cuvier's functional attitude to anatomy will emphasise that organic relation between the parts, that coherence of the systems of the body, to which I have already made reference in the discussion of functionalism. If we have detected a 'biological' basis to those compositional techniques deriving from Durand and carried on in the French Beaux Arts tradition, which, however radical originally, decayed at last into sterile and inhibiting formulae, this is not a characteristic which would have been recognised by the theorist of 'organic architecture', Louis Sullivan, in the retrospective view of a hundred years later. For Sullivan the additive procedures and 'elementary' character of Beaux Arts composition were 'the mere setting together of ready-made ideas, of conventional assumptions'. The Beaux Arts method is, he says 'a mechanical, not an organic process; it is, indeed, the very antithesis of an organic process'.[21] What the concept of 'organic' is which Sullivan comes to hold, we shall now begin to examine.

# 4

# The anatomical analogy: engineering structure and the animal skeleton

After the Revolution there was established in Paris a new *Muséum d'Histoire Naturelle*, which was created out of Buffon's old *Jardin du Roi*, and was more popularly known as the *Jardin des Plantes*. Twelve professorial chairs were assigned to the various branches of the subject, and filled by the leading life scientists of the day, including E. G. Saint-Hilaire, the geologist Brongniart, and the two most celebrated figures of all, the proto-evolutionist J. B. de Lamarck, and the man who is regarded as the effective founder of comparative anatomy, Georges Cuvier.[1]

Despite Lamarck's seniority in years, it was Cuvier who took the central position — in 1803 he was made perpetual secretary to the class of Physical and Mathematical Sciences of the National Institute — and who became the most respected and admired French biologist of the first half of the nineteenth century. Lamarck's fame, of which we shall hear more later, was due mainly to the posthumous revival of his 'transformist' ideas which occurred after the publication of *The Origin of Species* in 1859, and for which Darwin's opponents, more than Darwin himself, were responsible. In his own time Lamarck's 'zoological philosophy' was largely ignored — Cuvier thought all such evolutionary ideas 'extraordinary and incomprehensible'[2] — and he was known more for his taxonomic work on invertebrates.

There is a certain irony, therefore, and also a slight anachronism, in referring to Cuvier as a 'biologist', since the term 'biology' was coined by Lamarck and was not in general currency until much later. However, it is Cuvier who more properly deserves the title than Lamarck himself, because it is Cuvier who breaks from the speculative vitalist philosophies of the eighteenth century, and who brings to the study of life the objectivity and the empirical technique of the truly scientific attitude. We shall see, when we come to examine the history of evolutionary theory, how it is Cuvier — who believed strongly in the fixity and special creation of natural species, was firmly religious, and who regarded theories of the origin of species as meaningless metaphysics — who still, paradoxically, prepares the way for Darwin; more so than does Lamarck, however much he may be regarded in the conventional view as Darwin's evolutionary forerunner.

It is worth giving a brief description of the *Jardin des Plantes*, which was largely organised by Cuvier in person. It attracted many visitors, not only scientists, among whom was at least one highly influential writer on the applied arts, for whom the experience was formative. Despite its name, the garden included a menagerie of live animals (Cuvier designed the cages, and his brother Frederic was the keeper), and a large collection of fossils, animal skeletons, and preserved and stuffed species (5,000 types of fish alone), housed in fifteen rooms which communicated with Cuvier's own house. A series of displays demonstrated the organs and bodily systems, and their variations in different species; and in the 'great room' were skeletons of the biggest animals — giraffe, horse, whale and elephant.[3]

Cuvier's own anatomical work was devoted later in life to fishes and published in the eight volumes of the *Ichthyologie*, but earlier he worked principally on the larger mammals. The skeletons of the larger and more exotic animals also occupied his attention amongst fossil species, in his work in palaeontology, 'the zoology of the past'. C. C. Gillispie character-ises Cuvier on this count as a showman, an 'impresario of the dramatic and outré', keeping the more spectacular species to himself while relegating to his colleagues the lower ranks of the animal kingdom (and to Lamarck the lowest of all).[4]

What concerns us here, however, is not so much Cuvier's particular sub-ject matter — though that is not irrelevant — as the principles and frame of reference of his anatomical method. Yet again we must go back to Aristotle's natural history, which Cuvier's work follows directly in spirit (and in some respects in empirical observation). Cuvier takes from Aristotle a teleological, functional attitude to the description and explanation of anatomical form. He believes, like Aristotle, in the 'unalterable functional integrity' of the organism; that the various organs and parts all play necessary and com-plementary roles in supporting the animal's actions and way of life. Anatomy, that is the description of the 'structure of organic bodies' or parts, is thus meaningless without some functional explanation of the purpose and working of those parts. As William Coleman puts it in his study of Cuvier's life and work: 'The physiological expression of the directedness of vital processes was a characteristic mark of Cuvier's system of organic nature and it opened the path to the discovery of the structural bases and relative im-portance of the various animal functions.'[5]

I have mentioned Cuvier's belief that organic species were fixed, distinct and unchanging for all time. The clear purposefulness which was to be seen everywhere in the design of animals and plants bore witness to the benign wisdom and creative providence of God. Cuvier described this universal adaptation of organic form to the special habits, behaviour and surroundings of each creature — which would be explained in modern biology via the mechanisms elucidated by Darwinian evolutionary theory — by reference to the hypothesis of 'conditions of existence'. The 'conditions of existence' – 'principles which stated the fundamental characteristics of each and every creature' – corresponded more or less exactly to Aristotle's 'final causes'. They laid down in general terms a kind of hypothetical specification for or set of constraints on the creature, which its particular anatomical and physiological organisation was then divinely 'designed' to fulfil or obey.

Although logically the 'conditions of existence' ought to come first, and the anatomy and physiology of the animal would follow in consequence, in practice the anatomist could only work the other way round; could only infer the conditions of existence from the actual organs and structures which he found, and from the purposes and methods of operation which he deduced. The argument was therefore circular and so essentially tautologous.

Philosophical discussions of final causes, of the metaphysical problems of purpose and design in nature as a whole, were of no great interest to Cuvier. Nor was he prepared to mix religious with scientific explanation. It was sufficient for him that 'conditions of existence' should be embodied in the plan of nature from the creation; and he was content to proceed directly to the detailed examination of particular animals and particular organic structures on that assumption. But even if the idea now appears as a theoretical fiction, it was in Cuvier's work very far from being an unfruitful or unhelpful one, focussing attention as it did on the functional organisation of bodily structures and the intimate relationship of creatures and plants to their surrounding environments.

As corollaries of the 'conditions of existence', there followed Cuvier's two famous anatomical rules, the 'correlation of parts', and the 'subordination of characters'. By the 'correlation of parts' Cuvier meant the necessary functional interdependence between the various organs or systems of the body. Respiration supplies oxygen which being transferred through the lung walls to the blood is then circulated throughout the body; the circulation of the blood depends on the action of the muscular pump of the heart; this muscular contraction is controlled through nervous impulses from the brain; and so on. The presence of one organ or structure would necessarily imply the presence of one or several others; and any change in one would imply a correlated change in others. To quote Cuvier: 'All the organs of one and the same animal form a single system of which all the parts hold together, act and react upon each other; and there can be no modifications in any one of them that will not bring about analogous modifications in them all.'[6] This idea of the correlation of organs is not entirely new with Cuvier. We have seen it adumbrated in Aristotle. And it is already clearly formulated in the anatomical work of Cuvier's immediate predecessor Felix Vicq d'Azyr, who succeeded Buffon at the Academie Française and whose work Cuvier drew from extensively for his own comprehensive review volumes. Vicq d'Azyr asserts, for example, how 'there exist constant relations between the structure of the carnivores' teeth and that of their muscles, toes, claws, tongues, stomachs and intestines'.[7]

1 .    But for Cuvier the correlation of parts becomes the basis of a whole anatomical methodology, and he turns the comparative method of Vicq d'Azyr to the determination of the nature of these correlations. Cuvier resolved that since experiments with living animals would destroy that very systematic organisation, the delicate balance of interrelationships which the functional anatomist or physiologist was seeking to understand, he would adopt the strategy of regarding the whole range of existing species as a kind of ready-made set of experiments. By noting the repeated occurrence of certain structures in combination with each other, and related consistently to specific habitats and ways of life of animals, it would be possible to formulate the laws governing such relations, with a rigour, says Cuvier, ultimately matching those of the mathematical sciences.

2 .    By the second rule, the 'subordination of characters', was meant that certain of the organs or bodily systems had greater functional significance than others, and could thus be arranged in order of importance. In fact this principle is due to A.-L. de Jussieu, and had an originally classificatory purpose; the reference is to 'characters' in the sense of features selected for the purposes of taxonomy. With Cuvier the relevance of the rule to classification is still very great; but now the principles of classificatory organisation are functional ones, turning on the relative importance of the organs or systems to the working of the whole body, rather than on perhaps incidental and external features selected without regard to their functional meaning. For Vicq d'Azyr it had been the alimentary function which was most important to the animal. Cuvier changed his mind several times about the ranking of the bodily systems, thinking initially that reproduction and circulation were foremost. Later he saw digestion as being most important, and finally he came to give first place to the nervous system.[8]

Michel Foucault has analysed the consequences of the change from eighteenth-century methods of classificatory natural history to this systematic and functional approach which characterises Cuvier's comparative anatomy.[9] No longer is it visible, geometrical, unconnected and external properties of organisms which provide the criteria for assigning them to groups and families; it is now in a sense 'invisible' properties – those of function – hidden, in the case of the animal, deep in the body. Many external 'characters' of animals are related to rather minor functions and are capable of greater variation than are the more significant major organs in the interior. As Foucault puts it: 'Animal species differ at their peripheries, and resemble each other at their centres; they are connected by the inaccessible, and separated by the apparent.'[10]

Differences and similarities which are superficially observed are no longer a sure guide for taxonomy, since the exact nature of hair or fur, external colouring, the precise sizes of limbs, can all alter within limits without endangering the coordination and viability of the whole. As Cuvier says:

> we find more numerous varieties in measure as we depart from the principal organs and as we approach those of less importance; and when we arrive at the surface where the nature of things places the least essential parts — whose lesion would be the least dangerous — the number of varieties becomes so considerable that all the work of the naturalists has not yet been able to form any one sound idea on it.[11]

It is the principal organs which are invariant and which therefore serve as the basis of classification, while the subordinate characters are open to considerable variety. If external features — claws, teeth, hooves — *do* serve classificatory purposes, it is because they are connected by networks of functional relations to the larger bodily systems of which they are parts.

The implication of the two rules, but particularly that of the correlation of parts, was that the necessary and logical concurrence of certain typical sets of organs in typical bodily plans would be related in the broadest sense to the different *environments* of animals — to their types of food, their means of catching and ingesting it, to the meteorological conditions, to the different elements in which they moved. Herbivores, for example, would be equipped with particular kinds of teeth, which would imply the shape of the jaw, and hence the skull; the type of digestive system would also correspond, and so on. Especially active creatures such as birds, which consume large amounts of energy in flying, require corresponding breathing and eating habits, so determining the plan of the appropriate organs; while sluggish beasts like reptiles, which pass long periods without need of respiration, have much less well-developed respiratory systems — and being relatively inactive, their locomotive organs are in many cases also correspondingly modest. Thus a classification of species by functional systems of the body would simultaneously constitute a classification in environmental and behavioural terms.

On the other hand, it was a clear corollary of the 'correlation of parts' that certain combinations of organs or bodily structures were functionally quite impossible. 'The ruminant could not have a short, straight digestive tube — the eagle was forbidden webbed feet; the serpent had no external limbs — the cave-dwelling crustacean lacked acute eyesight.'[12] It was not that monsters had been a necessary product of the relentless permutation of all organs each with every other — and had been unable to survive. It was, for Cuvier, that they were simply a *logical* impossibility; they not only had not existed, they never could exist. In his words:

> it is evident that a suitable harmony between those organs which act upon each other, is a necessary condition to the existence of the being to which they

belong; and that if one of these functions were modified in a manner incompatible with the modifications of others, that being could not exist.[13]

Such animals as are found in nature, or which have existed historically but become extinct, represent for Cuvier all those possibilities which are coherent, or put another way, are not 'repugnant'. The distinctness of species which he emphasised had therefore a logical explanation, and the gaps between species were not accidental but represented areas of anatomical incompatibility, 'impossible combinations of organs or modifications': 'those of these modifications which cannot exist together are reciprocally excluded, whereas the others are brought into existence'.[14]

The interpretation extends, as mentioned, to Cuvier's categorisation of the fossil remains which were being excavated in the early years of the century (many as a direct result of the contemporary building boom: Cuvier's specimens came mostly from limestone quarries in Montmartre). These quite certainly did not belong to any species found still living. Cuvier, reluctant to relinquish the concept of fixity of species, put forward the explanation that of an originally much larger number of species, many had at various times become extinct through natural disasters or upheavals and in particular as a result of floods. The hypothesis of successive floodings was one among several possibilities which had been proposed by geologists as causes for the patterns of superimposed rock strata. The theory was known picturesquely, indeed dramatically, as 'castastrophic neptunism'. (Its rival, the explanation via forces of heat and pressure, was known as the theory of 'vulcanism'.)

Many of the fossil specimens recovered were incomplete, or consisted only of fragments or groups of bones. In other cases, bones from different species appeared to be mixed, and the palaeontologist was presented with the serious problem of piecing together the bits and deciding which bones fitted with which others. It was here that Cuvier's principle of the correlation of parts was clearly of the greatest usefulness; it 'provided the theoretical basis for the reconstruction of the lost species'.[15] With characteristic panache, Cuvier announced that he, the 'Antiquary of new species', had been 'obliged at once to learn how to restore these monuments of past times, and to decipher their meaning'.[16] The correlation of parts was his trumpet and with its call he would resurrect the dead.

It was his rather ambitious claim that the experienced palaeontologist would, with the aid of the theoretical rules of comparative anatomy, be able to infer the whole form of the unknown animal from rather limited fragmentary remains, and determine logically which bones must belong together (figure 7). Further, he would be able to fill out the skeleton with flesh, could form an idea, from the bones, of the creature's soft parts, and hence its whole manner of life. He describes this method in a famous passage — which we shall meet again, since it caught the imagination of writers on

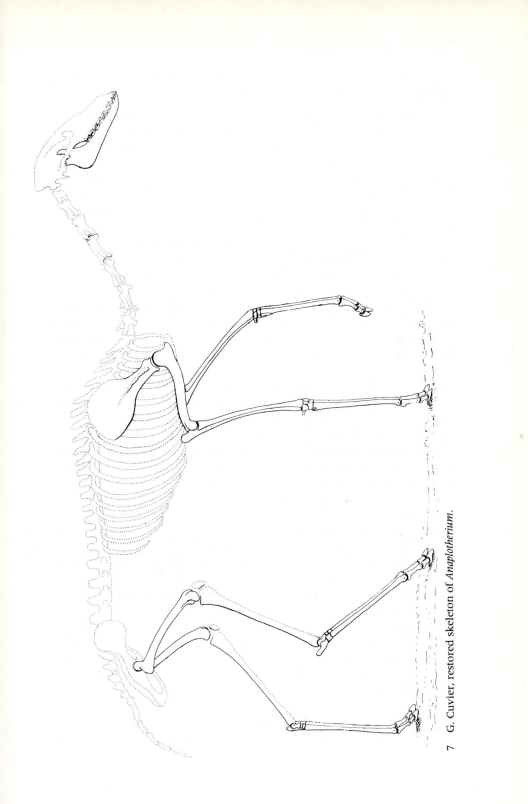

7  G. Cuvier, restored skeleton of *Anaplotherium*.

subjects quite outside biology and geology — in his book on fossils and pre-historic life, the *Recherches sur les Ossemens Fossiles*:

> In short, the shape and structure of the teeth regulate the forms of the condyle, of the shoulder-blade, and of the claws, in the same manner as the equation of a curve regulates all its other properties; and, as in regard to any particular curve, all its properties may be ascertained by assuming each separate property as the foundation of a particular equation; in the same manner, a claw, a shoulder-blade, a condyle, a leg or arm bone, or any other bone, separately considered, enables us to discover the description of teeth to which they have belonged, and so also reciprocally we may determine the forms of the other bones from the teeth. Thus, commencing our investigation by a careful survey of any one bone by itself, a person who is sufficiently master of the laws of organic structure, may, as it were, reconstruct the whole animal to which that bone had belonged.[17]

*[handwritten margin note: to approach the rigor of cause + effect of mathematics]*

This claim was something of an exaggeration, and in practice Cuvier was more tentative and careful about the conclusions he drew from actual fossil evidence. He depended more than the foregoing passage would suggest on arguments by direct analogy from known creatures rather than on abstract structural laws; and his success with anatomical reconstruction can be attributed as much to his enormous zoological experience and knowledge as to the application of his theoretical rules. It was nevertheless true that such clues as the shape of the teeth could alone tell 'a great deal about the nutrition and general economy of the animal'.[18] And the anatomical rules expressed a goal for exactness and certainty in biological understanding which, if not yet achieved, would be the task of the progressing science to achieve.

We are now prepared, by this exposition of Cuvier's methods and concepts in anatomy, to embark on an exploration of their influence on architectural theory, and of the analogies drawn in anatomical terms between the two fields. We can note the separate topics involved, for mnemonic purposes, as those of 'correlation of parts', 'coherence' or 'unity' in the organic body; the use of the anatomical rules for fossil reconstruction; the classification of species with reference to *function*; and the relation of organisms to their environments.

A word needs to be said first, however, about the problems of historical dislocation of which warning was given in chapter 1. Cuvier did his most important work in the first two decades of the century. He died in 1832 (the same year as Goethe). Cuvier's methods — of classification and analysis — are first held out explicitly as models for the study of buildings and useful artefacts, in France by E. E. Viollet-le-Duc, and in Switzerland by G. Semper, both writing from the mid-1850s. After that the same themes can be followed through right up to the end of the century. By that time Cuvier himself would have been little read for his theoretical views, and certainly not by architects.

I have chosen to present a set of general ideas in biology by means of this account of Cuvier's work alone. While Cuvier is certainly the leading biologist of the first half of the century, and a pivotal figure in the whole development of the subject, it would hardly be right to give him an exclusive importance. (In England it is the evidence of adaptation in nature adduced in William Paley's *Natural Theology*, and in geology the work of Charles Lyell, which are formative in, for example, the development of Darwin's thought.) Perhaps Cuvier, however, may be allowed to stand for this same set of ideas as they are transmitted through his own works, through others, and through works of biological popularisation, over a period of fifty years and more.

When we come to examine the influence of evolutionary biology in the form principally, of course, of the work of Darwin, we shall see how in architectural theory distant echoes of Cuvier are to be detected *simultaneously* with invocation of the new concepts of natural selection, survival of the fittest and so on. For the purposes of a theoretical analysis, whatever the confusion in the design and architectural literature, it seems better to separate the various strands and to follow them right through one at a time, rather than track all of them in parallel.

In its most naive expression the anatomical analogy as applied to buildings takes the form of a simple metaphorical comparison of the skeleton of the animal with the supporting structural framework of columns and beams or piers and vaults. (The further consequences suggested by this mere figure of speech develop into something more subtle.) Thus we have Horatio Greenough declaring (in the 1850s) that 'the principles of construction can be learned from the study of the skeletons and skins of animals and insects'.[19] Later, in the steel-frame architecture of the Chicago of the 1880s and 1890s, the separation of the building's 'skin' from its structural 'bones' is made complete, and the metaphor becomes especially apt.

For Le Corbusier, in whose writings biological analogy abounds, the traditional load-bearing wall construction of stone is to be compared with the restricting external bony shell of the tortoise or lobster. By contrast, the modern free-standing type of columnar structure of concrete or steel would correspond to an internal skeleton; while the screen walls whose function is not structural, but simply to divide space and keep out the elements, would be equivalent to membranes and skin.[20]

This comparison of structural arrangement in buildings with skeletal form in animals is to be found at least as early as 1770, when J.-R. Perronet said of Gothic cathedrals that

> The magic of these latter buildings consists largely in the fact that they were built, in some degree, to imitate the structure of animals; the high, delicate

columns, the tracery with transverse ribs, diagonal ribs and tiercerons, could be compared to the bones, and the small stones and voussoirs, only four or five inches thick, to the skin of these animals. These buildings could take on a life of their own, like a skeleton, or the ribs of a boat, which seem to be constructed on similar models.[21]

It is perhaps not just coincidental that such an analogy should have been made at a time when Vicq d'Azyr was initiating the functional approach to comparative anatomy. Perronet's image was dismissed in a riposte from the architect Patte, on the grounds that the static equilibrium of a construction in such a hard and unyielding material as stone could not be properly compared with the way the muscles and elastic, living structure of the body keep it in balance.[22] But it was a vivid and striking image all the same, one which was to be used repeatedly through the next hundred years, and with especial reference to the architecture of the Gothic cathedral (figure 8).

One of the recurrent themes of nineteenth-century architectural theory is the claim for certain historical buildings, but above all the French cathedrals of the twelfth and thirteenth centuries, that they exhibit — and indeed that their beauty results from — an absolute rationality and economy of structure. This is the so-called 'Gothic Rationalism'* of which Eugene Emmanuel Viollet-le-Duc was the greatest exponent. R. D. Middleton in a dissertation on 'Viollet-le-Duc and the Rational Gothic Tradition'[23] has traced the theme back to the same quoted passage from Perronet, where Perronet puts the view that in Gothic — unlike the mass and bulk which characterised for example Roman building — weight was pared down to an irreducible minimum, and opposing structural forces were exactly reconciled in the ingenious systems of counterbalanced vaulting, piers and buttresses which the Gothic builders had evolved.

The primary structural problem which the Gothic builders had set themselves was that of spanning the enclosed volume, of closing the roof of the church, while at the same time reducing to a minimum the area of supporting walls by which this roof was held up. The loads from the vault were brought together and concentrated onto a number of point supports, the columns, which transferred these forces to the ground. Meanwhile, the intervening area of wall which in Roman and Romanesque architecture would have played the main structural role, was in Gothic dissolved, removed and replaced by the progressively larger areas of glass which in the end came to fill the entire space between external buttresses. The form of the vault was thus all-important and determined the whole supporting system which it crowned.

Viollet-le-Duc saw the pattern of ribs in Gothic vaulting, gradually elaborated into a hierarchy of interlaced primary and secondary members, as

---

*For a discussion of the term 'rationalism' in this context, and its relation to 'functionalism' and 'functional determinism', see below p. 192.

8   A. Bartholomew, diagram comparing the counter-abutments of Gothic vaulting with the human skeleton.

expressing visually and indeed resisting structurally in the most economical possible way the exact pattern of distributed forces in the vault's warped surfaces. These ribs were collected together at the head of each column, and their number, relative sizes and positions, distributed around the main shaft, were thus determined by the pattern, proportion and dimensions of the whole vault. The compound profile of the column in cross-section was determined logically by the conformation of the roof whose imposed load was carried down that column (figure 9).

It was the underlying structural principles, the intellectual basis of Gothic building, which Viollet-le-Duc sought first of all to demonstrate in his writing. Although he was highly sensitive to those qualities of sacred Gothic architecture which heightened spiritual feelings, to its symbolic language and to the artistic expression of religious themes in its forms, decoration and carving; although he had certainly a 'sensuous and romantic appreciation of the style'[24] and disapproved of any attempts at systematising architectural style

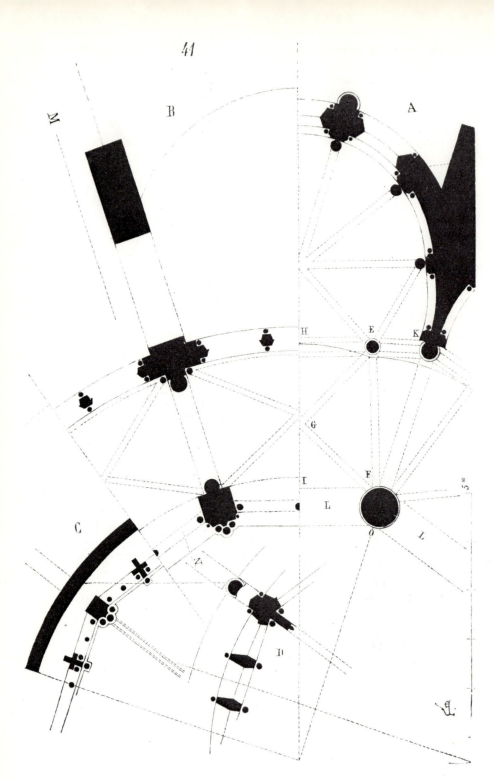

9   E. E. Viollet-le-Duc, plan drawings of apse at Notre-Dame de Châlons.

Viollet-le-Duc — the study of gothic principles for creating a new style

through sets of rigid or mathematical rules; still it was a fundamental understanding of function and structure which for Viollet-le-Duc was not only
the key to historical interpretation, but provided the lessons which could be
learned from Gothic and applied in modern building, in the creation of a new
style. Indeed it was not just the structural framework of the Gothic vault
which was to be seen to be designed on rational principles; and he would not
have concurred with the view that various apparently 'decorative' features
in Gothic were superfluous and functionless. Even the profiles of mouldings
and small details of the placing of masonry masses all played their own
functional parts, in throwing off rain, for example, and in providing counter-
weights to resist lateral thrusts.[25]

We can now see precisely what Viollet-le-Duc refers to when in a passage
from the *Dictionnaire Raisonné de l'Architecture Francaise* — the work in which
he expounds his rational philosophy of architectural structure — he says.
'Just as when seeing the leaf of a plant, one deduces from it the whole plant;
from the bone of an animal, the whole animal; so from seeing a cross-section
one deduces the architectural members; and from the members, the whole
monument.'[26]

This method of deduction, which clearly follows Cuvier's anatomical
principle of the 'correlation of parts', is illustrated admirably in the relation
of vault to column in Gothic. Since the pattern of ribs follows logically and
inevitably from the shape of the vault, and the exact profile of the column in
cross-section is determined by the ribs and how they are brought down onto
the head of the column; so in principle it would be possible, Viollet-le-Duc
is saying, for a skilled art historian cum engineer — such as himself — to work
through the process backwards, and from the one part of the structure alone
infer or reconstruct all the others.

Viollet-le-Duc does not quote many sources at all in his books, and the
references to Cuvier's rules and fossil reconstruction are indirect rather than
explicit. But we do know (from the catalogue of his library) that he owned a
copy of the *Leçons d'Anatomie Comparée*.[27] And there is at least one specific
reference to Cuvier in the *Dictionnaire*, in the section devoted to 'Restoration'.[28]

Viollet-le-Duc is known, besides by his theoretical writings, for his extensive work on the restoration of the Gothic monuments of France. One might
be led to expect, then, that this mention of Cuvier would be an allusion to the
possibility of using the anatomical rules, by analogy, in the reconstruction of
'architectural fossils': for rebuilding the 'monuments of past times', in Cuvier's
phrase. Curiously this is not the case, and it is Cuvier's general principles of
classification to which Viollet-le-Duc turns, discussion of which we shall
come to in due course.

It was for Viollet-le-Duc's British contemporary, the historian and writer
James Fergusson, to pick up, in his *True Principles of Beauty in Art*, the art-
historical implications as opposed to the lessons for structural design.

Fergusson does indeed see the possibility of something akin to Cuvier's rules for use in identifying archaeological remains and reconstructing ancient buildings: 'With the same facility with which a fossil impress or a bone does this for a geologist, does any true style of art enable the archaeologist to tell from a few fragments in what century the building to which it belonged was erected.'[29] *

We can follow similar ideas to America. Horatio Greenough has already been quoted on the constructional lessons to be learned from animal skeletons. The direct heirs to Greenough's functionalism in American criticism were Montgomery Schuyler and Leopold Eidlitz. The publication in America in 1875 of a translation by the architect Henry van Brunt of the *Entretiens sur l'Architecture* also made Viollet-le-Duc's Gothic 'structuralism' known to these writers and to an American public.[30]

Eidlitz was a practising architect with a profound interest in structural problems and an admiration for both German and French medieval building. His architectural theories, which focussed principally around questions of structure, were set out in his book *The Nature and Function of Art, More Especially of Architecture* which he published in 1881.[31] Eidlitz refers repeatedly to the building as an 'organism'; but he also speaks of separate constructional elements as 'subordinate structural organisms', in particular the pier, the flying buttress and the pinnacle of thirteenth-century Gothic building.[32] These structural elements express and correspond to their real function, for Eidlitz, in a way in which the appliqué structural motifs of Renaissance architecture, pilasters and pediments, do not.

Eidlitz had considerable influence on the architectural journalist Montgomery Schuyler. The two men were good friends, and Schuyler was the critical champion of Eidlitz's architectural work, which has since been largely destroyed or forgotten. Schuyler's oeuvre is uneven and he ranged over many topics, some of no great lasting interest. But his architectural criticism was informed always by an essentially rationalist and radical viewpoint, by the same opposition to mindless eclecticism and irrelevant historical pedantry in design that Eidlitz and Viollet-le-Duc shared, and by a great enthusiasm − in which he was ahead of other contemporary critics − for the achievements of the new American engineers, especially for bridges and skyscrapers.

An address delivered in Schenectady in 1894 and subsequently published in the *Architectural Record*, under the title 'Modern Architecture', provides the best concise statement of Schuyler's philosophy.[33] Many of the rationalist

---

* The zoologist C. F. A. Pantin has remarked on the practical importance which attached during the Second World War in some areas of operational research to the 'archaeological' reconstruction of mechanisms and their function from captured parts or fragments, somewhat along the lines of Cuvier's palaeontological method. *The Relations between the Sciences* (Cambridge, 1968), p. 44.

themes are rehearsed in this piece. As examples of the new problems, new conditions in architecture which Eidlitz had referred to in a rather abstract theoretical way, Schuyler discusses the very specific changes going on in the world of American commerce and technology — as for example the introduction of the steel frame and the mechanical elevator — which were demanding a new response from architects.

In so far as American architects achieved success in creating a new and appropriately modern style, Schuyler says, it tended to appear precisely in those areas (in office buildings, in the Chicago skyscrapers) where academic convention had of necessity to be cast aside. The problem which the new Chicago construction presented was difficult, but no more difficult than similar problems which faced architecture in the past. When the thirteenth-century Gothic builders were faced with the problem of resisting powerful lateral forces acting to spread the supporting walls and so risking collapse of the vault, they sought a practical solution by arranging diagonal shoring of masonry over the aisles on the outside — as Schuyler says, an unpromising and ungainly structural expedient. Nevertheless, by working at the problem of expressing this 'flying buttress', of displaying visually the function which it performed, after several generations the Gothic builders were able to make it speak.

> Made it speak? They made it sing, and there it is, a new architectural form, the flying buttress of a Gothic cathedral, an integral part of the most complicated and most complete organism ever produced by man, one of the organisms so like those of nature that Emerson might well say that —
>
> > Nature gladly gave them place
> > Adopted them into her race,
> > And granted them an equal date
> > With Andes and with Ararat.
>
> The analogy is more than poetically true. In art as in nature an organism is an assemblage of interdependent parts of which the structure is determined by the function and of which the form is an expression of the structure.[34]

Schuyler goes on to reproduce exactly the passage quoted earlier from Cuvier's *Recherches sur les Ossemens Fossiles* ('Let us hear Cuvier on natural organisms'), about the principles of palaeontological reconstruction. He says of Cuvier's rule of the correlation of parts that

> This character of the organisms of nature is shared by at least one of the organisms of art. A person sufficiently skilled in the laws of organic structure can reconstruct, from the cross-section of the pier of a Gothic cathedral, the whole structural system of which it is the nucleus and prefigurement. The design of such a building seems to me to be worthy, if any work of man is worthy, to be called a work of creative art. It is imitation not of the forms of nature but of the processes of nature.[35]

These kinds of ideas come originally, no doubt, from Viollet-le-Duc. Before leaving Schuyler it is worth mentioning one further example which he gives in his address, of the types of structural form which the engineers were producing as a kind of challenge to contemporary architects, and which were demanding equivalent architectural expression. It had been Eidlitz's prediction that such forms, created to fulfil unprecedented functions, would be novel and surprising even to their creators. Schuyler takes the same example which was to prove so useful to D'Arcy Thompson: that of the recently completed Forth Bridge in Scotland.* 'Is it conceivable', he asks, 'that this form could have occurred to a man who sat down to devise a new form, without reference to its basis and motive in the laws of organic structure?'[36]

*[handwritten left margin: the physiological analogy]*

We have seen how the particular image of Cuvier's method of restoration of fossil bones is used to convey the architectural idea that, in Gothic of all styles, but also elsewhere, the structural framework of the building forms a coherent and coordinated system in which the elements interact as the loads are transferred from one to the next. There could be comparable 'physiological' analogies made with other types of functional systems in buildings, though to my knowledge such analogies were not drawn by nineteenth-century writers nor linked with the name of Cuvier. We have to wait for Le Corbusier to find biological comparisons of the physiology of breathing with the ventilation of buildings; of the nervous system with the networks of electricity supply, communication and telephone services in a building or city, of the bowels with sewer pipes and refuse systems; and, favourite analogy of all, the circulation of the blood with the circulation of people or traffic.**

In succeeding chapters I will try to show how the idea of 'organic' coherence, or 'unity', so far conceived only in relation to engineering structure, is given a much wider and perhaps looser architectural connotation; how it serves to describe the relation of the internal functional organisation of a building to its immediate surroundings, or to its 'environment' understood in a rather broader and more abstract sense; and how the way is thus paved for a theory of architectural evolution. There is one somewhat more technical and specific aspect of biological analogy in architecture, however, which follows directly from the central concepts of Cuvier's anatomy, and although provid-

---

*In his discussion of the engineering of the quadruped skeleton (see p. 14), D'Arcy Thompson mentions that Professor Fidler, in his *Treatise on Bridge-Construction*, has a description of bridge types under the title 'The Comparative Anatomy of Bridges'. *On Growth and Form* (Cambridge, 1917; abridged edn, 1961), p. 242.

**Although Le Corbusier admits to a degree of confusion about how exactly some of the analogies are to be carried through: 'A plan arranges *organs* in order, thus creating an *organism* or *organisms*. The organs possess distinctive qualities, specific differences. What are they? Lungs, heart, stomach? The same question arises in architecture.' *My Work* (London, 1960), p. 155.

ing a slight digression should be treated first. This concerns the 'principle of similitude'.

## The principle of similitude

It was an important consequence of the 'correlation of parts' that functional relations would not only govern the necessary and simultaneous presence of various organs in systematic combination, but would also determine the proportions and dimensions of the overall *shape* of a creature. For example, a bird with twice the body dimensions of another would have a weight roughly eight times as great — in proportion to the volume. But if it were to be exactly of the same shape, simply 'scaled up' as it were, it would have a wing area only four times as large, yet needing to support the increased weight. It follows that proportions of wing to body size would have to be different in the larger bird to take account of this consideration. Several writers have pointed out the relevance of this kind of effect to systems of architectural proportion and to structural and engineering problems in building.

It was not Cuvier who originated the 'principle of similitude' in fact, although his studies set it in the whole framework of functional anatomy, and he refers to its effects. The principle is as old as Galileo, who first appreciated its workings and found many examples of its operation both in nature and in the world of engineering. The essence of the principle is that in bodies which are similarly constructed, i.e. of the same shape, the relations of the parts will vary with the size. The volume of bodies will vary with the cube of their linear dimensions, and so mass and weight will tend to vary similarly; while the total surface area, or the cross-sectional area of parts and hence their mechanical strength, will vary as the square of the dimensions.

In engineering the study of this class of problem is termed dimensional analysis; it has the implication that bridges, girders or other structures, which are of exactly similar design, will vary in strength for given thickness according to their absolute size. A model which is similar in every proportion to the full-size structure will thus not give a 'true-to-scale' representation of that structure's mechanical performance. Galileo remarks on noticing how in the Venetian Arsenal proportionately more scaffolding was used for the construction of a large boat than for a small one, because of its relatively greater weight for size.[37]

One nineteenth-century writer who was interested in the principle of similitude was Herbert Spencer, whose 'synthetic philosophy' and sociology were erected on a biological foundation, and whose original training and employment were as an engineer. Spencer showed how the effects of similitude set a limit on the dimensions of cells, thus explaining why animals both very large and very small are still made up of cells of much the same size. Spencer went on to apply the same ideas by analogy in sociology, where they suggested possible reasons for the sizes and relative cohesiveness of social groups.[38]

In the biological context, Galileo had shown a drawing of two bones of different length, but of strengths capable of supporting loads in proportion to their linear dimensions. The longer bone is much fatter in proportion than the shorter one (figure 10).[39] His illustration shows the reason, for example, for the legs of elephants being so fat; and why land creatures much larger than elephants are impossible, since the loads imposed during walking or running would become too great, and the necessary thickness of leg make for too clumsy an action. Whales and large fishes only avoid this problem because their bodies are supported in water and they are therefore not so subject to the effects of gravity on their skeletons. Hippopotamuses, like the larger prehistoric dinosaurs, are also helped by their partly aquatic habit.

Viollet-le-Duc drew attention to the way in which similar considerations ought to apply to columnar structures in building. Proportions, he says, are to be determined not in any absolute way but in relation to material, the design in question and its purpose.

> In the art of architecture, it is not possible to establish the following formula; that 2 is to 4 as 200 is to 400; because if you can put a lintel 4 metres in length onto columns 2 metres high, you would not be able to put, on two columns of 200 metres in height, a lintel of 400 metres. To change scale, the architect must change the method (*mode*), and style consists precisely in choosing the method appropriate to the scale — using that word in its widest definition.[40]

Eidlitz was among other nineteenth-century critics who made similar points. He gave a fuller mathematical explanation of the dimensional effects involved than did Viollet-le-Duc, in relation to the special question of the design of classical columns. The schools had always taught that the proportions of the classical orders were fixed according to prescribed ratios, and columns therefore should be of similar shape whatever their size. Eidlitz points out that to double the dimensions of a columnar structure involves an eightfold increase in the superimposed load on each column, which would require for equivalent strength a $2.83:1$ increase in the column's diameter, as opposed to a simple doubling. Nevertheless a constant geometrical proportion in column and entablature was an article of faith with the Renaissance school.[41]

Here then is one way in which architectural proportions, at least those of the structural members, might be determined in a relative manner and on the basis of *function*, rather than by the purely visually derived and absolute mathematical canons of the proportional theorists. At least two twentieth-century writers on design make the same point as Eidlitz about the classical

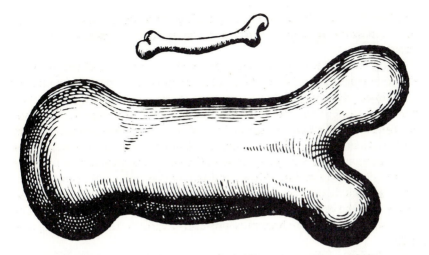

10   Galileo Galilei, diagram showing bones of different proportions, to illustrate the 'principle of similitude'.

orders: Trystan Edwards in *Style and Composition in Architecture*, who cites in evidence the varying proportion of the human body from baby to adult;[42] and Percy Nobbs, in *Design: A Treatise on the Discovery of Form*, a now forgotten philosophical book of the pre-war period, which nevertheless contains some very interesting and suggestive thoughts about questions of architectural form (figure 11).[43]

D'Arcy Thompson devotes most of a chapter — 'On Magnitude' — to the principle of similitude, which has many subtle and far-reaching consequences for the design of animals.[44] With organisms several properties vary with the cube of linear dimensions, including tissue respiration or combustion, and heat production; while varying with the square of the dimensions are the strengths of bones, muscles, and the stems of plants, breathing mechanisms (since these depend on the area of surface through which oxygen is absorbed), surfaces for food absorption in the stomach, and the loss of heat to the atmosphere from the skin.[45]

These facts provide the reasons why, *inter alia*, there is a lower limit on the size of warm-blooded creatures, and why smaller animals like mice must keep eating, and humming-birds, bees and some insects live on nectar, 'the richest and most concentrated of foods'; why fleas and grasshoppers can jump so high in relation to their size, but nevertheless the absolute height to which fleas, men and horses can all jump is much the same; why bigger birds must fly faster; why insects can walk on walls and on the ceiling; and why trees cannot be much taller than 300 feet; as well as numerous other

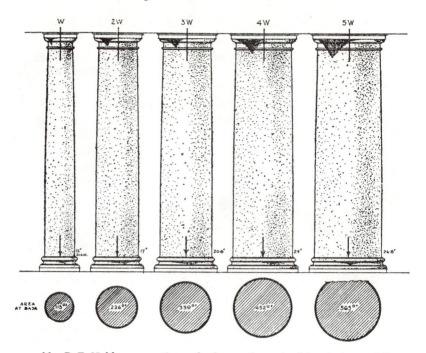

11   P. E. Nobbs, proportions of columns determined in relation to differing imposed loads.

surprising and powerful theoretical limitations on the variety of natural forms and the behaviour of animals.[46]

Some equivalent effects may be observed in architecture. The amount of space provided in a building is often conveniently expressed in terms of a total floor area. But this is misleading, since some constant or minimum floor-to-ceiling height is usually assumed, and the effective amount of accommodation is in reality a function of the built volume. Some other important properties of the architectural form are, however, related to area. The site area occupied may be important, while the building's outer surface area will certainly be, since this is related significantly to cost (the external 'skin' being an important element in total costs) as well as to loss of heat to the atmosphere through conduction, and to demands for a given area of glazing for the purposes of lighting. Nobbs discusses how, for this last kind of reason,

> the form of a two-hundred room house cannot be an enlargement of the form of a twenty-room house, nor that an enlargement of the form of a two-room house. A seedling with four small leaves is a very different thing, from the point of view of design, from a plant with a thousand large leaves and fifty blooms.[47]

He points out how the building form may be lengthened indefinitely to accommodate an increase in the number of rooms, or increased in height up to the limits of structural possibility; but that the depth is fixed by the daylight problem. Rather than a fixed depth dimension, we can express the requirement for daylight somewhat approximately as a requirement for a given area of wall surface per unit volume. We see how in very large office buildings this ratio is achieved by building in tall tower or elongated slab blocks, while in even larger buildings, such as Le Corbusier's monstrous crystalline skyscrapers for the 'Voisin' plan for Paris, the form is corrugated in a series of protruding fins in order to admit light to every part.[48] Something similar may be observed in the plan forms of such large buildings as hospitals, arranged in a series of radiating or branching wings.

The typical American central business district with skyscraper blocks organised in a grid layout — as in Manhattan — shows how, on a larger scale still, this effect of folding to increase surface area is carried beyond a system of corrugations in the horizontal plane only to become a system of separate vertical spikes. D'Arcy Thompson illustrates how for different reasons various body surfaces have their area increased by a similar conformation. Thus the villi on the lining of the intestine increase the surface available for absorption — much in the same way, D'Arcy Thompson says, that we increase the effective absorptive area of a bath towel by designing a fabric with numerous separate protruding loops of thread.* A coral reef is another natural example of a much increased surface area for given volume.[49]

One celebrated observation of Buckminster Fuller's about the geometrical organisation of Manhattan and its buildings in relation to *heating* problems, in contrast to lighting problems, is that an engineer could hardly have devised a more efficient form for getting rid of the heat which is so expensively and continuously produced in every building during the New York winter. The jagged skyline is like the cooling fins of a motorcycle engine. The one consideration works in opposition to the other; an increased surface area is required for light, but a decreased area is preferable on heat retention grounds. (During the summer, the thermal problem is, of course, the opposite one. It is desirable to lose heat, and for this the corrugated, high area form is preferable. In the New York climate, of the two problems winter heating and summer cooling, the summer is the greater.)

Fuller applies the principle of similitude to his own hemispherical 'geodesic' domes, showing how larger domes will lose heat less fast; for the same reason, on a much larger scale, that the earth is capable of maintaining a high internal temperature since the loss through cooling at the surface has relatively little effect[50] (although the thermal mass of a solid body like the earth is, of course, relatively much greater than that of a hollow structure

---

* When people say in disgust how tripe looks like face flannel, they are thus remarking on a functional as well as a formal similarity.

such as a dome, over and above the effect of size on the ratio of surface to volume).

One implication of the principle of similitude which does not seem to have struck Fuller, however, relates to his 'energetic-synergetic' system of geometry, which is intended among other things for use in the design of structures exhibiting an 'omni-directional equilibrium of forces'.[51] In nature it is only with very small organisms, such as the Radiolaria and other minute sea creatures, that the force of gravity ceases to be of relative importance (because of the high surface to volume ratio) and the main forces acting on the form (equally in every direction) are those of surface tension. As a result these creatures, alone in the organic world, take entirely and three-dimensionally symmetrical, often spherical, forms, some highly reminiscent of Fuller's geodesic structures.[52] At a smaller scale yet, the forms of some viruses, which are probably determined by constraints on the possible close-packing of similar sized units, and are certainly not influenced by gravity, also share the exact geometrical properties of Fuller's domes.[53] But at an architectural scale very different conditions prevail, and the uni-directional force of gravity is all-important; hence of course the horizontal and vertical geometry of the floors and walls of most conventional building.

Some recent investigations by Martin and March, mostly in the context of rectangular geometries, have studied some of those properties of idealised simplified 'built forms' which depend on the relationships existing between built volume and the areas of building surface and land covered.[54] These investigations, which are concerned with effects connected with the principle of similitude, have shown how much of our conventional wisdom about architectural forms and their use of land in relation to lighting considerations, for example, can be questioned. In many cases our tendency is to apply similar rules of thumb irrespective of absolute size or scale, and we find it very difficult to appreciate intuitively the complicated relationships obtaining when dimensions of length and height vary linearly, areal measures vary as the square, and volumes of buildings as the cube.

Following D'Arcy Thompson, the study of the problem of size and its consequences on organic form was very much developed in biology, by Julian Huxley and others, under the name of 'allometry'.[55] Huxley himself was particularly interested in giving mathematical treatment to the subject of the growth of organisms. It is a consequence of the principle of similitude that when creatures or plants increase (or decrease) in absolute size during their lifetimes, if the organisms are to maintain the precise same shape then the ratios of area and volume to linear dimension must change. Alternatively, and what happens most usually, the proportions and shape change to compensate functionally for the dimensional effects. Thus the proportions of head, trunk and limbs in human babies are very different from those of the mature

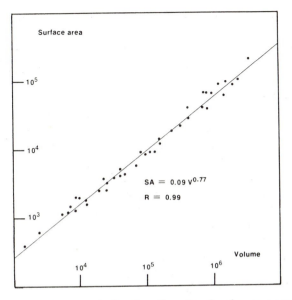

Surface area

10⁵

10⁴

10³

SA = 0.09 V⁰·⁷⁷

R = 0.99

Volume

10⁴  10⁵  10⁶

12   R. Bon, graph showing allometry of surface area versus volume (sample of forty buildings, measurements in feet).

adult body. Huxley and others have been interested, in their allometric studies, in the differential rates of growth by which these relative proportions of the various parts are altered during development.

Quite recently the same mathematical methods have been applied to the growth of human organisations such as commercial firms, and — in a small way — to architectural phenomena.[56] Bon, for example, has studied the ratio of surface area to volume in a sample of historical buildings, and showed a simple allometric relationship to apply, as a consequence of the flattening and elongation of the shape in the horizontal and vertical directions as described, with increasing absolute size (figure 12).[57]

Of course, in this case it is not the growth of a single building, at a series of time intervals, which is studied here, but rather the comparison of different buildings of varying sizes; but it is reasonable to imagine that the similar effect would be observed in the latter situation. (This is an important and obvious difference between natural and man-made structures, that the latter do not in general grow but must be assembled piece by piece into their final form. As a consequence there are engineering problems involved in maintaining the stability of a partially completed building structure, of a kind which natural organisms do not have to face.[58] If buildings *do* grow, it is by large occasional increments. Possibly, looking at a larger scale, the growth of

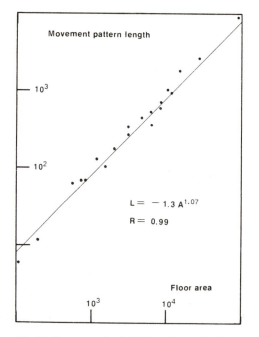

13   R. Bon, graph showing allometry of movement pattern length versus floor area (sample of twenty buildings, measurements in feet).

high density city districts of a 'natural' unplanned character might have more formal affinities with natural growth processes by the addition of cells than does any growth of a single building.)[59]

In Bon's studies, the correlation of the two variables of area and volume in logarithmic relationship, for the sample of forty buildings which he chose, was very close. Bon also looked at the floor area of each building as compared with the total length of 'movement pattern' — that is of corridors and other circulation routes — and here again found a similar logarithmic relationship to apply quite precisely (figure 13). In this case the significance of the linear measure of the total length of routes is that one would expect these means of access to penetrate to all parts of the floor area of the building at a more or less even 'density', irrespective of the building's absolute size.

# 5

# The ecological analogy: the environments of artefacts and organisms

This account of the 'principle of similitude' and its effects has served to show the relationship between certain of the functions of the organic body and its shape or form; and to demonstrate a similar relationship applying between certain functions of buildings, and their shapes. These have been rather general architectural functions, applying to buildings of almost all kinds: the provision of usable space, and its relation to site area occupied; the retention or loss of heat, and the admission of daylight, as they affect surface area of walls and roof; and the circulation of the occupants along corridors, on stairs and in lifts.

There would clearly be many other ways, having nothing particular to do with such dimensional effects, in which the shapes of buildings would correspond to, and could be made to express, the specific functions which they serve in controlling the climate, and in accommodating private and social activities. These might have to do with the size, shapes and relative disposition of rooms, the placing of doors and windows, the pitches and overhangs of roofs — the possibilities are virtually endless.

The differences resulting from the accommodation of different types of social activity might be expected to give rise to an association of characteristic overall shapes of building with these respective specialised uses: theatres, railway stations, office buildings and so on. At the same time it might be argued that the weather-resisting functions of architecture would also have their effects on form; and so different building shapes would be found to be associated with different climatic conditions — whether the main problem be cooling the interior, keeping it warm, keeping out rain and snow, or whatever. By similar arguments the separate functional elements or individual spaces of buildings would have their typical forms; and equally, in the field of the applied arts, all kinds of tools, implements, domestic utensils and the like, would also have their characteristic geometrical shapes, suitable for their different purposes.

In Cuvier's comparative anatomy the coordination of the internal parts of the body was seen to be associated with the external conditions or environment of the animal. Creatures subsisting on a certain kind of food would have a set of alimentary and digestive organs to match; animals living in water, sea or air would have appropriate organs of locomotion. It is difficult and possibly meaningless to try to define what the 'function' of an animal in overall terms is — perhaps, in the Darwinian view, survival and reproduction of its own kind — but evidently the separate organs of the body can be said to serve definite functions, and these functions are related directly or indirectly to the nature of the creature's environment — fins for swimming, certain kinds of teeth for eating meat or grass, and so on.

We have here the clear basis for a rather simple 'ecological' analogy of a kind that is almost too familiar in the literature of nineteenth-century functionalism and in the modern movement: in both animals and arte- facts, form is related to function, and function is related to environment. (The term 'ecological' would be anachronistic as applied to Cuvier's work; though in derivation appropriate enough for an architectural analogy.) The degree to which form suits or is appropriate to function and environ- ment in either case might be expressed in terms of 'adaptation' or else (after Darwin and Spencer) in terms of 'fitness'.

Thus Greenough says, of the search for constructional principles for architecture in the forms of beasts and birds:

> are we not as forcibly struck by their variety as by their beauty? There is no arbitrary law of proportion, no unbending model of form. There is scarce a part of the animal organisation which we do not find elongated or shortened, increased, diminished, or suppressed, as the wants of the genus or species dictate, as their exposure or their work may require.[1]

'The law of adaptation', Greenough declares, 'is the fundamental law of nature in all structure'.[2] Although the variety of forms in nature might seem capricious to the casual observer, though they might seem to be evidence of 'Omnipotence at play for mere variety's sake',[3] in fact every detail of organic form, he argues, has its functional purpose — even the colours of plants and flowers, which serve to attract and guide pollinating insects, or the colour- ing of animals for the purposes of disguise or aggressive appearance. 'If there be any principle of structure more plainly inculcated in the works of the Creator than all others, it is the principle of unflinching adaptation of forms to functions.'[4] By a study of this principle of adaptation in nature, the archi- tect may arrive at sound principles in building. This will entail a study of the climate which a building will be exposed to, of the site for which it is intended, of the nature of the institution which it houses, and of the varied wants of the building's users.

Leopold Eidlitz declares in similar vein how 'In nature forms are the out- come of environment. Environment determines function, and forms are the result of function.'[5] Building forms must be adapted in an equivalent way to the 'environment' in which they are situated, through the skill of the architect 'until the functions resulting [from this environment] are fully expressed in the [architectural] organism'.[6]

Probably the most famous and certainly the most abbreviated statement of the whole idea is Louis Sullivan's well-known, indeed notorious, slogan 'Form follows function', which we shall have occasion to examine more fully later on. (The trouble arises out of the use of the word 'follows'. Stated as 'Form *is related to* function' the phrase would be unexceptionable, though hardly as catchy. Perhaps Sullivan was betrayed by a weakness for alliteration.)

Two sections in Sullivan's long series of *Kindergarten Chats*, which are cast in the form of a kind of dramatic dialogue between a teacher of architecture (Sullivan) and his young student, carry the title 'Function and Form'.[7] The relationship between form and function is displayed in all of natural creation, says Sullivan, through the persona of the teacher figure. Trees are his most frequent example, but equally this relation is seen in animal or mineral nature, in human life, indeed in everything which 'the mind can take hold of'. As he says, in nature 'it stands to reason that a thing looks like what it is, and vice versa, it is what it looks like'.[8]  *evidence* (handwritten)

As a prescriptive functionalist model for architectural design, this is quite straightforward and uncomplicated. The purpose of a building should be clearly set out in its general appearance, the structure should be logical and comprehensible, it should be evident immediately what kind of business or activity the building houses. Echoing his master's voice, the student in the *Kindergarten Chats* suggests that:

> if we call a building a form, then there should be a function, a purpose, a reason for each building, a definite explainable relation between the form, the development of each building, and the causes that bring it into that particular shape; and that the building, to be good architecture, must, first of all, clearly correspond with its function, must be its image, as you [the teacher] would say.[9]

If the 'ecological' analogy is developed in any detail, however, the question arises as to what exactly the 'environment' of a building or other artefact consists of, or refers to. There will be no difficulty in allowing the inclusion of the meteorological environment, in the case of buildings. Account must also be taken of the physical environment in the sense of the ground area or three-dimensional space available, to which a building must obviously be 'fitted' in a literal geometrical sense. The same is true for many smaller artefacts which must fit, match or pack together with other artefacts, with natural objects, or with the shape of the human body (e.g. clothes, shoes, furniture, the handles of tools).

Then there is the matter of the material and technological 'environment'

the environment's 'impact' — -meteorology
-bldg. mat'ls?
-social
-economic
-cultural

60    *The evolution of designs*

of the artefact, which will affect the available materials from which it may be constructed, and the tools and manufacturing processes which can be used to make it. There is little need to elaborate on the way in which different materials of construction and techniques of manufacture can have their effects on the resulting forms of buildings or other useful objects. Here perhaps is one aspect in which the detailed analogy with plants or animals holds good, since the material limitations on structure are strictly comparable — though the processes of 'manufacture' of organic bodies are hardly so.

Beyond these physical and material factors in the environment of the artefact, we come to what are clearly highly important though rather indeterminate and more abstract 'environmental' components. These are the social, economic and cultural 'environments' in which the requirements for the artefact are created, to serve activities and tastes; and where limits are placed on the possible expenditure of materials and time in its production. Without these there would be no functions for the object in the first place. There is possibly a religious 'environment' as part of the cultural. And it might even be suggested that the personality and skill of the designer or artisan form part of the environment of the designed object; though more reasonably they could be seen as mediating *between* artefact and environment, and constituting the agencies by which the adaptation or fit of one to the other is produced.

If there are different environments, for buildings let us say, in these terms, obtaining in different geographical areas or in different historical periods, then such building forms can be expected to vary correspondingly — this assuming that the forms are well-adapted to the prevailing circumstances in every case. Forms for identical or closely related functions will be geometrically similar, thus giving rise to the appearance of repeated instances of artefact 'types'. And if there is a degree of uniformity in the conditions — social, cultural, material, technological — affecting *all* artefacts in a given place and time, so it might be expected that even buildings or useful objects of different functions would still nevertheless possess some 'stylistic' features in common; so providing an explanation of stylistic periods and regional characters in architecture and the applied arts as a whole.

It is essentially these concepts, although expressed in rather less biological language, that are to be found in Viollet-le-Duc's exposition, in the *Dictionnaire*, of the significance for him of the two words 'Style' and 'Unité'.[10] *Style* in general is what is achieved by adherence in design to logical, structural or functional principles (*principes*). In nature the forms of animals or plants are governed by such principles. An artefact, or a creature, which is well-adapted, will have style. 'If we follow all the phases of inorganic and organic creation, we shall soon recognise the logical order, in its most varied and even apparently different aspects, which results from a *principe*, from an *a priori* law, from which it never departs.'[11]

le-Duc 'style' achieved by adherence to 'principes' (of struct., funct.) a priori laws

True style in architecture will be produced by keeping to equivalent principles. It is thus something which is produced, not automatically for sure — it requires thought, effort and skill — but as a kind of side-effect of the successful reconciliation, and expression, of function and structure. Style is not consciously aimed at, but grows like a plant according to fixed rules. It is certainly not 'a sort of spice which one takes from a bag to sprinkle over those works which, by themselves, would lack any savour'.[12]

The greatest historical *styles* in architecture — for Viollet-le-Duc the buildings of the Greeks, of the Romans, and the medieval architecture of France — are those in which there exists a unity of intention and conception, a unity of form with constructional method; and hence which, in their different ways, all possess *style*. The monuments from the various periods are 'highly dissimilar', Viollet-le-Duc says,

> and they are dissimilar because they obey the law of unity based on structure. The structural method changes and the form must necessarily alter, but there is not one Greek unity, one Roman unity, one medieval unity. An oak tree bears no great resemblance to the base of a fern, nor does a horse to a rabbit; plants and animals submit nevertheless to the principle of organic unity which rules all organised individuals.[13]

Several points should be noticed about this argument in general, and about Viollet-le-Duc's version in particular. First is that a connection is now established between the external 'environmental' conditions in which a building is produced, and that coordination or coherence, that necessary relation of the parts, which in the previous 'anatomical' discussion we had treated as wholly internal to the body or the building in itself. Cuvier had related the 'conditions of existence' to the 'correlation of parts'. This relation now has its counterpart in the architectural analogy.

For Viollet-le-Duc a building, or all the buildings of a historical period, if they possess *style*, will do so because they form a *unity*. The word unity has no doubt larger (and vaguer) aesthetic (and scientific) significance for Viollet-le-Duc; he says that 'creation is unity; chaos, the absence of unity',[14] and at one point discusses unity in terms of a unification of all the laws of physical science. But I at least interpret one of its connotations as referring to the internal coordination which Viollet-le-Duc clearly recognised as being common to animal anatomy and architectural structure; and this interpretation seems to be supported by the references to architectural unity in connection with structural methods and materials in building.

On the other hand it would be wrong to imply that Viollet-le-Duc imagined a complete determinism in the way in which the style of building reflected the changes in 'environment', in function or in structural methods. On the contrary it was the highest achievement of art to produce this unity, this adaptation of form to purpose (which was by no means to be found in

'UNITY' = internal 'correlation of parts' (as in Cuvier) — ie structurally principaled, functionally correct

every historical style at every period); it could be brought about, as mentioned, only by the application of intelligence and reason, and through artistic sensitivity.

The same point is taken up by Eidlitz, whose definition of architectural style is very close to Viollet-le-Duc's. Style for Eidlitz is a result of adhering to definite *ideas* (the equivalent of Viollet-le-Duc's *principes*) and of working these out according to the nature of the chosen materials. It is also a result of 'progress in artistic ability to express ideas in matter architecturally'.[15] The implication of this last point is that logical analysis of function and structure is not enough to ensure that the reasoning behind the design is fully *expressed* in its appearance; and that this visual exposition of the building's 'argument' is a matter of artistic skill, rather than some completely necessary consequence of the application of reasoning alone.

*not determin-istic*

It follows as a corollary that in those periods of architectural history in which forms were ill-adapted to function and circumstance, because architects had failed in reasoning or in expressive power, then their buildings would exhibit an awkwardness and an incoherence of their parts. Such periods would give birth to breeds of architectural monsters.

*lacking expression, having awkwardness, incoherence = 'monsters'*

Greenough had described contemporary American building as a kind of absurd and degraded architectural circus. To clap Greek pediments on to Wall Street banks and force billiard halls behind temple facades was as if the lion were shaved and called a dog, or the unicorn harnessed to the plough.[16] For Sullivan the architectural animals of commercial America are not just dressed up; they are positively deformed. He pictures the clothing of steel framed buildings in masonry forms which refer to quite other structural methods, as producing strange hybrids. This passage irresistibly calls to mind Cuvier and the 'repugnance' of impossible organic combinations.

*American monsters ↓ impossible (unprincipled) combinations*

> Imagine for instance:
>   Horse-eagles.
>   Pumpkin-bearing frogs.
>   Frog-bearing pea vines.
>   Tarantula-potatoes.
>   Sparrows in the form of whales, picking up crumbs in the street. If these combinations seem incongruous and weird, I assure you in all seriousness that they are not a whit more so than the curiosities encountered with such frequency by the student of what nowadays passes for architecture.[17]

We left the question of architectural classification in an earlier chapter at a point where the practical need for classification seemed to be presented by the emergence of new social functions for buildings; but where paradoxically enough the methods of botanical taxonomy, which were arguably taken as a model for classification, turned purely on features of geometrical or formal similarity or difference between plant species. This 'ecological' conception of the relation of the forms of buildings and other artefacts, via their practical functions, to the social, cultural and material environments in which they are produced, offers the possibility for a truly *functional* classificatory method based on the kinds of social activity served or accommodated, on materials and techniques of construction, on geographical variations in climate — in a word on 'environmental' factors of all kinds.

Thus we find Viollet-le-Duc's criteria for classifying buildings to be essentially functional and material ones. We have noted earlier how Viollet-le-Duc turned to the general principles of Cuvier's systematic arrangement of animal species in the 'Restoration' entry in the *Dictionnaire*. What such principles would mean in this architectural application, he develops further in the section on 'Unité'.[18] Like Durand, he is concerned with drawing conclusions from a classification of architectural history, for an approach or method in the design of new buildings. What use is it, he asks, for a man to inherit a splendid library, unless he can sort it into some kind of order, and so be able to make use of it? Equally, what use can the architect make of the past, how can he organise the classification of his architectural library, so as to give substance to the hope that out of it all, 'il sortira l'architecture de l'avenir'?

On what criteria would he make this classification of the buildings described? He would look, Viollet-le-Duc says, at the various human and social needs satisfied in each case: shelter, assembly, the accommodation of man's various occupations. Then he would look at the manner in which these needs are satisfied: from what materials the building is made, whether it is a permanent or temporary structure, and so on. It would thus be a functional classification, based not exclusively or necessarily on similarities of appearance, but on similarities between the purposes of buildings and between the ways in which they are constructed to fulfil these purposes.

When it comes to practical application of his own prescriptions, it seems as though Viollet-le-Duc placed more emphasis on materials and their effect on engineering structure than on anything else. He says of the succession of Greek, Roman and Gothic that 'the structural method changes and the form must necessarily alter'; and it certainly seems that his own published projects, with their surprising tilted columns and boldly expressed cast iron, are more intended to show how the forms of a new architecture are to be developed out of the new industrial materials of the nineteenth century, than out of the new social order and its functional requirements.* (Although these too are given their place, as for instance in

---

* There is a certain sad irony in the way in which these awkward designs fail to achieve just that unity which Viollet-le-Duc had emphasised as so essential. As Sir John Summerson says: 'It is all marvellously clever ... but the result is not very moving. It does lack style. It is rather like a language invented *ad hoc*; a sort of esperanto evolved from the salient characteristics of other languages but lacking the vital unity which any one language possesses' (*Heavenly Mansions, and other Essays on Architecture* (London, 1949), p. 156). Or in our terms a creature of Dr Frankenstein, from stolen limbs and organs.

the discussion of symmetry and the planning of houses in the lecture on 'Domestic Architecture' in the *Entretiens*.)[19]

In slight contrast to but still in fundamental sympathy with Viollet-le-Duc, is the position of E. L. Garbett, whose *Rudimentary Treatise* on architecture appeared in 1850 and was read appreciatively by Ralph Waldo Emerson and by Greenough.[20] Garbett thought that a new style for the nineteenth century was only justified by the introduction of a new constructional *principle* – and not by new materials as such. The new principle was that of the *truss*, out of whose use would come a 'tensile' architecture, as distinct from the 'depressile' architecture of the beam (i.e. Greek), and the 'compressile' architecture of the arch (Gothic).

In Gottfried Semper's writings, by comparison with Viollet-le-Duc, there is an overriding preoccupation with systematisation and classification; and with Semper too the reference to Cuvier in this connection is much more explicit and more extensive. Viollet-le-Duc and Semper were close contemporaries. It is quite possible to imagine a modest degree of mutual influence, since we know that Viollet-le-Duc owned a copy of Semper's great work *Der Stil*;[21] and in *Der Stil* there are certainly many references to Viollet-le-Duc.* The two part company, however, in the specific historical periods which they regard respectively as best exemplifying true style; for Viollet-le-Duc it is of course the Gothic, while Semper's admiration – coming from his classical German education – is for the Greeks. And Semper's main emphasis in his writing is on handicrafts and the design of household objects, rather than on architecture. Indeed the two completed volumes of *Der Stil* are devoted entirely to the subject of craft work and decoration, while a third, projected volume on architecture was never completed.

Semper's definition of style is nevertheless rather close to Viollet-le-Duc's. It varies in precise formulation at different stages in the development of his thought; but it turns always on the relation of a work to the circumstances or environment in which it is created, and on the role of the artist in responding to and expressing these circumstances. Thus in the pamphlet *Wissenschaft, Industrie und Kunst*[22] of 1852, style is defined as 'the basic idea [of a work] raised to artistic significance'; in which process the artist must have regard to tools, materials and physical climate, and in which the influence of time, place and culture will also be felt.

Elsewhere he includes amongst these 'environmental' influences on style, the prevailing social, political and religious climates of each country and period.[23] Style is 'the conformity of an art object with the circumstances of its origin and the conditions and circumstances of its development'.[24]

Semper even has an 'algebraic' formulation of the nature of style,[25] which

---

* According to Lawrence Harvey, though, Semper regarded Viollet-le-Duc as an enemy. 'Semper's Theory of Evolution in Architectural Ornament', *Transactions of the Royal Institute of British Architects*, 1 (1885), 29–54. See p. 31.

he expresses thus:                     *Semper's defn. of STYLE*

$$Y = \text{function } F \,(x, y, z, \text{ etc.}).$$

Y is any of a range of possible particular styles, and in each case this style is
a function (in the algebraic sense) of the function (in the utilitarian sense) of
the object in question, modified by a series of variables $x, y, z$ etc. These
variables stand for the sort of material and cultural factors already listed.
Thus objects with a common function — favourite examples are water
vessels or drinking cups — which are made of different materials, by different techniques, by different peoples, at different periods, will have a
certain essential form and set of geometric characters in common. Semper
refers to these common formal properties of objects of similar function by the
word 'type' or 'motif'.[26] Meanwhile the 'environmental' differences will
have their effects in transforming or modifying the basic type — by minute
or continuously varying degrees, in principle — so resulting in the formal
differences by which the style in question is characterised. Both cultural
and material factors are influential on historical styles; but it is by attending
to the expression of the material conditions, in architecture and the practical
arts, that the designer will achieve style in Semper's general and laudatory
sense.

Semper's general formulation of what constitutes style, and Viollet-le-    *Zeit-*
Duc's too, in so far as they take account of social, cultural and historical    *geist*
factors, serve to align them with a much broader and more widely held
theory of artistic style as the product of the cultural milieu or *Zeitgeist*. As
L. D. Ettlinger says:

> Ever since the late eighteenth century, historians and archaeologists had
> concerned themselves with the problem of national styles and had looked
> for causal connections between forms and the spirit of the people who had
> made them. In Germany, Winckelmann, Herder, the Romantics, and above
> all Hegel had tried in various ways to show that each work of art is the
> tangible expression of a nation, and conversely that the physiognomy of
> each work of art or building reveals the deepest thoughts and feelings of its
> makers.[27]

There is a strong component of this tradition of ideas in Semper's lecture
on *Architecture and Civilisation* given in London in 1853.[28] There is something
of it in Viollet-le-Duc's historical analyses, especially in his interpretation
of the social background of French Gothic. In England the same concepts
would be associated principally in the architectural context with the name
of Pugin. For some later but representative statements, we might instance
Auguste Choisy's remark in his *Histoire de l'Architecture* that 'Buildings
classify themselves as witnesses fixing the way of life and the moral condition
of humanity age by age';[29] or Sullivan's allusion in an essay 'What is Architec-

*bldgs. as witnesses*

ture?' to buildings as 'the product and index of the thought of the people of the time and place'.[30]

It is not my present purpose to explore these ideas in any detail.[31] Their history is complicated and diffuse, and in the end there is nothing especially biological about such a loose 'environmental' metaphor. (It accounts for a large part, however, of what Sullivan and Frank Lloyd Wright meant by an 'organic' architecture: that it should grow naturally out of the society which produced it. For both men this implied a distinct political involvement, and the search for a proper architecture of democracy.) There will be more to be said on the subject when we come to the (closely related) metaphor of the *progress* of historical styles as a process of artistic evolution.

Instead I propose to concentrate here on the material and technological influences on style; and it is in any case these, and not the cultural, which Semper identifies as the keys to his classification. The whole structure of *Der Stil* is on a systematic plan, with the forms of handicraft production classified primarily on the basis of materials — textiles, ceramics, wood and stone construction — and with architecture classified similarly four ways. In Semper's scheme the various parts of the building correspond to his four basic materials: wood construction in the roof and stone for the foundations and basement, while by a somewhat forced and unconvincing argument the central hearth with its cooking vessels is related to ceramics, and the partition walls to textiles.[32]

Actually it is not strictly correct to say that materials of construction provide the criteria for classification in Semper's scheme; since the materials in question are associated by Semper in each case with characteristic properties affecting their strengths, their structural uses, and therefore the ways in which they are variously worked and assembled.[33]

The principle of textile materials is that of thin, pliable, tough fibres, which may be plaited or woven. Ceramics have the property before firing of a great plasticity, capable of being moulded; then they are hardened into permanent shape. Carpentry and joinery make use of the characteristic properties of timber — that it comes in long pieces of high elasticity with a certain resistance to bending — by combining these pieces into rigid frameworks. In masonry, finally, the pieces are hard, very strong in compression, shaped by carving, and piled together into assemblies of blocks. These qualities and methods of assembly would thus serve to classify other materials — the most obvious omission being metals — with the four basic types. For example, metal might be moulded, like ceramics; or worked into bars and joined in frameworks, like timber.

In a manuscript devoted largely to the classification of works in metal, dated 1854, Semper sets out the plan for an ideal or universal museum, which is organised spatially according to his four-way system.[34] He admits that no real museum could or even should aspire to universality; but he does think that every actual museum should nevertheless be imagined as part of such an ideal and all-encompassing collection, and that it should be laid out accordingly. Semper's plan is for a square building whose sides represent the four fundamental materials or material principles. The four corners stand for appropriate combinations of materials in pairs; and at the centre of the square are those works in which all four materials are combined, as typically in architecture.

It is not especially important here whether the categories of Semper's classification are useful or convincing ones in detail. What is relevant is the overall principle of classification; and it is clear that this is first of all by function, and in second place by material and technological factors.

We can now turn back to biology, and examine what Semper saw in the classificatory methods of Cuvier. Semper had visited and been much impressed by the zoological exhibits in the *Jardin des Plantes* in 1826.[35] He also makes plain, by direct reference and in discussions of 'palaeozoology' in his writings, his familiarity with Cuvier's published works. He describes Cuvier's museum, and makes the analogy with a proposed comparative method of analysis in art and architecture, in a lecture which he gave at Marlborough House during his stay in England in the 1850s. He says:

> In this magnificent collection ... we perceive the *types* for all the most implicated forms of the animal empire, we see progressing nature, with all its variety and immense richness, most sparing and economical in its fundamental forms and motives; we see the same skeleton repeating itself continuously, but with innumerable varieties, modified by gradual developments of the individuals and by the conditions of existence which they had to fulfil ... A method, analogous to that which Cuvier followed, applied to art, and especially to architecture would at least contribute towards getting a clear insight over its whole province and perhaps also form the basis of a doctrine of *style* and a sort of *topic* or method, how to invent ... [36]

This last sentence is particularly suggestive, in the way in which Semper sees such a procedure leading beyond just analytic classification, to provide a basis for synthetic methods for design. (Elsewhere Semper makes reference, in a similar context, to Durand's planning system, but with the stricture, like Sullivan's, that his method is of a mechanical, additive nature only, and cannot produce that organic coherence which must characterise true types.)[37]

So far as I know neither Semper nor Viollet-le-Duc make explicit reference to the classificatory principle of the 'subordination of characters' or to Cuvier's use of it. The fact is, though, that the analogy with the applied arts and architecture allows for the interpretation of this idea as much as it had for the correlation of parts. The meaning of the subordination of characters was, we remember, that certain organs or parts of the body were of more

*'Subordination of characters'*
*(increasing variation in subservient parts)*

central importance to the functioning of the whole — as for example the brain and nervous system, or the heart and circulatory system — than were others; and that there were fewer opportunities for variation in these key functional parts than in the less significant peripheral or surface features.

In rationalism in architecture the equivalent of such a rule would be that certain important structural characters or members would be standardised, invariant between buildings of similar function and construction — as perhaps the basic structural elements of the vaulting system of the Gothic cathedrals — while surface features, decoration and small detail could be the subject of considerable capricious variation. This interpretation would certainly be in agreement with Viollet-le-Duc's views on the subject, and something equivalent could reasonably be argued as an implication of Semper's. The consequence would follow, for a functional classification of artefacts and buildings, that this should be made on the basis of fundamental similarities of function and structural arrangement, with rather little reference to superficial characters of minor functional significance.

We have now come to a crucial point in this whole discussion of the question of architectural or 'artificial' classification; and it is one which needs some clarification, since Semper in particular is rather confused or inconsistent here.

*variety of criteria used for grouping similarities*

It is clear that a classification of artefacts or buildings could be made in any of a very large number of ways, according to the interests of the classifier and the purposes for which the classification is made. Such classifications need have no bearing on the *form* of the objects whatsoever; they might be according to the artists who designed the objects, their date of manufacture, who they belonged to, or any of a hundred other such properties or characters. When a classification is made, as is Semper's, according to function and materials, then objects are still not classed together by virtue of their similarity of form *in itself*; but only in so far as the similarities of function and of materials of manufacture, by which the grouping *is made*, give rise to similarities of form — inasmuch as form follows function.

*given like function, like appearance may result from functional constraint (ecology) from 'copying model'*

There are, however, two plausible reasons, aside from pure coincidence, why artefacts of related function might have similar geometric form or appearance. The first is this constraint which the local circumstances of material, manufacture and function impose upon the form — whether a cup is made of glass or clay, whether it is moulded or thrown, what drink it is intended to hold, what ceremonial or social convention may attach to its use, and so on. Under equivalent conditions, the resulting forms might be expected to be comparable. The second reason for similarities of form in artefacts is a 'genetic' one: that one object has been *copied* in its manufacture from another of similar function — the glassblower or potter making the drinking cup has taken another cup, either an actual cup or an image of a cup in his memory, as his model in producing the new one. Obviously the two explanations might and very likely would coincide in one and the same artefact; but the conceptual separation is still most important.

The point is a crucial one, in that there is no real temporal or historical component in the first case, while there most definitely is in the second. In the simple 'ecological' analogy in the applied arts generally, forms and styles are to be related to 'environmental' conditions occurring at different points in time. If the 'environment' changes between one historical date and another, so would the forms and style; but this is not a matter of any continuous or autonomous historical process in the forms and styles themselves. Should the environmental conditions change back to what they were precisely at some previous point in time, then in principle – though the argument is perhaps a little unrealistic – so should the forms of artefacts revert exactly.

Where the similarity of form is to be attributed to the fact of copying, then this immediately implies a process extending over time as designs are copied and copied again; and what is more it is a directional and not a reversible process which is involved. We are verging here on an evolutionary explanation; and it is in this distinction between the explanation of similarities of form in terms of similarities of environment, and their explanation in terms of copying – which in the biological analogy would correspond to heredity – that the wide gap between Cuvier and Darwin opens.

Cuvier was strongly committed as we have seen to the view that organic species were distinct and undiverging for all time. There was thus for Cuvier a real basis to classification at the species level; the criterion being that interbreeding was possible only between members of the same species, or at least that only these unions could produce fertile offspring. Separate species had a 'mutual aversion' which prevented them mating; and within each species all individuals were descendants of a common ancestral stock. This was a hypothetical definition which it was difficult to verify by observation or experiment, but it does nevertheless remain essentially the same criterion by which species are distinguished in principle in zoology today. (The difference being of course that modern biology believes that one species *can* gradually separate, it can evolve, into two or more species sufficiently distinct, in time, for interbreeding to become impossible.) Cuvier could not deny the fact that within one species, slight variations of form, size, colour and so on were universally to be found – something which we know well from our own species. But it was his view that these occurred in what were, according to the principle of the subordination of characters, the less significant and more superficial features of the animal. Meanwhile the organs of primary importance were strictly invariable.

While Cuvier might then have attributed similarities of appearance in the same species to the effects of heredity, this was not in fact the main basis for his explanation at all. The cause for him was rather to be found in the stability

of the animal's conditions of existence. And at the higher levels of classification — those of classes, orders and genera — this was necessarily the whole
of Cuvier's explanation. Such groupings were artificial ones, made only for
the convenience of the naturalist or zoologist; and in so far as they had any
foundation in reality, it was because they arose as secondary effects of certain
common features of the environments of groups of species, of their conditions
of existence — that all fishes live in the sea, that all birds must have an
aerodynamic form, etc.

The alternative or additional explanation for the general similarities of
species in the larger and higher classificatory groups — the families, orders,
classes and phyla — and one quite unacceptable to Cuvier, was that suggested
(unwittingly) in the phrase used by Aristotle when he described such groups
as possessing a degree of 'family resemblance'. It was of course that, as
individuals shared a common descent within species, so species shared a
common descent within phyla. Not that Darwin and other evolutionary
thinkers denied the relation of organism to environment; indeed it was
precisely this which they were concerned to explain. But in Darwinian
theory it is through 'copying' or hereditary processes that the adaptation to
environment is achieved.

We are coming to the point where it will be necessary to embark on a
full-scale account of the evolutionary analogy in architecture and handicrafts. We can anticipate a little, however, in this discussion of classification
in the work of Semper and Viollet-le-Duc, to point out the ways in which the
strictly 'ecological' and 'evolutionary' aspects of biological analogy are there
confounded or compounded.

For Viollet-le-Duc the point is well illustrated in his view of Gothic. In
the entry in the *Dictionnaire* under 'Cathédrale' there appears, amid detailed
descriptive analyses of a number of particular French cathedrals, a figure
which illustrates a hypothetical cathedral (figure 14).[38] Although it follows
broadly the original, though never completely executed, design for Rheims,
Viollet-le-Duc makes it clear that the drawing is intended to show the arrangement *typical* of French thirteenth-century cathedrals collectively. The
idea is not original to Viollet-le-Duc; there was a tradition of such drawings
going back to guide books of the seventeenth century.[39]

Hubert Damisch in his essay *L'Architecture Raisonnée* calls Viollet-le-Duc's
version 'La cathédrale idéale', an ideal or theoretical model of the Gothic
cathedral.[40] His interpretation of the drawing is that it is intended by
Viollet-le-Duc as a conceptual tool, designed to reveal the structural principles which are common to all the cathedrals actually built, these real
buildings representing a series of variations on or transformations (*multiples
réalisations*) of the one basic theoretical type.[41] It has something of the
character of Goethe's archetypal plant, but conceived in a rather different
spirit and for a very different purpose.

14   E. E. Viollet-le-Duc, 'Cathédrale idéale'.

Viollet-le-Duc's cathedral archetype is not thought of as corresponding to some sort of ultimate or Platonic essence. Nor is it suggested that this ideal type was in any way imagined to exist in the conscious minds of the cathedral builders. It is intended rather as a conceptual or didactic classificatory device, to aid understanding.

The 'ideal cathedral' offers explanation because it provides a rational exposition of the structural and functional logic of every member — the vault, the pier, the flying buttress and all the other parts — and their assembly into a coherent, coordinated structural system. Inasmuch as all cathedrals shared the same general function, and employed similar constructional techniques and materials, so their basic structural forms would be similar, and would correspond to the ideal plan. Any variations would result from one of two possible kinds of changes. The first would be changes in these determining factors, i.e. 'environmental' changes.

But a second kind of change is attributed by Viollet-le-Duc to the varying degrees of success with which succeeding generations of builders achieved a true rapport between structure, function and form, a 'unity of intention and conception'. It was quite possible that this degree of success might be greater at each subsequent attempt, as each generation copied old forms but introduced improvements by stages; and so a progression of forms towards some ever more perfect resolution would be evident. Here then is Viollet-le-Duc's evolutionary interpretation of the overall progress of Gothic; he talks of medieval architecture as a whole being an organism 'which develops and progresses as nature does in the creation of beings; starting from a very simple principle which it then modifies, which it perfects, which it makes more complicated, but without ever destroying the original essence'.[42]

Although the reference here is specifically to the progress of medieval cathedral building, it would be true to say that similar arguments are to be found in Viollet-le-Duc's descriptions of, for example, the development of the Greek temple form. Thus in the *Entretiens* he describes how

> in Classic times, Greek genius attained a relative perfection only by a series of experiments tending always in the same direction. Thus, by how many successive modifications of the Doric order was that perfection attained which is exhibited in the Parthenon! We recognise many, though we do not know them all.[43]

Turning now to Semper: he is actually reported to have conceived the idea of organic evolution on the occasion, ironically enough, of his visit to the *Jardin des Plantes* — or rather to have recalled to mind then a quotation from Seneca which he regarded as anticipating Darwin.[44] And despite the fact that it is Cuvier's museum which is held out as the model for classification in the applied arts, the truth is that Semper's theory incorporates a substantial evolutionary or historical component within it. His idea of a type or motif, as we have seen, is related to constancy of function; and he writes of those 'traditional forms which over the centuries have proved themselves to be unshakably true expressions of types'.[45] But at the same time he makes a definite claim that in certain types, particularly those associated with his four key materials, lie the *historical origins* of the applied arts and architecture; and that in the subsequent progress of these arts the original types have been continuously elaborated and differentiated.

It seems that a particular Caribbean house which was on show amongst the ethnographic collections in the Great Exhibition of 1851 was important in suggesting to Semper the idea for the 'four elements of architecture', a concept which he developed in a little book published in the same year.[46] The four archetypal elements are combined together into the *Urhutte*, the archetypal building from which all architecture in theory began. (There is an allusion here, it appears, to Goethe's *Urformen*.[47] The similar idea appears in *Der Stil* and elsewhere, in the concept of type-forms in handicrafts, such as the textile mat which Semper regards as the origin of the partition wall in architecture.)

*[margin note: Semper's 'urhutte' archetypal bldg.]*

Later Semper read *The Origin of Species*, and according to Ettlinger 'stressed certain parallels to his own theories, without however wishing to transfer Darwin's method altogether to the arts'.[48] He thought that the origins and progress of the art of building were 'as . . . entitled to an investigation as are the natural sciences or comparative philology'.[49] And he saw the value in such a study as providing something for architecture which it could not in the sciences; and that was, rules and principles to be used in design. In the evolutionary view, 'Building styles . . . are not invented, but develop in various departures from a few primitive types, according to the laws of natural breeding, of transmission and adoption. Thus the development is similar to the evolutions in the province of organic creation.'[50]

Where Semper believed that the Darwinian analogy failed to hold — and it is the core of the various evolutionary fallacies which I shall analyse at some length in later chapters — was in the role of the human designer in the origin of building styles and forms.

> The old monuments are very correctly designated as fossil shells of extinct organisms of society, but these shells did not grow into the back of the latter, like snail shells, nor did they shoot up like coral reefs according to some blind process of nature. They are free creations of man, who used intelligence, observation of nature, genius, will, knowledge and power, in their production.[51]

# 6

# The Darwinian analogy: trial and error in the evolution of organisms and artefacts

*1858  origin of Species*

It will suit the argument here to turn to Darwin and *The Origin of Species*, and to leave an account of some of his predecessors until afterwards. There is even some historical justification in this apparently anti-historical procedure, since the views of many of these precursors of Darwin only became known to a general and non-technical public after Darwin's own ideas were widely publicised. Darwin himself was partly instrumental in this process by publishing in the third and subsequent editions of the *Origin* a list of thirty-four authors, including his own grandfather Erasmus, who had anticipated his thoughts in some aspect or other. Many of these were previously unknown even to Darwin, and were brought to his attention by others. And although the subject of evolution was discussed in biological circles from the early 1800s and indeed even earlier, it was only in the 1860s that the real impact of evolutionary thinking was felt in other subjects, amongst them architecture, design and, as we shall see, archaeology and ethnology.

Darwin and Wallace presented their theories to the scientific community in twin papers to the Linnaean Society in 1858. There followed one year later the publication of *On the Origin of Species by Means of Natural Selection*, without doubt the most important event in nineteenth-century biology.[1] In the *Origin* Darwin draws out some general observations from an enormous accumulation of zoological and botanical data. The first is that most living creatures produce very many more offspring than is required simply to replace their number. A population, if account is taken of numbers of births alone, would tend to increase in geometric ratio.

> There is no exception to the rule that every organic being naturally increases at so high a rate, that if not destroyed, the earth would soon be covered by the progeny of a single pair. Even slow-breeding man has doubled in twenty-five years, and at this rate, in a few thousand years, there would literally not be standing room for his progeny.[2]

Despite this, although dramatic fluctuations certainly do occur in animal and plant populations, in general the number of any one species remains roughly the same from one generation to the next. It follows from these two observations that a struggle for survival must take place. This struggle might go on not only in the competition of young to achieve maturity. It could include a competition for reproductive advantage, through success in mating, greater fertility or in other ways.

The third important observation which Darwin makes from his accumulated studies of nature is the fact of variation. Within any one species all individuals are not exactly identical; they vary in all sorts of ways, some of which may confer an advantage in the struggle for survival, others a disadvantage. As a result a higher proportion of those individuals possessing a given advantage will achieve full development and reproduce; while those less well-suited will tend to fail to do so. And where such features are transmitted through inheritance, then the adaptive variation will tend to spread through the population, and be perpetuated, while the disadvantageous variation will disappear.

It is not a requirement of Darwin's theory that only the beneficial characteristics be inherited. It is sufficient that *all* variations be passed on, irrespective of their value to the animal or species, since only the beneficial ones will be retained in the end by selection. This is the 'survival of the fittest' (Herbert Spencer invented the phrase), the process of natural selection by which the forms of organisms are continually adapted and adjusted to their surrounding environment. It is not forces from the environment which mould the organism from outside, but a series of spontaneous changes coming from within which are then 'tested' against the environment; those which constitute improvements, or confer greater fitness, are preserved.

Darwin had drawn some of his inspiration here from a close study of the methods used by animal and plant breeders to produce modifications in domestic species — or even, apparently, new species altogether — by techniques of 'artificial selection';[3] and, Darwin says, he so named 'natural selection' as an equivalent process in nature. Plant breeders, for example, are not able to steer the gradual modification of a species along the required path by any direct action on their part. They must simply breed large numbers of plants, wait until they spot individual plants which have, in some minor degree, the kind of character they are aiming for, select those plants for further breeding, and so on.

Artificial selection tends to be applied to those external features of the animal or plant's appearance which the breeder can readily detect. In the case of pigeons, for example, these might be wholly frivolous features, such as the fantail, or the curious head-over-heels falling motion of the flight of the tumbler. But in other cases the characters selected for are ones which are to man's practical advantage, rather than just those which catch his whim: size and flavour in fruit and vegetables, colour, size and scent in flowers, strength or speed in horses, all kinds of useful habits or instinctual skills in dogs. Natural selection would be able to act on very minute variations of internal as well as external structure, which the breeder of domestic species would not necessarily be able to pick out. It would act always for the animal's own benefit. It would also have been acting over enormously greater spans of time.

Lyell's book, *Principles of Geology,*[4] provided Darwin with overwhelming evidence of the extreme antiquity of the earth; and it did this in part by reference to palaeontological evidence and the succession of fossil species – so indicating at the same time the very remote historical origins and progressive transformations of life itself. Lyell marshalled the arguments which were to prove conclusive in favour of uniformitarianism: the theory, due to the eighteenth-century geologist James Hutton, that the present state of the earth's surface and the formations of its strata are due to processes essentially similar to those still observable, such as erosion, volcanic action and earthquakes, acting over extremely protracted periods – and not due to cataclysmic or catastrophic events, such as great floods, of a singular and unrepeated nature. It was to such catastrophes that Cuvier among others had attributed the disappearance of the extinct species. Lyell's privately expressed ambition in writing the *Principles of Geology* was 'to sink the diluvialists',[5] and in this he was eminently successful.

Part of Cuvier's argument against evolution had been that there was not sufficient time in the earth's history for the changes required. He had pointed to the mummified animals recently found in Egypt, two to three thousand years old, which were identical with modern specimens.[6] The date of the most recent catastrophic flooding Cuvier had put at only five or six thousand years before the present. After Lyell these arguments against evolution on the basis of a lack of available time lost most of their force.

There has been much discussion in biology of what exactly is the nature of the 'fitness' to which the 'survival of the fittest' should be taken to refer. In the mathematical analysis of modern evolutionary genetics the rather imprecise term 'fittest' has been replaced by using purely numerical measures of reproductive success (in sexual reproduction the average number of off-spring per breeding pair[7]). Fitness is interpreted simply as 'fitness for survival'. It has been quite justifiably pointed out that this reduces the 'survival of the fittest' to a tautology; the phrase comes to mean no more than 'the survival of those which survive'.[8] The real issue, of what characteristics it is which endow their possessors with the reproductive advantage, is side-stepped.

But the capacity to reproduce and to survive as individuals and as a species depends in turn on fitness understood in a much more common-sense and everyday meaning, even if this fitness is not so directly susceptible to exact quantification. Thus fitness might be found in a whole range of attributes: in an animal being better fitted for finding food, better fitted for moving about, better camouflaged to evade predators, more attractive to possible mates, more fecund — any quality which contributes to the animal's success in avoiding early death and producing offspring.

In organic evolution the single dominating goal towards which all adaptations are aimed is that of survival. This goal is achieved by a series of adaptations of the various parts, which improve their contribution to supporting and furthering the main aim. So there may be 'fitness' in a quite ordinary sense conferred on the animal by the possession of longer or stronger legs, sharper eyes, sharper teeth or sharper wits.

It is important to realise, however, that fitness is not an absolute quality, but always a relative attribute — relative to the particular environment in which the animal or plant finds itself. What confers fitness in one set of circumstances may be a disadvantage in another. If there is one successful species in any given area which exploits a certain kind of food to the extent where supplies become scarce, then it will be advantageous for another species to exploit a different food. To be the same light colour as the barks of trees, and thus be camouflaged from predatory birds, is an adaptation which confers fitness on certain moths. But when that bark is darkened by industrial smoke, it is then advantageous or more 'fit' for the moth to be black in colour; and the evolutionary process selects for this new adaptation.

With Cuvier the design of nature, the harmonious and fitting way in which each animal matched its conditions of existence, was all taken for granted; it was all part of the beneficence of God's creation, and provided the starting point for investigation and analysis. The same providentialism was if anything stronger amongst British biologists in the first half of the century, several of whom combined clerical positions with the pursuit of natural history. I have already mentioned William Paley's *Natural Theology*[9] of 1802, which was an extended treatment of this argument for the existence of God, the 'argument from design.' This book and Paley's *Evidences of Christianity* were read by Darwin at Cambridge. In the 1830s the Royal Society sponsored a set of popular books, the *Bridgewater Treatises*, written by scientists and clergymen, including the anatomist Charles Bell and the geologist William Buckland.[10] The express purpose of these was to demonstrate 'the power, wisdom and goodness of God as manifested in the Creation'.

As several historians of science have pointed out, there is not so much of a philosophical or conceptual gap between Darwin and his contemporary religious opponents as popular opinion would suppose. There is a common framework of ideas shared by both sides. What Darwin achieves is a kind of inversion within this accepted framework. Where previously design and adaptation had been taken as the points of departure of natural history, the causes of the phenomena which were to be examined, Darwin turns adaptation into an effect. As C. C. Gillispie argues, the problem of adaptation was crucial

*teleological*

*phenomenon*

*adaptation / as effect (Darwin) vs cause (theology) → mystery*

because the case in favour of purpose, the conception of biology as the science of the goal-directed, rested precisely there, on the ancient and reasonable observation that animals seem to be made in order to fit their circumstances and in order to live the lives they do lead, with the right equipment, the right instincts, and the right habits. Darwin did better than solve the problem of adaptation. He abolished it. He turned it from a cause, in the sense of final cause or evidence of a designing purpose, into an effect, in the Newtonian or physical sense of effect, which is to say that adaptation became a fact or phenomenon to be analyzed, rather than a mystery to be plumbed.[11]

What was particularly shocking in Darwin's theory for his more sophisticated Christian adversaries was thus not the assault on the traditional biblical account of the creation, but rather that the entire structure of argument, which had previously served to demonstrate the existence and wisdom of God, was appropriated from them and turned against them. God was replaced, as the agency responsible for adaptation, by natural selection. As W. F. Cannon expresses it, Darwin stole away the universe of the theologians.[12]

It was equally unacceptable and incomprehensible, for many philosophical opponents of Darwin, that he gave no convincing explanation of the sources of variation in organic form which are a crucial feature of his theory, and which would now be explained as deriving from genetic recombination and ultimately from mutations of the genes. It was only necessary, however, for Darwin to regard variations as though they occurred haphazardly; and although at different stages he offered some possible explanations of their cause, this was not strictly essential to his position, and variations could without harm to the main theory be treated as perfectly random and spontaneous. Other theories of evolution, principally Lamarck's as we shall see, devoted great attention to the problem of how variations might be produced. Darwin could simply ignore the question. But for him to place this random undirectedness at the very heart of the evolutionary mechanism was to many of Darwin's critics to render the whole process meaningless and purposeless.

*applied Darwinism*

The impact of Darwinism, first in theology, religion and philosophy, and subsequently in many more areas of intellectual activity, is very well known. Ideas of evolution were applied — not for the first time, but now with especial vigour — to human history, to the history of ideas and the growth of science, in art criticism, in linguistics, economics and social theory (from which some of Darwin's ideas had first come — notably through his reading, 'for amusement', Malthus's *Essay on the Principle of Population*, which had suggested to him the mechanism of selection, through the growth in numbers of a species and the consequent competition for food and resources[13]). The effect on such embryonic subjects as anthropology, sociology and psychology was overwhelming; and the whole basis of these emerging disciplines was set out or reorganised upon a biological, evolutionary foundation.

We will have occasion to follow some of these developments, if very briefly, when it comes to examining the fallacies underlying evolutionary analogies in architecture and design. But let us first see how the detailed mechanisms of the Darwinian theory are transposed into two fields which deal with material artefacts: architectural theory, and the study of material culture in archaeology and ethnology. It was a long time before the waves spreading out from the Darwinian commotion reached some of the more remote backwaters of architectural and design philosophy. But their full force was felt straight away in those areas of the study of man which were so much closer to biology.

In many respects of course the subject matter of both, architectural or design theory and archaeology, is the same: the study of tools or useful objects, of buildings and settlements. Perhaps to practising designers, or to students of architecture, the suggestion that a gradual process of evolution could result in as good or better forms than those devised by the free play of imagination was an affront to their sense of the role of creative individuality, and so to their self-esteem. The evolutionary view stressed cooperative activity in design, the importance of tradition and the inheritance of the past; a gradualist, reforming rather than revolutionary philosophy. It did not give the same weight to originality, novelty and the personal as did the Romantic concept of the artist's function. Perhaps in relation to the art and culture of distant peoples and the distant past these sensitive issues did not arise.

However this may be, it was the anthropologists and archaeologists who pioneered a scientific and explicitly Darwinian study of the way in which tools and buildings − in primitive cultures at least − are produced and developed. They were the first to bring these artefacts within the scope of Herbert Simon's 'sciences of the artificial'.

How is the analogy made, precisely, between Darwin's concept of organic evolution and the technological evolution of artefacts? The first step, as we saw with Semper and Viollet-le-Duc, is to equate heredity with copying. New tools or buildings are copied from old models, with every effort made to ensure the exact reproduction of the traditional design. One of the reasons for the particular appropriateness of Darwinian analogy to the study of primitive societies and manufactures is that there is arguably in such societies a great measure of social stability and a considerable conservatism in the methods of the primitive craftsman, stabilities which are further reinforced by tradition and taboo. More controversially, the primitive artisan may be argued to have weaker powers of creative imagination than his modern counterpart, or to lack the inventive or innovative urge. Such factors serve to stabilise designs and to discourage radical change; and this stability is the counterpart in technological terms of the stability of form in organisms conferred by genetic inheritance.

One must imagine, nevertheless, that for various reasons — lack of skill on the part of the maker, the refractory nature of materials, and so on — these copies are not exact in every detail, and that slight variations of form creep in as a result. These correspond to the variations between individuals in organic species which play the crucial role in Darwin's theory.

When the various implements or tools are put into use they are subjected thereby to a variety of tests, of their strength, sharpness, impermeability to water, whatever characteristics there are which confer appropriateness or fitness on that utensil — hammer, knife, pot — for its particular function. Large numbers of the same design are made; and those designs which have some slight variation in form which confers a particular advantage, an increased fitness, will tend to be preserved or selected. They will either tend to survive longer, because of their greater strength, for example; or perhaps they will be preferred as models when it comes to copying their forms in new tools.

One should notice that, as with Darwin's theory in relation to organic species, it is not necessary to the success of the process that all variations in form between copies should necessarily be beneficial or constitute an improvement. It is possible that variations be introduced simply accidentally, 'at random'; and the mechanism of selection will ensure the spread of the advantageous feature, and the elimination of the disadvantageous.

One feature that *is* necessary, in both cases, is that there should be long periods of time over which the evolutionary process can take its course; and that during these periods the environment (in the case of organism) or function (in the case of artefact) should not be subject to any extremely rapid changes. It was reasonable to imagine that, in the primitive societies from which the anthropologists and archaeologists took their examples, this condition was generally satisfied. Because the variations in form confer such very minor advantages, and only on a statistical basis, it takes time for selection to act. If large changes or variations were made at once, or many changes at a time, then the whole coherence and hence the viability (of the organism) or the functioning (of the artefact) would be jeopardised.

It is amusing to note in this context the architectural metaphor involved in one of the repeated and rather easy jibes made against Darwin. This was that his theory amounted to much the same as saying that if one were to throw a heap of bricks up in the air, repeatedly, then by the effect of 'random variations' they would be bound at some time or other, after a lot of trials, to come down in the form of a house. The analogy is of course false from the beginning. Darwin never suggested that large numbers of variations occurred simultaneously to the whole form and organisation of the creature or plant. Quite the contrary. It would be more truly analogous to his argument to imagine the design of a house being produced through the occasional random change of the position of one brick or one feature at a time, *while all the others remained fixed*; that element being retained in its new position if this turned out to be more appropriate in use. This is indeed not so far from the tolerably plausible and workable theory of the evolution of primitive architecture, or at least of simple artefacts, which was actually propounded in archaeology.

The analogy from organic evolution as applied to human manufactures, it will be observed, puts a new interpretation on the kind of relation which we have previously examined between an individual artefact and the general *type* of which that artefact is but one example. The type is what is transmitted in copying. It is the set of 'genetic instructions' which are somehow passed from one generation of craftsmen to another. We shall have cause to look at the implications of this aspect of the analogy rather closely later on. Suffice it to say here that the analogy suggests that artefacts themselves in some sense serve to carry *information* about their own functioning and manufacture, through time; and also that such information passes through the heads of craftsmen, and that there exists in the mind of the craftsman in some form the type, or image, or model for a species of artefact, which guides him when he comes to make a new copy.

It is not individual artefacts which evolve. It is abstract *designs*, of which particular artefacts are concrete realisations. The distinction corresponds to that made in biology, considerably after Darwin, between the *genotype*, which is the 'description' of the species transmitted through biological heredity, and the *phenotype*, which is the physical embodiment of what is described in the individual organic body. This is another point which will be taken up again.

We can now note how in the biological sphere this distinction serves to make clear the difference between those variations in the body of the individual animal which are heritable, and those which are not. The 'set of instructions' embodied in the genes, the genotype, is carried into effect in the development and growth of the individual, the phenotype. But the developmental process is not an absolutely fixed and predetermined programme; it has a certain flexibility. The direction which it takes within this permissible area of free play is conditioned by the immediate environment in which the animal grows up. Thus if the animal is nourished more or less adequately, or on different sorts of foods for example, it may be stunted or enlarged in size, or affected in hair, skin colour etc. Such variations of bodily form are not then transmitted to that individual's offspring.

Going back to the application to artefacts, we can possibly see something analogous. We might imagine an abstract design transmitted culturally, for a type of building or object. When it comes to making a particular artefact, then the design is realised; but it is realised with the available materials, with the tools immediately to hand, and in the case of buildings on some specific site with its own special features. All these 'environmental' factors acting on the manufacture or 'development' of the artefact will plausibly have their effects in slight changes or variations in form from one object of the given type to another. (Whether such 'variations' would be 'inherited' in the techno-logical case is, however, a rather more vexed question.)

One very vivid and telling example of this distinction of 'phenotype' from 'genotype' in architecture, which is due to Hillier and Leaman,[14] is that pro-vided by the design of the military encampment — perhaps the Roman camp. Here there existed a standard arrangement which was embodied no doubt quite literally in a set of explicit instructions — in 'standing orders' — and which was realised on particular occasions on many sites in widely scattered parts of the Empire. Due to differences in topography, building materials and so on, these realisations would all have been different in minor detail, though all built to the same underlying design. It is perhaps possible that this idea provides us with one way of understanding the very characteristic feature of primitive and vernacular architecture: that within a pattern of overall similarity between one building of given function in some culture and an-other, there will nevertheless often be considerable variations of detail.* (Other interpretations in terms of different choices on the part of builders or occupants, small functional differences etc., are equally possible.)

The essence of the Darwinian theory lies in the concept of trial and error; the trials being provided by variations, and the errors being detected and removed by selection. Before Darwin, similarities of form in the organic body had been seen to be associated with similarities of environment — even though this relation might not, as in the case of Cuvier or the natural theolo-gians, have been generally regarded as a causal one (causal in the Newtonian sense — as distinct from the kind of teleological explanation offered by Aristotle's 'final' causes).

Darwin had shown how similarities due to heredity or historical origin could be connected with similarities due to adaptation to similar environ-mental conditions. Adaptation to environment was *produced* through trial and error, and the successful results retained and passed on through heredity. Animals of different species might be similar because those species had an immediate historical connection through the evolutionary 'family tree'; they

---

*This fact may possibly have a great deal to do with the aesthetic attraction of vernacular architecture. Unity in diversity, 'likeness tempered with differences' (Gerard Manley Hopkins's phrase), variation according to a theme; these are properties which many critics and writers on aesthetics have diagnosed as being essential to the beauty both of works of art and of natural phenomena. There is a quality of 'freedom within rules', of order in the gross combined with unique-ness and variety in the detail, a non-mechanical, unpredictable but nevertheless generally controlled effect, which seems to be the source of some basic aesthetic satisfaction. A most attractive essay on this theme in relation to organic form is Paul Weiss, 'Beauty and the Beast: Life and the Rule of Order', *Scientific Monthly*, 81 (1955), 286–99.

might be similar because they shared similar ways of life and occupied similar ecological 'niches'; or they might be similar for both reasons together, because of the one fact being causally related to the other. (This is not by any means to say that all species which occupy similar environmental conditions are necessarily closely related evolutionarily.)

There is a very general idea that technical progress in building, the accumulation of structural, material and engineering knowledge and the refinement of constructional form and technique, have been the product of extended historical processes of trial and error by many generations of architects and craftsmen. This idea occurs very widely in the theoretical literature of the nineteenth century, and cannot indeed be attributed to any specifically Darwinian analogy, especially since it is to be found well developed before 1859.

Viollet-le-Duc's remarks on the structural (and artistic) evolution of Gothic and of the Greek temple have been quoted in chapter 5. James Fergusson in his *True Principles of Beauty in Art* (1849) has a whole chapter devoted to 'Progress in Art'.[15] Where better can such progress be observed than in medieval architecture from the twelfth to the fourteenth centuries? The critic will find here 'a series of buildings one succeeding the other, and the last containing not only all the improvements before introduced into all the former examples, but contributing something new itself towards perfecting a style'.[16] These buildings occupied the attention of not just a series of individual architects, but a whole mass of people, clergy as well as masons and mechanics, who worked together in a common effort. Both the overall form and the separate architectural details are subject to this process of improvement:

> the rude and heavy Norman pier was gradually lightened and refined into the clustered shaft of the later Gothic; . . . the low rude waggon-vault expanded into the fairy roof of tracery, and the small timid opening in the wall, which was a window in the earlier churches, became 'a transparent wall of gorgeous hues'.[17]

In every case it is not the contributions of individual geniuses alone which are the source of progress; it is the existence of an organised system in which each generation builds on the achievements of its predecessors, and knowledge and skill are built up cumulatively. Fergusson slips without remark or pause from discussion of progress in artistic style or in the solution of an aesthetic problem, to discussion of progress in scientific knowledge; indeed the two are assumed to be equivalent processes. Thus in astronomy, geology or chemistry, progress is made, for Fergusson, in essentially the same way as in medieval architecture.

Every new worker in these scientific fields starts from the level reached through the collective effort of all those who have laboured before him. He does not have to bother with the failures, the rejected efforts of previous workers; he can know how to avoid their mistakes. Even the beginner in contemporary astronomy or physics, says Fergusson, knows more than Newton, and, whatever his talents, cannot help but move knowledge forward in some slight degree beyond where it stood before. Though the genius of the greatest scientists can revolutionise their subject, they too must still build on what has already been done. (We are reminded of Newton's own remark, that if he had been able to see further, it was because he had stood on the shoulders of giants.) Not only in the sciences is this true. It applies equally in the useful arts, as for example in ship-building. (The comparison between the design of ships and of cathedrals is a popular one in the rationalist literature.) From the ships used by William the Conqueror to invade England, to contemporary 120-gun warships, Fergusson says,

> We have a steady progression through eight centuries, and it would be difficult to calculate how many millions of brains of all calibres, not only in every port of Europe but of America also, it has required to produce this great result. We neither care nor know who did it, more than we do know or should care who built our great cathedrals: they are the result of the same system, and not individual inventions, and can only be reproduced by causes similar to those which first created them.[18]

Technological progress in all areas is of the same nature, in engineering, bridge-building, the mechanisation of agriculture. Sometimes a notable and imaginative inventor appears and makes great advances, but all the time thousands of anonymous craftsmen and mechanics are each making small steps forward, so that their combined efforts more than surpass the achievements of the odd few whose names are remembered.

Fergusson even proposes a method whereby the slow evolutionary progress of medieval architecture could be emulated in modern-day design. He illustrates his proposals by reference to an imaginary competition for an 'Anglo-Protestant' church.[19] The best entry in the competition is to be selected and built. Immediately, its defects will become apparent: 'it is too high or too low, not sufficiently lighted, or there is a glare in one part and obscurity in another; it is not adapted for hearing the voice of the ministrant, or for seeing the service; the cornices are too heavy, the ornaments inappropriate, and so on'.[20] When it comes to building a new church, then, the same design is repeated exactly but with changes made to remedy these defects, and so on in a third, a fourth, a fifth; so that by the time the tenth is reached, says Fergusson, it will 'certainly be a very perfect building'. When over a century the talents, taste and experience of a hundred or even a thousand ordinary men are built into the design, the result will be something that not even an individual of the greatest genius could match.

Horatio Greenough, writing at almost exactly the same time as Fergusson ~ethnology~
(his collected essays appeared in 1852), makes the same comparison with
the 'perfect organisation' of boat design as Fergusson does. He points to other
such models in the designs of primitive tools, as for example the war club of
the South Sea islander. In these designs the architect may see the sort of
natural, unpretentious, direct adaptation of forms to uses which he too should
be able to achieve, if he would only use some 'plain good sense', as Greenough
says, instead of looking always to historical authority. The savage making
his club shapes the handle to a convenient curve, he gives the head its weight
and cutting edge. The resulting grace of form and subtle outline come at the
end of a long series of improvements, a kind of technical equivalent of organic
evolution. 'Weight is shaken off where strength is less needed . . . functions
are made to approach without impeding each other . . . till the straggling and
cumbersome machine becomes the compact, effective and beautiful engine.'[21]
The design of ships has gone through this same evolutionary process.

> If you will trace the ship through its various stages of improvement, from the
> dugout canoe and the old galley to the latest type of the sloop-of-war, you
> will remark that every advance in performance has been an advance in expres-
> sion in grace, in beauty, or grandeur, according to the function of the craft.[22]

Here the forms are tested in their environment in a very real sense, Greenough
maintains, against forces which are much more severe than those acting on
architectural forms. The responsibilities which weigh on shipbuilders have
forced them to devise designs well fitted to withstand the destructive pressure of wind and waves. If only architects had had such responsibilities, then
modern architecture would be as much superior to the Parthenon as the latest
clipper ships were to the galley of the Argonauts.

All this evolutionary analogy so far, from Fergusson and from Greenough,
is prior to the publication of *The Origin of Species.** (Later we come across
almost identical remarks to those of Viollet-le-Duc and Fergusson about the

---

* Subsequently, in the 1860s, Fergusson was to develop a more serious biological and
anthropological interest in evolution. His *History of Modern Architecture* (London,
1862) contained an appendix on 'Ethnology from an Architectural Point of View';
although, sadly, the book received an extremely severe notice ('utterly incompetent',
'lamentable ignorance') in the *Anthropological Review*, 1 (1863), 216—77, softened only
by the fact that the criticism was directed specifically at the appendix, rather than at
Fergusson's architectural scholarship. Perhaps in response to this, and in an effort
to improve his ethnology, he was in the late 1860s attending meetings of the
Ethnological Society of London — although he does not seem to have been a
member — and contributing to the Society's *Journal*, 1 (1868—9), 140—1; and to
discussion (see 2 (1870—1), 82). It is thus more than likely that he would have
come to know General Pitt-Rivers (then Colonel Lane Fox) who was Honorary
General Secretary of the Society, and whose studies of the evolution of primitive
artefacts are discussed in detail below (see pp. 87—94). Other Ethnological
Society officers were the cultural evolutionist E. B. Tylor, and Darwin's champion
T. H. Huxley, who was President.

evolution of medieval cathedrals, in both Eidlitz and Schuyler. Sullivan talks in exactly equivalent terms about the evolution in different periods of the basic structural elements of architecture: the pier, the lintel, the arch. They have been developed by 'successive men in successive times, by a series of rough approximations'.)[23] There is no suggestion at this stage of a detailed similarity of mechanism by which the two types of evolution, technical and organic, proceed, beyond the very broad notion of trial and error carried on over long stretches of time. The references to 'evolution' signify progress or development conceived of in a quite ordinary everyday sense, as much as they carry any specifically biological connotation. In the 1860s, however, the situation is very different, and a deliberately biological theory of artefacts and their evolution is elaborated in considerable detail. It is, as mentioned, the anthropologists who are responsible; and it is to them we should now turn.

One fact that is quite striking about the beginnings of scientific anthropology in the latter half of the nineteenth century is how many of its important figures were formerly or simultaneously biologists, turning from the study of animal and plant worlds to the study of man. There was Darwin himself with his *Descent of Man*;[24] although Darwin's anthropological concerns were more strictly physical than cultural. Sir John Lubbock, Lord Avebury, a family friend of Darwin, combined interests in natural history, archaeology and anthropology with a host of other pursuits, intellectual, commercial and political. His principal anthropological works are *Prehistoric Times* and *The Origin of Civilisation*;[25] he worked as an assistant to Darwin as well as making pioneering studies in animal behaviour of his own; and in archaeology his wide-ranging interests involved him among other things in saving the Avebury stone circle for posterity — hence his title.

It is perhaps only to be expected that those who embarked on the construction of large-scale philosophical theories of the development of human culture according to explicit evolutionary schemes, such as Herbert Spencer and the American L. H. Morgan (author of *Ancient Society: Researches in the Lines of Human Progress through Barbarism in Civilisation*[26]), might have come to anthropology or sociology via biological science.

E. B. Tylor, the third in this trio of great cultural evolutionists and author of *Primitive Culture*,[27] became the holder of the first lectureship in anthropology in Britain. The post was established in connection with the setting up in Oxford of the ethnographical museum formed from the collection of Colonel Lane Fox, and which is now the Pitt Rivers Museum.* This was one of the first scientifically organised collections of primitive artefacts and it too was

---

* Lane Fox became later in life Lieutenant-General Lane-Fox Pitt-Rivers. It will be convenient to refer to him as Pitt-Rivers from here on, despite any anachronism, this being the name by which he has become generally known. (John Lubbock married Pitt-Rivers's daughter.)

set out on an evolutionary plan. According to the Museum's first curator Henry Balfour (a Fellow of the Zoological Society),

> Colonel Lane Fox strongly advocated the application of the reasoning methods of biology to the study of the origin, phylogeny, and etionomics of the arts of mankind, and his own collection demonstrated that the products of human intelligence can conveniently be classified into families, genera, species, and varieties, and *must* be so grouped if their affinities and developments are to be investigated.[28]

Finally, Alfred Haddon, the virtual founder of the department of anthropology at Cambridge, whose name is remembered by the Haddon Library which he created, was before that Professor of Zoology at Dublin. It was on the zoological expeditions which he made to New Guinea that Haddon originally came into contact with the primitive peoples whose way of life he was subsequently to study.[29]

The idea for a collection of implements, tools and other of man's useful inventions first occurred to Pitt-Rivers some time about 1851[30] — suggested in part, one might surmise, by seeing the ethnographic exhibits at the Great Exhibition. He therefore entered very early into the field of scientific evolutionary investigation of ancient culture. His main inspiration in starting the collection, he says, had come from his military work, where he had been concerned with problems of the improvement of firearms at a time when the Army was at last abandoning the old 'Tower' musket.[31] He had been very forcibly impressed, when he came to look at the historical development of modern weapons in detail, by how very gradual and slow a process this was, and by what very small increases in efficiency and small alterations in the detailed organisation of the weapons' construction it advanced.

Later Pitt-Rivers was to lecture at length on the subject of the evolution of weapons ('Primitive Warfare')[32] to the Royal United Service Institution, whose own historical museum provided material for his investigations. It occurred to him that the same slow evolution might be found in other kinds of tools, both modern and ancient. As Henry Balfour describes, 'Through noticing the unfailing regularity of this process of gradual *evolution* in the case of firearms, he was led to believe that the same principles must probably govern the development of the other arts, appliances and ideas of mankind.'[33] Because of various purely practical advantages, Pitt-Rivers decided to confine his collection to artefacts from primitive cultures. These objects would be simpler, less numerous and less bulky than their modern equivalents; it might be possible to trace the history in some cases right back to the absolute origins of some series of forms; and he thought that there was a greater likelihood of obtaining a continuous series of artefacts with whole ranges of intermediate stages between distinct forms. It was thus for convenience that he turned to primitive cultures for his examples, rather than any initial purely anthropological interests as such. Pitt-Rivers emphasised that the purpose of his collection was for instruction, and not, as many previous collections had been, to display just the beauty of primitive art or its curiosity. Objects in those collections had been picked up at random, mostly by sailors in foreign seaports, and had not been arranged scientifically in any way, except perhaps by place of origin. Pitt-Rivers's purpose was to collect and classify artefacts in such a way as to provide a theoretical de-monstration of their relationships and historical origins, according to well-defined principles which we will examine shortly.

The reason why Pitt-Rivers imagined that he might be able to discover objects in continuous series of only slightly altered forms in the cultures of savage or primitive peoples, was the simple one already indicated that here the progress would be so much slower than in modern, more advanced technology. Both he and Balfour stress the 'innate conservatism' of the human species, but especially among primitives. These peoples have great difficulty in emancipating themselves from tradition and received ideas. E. B. Tylor makes the same point: 'The savage is firmly, obstinately con-servative. No man appeals with more unhesitating confidence to the great precedent-makers of the past; the wisdom of his ancestors can control against the most obvious evidence of his own opinions and actions.'[34]

This 'innate conservatism' served to ensure that the development of arte-facts would be very slow in early cultures; that their forms would be trans-mitted from one generation to the next very little changed, either by the handing on of craft skills via teaching and example, or else by always copying old forms when a new tool was made. There would be no sudden jumps or gaps in the series; so it might turn out that apparently quite separate and distinct implements, of quite different appearance and function, could in fact be 'genetically' related through a whole number of transitional forms — some-thing that Pitt-Rivers, Balfour and others were able to demonstrate convin-cingly in some quite surprising instances.

One of the most fascinating demonstrations Henry Balfour gives of what is, on the face of it, a very improbable 'family relationship' of this kind, is the connection between the archer's bow and stringed musical instruments, in particular different forms of harp. He describes this in a pamphlet *The Natural History of the Musical Bow*,[35] where he is able to show a continuous progression of only slightly changed forms at every step in the series, but of which the starting point and the end point are far apart in both form and function. Most of the examples of intermediate forms he produces to support the hypothesis of this evolutionary relationship were to be found in use by various living peoples, mainly in different parts of West Africa.

At first the archery bow serves a double purpose, being stopped along its length with a looped thong to provide a simple two-noted instrument for making rhythmic music. Later a similar type of bow is attached to a gourd resonator, and serves only the purpose of music-making. Several bows are then attached to the same gourd side by side, to give a range of notes. The strings subsequently are fixed to a single curved support instead of separate bows; but at this intermediate stage the lines of attachment at the two ends are at right-angles, so the strings do not lie in the same plane but describe a kind of warped surface.

As Balfour says, it is remarkable that such a bizarre, hybrid instrument, suggesting as it does 'a banjo at one end and a harp at the other', should have survived at all – unless it be for the express purpose of helping the ethnologist to reconstruct the series – since it is an 'almost aggressively inefficient form' and seems simply to exist to make the transition to the next and final stage. Here the strings are brought all into the same plane; and the 'fore-pillar' is added to complete the rigid frame of what is now recognisable as a primitive harp.

One odd feature to which Balfour draws attention is the fact that this fore-pillar was only introduced very late, and that without it, in earlier forms, the effect of tightening or loosening one string is to pull all the others out of tune. Despite this severe defect, and notwithstanding the fact that several other types of contemporary stringed instruments had surrounding rigid frames, it seems that the strong forces of tradition controlling the design were sufficient to distract its builders for a long time from the obviously advantageous modification which conscious analogy with other forms should, we might imagine, have suggested.

It was one of the chief criticisms made of Darwin's theory of organic evolution that there were obvious gaps between known existing species; gaps which it might be rather difficult to imagine bridged by complete series of intermediate forms. Nor did palaeontology, in his time, give very full support to the claim which Darwin made that such transitional links must have existed in the past, and have since become extinct. This criticism Darwin had anticipated and attempted to answer in a chapter in *The Origin of Species*, 'On the Imperfection of the Geological Record'.[36] It was necessary for him to assume that *natura non facit saltum*,[37] that the progress of natural evolution is always gradual and by slight improvements. (There has been much debate on the subject of the speed and smoothness of evolution since Darwin; and suggestions have been advanced as to how relatively large and rapid changes might be possible within the basic framework of the Darwinian theory.[38] Many of the problems of the 'imperfection' of the fossil record remain today. At a certain level, however, all biologists must obviously agree about the essential continuity of the evolutionary process.)

It is Balfour and Pitt-Rivers's suggestion that this gradual evolution applies also to primitive artefacts; and that only the disappearance of the inter-mediate forms, like the extinction of transitional species of animals or plants, gives the false impression that these objects were separately and independently 'invented'. Balfour was convinced furthermore that even modern 'so-called "inventions"' would be found to grow by very small stages also, if their evolution could only be studied in detail in the same way. The difficulty was that very few of the intermediate stages are ever recorded or displayed to public view ('we are not as a rule privileged to watch behind the scenes'). They are ephemeral and occur only in the designer's mind or in experimental versions of the invention which are very soon destroyed or modified again.[39]

A further problem was that, while some isolated primitive cultures might exist for very long periods without contact with the outside world and so be subject to no external influences, in the modern world such contacts and exchanges of ideas would be going on constantly, not confined by strict geographical limits. What is more, with the advent of writing and of printing, this transfer of ideas could jump the barriers of time as well as space; a concept recorded in print in one century might not be followed up until the next. And such complex sequences or trains of influences would be virtually impossible ever to retrace.

Thus Balfour and Pitt-Rivers's theory of technological evolution stressed continuity and temporal sequence above all in understanding the relations between artefacts. It might be possible to compare tools of similar function collected from different times, or from different parts of the world; but it was important to appreciate that in its historical origin one type of utensil or tool for a given purpose could be related genetically to another not only of different form but of different function too. It was not a matter of forms being progressively fitted, through trial and error, to some fixed and predetermined function. The *function evolved* along with the form.

The same was true of organic evolution; and indeed the possibility of extreme changes — via long transitional series of intermediate steps — in the functions of organs provided a solution to some of Darwin's further difficulties to his theory. How could any gradual transitions be made, for example, between the forms of underwater creatures such as fish, and those of air-breathing land animals? Where did the lungs come from? An equivalent problem was how land creatures could evolve the organs of flight by gradual stages, and so take to the air as birds.

Darwin pointed to the fact, accepted at his time among physiologists, that the *swimbladder* in certain fishes is homologous — that is to say it occupies a corresponding place in the overall organisation of the body — to the lungs of higher vertebrates. The swimbladder is an organ which adjusts buoyancy. It is supplied with air through a duct, and lies closely in the body alongside the gills or branchiae, through which the fish breathes air dissolved in the water. In some fishes the two organs, swimbladder and gill, are used for respiration together, the one for free air, the other dissolved air. According to Darwin it is the swimbladder which has been converted by evolution, both in function and in form, to become the lung in land animals. 'The illustration', he says, '... is a good one, because it shows us clearly the highly important fact that an organ originally constructed for one purpose, namely flotation, may be converted into one for a wholly different purpose, namely respiration'.[40]

Pitt-Rivers's scheme of classification thus needed to cope with the two dimensions of space and time. Objects from a given geographical region would be grouped separately, and in principle so would objects from the same historical period. But the matter was seriously complicated, first of all, by the fact that objects of similar form and/or function were to be found in widely separated countries (and no doubt at widely varying dates); and second by the fact that the chains of genetic connection which linked objects of similar and different functions together could themselves be extended not only in time, but also in space. It was clear that the processes of successive copying of artefacts would not be fixed spatially – unless some society was completely static and isolated. But this would be unusual, and most often it would be expected that technical inventions would spread or diffuse, as different peoples migrated bodily or exchanged artefacts through trade or war.

In practice it is perhaps fair to say that Pitt-Rivers did not entirely resolve this problem of the simultaneous classification of artefacts by form, function, place and date of origin and by evolutionary connection to each other; but it is fair too to admit that the problem was a very difficult one. The elements of all these classificatory criteria are present, however, in the lecture on the 'Principles of Classification'[41] which Pitt-Rivers gave in 1874, and which Balfour summarises as follows:

> he adopted a *principal* system of groups into which objects of like form or function from all over the world were associated to form series, each of which illustrated as completely as possible the varieties under which a given art, industry or appliance occurred. Within these main groups objects belonging to the same region were usually associated together in local sub-groups. And wherever amongst the implements or other objects exhibited in a given series there seemed to be suggested a sequence of ideas, shedding light upon the probable stages in the evolution of this particular class, these objects were specially brought into juxtaposition.[42]

The grouping to illustrate sequences was applied especially to objects coming from the same geographical area, since it was reasonable to assume in these cases that they corresponded to an actual historical transfer and development of ideas. But sequences were also made up from similar artefacts found in different parts of the country – from the different tribes of Australia, for example (figure 15).

At the beginnings of the series Pitt-Rivers placed those objects and tools which most closely resembled natural forms, from which they might have been derived – cutting tools and scrapers from sharp stones, spoons or

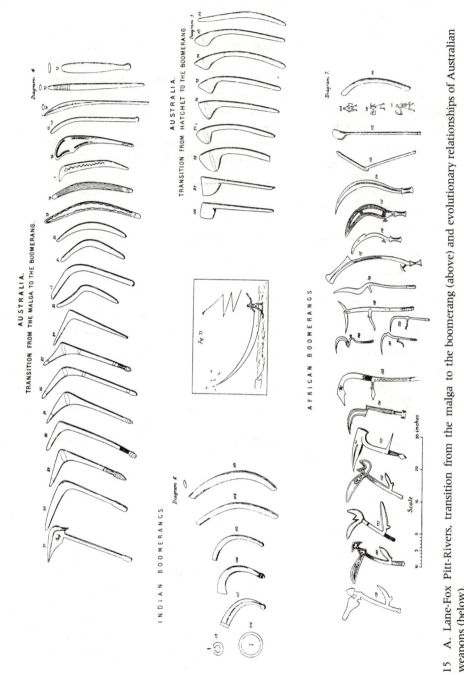

15  A. Lane-Fox Pitt-Rivers, transition from the malga to the boomerang (above) and evolutionary relationships of Australian weapons (below).

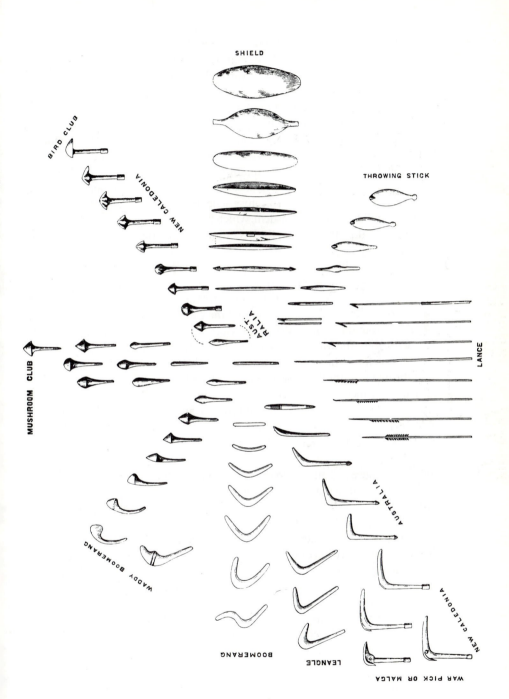

knives from seashells, clubs from sticks, and pots from gourds. First the naturally found object was assumed to be used as a tool without alteration; then its form was modified, elaborated or imitated in other materials. The more developed tools and objects were placed in order so as to illustrate progressive transitions to more complex and specialised forms.

Pitt-Rivers began his collection with firearms and other weapons, and at first it was accommodated in his own house. From 1874 to 1878 it was on public display in the Bethnal Green branch of the South Kensington Museum.[43] From there it was moved to South Kensington, and in 1883 Pitt-Rivers offered it to Oxford. The building erected to house it at Oxford, though of some interest architecturally,* bears no particular correspondence in its layout to Pitt-Rivers's classificatory scheme; but a quite recent proposal for a new building for the musuem, which has not so far been carried out, has a plan which directly matches the basic dimensions of the organisation of the collection itself.

The new building would be circular, and the displays arranged concentrically in rings. Distances outward from the centre represent the time dimension, while the different countries of origin of the exhibits — the space dimension — are represented by points around the circle. The visitor moving round the plan, around the rings, would therefore be able to see contemporaneous products from the different geographical cultures. Alternatively, moving straight out from the centre (representing a point in time at the very beginning of man's cultural development — signified, in the plan, by a botanical garden of primeval plant species) he would follow, in historical sequence, successive developments in the culture and artefacts of each given area. (Even better, though virtually impossible to realise architecturally, would be a three-dimensional layout, with two dimensions (in plan) to represent the surface of the earth, and the third (which would have to be vertical) to represent time. Such an arrangement would in principle allow 'genetic' connections to be shown as they extended through time *and* space.)

It is instructive to contrast the layout of this 'ideal' version of the Pitt-Rivers collection with Gottfried Semper's plan for *his* ideal museum discussed in chapter 5. The two schemes are obviously direct reflections of the transition of interest which we have been following from the 'environmental' influences emphasised in Semper's classification by function and materials, to the 'evolutionary' connections stressed in Pitt-Rivers's chronological series. In point of fact Semper was aware of the necessity of showing in a comparative arrangement other connections than those of function and manufacture; and although his own museum plan does not allow it, he attaches, as we might expect, almost as much importance to historical connections as to compar-

*An addition by T. N. Deane and Son, in 1885–6, to Benjamin Woodward's iron and glass Italian Gothic University Museum building of 1855–60.

isons which are simultaneous in time. As he says:

> A complete and universal collection must give, so to speak the longitudinal
> Section — the transverse Section and the plan of the entire Science of Culture;
> it must show how things were done in all times; how they are done at present
> in all Countries of the Earth; and why they are done in one or another way,
> according to circumstances; it must give the history, the ethnography and the
> philosophy of culture.[44]

*[handwritten margin note: Semper's museum]*

Objects of different materials and different functions will be linked in their origins and so will serve to connect the 'special collections' which are classified functionally and materially. Semper even argues that his primary four-way division by materials and manufacturing technique 'does not exclude historical and ethnographical distinctions',[45] which may be introduced as secondary principles of arrangement.

As a slight diversion from the main argument we might pause to remark here on certain historical connections between the archaeological and anthropological circles in which Pitt-Rivers moved, and the acquaintances and contacts of Semper. Semper not only had a direct personal interest in archaeology, where he was concerned mainly with the question of polychromatic decoration in Classical architecture; he was also well-read in archaeology and ethnology generally, as references in *Der Stil* amply indicate. One of the principal influences on Semper here was Gustav Klemm, author of *Allgemeine Kultur-Geschichte der Menschheit*[46] — indeed it is likely that the two men were acquainted.[47] Klemm was one of the pioneers of analytic archaeology, and was an early cultural evolutionist with a particular interest in primitive artefacts, especially weapons. E. B. Tylor in his *Primitive Culture* pairs the names of Klemm and Pitt-Rivers for their parallel interests in the development of weapons according to 'biological' and evolutionary principles.[48]

In 1851 Semper came to England, and contributed to the design of certain sections of the Great Exhibition — at the direct invitation, so it seems, of Prince Albert.[49] He moved at this time in the group of designers and architects involved with the Exhibition; such men as Owen Jones, Richard Redgrave and Henry Cole. Owen Jones and Semper must have been particularly close, because of their common interest in polychromy, and their work together on colour schemes for the Crystal Palace. Besides the objects of contemporary manufacture on show there were as already mentioned a great number of ethnographic exhibits, including Semper's Caribbean *Urhutte*.

When the Exhibition closed many of the objects were taken to Marlborough House, which formed the headquarters of the newly established Department of Science and Art, set up in 1853 with the purpose of continuing to promote the educational and scientific objectives which had been behind the Exhibition. Later, in 1856, the Department of Science and Art and the collections were all moved to premises in South Kensington, where they formed the nucleus of the present Victoria and Albert and Science Museums.[50] Semper was asked to give lectures at Marlborough House and it was during this period also that he worked on the preparation of *Der Stil*.[51]

Many of the illustrations of handicraft objects in *Der Stil* are taken from the collections of the British Museum, and there are references to British archaeologists and archaeological journals throughout the book. The subject of one of the Marlborough House lectures – in which much of the theoretical argument of *Der Stil* was first formulated – is metal-working technique, as exemplified in exhibits in the collection of weapons on show at Windsor Castle.[52] In Owen Jones's famous *Grammar of Ornament* (published in 1856), the examples of 'ornament of savage tribes' – carved decoration on paddles, adzes, shields and clubs – are many of them, especially those in plate 2, drawn from the collection of weapons belonging to the Royal United Service Museum.[53] This is the same museum, we remember, from which Pitt-Rivers drew many of *his* examples, and where he gave his lectures on weapons. Pitt-Rivers, as we also saw, later put his collection on display under the auspices of the South Kensington Museum.

There is therefore evidence of close contact, at least in the middle 1860s, between Henry Cole and his circle and Pitt-Rivers. During this period Cole was working at South Kensington, and Pitt-Rivers and Cole were both Fellows of the Anthropological Society of London; a society which also included in its membership many biologists, such as the Lamarckist St George Mivart, and which boasted as Honorary Fellows Darwin, Owen and Milne-Edwards.[54]

Semper himself had left England in 1855, and there is no direct evidence, for example in *Der Stil*, that he was aware of Pitt-Rivers's activities. It is also important to bear in mind the way in which publication of *The Origin of Species* at the end of the decade brought together scholars from many previously isolated disciplines within the broad framework offered by Darwin's theory. What is undeniable, however, is that Semper and Pitt-Rivers were both working, from their different points of view, art-historical and archaeological, on theoretical schemes for the 'biological' study of handicrafts; working in the same intellectual milieu, at the same time, and drawing much of their raw data from those same collections of early artefacts which were available for study in London in the 1850s.

There were some rather broad and difficult conceptual and methodological issues raised by Pitt-Rivers's approach to classification, and which were the subject of a much wider debate in later nineteenth-century evolutionary anthropology generally. The first of these arose out of the fact that the great majority of specimens came, naturally enough, from *contemporary* groups of (culturally and technologically) primitive peoples, and could not themselves therefore be put directly into truly historical sequences.

It was conceivable that a proportion of tools still in use might be survivals from an earlier stage, co-existing side by side with their evolutionary 'descendants' and not, for some reason, functionally superseded — though it would be difficult to determine that this was the case. More importantly there were the genuinely ancient artefacts which had been discovered by archaeology; as was the case, for example, with all the stone implements from the Palaeolithic cultures. The biological parallel here was with the fossil species; and so we should not be too surprised to find both Balfour and Pitt-Rivers introducing the subject of palaeontology and Cuvier's rules once more.[55]

The analogy takes a slightly new twist, however, in that what is now emphasised in the analogy with zoological reconstruction of the lost species is the role played — as it undoubtedly was in Cuvier's case — by *comparison* with existing, living species. The archaeologist makes a similar comparison of 'fossil' artefacts with tools still in use by contemporary primitives; and in this way he is able to infer the state of culture and technological milieu to which the buried artefacts belonged. 'What the palaeontologist does for zoology, the prehistorian does for anthropology.'

This [comparative method] then assumes in effect that living primitive peoples may be taken as comparable with historical peoples who at some previous date existed at an equivalent level of technological or cultural development. In its most extreme form the method makes the assumption of a *unilinear* and standard path of cultural evolution, of which present-day primitives represent distinct historical stages, some of them having lagged behind others in the speed of their progress. It was thus imagined that the whole sequence could be reconstructed by interpolation between the various observed stages. Living primitive peoples were, on this theory, like cinematic stills taken from various points throughout the film of the evolution of culture.

Morgan and Lubbock both argued from the comparative method, whose basic assumption tended to be that simpler forms could be taken to be older ones.[56] Lubbock in particular makes the analogy quite explicitly between comparative analysis in ethnology and archaeology, and the same procedure in biology and geology. In the reaction against evolutionary anthropology which occurred in the 1920s and 1930s, the method came under serious and abusive attack. This is not the place to try to enter into the arguments involved; but suffice it to say that comparative analysis, although it may have had its dangers, when used sensibly and critically can be a perfectly justifiable procedure, as modern anthropological theorists now acknowledge.

Again, there was considerable criticism of Morgan, Tylor and Spencer by later workers for what was allegedly their conception of cultural evolution as a single track process: everywhere the same, from 'savagery' through 'barbarism' to civilisation (in Morgan's terms), and each stage with its associated cultural forms, its typical technology and social organisation, through which all humanity was assumed to pass. It seems clear in more sober retrospect, however, that this was a highly simplified caricature of their position, promoted for polemical purposes; and if they perhaps carried the theory of parallel development in separate cultures to excess, they by no means denied the effects of diffusion between cultures, or the fact of divergences between them.[57]

A further and closely related issue of contention arose concerning the discovery in geographically separated cultures of artefacts — or customs, or social forms — with a very striking similarity of appearance. Some examples discussed by Tylor were the piston bellows of Madagascar and Indonesia; the use of the bow and arrow in the Old and the New World; and the game of 'parcheesi' played in both Mexico and India.[58] Was it to be inferred that such occurrences were evidence of contact between these respective peoples? An explanation along these lines tended naturally to carry more weight the more esoteric or bizarre the artefacts or forms of behaviour involved and the more precise the resemblances. On the other hand, it might be supposed with certain types of device of a very general usefulness — such as the bow and arrow — that they had been independently invented in two or more places.

The debate on this question of the relative roles in cultural evolution of diffusion versus independent invention is one that has also absorbed an enormous amount of anthropological attention; and again I do not propose to attempt a summary. What *is* relevant here, however, is to look at the specifically biological analogy with the cultural problem, which is one that Pitt-Rivers himself pointed out.

A very useful anatomical distinction, made originally by Richard Owen, was between what he termed *analogies* of structure, and *homologies*.[59] Analogy was a resemblance of structure arising from an identity of function; as for instance between the wings of insects, bats and birds. Another example is provided by the facial features of the frog, the hippopotamus and the crocodile. In all three cases the head is so shaped that the animal may lie in the water completely submerged with only the eyes and nostrils showing above the surface.

As for homology, its explanation, before Darwin, was not so immediately clear. It was nevertheless quite apparent that between different genera and within the various phyla there were overall similarities or homologies in the bodily plans of animals, in that corresponding parts appeared in corresponding places in the animals' organisation, but serving possibly different functions. In Owen's definitions:

> 'ANALOGUE — A part or organ in one animal which has the same function as another part or organ in a different animal.

'HOMOLOGUE' — The same organ in different animals under every variety of form and function.[60]

It was the 'family resemblances' between species which formed the basis of Aristotle's classification system; and it was these same homologies of structure which had suggested to *Naturphilosophie* the idea of organic archetypes. (Owen himself was not an evolutionist, but was very close to *Naturphilosophie*; he rather gracelessly and grudgingly bowed to Darwin in the 1860s when it became clear which way biological opinion was moving.) The family resemblances are generally more pronounced in animal embryos, and homologous organs develop from corresponding embryonic parts. As an example, the arm in man is homologous with the front leg in quadrupeds, and with the wing in birds. The explanation Darwin offered of homology was descent from common ancestors, with a transitional series of intermediate forms in which the organ's function as well as its detailed form might have changed.

This biological distinction between analogy and homology was carried over into ethnology (so that we now have an analogy for 'analogy'!). In his collection Pitt-Rivers had sometimes juxtaposed objects from different geographical cultures, different countries, which had considerable similarity of appearance and purpose. This did not mean, as Henry Balfour emphasises, that he was insensitive to the problem of whether such similarities could be due to actual contacts between the peoples in question, to cultural diffusion and the historical spread of ideas through trade and migration (homologies); or whether, on the other hand, they could be evidence simply of separate peoples passing independently through similar cultural stages, or finding similar solutions to more or less universal technical problems (analogies). To quote from Balfour:

> It must not be supposed ... that he [Pitt-Rivers] was unaware of the danger of possibly mistaking mere accidental resemblances for morphological affinities, and that he assumed that *because* two objects, perhaps from widely separated regions, appeared more or less identical in form, and possibly in use, they were necessarily to be considered as members of one phylogenetic group. On the contrary, in the grouping of his specimens according to their form and function, he was anxious to assist as far as possible in throwing light upon the question of the monogenesis or polygenesis of certain arts and appliances, and to discover whether they are exotic or indigenous in the regions in which they are now found, and, in fact, to distinguish between mere analogies and true homologies. If we accept the theory of the monogenesis of the human race, as most of us undoubtedly do, we must be prepared to admit that there prevails a condition of unity in the tendencies of the human mind to respond in a similar manner to similar stimuli. Like conditions beget like results; and thus instances of independent invention of similar objects are liable to arise.[61]

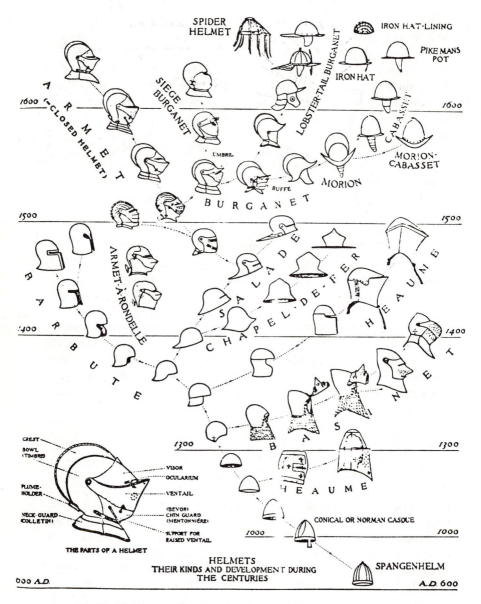

16   Bashford Dean, diagram showing historical evolution of helmet design.

17  A. L. Kroeber, 'The tree of organic phylogeny with its characteristic branch pattern' (left) and 'The tree of cultural phylogeny with *its* characteristic reticulated branch pattern' (right).

Balfour himself considered that the supposition of 'independent invention' should be entertained only when all possibilities of actual influence or connection have been exhausted. He urges caution in coming to any assumption of a generally standard sequence of stages in cultural evolution, or a supposed 'phylogenetic unity of the human species'.[62] That is, he is more disposed to find homologies than true analogies.

One significant contrast between technological and organic evolution, recognised by the cultural evolutionists, was that which was signalled by the difference in shape between the 'family tree' of organic species and the 'family tree' of artefacts. From the definition of an organic species, it followed that once having diverged to the point of splitting into two or more distinct species, these separate branches could never in the future join up again to reform the original species nor could they ever merge with others. New species could be created only by the splitting apart of old ones; and so the branches of the tree of natural evolution were like those of a real tree (or a graph-theoretic tree), always diverging, never rejoining.

With useful objects or tools such a situation did not appear to apply. It seemed perfectly possible — and indeed many actual examples presented themselves — that a new type of artefact might be produced by bringing together two previously separate types; or perhaps by combining selected parts of several already evolved artefacts. A number of recent writers on the subject of mechanical invention have proposed that this joining together of two previously unrelated devices in a kind of technological metaphor or pun constitutes the very essence of the inventive process. Thus Arthur Koestler speaks of the 'bisociation of matrices', the bringing together of two previously distant frames of reference, in every creative synthesis; and offers as one example the invention of the printing press as being a novel combination of two already evolved but formerly quite distinct machines or tools — the engraved or raised seal (providing the model for the type-cast letter) and the wine or olive press.[63] Donald Schon describes inventive processes of many kinds, in science and in language as well as in technology, in terms of a 'displacement of concepts', whereby an idea, a word or an artefact is removed from its habitual context and transferred to some novel application.[64]

The convergent pattern uniquely characteristic of cultural evolution (in its other aspects as well as in material culture) is rather fancifully pictured in a diagram by the anthropologist Alfred Kroeber, which shows the tree of 'cultural phylogeny' with a network of crossing and rejoining branches (figure 17).[65] In this combinatorial and convergent aspect of the invention or development of new kinds of artefacts the analogy with the production of novelty in biological evolution begins seriously to break down.

# 7

# The evolution of decoration

We will shortly come to look at how the Darwinian analogy was taken up by architects and design theorists, interested in turning it not to the academic study of the applied arts of the past, but in applying it practically to the design of new buildings and new machines. However, it will suit the sequence of the argument to examine first a different topic, one which much preoccupied the evolutionary anthropologists, especially Balfour and Pitt-Rivers, and which had its relevance to architectural history as well as to the art of primitive peoples. This was the question of the evolution of decorative motifs and patterns, such as those found on pots, weapons, fabrics or buildings. Here again it seemed to several of the nineteenth-century students of the subject that changes in decoration, like the changes in the overall forms of useful artefacts, were produced in very gradual stages; and that motifs were transmitted through a similar process of successive copying with slight modification.

Various of the features of artificial evolution which have been already remarked on are once more in evidence in the examples of decoration which were collected together by Balfour in his *Evolution of Decorative Art*,[1] by Alfred Haddon in his *Evolution in Art*,[2] and by several other authors. These examples demonstrated, they argued, the apparent extreme conservatism of the primitive designer and his unwillingness to make severe alterations to traditional forms, so that novelty was again introduced only in stages. The origins or at least precursors of particular decorative forms were to be discovered by tracing them back through continuous series of always slightly differing copies. And such chains of 'genetically' connected designs might begin and end with examples so widely different that, unless the intermediate links were known, it would not be imagined that they were in any way related.

Henry Balfour distinguishes several hypothetical stages in a general evolutionary sequence.[3] In the first place very simple and early ornament is produced by some emphasis of the natural characteristics of the material from which the object is made. In tools carved from wood it may be that the grain or prominent knots are picked out by colouring.[4] On stripped bamboo or reed stems used for arrows or spears, for example, the regularly spaced bands or nodes marking the branching-off points of the leaves, which in themselves produce a simple decorative pattern, are smoothed and coloured to enhance the natural effect.[5] There is plenty of evidence to show that all kinds of natural objects which are in some way curious, shiny, oddly coloured, rare or of regular geometrical form — such as pebbles, shells, seeds or animal teeth — were collected for their own sake by early peoples (as they are by contemporary primitives, indeed by modern artists and collectors), and employed for decoration as necklaces, bangles, or attached to clothes.

Balfour calls his first stages in the evolution of decoration an *adaptive* stage, 'that is, man simply accepted and adapted effects which were accidentally suggested to him'.[6] In the second stage, the natural effect is *imitated* artificially, in places other than where it occurs naturally. This leads directly to the third stage, that of *successive copying*;[7] for where the natural design has been once copied, that copy can be copied again, and so the motif takes on 'a life of its own'. As the copying process goes on, so the design varies, for a number of possible reasons. The first possibility has already been discussed in connection with the functional evolution of implements; that of sheer technical inadequacy on the part of those making the copies, or through the exigencies of materials, differences in tools used and so on. Balfour calls this 'unconscious variation'.[8]

Although it is difficult to find complete graded sequences of surviving examples to illustrate copying going on in design — just as it was difficult, to Darwin's regret, to find continuously varying series of fossil specimens in palaeontology — nevertheless many such series *do* exist, and there is no doubt that this is a widespread phenomenon and the source of much rich variety and apparent 'invention' in primitive decoration. If a second motif is copied from a first, a third from the second, and so on, and if the makers of later versions have no access to the early members of the sequence for reference, then the character of the design can quite rapidly diverge and take on new appearances.

In order to test this process by experiment Pitt-Rivers had tried out the method of successive copying in some practical trials amongst his colleagues and friends. As Haddon describes:

> The credit of first applying this principle in art is due to General Pitt-Rivers. He gave a certain drawing to some one (A) to copy; his rendering was sent on to another person (B) to copy, this copy was handed on to a third individual (C), and so on, each copyist having only the preceding person's performance before him. In each case fresh variations occur according to the greater or less imitative skill of the artist. The General has collected some very curious examples of series of this kind.[9]

Inspired by the General's example, Balfour had also tried the same experiment for himself, and illustrates two of the resulting series in *The Evolution of Decorative Art*. In the first place the model taken for copying is a sketch of the

*[handwritten margin notes: 'heredity' – not really analogous    evolution ie no 'selection']*

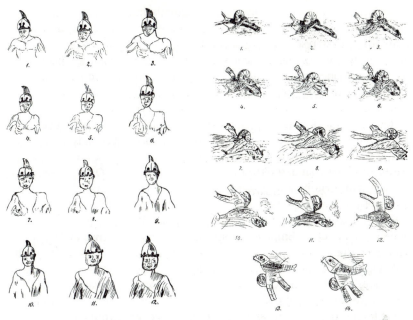

18  Examples of successive copying of drawings by different individuals, each working from the immediately preceding copy, without reference to the original.

head and shoulders of a bust of Patroclus, from the Aegina Marbles[10] (figure 18, left). The figure is bare-chested but wears a helmet. As the series of copies progresses the heavily emphasised pectoral muscles of early versions are developed into full breasts and the figure changes sex from male to female. Subsequently the collar-bones droop lower to a V-shape and are interpreted as the neckline of a cloak. The plume of the helmet shrinks to a tiny tuft and the eye-holes of the visor turn into circular decorations.

Rather more bizarre is a second sequence in which the original design depicts a snail crawling over a twig[11] (figure 18, right). Here there is more room for ambiguity and misinterpretation. By the ninth drawing snail and twig have merged into a single object, and it is difficult to say definitely what is represented. By drawing number twelve the shell has separated completely from the body of the snail, which is almost fish-like now. At this stage the drawing turns *upside-down* — since there was nothing on the paper or drawing to suggest to the copyist which was properly top or bottom — and is interpreted as a bird, whose head has come originally from the cross-section of the broken-off twig and its eye from the growth rings. The twin eye-stalks of the snail have become the bird's forked tail, while the shell is turned into some kind of excrescence or wart on the bird's legs. These legs themselves derive from the original branched twig. As Balfour exclaims, 'This truly is "evolution made easy" !' — from mollusc to bird in only a dozen steps.

If this 'laboratory' example of successive copying should seem contrived or unrealistic in relation to the evolution of primitive decoration, both Balfour and Pitt-Rivers have authentic examples from anthropology and archaeology which demonstrate what are on the face of it equally improbable and extreme transformations through gradual distortion. One series which they both cite is that described by John Evans in a paper 'On the Coinage of the Ancient Britons and Natural Selection'.[12] This illustrates local crude copies of original foreign and classical models.

One sequence shows versions of a gold coin of Philip of Macedon, with a wreathed head of the Emperor on one side and a chariot, driver and horses on the other (figure 19). The Emperor's face rather quickly disappears in the copying, leaving the wreath only. The wreath then undergoes all sorts of remarkable transmogrifications, becoming coarsened in treatment into patterns of rectangles and ovals, turning thence into ears of wheat or barley; while the Emperor's own ear at the centre changes into symmetrical crescent moons, which in their turn attract matching stars. As for the fate of the chariot design on the reverse, it is worth quoting Pitt-River's own, somewhat whimsical, description:

> the chariot and horses dwindled into a single horse, the chariot disappeared, leaving only the wheels, the driver became elevated, not elevated after the manner unfortunately too common among London drivers, but elevated after the manner of Spiritualists, except you see he had the precaution to take on a pair of wings, differing also both from the London driver and the Spiritualists, inasmuch as instead of having lost his head he has lost his body, and nothing but the head remains; the body of the horse then gradually disappears, leaving only four lines to denote the legs.[13]

Thus Henry Balfour's first possible reason for a design varying in subsequent copies — that of 'unconscious variation' through accidental inexact copying — can perhaps be illustrated by the series of coins and drawings just described. With Balfour's second possible reason for change, which he calls 'conscious variation' — and of which there is very possibly an element with the coins — there is by contrast some definite intention to alter or improve on the previous version, rather than just to reproduce it (if not with complete success) in facsimile.

It will be observed that in the analogy of changes in these decorative designs with the evolution of organic species, there is one central aspect in which the Darwinian theory fails to apply, at least in any wholly convincing way — that is, in any analogy with the mechanism of *selection* according to

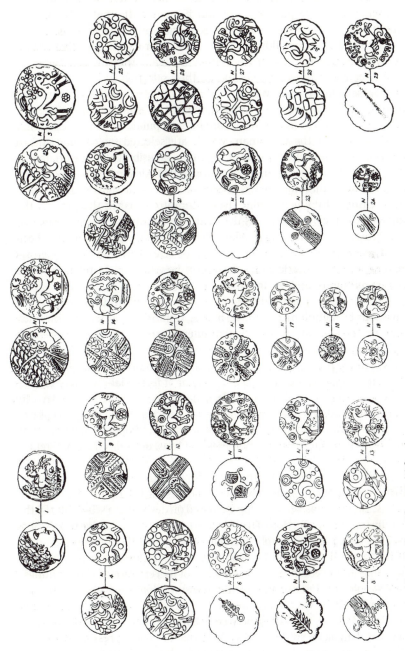

19　J. Evans, evolution of motifs on British coins.

fitness. With useful objects of specified functions the test of their fitness is made when they are put into use; and if they fail the test, this failure is manifest and unarguable. The pot cracks on the fire, the hand tool is difficult to hold, the roof of the building leaks. On the other hand decorative designs have by definition no such practical usefulness; and thus there are no equivalent objective or functional criteria for their selection.

Of course one might say that a process of selection does go on with such designs, but according to other standards, presumably aesthetic ones. It is those patterns or motifs which are most popular, or which best satisfy the critical eye of the craftsman, which are selected for copying and so preserved and multiplied. There is a certain plausibility in this argument. It has been used, for example, by Christopher Alexander to explain the beauty of the traditional designs of Slovakian peasant shawls, and to provide a reason why when aniline dyes were introduced in this century the quality of their colour schemes declined disastrously (to the sophisticated eye at least).[14] This is because, Alexander argues, the old colours had been arrived at through an extended process of selection; and there has not been an equivalent period for selection to be exercised in relation to the new possibilities offered by the new dyes.

Alexander says that the phenomenon of the decline in quality of the shawls was brought to his attention by E.H. Gombrich — although Gombrich is not responsible for the particular interpretation. However, Gombrich himself, and at his inspiration Karl Popper, have both made an analysis of the artist's creative procedures in the composition of the individual work, which sees them as having a certain 'Darwinian' or at least trial-and-error character.[15] The artist tentatively tries an effect, maybe even produces it accidentally (a variation), subjects it to critical appraisal (selection), and either keeps it or changes it again. The process offers one example of Popper's famous many-purpose cycle of alternating hypotheses and tests, of 'conjectures and refutations'.

This, however, is moving rather far away from the more strictly evolutionary conception of the anthropological students of decoration, who saw critical assessment or selection being exercised on designs as a whole, not by the artist during the production of the single artefact. The productive process was imagined rather as one simply of careful, if very slightly imprecise, copying.

If this general theory of the evolution of decoration is accepted (and we shall come in due course to some criticism of its very serious shortcomings), then it would seem reasonable within its assumptions to suggest that the aesthetic standards by which selection of designs would be carried on might be very variable ones, not only between individuals but also over time. In biological language we might say that the 'selection pressure' would be rather low by comparison with functional objects; and that evolutionary series in decoration could be expected to move off down meandering paths in almost any direction, as though selection was never holding the forms or patterns to some few definite courses. This is indeed what is observed.

When Balfour allows the possibility of the artisan making conscious variations of motifs, then he makes a most important, if entirely reasonable, departure from the strict terms of an analogy with Darwin's theory. In organic evolution, of course, the variations are 'blind', they are perfectly random; and they bear no necessary relation to the way of life of the organism or to its adaptation to the environment. It is only those variations which *turn out*, fortuitously, to be advantageous ones in the selective process which are then retained and inherited. A rigorously Darwinian analogy in the evolution of decoration (or of functional objects) would have to assume that all changes in their forms were introduced entirely accidentally and without any forethought or deliberate intention. This is quite plainly a most implausible suggestion.

The nearest one might perhaps approach to this situation is in the kind of artificial experiments with copying of the kind which Pitt-Rivers organised. Here the participants were instructed precisely to try to reproduce the given motifs as best they could, and not deliberately to alter them. Even in this case, though, it is apparent that changes which occur in the designs are not absolutely accidental or random ones.

If one reflects on what is happening in Pitt-Rivers's copying exercise, it becomes clear that there is actually no real equivalent of selection in the biological sense in it at all, and that it is in fact an experiment in pure 'heredity'. To mimic the selective process in organic evolution it would be necessary to have each copyist make *many* copies of the same design; to subject these to some sort of comparative critical appraisal; on the basis of this, to select one or a few versions only; to copy these again many times, and so on. Since there is nothing of this kind in Pitt-Rivers's method, one might imagine that technically unaccomplished copying and consequent small errors *on their own* would simply tend to result ultimately in a loss of detail, a loss of meaning, and a gradual degradation and ultimate disappearance of the original design.

There are some indications of this in the examples which have been illustrated. But it is by no means the general rule and, as the examples show, it is equally possible that designs will undergo strange and wonderful reinterpretations and elaborations, by which new features are added, new meanings are acquired, new forms are generated. I myself have tried repeating some similar experiments — something worth doing in its own right since the results are generally amusing, and psychologically very mysterious — and have found that with fairly skilled copyists instructed to make as exact reproductions as they are capable of, it requires only fifteen or twenty copyings to produce versions which, though still recognisable, are widely different, and yet not substantially degraded in detail from the starting design.

What is happening, evidently, is that fortuitous details of the design thrown up accidentally are being picked on and developed, perhaps subconsciously, or expanded into new features, while others are being omitted. There is *interpretation* and hence selection going on in the copying process itself. Often there may be an ambiguity in a design with some representational element, where a detail may be capable of being read with more than one meaning; and the copyist attaches a different significance from that which it held before. If the *same* design is set off on the copying process more than once, then the end results of the different trials can be very far apart — so illustrating the point about the 'low selection pressure' and the vagaries of these evolutionary series. On the other hand, one remarkable feature in certain instances is that definite trends are observable in the progressive transformation of some drawings; for instance, certain parts of a design may be subjected to a continuous directional movement relative to others. It follows that changes in this case are not due to the way in which different individual copyists each have their own special interpretations of the similar motif; but on the contrary, that all copyists are introducing the *same* systematic type of deformation or transformation. Without such general bias, one could only expect a kind of random indeterminate movement of the parts. (It is curious, incidentally, that the Surrealists do not appear to have caught hold of this idea for making drawings, since it provides an ideal pictorial equivalent to their techniques of 'automatic writing'.)

Many instances of such reinterpretations of decorative features at some stage during a continuous sequence are provided by Haddon, Balfour and Pitt-Rivers. There is not space here to describe any number of these in great detail, but some brief illustrations will suffice to show the typical features. One example is given by the designs drawn on paddle blades by the New Irelanders, a people from New Guinea.[16] Pitt-Rivers had found a more or less continuous development in these ornamental drawings starting from a quite naturalistic human figure, whose body dwindles in the end to a mere tapered handle-like form without arms or legs; the eyes change into a kind of leafy tuft like the head of a pineapple, and then disappear; the nose becomes a large diamond shape, later pulled out into moustache-like features; and in the end nothing is left but a simple crescent at the end of the handle — like the lingering smile of the Cheshire cat.[17] Beginning and end of the series bear no discernible relations whatsoever one to the other in the absence of the connecting links.

Another case where an originally representational drawing of the human figure has been abstracted into a purely geometrical design is in the decoration of spear shafts from the Solomon Islands.[18] In this instance, illustrated by Balfour, it is the mouth rather than the nose which dominates, and which ultimately devours the remainder of the design. First it becomes a double chevron, then progressively these chevrons are multiplied, finally inverted

*[margin note: subconscious interpretation in copying]*

*[margin note: biased tendency]*

into a symmetrical pattern, so that all vestiges of the original figure drawing disappear — with the exception of the legs which survive to mark the 'family relationship' of the whole series. As Balfour points out, one cannot necessarily assume that the known examples of these types of decoration represent a continuous single linear sequence of copying. Some would probably have to be placed on different but adjacent branches of a genealogical or evolutionary tree; a tree, however, since it is a cultural one, whose branches might divide, intertwine, rejoin and then perhaps divide again.

A final example may be taken from pottery. A quite widespread style of decorating jugs, for water or wine, is once again as representations of the human figure. In this case the whole vessel forms a kind of rotund statue of which either the neck or the lid becomes the head. The 'Toby' jug is a well-known modern example, but the idea is very ancient and such jugs have been found in Peru and Ecuador, in Cyprus, and by Schliemann in his excavations at Troy and Mycenae.[19] Although one might well imagine a progress from unornamented or geometric form to figuration — the basic functional shape of the vessel with its 'neck' and 'pot belly' suggesting the addition of decoration to turn it into a recognisably human image — there is evidence of the reverse process also taking place, and of highly elaborate and realistic representations degenerating later into schematic and rather dilatory decoration whose original nature has been quite forgotten.

In the Peruvian examples from the Pitt-Rivers collection a clear series of progressive degeneration can be seen;[20] and little remains of the human features in later examples except for the two small protrusions which were once the feet (figure 20). Meanwhile either the ears, or in some cases the arms, survive as symmetrical handles, or as holes for carrying-loops of string. It is the remaining vestigial feet which show that the series is a degenerating one and suggest that the decorative features have turned into functional ones, as with the arms turned to handles, rather than the other way round.

20  Anthropomorphic designs in Peruvian pottery vessels, from the Pitt-Rivers collection.

In the Cypriot vases, two small conical bosses or protuberances of a similar kind to the Peruvian 'feet', placed to one side of the vessel, also persist in degenerate forms; and in a paper on 'Archaic Survivals in Cyprus', R. H. Lang reports that even in the late nineteenth century potters in that country would still add two blobs of clay to a newly finished jug, without being able to offer any explanation save that this was a standard and traditional form of decoration.[21] The problem of their meaning is solved by a comparison with vases up to 2,500 years older found by archaeologists in the same area. These take the form of finely modelled female figures. The two protrusions are not the lady's feet, but her breasts.

In Schliemann's vases from Troy, the early forms are much cruder, but still recognisably human and female. In this case, however, the details of the head move to a detachable lid, so that without the lid the significance of the two rudimentary breasts is not obvious. Should vases of this type have been copied without their lids, it is not surprising that the original meaning of their decoration might have been forgotten. That in time they became a purely non-figurative form of ornament is proved by one example found by Schliemann, which has three such 'breasts'.

In the case of the Peruvian pots we saw that a representational and decorative form, the arm of a human figure, was put subsequently (or perhaps simultaneously) to a functional purpose, that of serving as a handle. It is much more usual, however, in the evolution of decoration to find the opposite process going on: that is to say, what is at one stage a characteristic of the construction, or a functional feature of an artefact, turns subsequently into a 'purely decorative' motif. In the biological analogy, such a form of ornament on useful objects would correspond to those vestigial organs or survivals which are sometimes to be found in the animal body as for example the finger- and toenails or the rudimentary remains of the tail in man.

As an example from primitive manufacture, we may imagine that a certain people make daggers or knives by lashing stone blades onto wooden handles by means of diagonal bindings of string or fibre. At some later stage it becomes possible, and more efficient, to make the implement in one piece, or to joint the blade to the handle with pins or sockets, say, so making the lashing unnecessary. It is frequently to be observed in such instances that the zig-zag linear pattern of the string binding is then imitated by incised or painted decoration.[22] One may suppose that this is so the new design should conform to the old image or stereotype of what is appropriate for such knives to look like (figure 21).

The term 'skeuomorph' was introduced by H. Colley March to describe this kind of decorative form deriving from structure.[23] 'Skeuomorphs' occur in pottery vessels which reproduce the characters of string and basket construction.[24] In very primitive work of poor quality where the wet clay has not the strength to retain its proper shape, the pot is bound round with plaited decoration as vestigial structure — 'skeumorphic' theory of decor. (Semper)

21    Skeuomorphs of binding.

or twisted bands during the firing. These bands, when removed, leave characteristic regular markings imprinted in the surface of the clay. In later copies where, through improvements in the methods of working clay, the restraining bands are no longer necessary, the patterns nevertheless are retained for decoration and are artificially imitated by modelling and incision of the clay by hand.

It is possible to find series of a similar kind in which, first of all, baskets are lined with clay and then dried in the sun, so that they will hold liquids, or else hot coals and raw food placed together in the vessels for roasting. Then the clay linings are separated from the basketry frames in which they are moulded, so that they take on not only the characteristic shape of the baskets, but are impressed also with their texture. Finally these beautiful and originally incidental ornamental patterns in clay are deliberately copied in applied decoration.

Examples of a comparable character from the Pitt-Rivers collection show the imitation of since-vanished string supports for pots made from gourds, by means of coloured line patterns drawn on their surface.[25] Equivalent series from Cyprus demonstrate an identical transference of the interlaced patterns of supporting cord handles onto the surface of clay pots as conventional ornament. Iroquois vessels made of birch or linden bark sections, carefully sewn together along the seams so as to give an angular shape with distinct facets, are unmistakably copied in their general form in earthenware at later dates, and the stitching pattern is converted into incised decoration.[26]

One example provided by Balfour of the form of a natural object used as a tool persisting into its artificial replacement is the large clam shells used by the Andaman Islanders as dishes.[27] The shape of the shell as found is something like that of a leaf, with one end rounded and broad, and the other pointed and narrow, providing a convenient, ready-made handle. Later wooden dishes copy the original shell form, and in some cases are given a second pointed handle, so becoming roughly almond-shaped and thus symmetrical. The asymmetry of the old clam dish is preserved, however, in a curious and otherwise mysterious decoration: a curved line in a red wax is added to *one end* of the wooden platter only. In Balfour's description:

> It is not balanced at the other end with a similar line, and it is perfectly evident that it has been introduced to recall the outline of the shell, which had established a claim to be remembered by having discharged its function in a creditable manner before the wooden copy was introduced.[28]

Some more modern instances of skeuomorphs which are often quoted are those to be found in clothing, such as the necktie, or the lapels on jackets. How else than as 'vestigial organs', asks P. B. Medawar, 'should we describe those functionless buttons on the cuffs of mens' coats?'.[29]* A favourite example amongst the architects of the modern movement, such as Le Corbusier, was the design of early cars or railway coaches taking the forms of horse-drawn carriages.[30] Hermann Muthesius mentions how the first gaslights (and, he might have added, not only the first!) simulated the appearance of candles.[31] The designs of modern cheap Italian wine flasks display a kind of double skeuomorph. Originally the flasks were blown, into globular form, and they needed their raffia jackets to provide them with flat bases on which they could stand. Now the flasks are moulded, so they could well have flat bases

*Adolf Loos, that well-known enemy of ornament, is reputed to have been most particular that the cuff buttons on his own suits be functional, and should allow for the cuffs to be rolled back — as was the original purpose — when eating messy foods, for example.

*vestigial vegetal patterns in constrn.*
*functionally superseded yet surviving in image*

incorporated. But they still keep their supporting jackets, which imitate the forms of the plaited raffia in plastic. In Samuel Butler's satirical Utopian romance *Erewhon*[32] — a book to which we shall return — there is an illustration of a vestigial organ of a related kind in the tobacco pipe: that is, the circular rim, like that of a cup, on which at one time the pipe could be rested, still burning, on the table — but which has gradually since shrunk to a small protuberance, and then into 'an ornamental leaf or scroll, or even a butterfly' before disappearing altogether.[33]

We might expect that one area in which 'skeuomorphic' decoration would be widely found would be in architecture;[34] and here indeed the examples are almost innumerable. Some instances of evolution in architectural decoration are to be found, it is true, in those motifs which derive originally from natural, often vegetable forms, and which have no particular structural significance. These patterns have often undergone considerable abstraction and formalisation, so that again their origin is not obvious. Such a case is the widely found classical 'egg-and-dart' pattern, which seems to originate from a highly schematised, probably Egyptian, lotus design.[35] Connection has also been traced between the spiral volutes of the Greek Ionic capital and Assyrian 'palmette' capitals, as well as back to the Egyptian lotus again.[36] Besides this source, though, and the decorative possibilities arising from the textures of building materials, it would not be going too far to say that almost all other architectural decoration (not counting applied sculpture and mural painting) has its origin in structure; either in the survival of functionally superseded forms, or in the application of previously structural forms to contexts where they are then structurally functionless.

In Semper's view there is certainly an evolution in architectural ornament, and its forms can be referred back to ancient prototypes, which in his opinion are those of handicrafts and clothing. Hence the arrangement of the three volumes of *Der Stil*, to cover respectively textiles, ceramics, and architecture (in the uncompleted last book), reflects a theoretical argument which is in part to do with the origins of architectural decoration being traceable ultimately to the patterns on garments and pottery. There is for Semper no simple and standardised process through which this evolution goes; it is very hard to retrace its paths; chronology even if known is not a sure guide (because of the fact of survivals); and it is not permissible to assume that a simpler form is necessarily an older one.

On the other hand Semper does definitely acknowledge the phenomenon of skeuomorphs. He remarks on how constructional features may be emphasised or exploited deliberately for decorative effect — for instance the ornamental sewn seam, a decoration widely used among the American Indians. And it is very frequently the case, according to Semper, that a pattern executed in one material is then imitated in another, as for instance floor mosaics imitating carpets, or wall tiles imitating wall cloths.

It should not be suggested, however, that this was Semper's universal explanation of the source of architectural ornament. His view was that decoration for the most part serves and always has served to clothe and dignify the essential structure of buildings. One of the most original and debatable points in Semper's architectural theory is his belief that the wall in architecture has its beginnings in textiles. Hangings were draped around and between the structural framework of the columns in Assyrian, Egyptian, Greek and Roman buildings; and while these draperies might have served some practical functions, to provide privacy or shade, they were principally intended, says Semper, to grace the structure with colour and pattern. If he is right in following an evolution from these textile hangings to the permanent partition wall (with its applied decoration), then this is in a sense the very opposite of a skeuomorph — it is a structural element derived from a decorative one.

For a contrasting view of ornament in architecture, as being almost universally skeuomorphic, we can take Banister Fletcher's *The Influence of Material on Architecture* (1897)[37] which might almost serve in other ways as Semper's missing third volume —were it not for its brevity and for an extreme materialism which, despite appearances, Semper does not in the last analysis subscribe to. As Fletcher says,

> Many constructive features offer to us a manifestation of the tendency, always existing, which consisted in transforming into a decorative feature that which previously was only a practical need. In all styles certain combinations went gradually from the domain of the art of building, to pass into that of decoration, and thus the spirit of architecture was modified insensibly.[38]

Frequently cited types of skeuomorph in architecture occur in the copying of the forms of timber building in stone; and of these Fletcher has numerous examples, from the Egyptians and Persians through to English church building of the Norman period. In the latter case the 'billet' patterns of stone strips which are applied in rectangular or diagonal lattices imitate the structural members of timber framing. The best-known example is the tower of the church at Earl's Barton in Northamptonshire.

There has been much scholarly dispute over one particular instance of timber forms being copied in masonry, and that is whether such is the origin of the general form and of many of the details of the classical Greek temple. Fletcher summarises the literature in a chapter entitled 'Greece: Timber to Stone and Marble'.[39] There seems to be little disagreement in the end that at least some of the features of columns and entablature have this derivation (one dissenter being Garbett who, with his structural theory of the basis of style, dismisses the whole wooden theory as 'an insolent libel'). The earliest opinions on the subject are provided by Vitruvius, who states very clearly that the origins of triglyphs and metopes are in the exposed ends of, and gaps between, timber beams and rafters.[40]

Some light was thrown on the whole issue by the discovery in the early nineteenth century of rock-cut tombs in Asia Minor, which were quite indisputably the precise reproduction of wooden buildings in stone, and which prefigured in several ways the appearances of the classical temple (figure 22). In tombs found by Fellows in Lycia the characteristics of timberwork are copied exactly, right down to the details of mortice and tenon joints.[41] The roof construction in one tomb imitates the form of untrimmed timber poles laid side by side over the chamber, with ends protruding in a row of cylindrical projections. At the ends of the row are larger, squared members. In a second tomb the whole row of roof joists is squared; in Haddon's words 'we witness, as Dr March points out, the origin of the well-known Greek ornament called "guttae"',[42] which appear like rows of small, regularly spaced applied cubes, but in their evolutionary ancestry are related to these protruding rows of the ends of joists.* (March was the author of a paper on 'The Meaning of Ornament, or its Archaeology and its Psychology'[43], to which this allusion refers, and which discusses several instances of architectural skeuomorphs.)

The gable end on this same tomb takes its shape from the triangular truss which would have supported a pitched wooden roof. Here is the origin of the Greek pediment and of a decorative form which has continued to adorn doors, windows, openings, and furniture to this day. The wooden ridge beam, although not carried over to the Greek temple, can still be seen in a third tomb from this area.[44] In this case the building copied has an elongated plan, and the pattern of guttae is carried only down the long sides, as is quite proper for a system of construction where joists, of which they are vestiges, would have spanned across the short dimension.

From the gable end it is clear that the building is of a single storey only, since the doors are carried up to the full height. On the long walls, however, are carved a second line of protruding joist ends, marking an intermediate storey. The stone structure copies a wooden one; and the line of guttae marks a floor level which is non-existent. Here is an example of one very common architectural feature, the 'string course', which, although it often serves no strictly functional purpose, is often applied externally to mark the storey levels, and to break up a wall surface into horizontal bands.

The respective attitudes of Semper and Viollet-le-Duc to the wooden theory are interesting. Semper was clearly embarrassed by the element of structural and material deception implied, but was at the same time concerned that his analysis should not seem to diminish the supreme architectural achievement

*Semper + le-Duc perjorative tone to the skeu.*

---

* As evidence of the longevity of this ornamental form, we could take the example of the standard British post box. This was, and is, referred to as a 'pillar box' because of its original Victorian design as a free-standing classical column with circular entablature. Cylindrical post boxes of late design, up to the 1950s, still carried vestigial reminders of this origin, including base, capital and the dentils of the classical cornice around the rim of the domed cap to the box.

22　Skeuomorphs of timber construction in architecture.

of the Greek builders. He was quite willing to acknowledge, as we have seen, that decorative patterns in one material might legitimately be reproduced in another. And as an ardent supporter of the theory that the temples were, when first built, covered with polychromatic painting, he was able to assume that their actual materials of construction were thereby concealed, and so artistically less significant. Semper's argument in the end turns on the claim that the essential poetic and symbolic form of the original wooden temple is 'de-materialised', as one might say; it is carried into the realm of the ideal, and is only conveyed symbolically to the spectator through the expressive means of the actual stone material, whose particular nature thus becomes in the context almost irrelevant.[45]

The problem was an even harder one for Viollet-le-Duc, who had argued, we remember, for a functional and structural explanation of many of what others might see as 'decorative' details of Gothic; and was concerned to do the same for Greek architecture. He puts on a straight face and argues the rationale of the Doric temple form right through according to masonry construction — a real bravura tour-de-force in the circumstances. One strong point he has in his favour is the appearance of triglyphs on all four sides of the building, which in a structural interpretation in timber would be paradoxical (since the roof beams to which they owe their derivation would run in one direction only).[46]

However, Viollet-le-Duc is not unaware of the evidence in support of wooden origins for classical architecture. He discusses the subject in his book *Habitations of Man in all Ages*,[47] and he has a plate of one of Fellows's tombs in the *Discourses on Architecture*.[48] He is prepared to allow a wooden derivation for the Ionic order; but about Doric he remains adamant, and he defends his position by drawing attention to the fact that the earlier the examples studied, the further they depart from a resemblance to timber forms, and the closer they conform to distinctly masonry methods of construction.

Many of the 'wooden' skeuomorphs of Greek building are naturally carried through to the Renaissance; indeed much of the whole apparatus of the Classical orders as employed in Renaissance architecture can be regarded as skeuomorphic. This in a different sense, however, since it is not just that timber forms are copied in stone, but that structural forms themselves are used decoratively or symbolically, applied to the surface, and not in fact performing the supporting functions to which they refer. The pilaster, for example, which imitates the structural form of a free-standing column, has itself no structural role; nor, often, does the pediment over the window or door which the pilaster 'supports'. Other classical elements which lose their structural purpose and turn into decoration are the string course, as mentioned, and the keystone of the masonry arch, which is transposed into brick construction, and even appears on openings which are not arched at all but supported on lintels.

*[margin note: Renaissance highly skeuomorphic use of classical orders]*

The fact of these various structural deceptions serves to account for some of the antipathy towards Renaissance architecture which was widespread among nineteenth-century rationalists. (Another objection was that the Renaissance style, being a historical revival, could not therefore be a true expression of the 'environmental' circumstances of its time.) For Fletcher the progress of historical styles in architecture is marked by, and in fact forced by, a change from the use of one material to another. 'Vestigial' survivals, skeuomorphs, occur during the transitional phases, but are signs of the immaturity of the new style and the lingering influence of the old. Thus 'It was only in the infancy of stone architecture that men adhered to wooden forms; as soon as habit gave them familiarity with the new material, they abandoned the incongruities of the wooden style, and all traces of the original form passed away.'[49] It is a sign of the new style having achieved its true maturity, for Fletcher, that the new material is fully expressed and there is no vestige of the old remaining. One might fairly attribute a similar view to Viollet-le-Duc.

This attitude to skeuomorphs, as unwanted and anachronistic survivals of obsolete functions, carries on in this century into the modern movement. For instance, Hermann Muthesius in an essay of 1913 on 'The Problem of Form in Engineering'[50] describes how in the history of technology it is unusual for some new invention to find its 'definitive form' immediately it first appears. More usually it is given the familiar form of its functional predecessor — his example of the candle-shaped gas-lamp is from this same article — and only after a period of time is this historical dress thrown off, and the proper functional form achieved for the new type. With ocean liners and express trains 'it has taken the work of generations to get to that form which today we regard as self-evident and as expressing the essence of the object'.[51]

In a set of photographs of automobiles which Le Corbusier illustrates in *La Ville Radieuse*, the series starts chronologically from a horse-drawn carriage and shows the lingering influence of carriage design right through to contemporary cars of the thirties.[52] The moral is a similar one: that the new form of transport requires a reorganisation, a rethinking of old forms, which the continuation of the carriage-building tradition has failed to achieve.

> When we leave one function behind in order to take up another; when for instance we stop swimming in order to walk, when we stop walking in order to fly, we break up the established muscular harmonies and we fall — unless by reacting with wisdom and perseverance, we create a new harmony wherein all the relationships are new but wherein coherence and unity of principle brings ease and proper functioning — real efficiency.[53]

(We can pick up echoes of Viollet-le-Duc here in the talk of 'coherence' and 'unity'.)

In an account which makes explicit the parallel with survivals in biological form, the Czech architect Karel Honzík refers to 'the many instances which Rémy de Goncourt* cites of how form tends to outlive function', such as the claws of the stag-beetle, which have become 'a useless ornament'. 'The persistence of form! Do we not know the force of this truism in every walk of life? From time to time we succeed in shaking off old forms that have become so much ballast or dead lumber.'[54]

The fact of the existence of vestigial or 'useless' organs in animals carries an important corollary. It follows that the form of the animal is not entirely and in every respect the product of adaptation to environment, but that there

---

*I presume Honzík means Rémy de Gourmont.

is a certain 'slack' or looseness in this relationship. The effects of selection might be such as to reduce the size or encourage the disappearance of certain features which have become disadvantageous or non-advantageous, up to a certain point. But beyond this point their retention causes no particular harm to the animal, and thus they may persist indefinitely.

From a rather different point of view, we can see also that the fact of evolution in itself is arguably incompatible with a very close adaptation of organic form to environment. It was the classical, originally Aristotelian, concept of the functional adaptation of organisms, as of the beauty of works of art, that their perfection was such that anything added or taken away would mean a change for the worse. We see that this was an essentially static view and that if any changes *are* to take place over time, then a certain evolutionary plasticity must be allowed to the form without thereby jeopardising the organism's functional performance.

Without a degree of flexibility in the form, the organism would be 'locked in' to some particular fixed morphological arrangement, and would be denied further evolutionary progress. (There is some evidence to suggest that this has happened in a quite literal sense, in organic evolution, to some of those organisms which possess a hard external carapace – such as the tortoise and certain insects - and which have become 'trapped' phylogenetically inside this rigid shell.)[55] The only alternative theory would be that changes in the animal body are rigidly correlated with environmental changes, and that it is only in the presence of the one that the other can occur.

It would follow that many of what appear to be 'decorative' features of the forms of plants and animals indeed have no vital function, and are either fortuitous or else are survivals of previously functional adaptations whose use has become obsolete. The argument is a difficult one, since it is well established that much of what is often regarded as 'decorative' in the organic body carries very practical functions (in sexual selection) which are precisely related to this aesthetic attractiveness.

Not only is there this 'decoration' evolved by animals for the purposes of sexual display. There are the markings by which some animals recognise other members of their own species, or can mimic the appearance of others, to deceive predators; and, as natural forms of 'ornament' par excellence, there are the colours and patterns which serve to identify or advertise plants to pollinating insects, and with which they 'compete' for the insects' attention.

J. Maynard Smith has a curious illustration of 'the analogies between advertisements and the competitive signals of animals on the one hand and between signboards and non-competitive animal signs on the other'.[56] He juxtaposes a peacock's tail feather display with an elaborate advertisement, urging 'Come to Brighton' over a rising sun design. Meanwhile the chaste plumage of the black-headed gull is set against a simple signpost pointing the way to Brighton. There must be plenty of artificial 'decoration', either of household objects or in architecture, which has either advertising or informative functions of these similar kinds.

But although much of the 'decoration' of animals and plants in reality serves such practical ends, the fact remains that there do exist some truly useless vestigial organs - even if, like the vermiform appendix in man, these might not always be very ornamental ones. The theorists of the evolution of decoration on artefacts held to the contrasting view that ornament there was very generally useless, and indeed represented the antithesis or complement of function. The fact that decoration of a 'non-functional' character survived at all on objects of practical use, was a demonstration — as with animals — that the forms of these objects were not defined entirely and precisely by their practical functions.

There was, to put it figuratively, a kind of inner 'kernel' constrained by function, surrounded by an outer 'shell' in which a degree of variation in appearance was allowable, and therefore within which decoration could have free play. (The argument is reminiscent of Cuvier's idea that variations were possible only in the peripheral organs; though of course Cuvier could not have allowed the idea of vestigial survivals, in this zone of variability.) Thus the French anthropologist A. Leroi-Gourhan claims that a great part of the decoration of artefacts can be regarded as lying within such a 'non-functional envelope': 'with the animal as well as man [i.e. man-made objects], the non-functional envelope is made up of survivals, the marks of a phylogenetic origin, for the one linked to the past of the species, for the other to the past of the culture'.[57]

Where the practical demands on form were diminished, so the argument ran, then the area available for decorative elaboration was correspondingly increased, and ornament was liable to break out in luxuriant profusion. Examples of this were offered by those primitive weapons such as axes or maces which had turned gradually into objects of symbolic or emblematic purpose only. As Henry Balfour put it:

> While, in the decoration of useful objects by savage artists, we find to a very great extent a true balance of ornament and form, we must, *per contra*, admit that, frequently associated with, and resulting from, very elaborate decoration is the degeneration of the utility of the implement. That is to say, among those savage races which are much addicted to elaborate fanciful decorations, the application of such ornamentation to useful objects is frequently carried so far, as to render them unfit for use, and they thus became mere ceremonial or processional emblems.[58]

(Balfour does not seem to allow the alternative and much more plausible explanation that, in such objects as are reserved purely for ceremonial or display, the *opportunity* is offered for extensive ornament.)

Balfour has a series of stone-bladed adzes from Polynesia to illustrate the process.[59] The first adze, the basic functional instrument, has a plain wooden handle with a black basalt blade attached by bindings. In a second example, used for ceremony, the handle is both lengthened and thickened to a degree that renders it quite unwieldy for practical use, but provides an enlarged field for fine filigree decoration. In the third case, although the head remains unchanged as a reminder of the original function of the tool, the handle has now become a great pyramidal pedestal, covered with complex geometric ornament over its whole surface. A rather similar example is provided by the modern civic mace, a highly decorated version of the crude wooden or metal club; and another by votive axes, whose blades are decorated with perforations in fretwork designs to a point where their strength is wholly removed. All this takes place in a greatly enlarged area of 'free movement' of the kind which has been described.

The distinction between objects of a utilitarian nature and those which are ceremonial or decorative was clearly one of degree only. We might expect that these writers would find some corresponding gradation in the opportunities offered for variety of form and extent of decoration. The archaeologist V. Gordon Childe suggests something of this sort when he remarks that the number of ways of making a flint knife or simple tool are rather few, restricted by the demands of function and the possible means of manufacture; whereas the range of possibilities for laying out the plan of a farmhouse, or of designing receptacles for corpses, is rather greater.[60] (The wider the possible variety, the more useful is that kind of artefact for archaeological classification and dating, since dissimilarities of type in highly decorated objects will in general be greater, and any similarities will be due to homology rather than to analogy.)

# 8

# Tools as organs or as extensions of the physical body

We now leave the question of decoration, and return to the evolutionary analogy as it was applied solely to the utilitarian aspects of artefacts. We have looked so far at the material products of man's invention and handicraft as though their evolution might be seen as analogous to and so parallel with the evolution of organisms. But there is a quite distinct and alternative way in which evolutionary theory can be applied to artefacts. This is in the proposal that tools, or machines, or other implements, are in fact *part of* the evolution of one particular species of animal, i.e. man; that they are, so to speak, extensions of or substitutes for the various organs of his own physical body.

*[margin note: exosomatic evolutionary phenomenon whereby man's (mechanical) appendages evolve]*

In this view there are in human evolution two kinds of hereditary processes going on at once. The two types have been distinguished by the use of two terms originally due to the theoretical biologist and demographer Alfred Lotka.[1] The first, genetical type of heredity, which man shares with all other creatures, Lotka calls 'endosomatic' or within the body; while the second type, unique to man and which is comprised by culture including material artefacts, he calls 'exosomatic' or outside the body.

The word 'exosomatic' hints at the notion of artefacts constituting a kind of shell or skin around man's body, interposed by him between his naked self and the environment around. As P. B. Medawar puts it, tools are 'appendages, exosomatic organs if you like, that evolve with us'.[2]

The image is very natural in relation to clothes, substituting for the function of skin — and by extension architecture. The simplest hand tools would extend or modify the functions of the hands themselves, while others might substitute for fingers or arms. And the bicycle or car replaces or improves on some functions of the legs. These are pieces of personal equipment which amplify the power or otherwise extend the muscular capacities of the body. On a larger scale such inventions as the telephone or broadcasting systems would serve to increase the range of man's voice, hearing and sight, while access to a library or computer network would amplify his memory and mental power.

There is thus a very metaphorical sense in which one might see man and his material creations together as some kind of hybrid mechanical/organic creature, in which the processes of evolution go on at some speed in the mechanical parts by comparison with very much slower changes in the organic parts. From this point of view cultural evolution and specifically technological evolution is seen as a continuing phase of biological evolution in man, proceeding by different mechanisms, and overlaid onto the Darwinian, genetic process.

In order to understand some of the historical origins of this conception, and to mount a critical analysis, it is necessary at this point to go back as promised to some of the predecessors of Darwin; and in particular to examine the 'transformist' theories of Lamarck. Though Lamarck and Darwin are often linked in histories of the development of evolutionary thought, and although Darwin after the publication of the *Origin* was prepared to acknowledge the possible validity of some aspects of Lamarck's theory, in fact the two men are more properly set in quite different philosophical and scientific traditions.

Lamarck's debt to classical thought is to the Stoics rather than to Aristotle, and his 'zoological philosophy' begins from the doctrines of Stoic metaphysics, that the principles of the world are activity and continuity, and that all nature is connected into an organised and purposive whole.[3] It is *pneuma*, the spirit or breath of life, which for the Stoics effects this animation of material, and which is the unifying force that binds the world together.

Where in the Christian concept of nature, purpose and design were the work of God, in the naturalist philosophy to which such biological thinkers of the Enlightenment as Diderot and Buffon adhered, it was nature itself which possessed or was the source of moral purpose. Indeed for Diderot there was no sense in which the physical aspects of nature could be separated from the moral. C. C. Gillispie describes how, in this way,

> the romantic nature philosophy of the Enlightenment . . . revived the ancient, the pagan sense of cosmic organism. Such was Goethe's innate, indwelling order, the bodily expression of identity and personality. Individual animals participate in life process, in this sense, as organs do in the life of the single body. But (as will appear in the example of Lamarck) there is no correlation between this and a theological view of nature. On the contrary, the organismic is a self-sufficient order. It may be a moral order, but such morality will be naturalistic, never theistic. Diderot was an atheist, Goethe was no Christian.[4]

Lamarck, according to Gillispie, was the 'intellectual successor to Diderot and Buffon'. His theory of evolution neither required nor gave any explanation of the fact of design or progress in nature, since it started from the assumption that these were intrinsic to the force of the life process which expressed itself in organisms. What was required was an account of how the life force came into conflict with inert physical matter and was diverted into various 'channels of necessity'. This interaction of the life process with the contingencies and exigencies of materials and environment resulted in the production of those various different forms of life, the species, which are actually observed. Hence the basic tenet of Lamarck's theory: that it is changes in the environment which are responsible for eliciting corresponding changes in the animal or plant. As Gillispie puts it: 'the environment is a shifting set of circumstances and opportunities to which the organism responds creatively, ... as an expression of its whole nature as a living thing.'[5]

Lamarck's transformism takes the static ladder of creation of eighteenth-century natural history and sets it in motion. But this is not the kind of motion which we saw in Bonnet's *Echelle des Etres*, where the species moved up the hierarchy of creation unchanged, and in orderly sequence. Lamarck's image of evolution is rather of a movement where organisms are always struggling upwards against the constricting and disorderly forces of inorganic material, and changing, progressing as they go. Their progress 'erodes' channels in the physical environment, and the dead remnants of the life process fall back to the foot of the ladder where they are once more incorporated into the upward movement.

In this way Lamarck lays emphasis on the *direct* effects of environment upon the organism, and on the efforts of the individual animal somehow to adapt itself to its surroundings. He proposes that the origins of the adaptation of the organs or features of animals and plants lie in the so-called 'inheritance of acquired characters'. During the life of the individual, the effect of various mechanical and other forces in the surrounding environment is to mould the form and structure of the parts into a more efficient and convenient shape. Parts or organs in frequent use become more highly developed. Others, falling into disuse, dwindle and disappear. These effects are passed on by some hereditary means to the descendants; and so, gradually, the marvellous adaptive complexity that we observe in nature is accumulated.

Lamarck summarises these aspects of his theory in three rules:

> The production of a new organ in an animal body results from the arising and continuance of a new need, and from the new movement which this need brings into being and sustains.

> The degree of development of organs and their force of action are always proportionate to the use made of these organs.

> All that has been acquired, imprinted or changed in the organisation of the individual during the course of its life is preserved by generation and transmitted to the new individuals that descend from the individual so modified [inheritance of acquired characters].[6]

*Lamarck's theory of environmental shaping*
*(discredited by modern genetic theory which proves*
*envt. has no effect on genetics.)*

It is the way of life, therefore, of the organism which, for Lamarck, determines its form, rather than the other way round. As Lamarck puts it:

> It is not the organs — that is to say, the form and character of the animal's bodily parts — which have given rise to its habits and peculiar properties, but, on the contrary, it is its habits and manner of life and the conditions in which its ancestors lived that has in the course of time fashioned its bodily form, its organs and its qualities.[7]

In human evolution it is, traditionally, the blacksmith who is brought forward to give evidence on behalf of Lamarckian inheritance. The great development of his arm muscles, acquired during years of work at the forge, is supposed to be passed on to the strapping sons who carry on the business.

The Lamarckian view is in many ways an eminently plausible one. As Medawar says, 'It is an intelligent and forthright doctrine, and, in ignorance of genetics, an alternative is difficult to propound.'[8] It is not only an intelligible theory, but somehow just and reasonable, that the offspring should inherit the benefits won by their parents in their hard battle with life. Unfortunately, in the light of the neo-Darwinian evolutionary genetics of the first half of this century, it has since been rejected as untrue. Neither Lamarck nor Darwin had access to any detailed knowledge of the workings of the hereditary process at the level of microscopic and molecular structures. Darwin himself, in fact, gave some support as indicated to Lamarck's idea of 'acquired characters'. But gradually, after his time, the area in which recourse could be taken to Lamarckian principles for explanation was gradually diminished; until with the new synthesis of genetics with whole areas of biological knowledge in the twenties and thirties, Lamarck — at least so far as the mainstream of biology was concerned — was wholly refuted.

The evidence was rather that the units of heredity, the genes, were highly stable, not subject to direct influence from the animal or plant's environment during its lifetime at all. They were passed on to the descendants absolutely unchanged (although, in sexual reproduction, in somewhat different mixtures and recombinations), with the exception of occasional abrupt changes whose frequency appeared to be random and whose cause was, in relation to the animal's pattern of life, largely accidental and external. *MODERN THEORY of molecular genetics*

With the discoveries of modern biochemistry it has been shown that this precision of the hereditary mechanism, the great fidelity with which offspring resemble their parents, is due, ultimately, to the chemical stability of the DNA molecule. Only a single molecule could provide in so small a space a stable structure, where the hereditary information might be safely encoded and preserved with only minor changes over many thousands of generations.

The refutation of Lamarckism has its interpretation in molecular genetics, in what Crick has called the 'central dogma'. The primary function of the genetic code embodied in the DNA is to determine the presence of particular proteins, mostly enzymes, which control in turn the processes of chemical activity in the cell, and thus ultimately determine the development, maintenance and functioning of organs and of the organism as a whole. The central dogma states, roughly, that information can pass only in one direction, from the DNA to the protein and not vice versa. Any changes in the amounts and disposition of protein molecules caused by conditions in the environment of the individual (Lamarck's 'acquired characters') cannot effect an equivalent change in the hereditary material, the DNA.

*conclusive refutation* [margin annotation]

While Darwin had been criticised for the random element implicit in the contribution of variations to evolution in his theory, Lamarck had on the other hand been ridiculed for his implication that the adaptation of organs is the result of a kind of sustained willing or effort on the part of creatures; as though 'creatures produced new organs, or transformed old ones, by simply *wanting* hard enough and long enough'.[9] As has been shown by H. G. Cannon, it was possibly partly because Lamarck's word *besoins*, meaning an animal's functional *needs*, had been translated by Lyell and others as 'wants', hence desires, that he fell foul of this kind of criticism.[10] (It was Lyell who first introduced Lamarck's ideas to an English audience – even if only to subject them to attack.) And despite the insistence of C. C. Gillispie that Lamarck was not a vitalist – he argues that Lamarck's concept of the vital force was not at all mysterious, but was related to *combustion*, i.e. that it had a strictly physical basis[11] – the fact is that many of Lamarck's critics have found a vitalist flavour in his writings. For instance, he talks of an unconscious *sentiment interieur* in the higher animals, and of the forces of life as distinct from mechanical, non-vital forces. This was probably of comparable importance in contributing to his scientific eclipse.

Lamarck's theory, as applied to organic evolution, is now generally discredited, and without supporters (with the exception of some valiant rearguard action being fought mainly by Arthur Koestler). It is not possible for bodily changes resulting from activities of the individual during its lifetime to affect the genetic material directly – that is to say it is not possible for Lamarck's 'acquired characters' to be inherited. The distinction between the two hypothesised styles of heredity, Darwinian and Lamarckian, has been characterised by Medawar (following J. Lederberg) as the distinction between an 'elective' and an 'instructive' process.[12]

Lamarckism was essentially an 'instructive' theory of evolution. An organism, so the theory suggested, somehow received instructions from its environment (acquired characters), and the information gained from these instructions could be passed on, genetically, to the next generation. But this is not a true picture, and instead the environment is now known to act in an 'elective' way, to bring out or choose genetic potentialities offered by the organism. In Medawar's words: 'So far as we know, the relationship between organism and environment in the evolutionary process is an elective relationship. The environment does *not* imprint genetical instructions upon living things.'[13]

In the lecture from which this quotation is drawn, Medawar is concerned first of all to point up this central difference of the Lamarckian from the Darwinian (or more properly 'neo-Darwinian') theory of heredity. But Medawar has a second purpose also, and that is to show simultaneously the essential difference between organic evolution and human cultural evolution. In the first case, natural evolution, we have the (properly speaking) genetic process, where the environment acts 'electively' in relation to changes in the organism. In the second, cultural case, we have a process in which the (metaphorically speaking) 'hereditary material' consists of mental concepts, or information in records, books and artefacts — and passes through such information channels as teaching and the oral tradition. Here the relationship of the 'cultural environment' to the individual is quite literally an 'instructive' one. The individual gains information about the world by being taught by his parents, in school, and through his experience of life in general.

We remember the blacksmith, who Lamarckists thought could pass on his well-developed biceps to his son. This he cannot do. But what he certainly *can* do is to pass on to them his skill and knowledge of the blacksmith's craft (as well as his tools and the smithy). In this respect his *culturally* 'acquired characters' — what he has learned of his trade from his predecessors, and through his own experience —*can* be inherited by his successors. We see then that Lamarckism, or at least the inheritance of acquired characters, was a theory which, while incorrect in relation to organic evolution where it was applied, turned out to be true when applied to culture.

One reason why Lamarck fell into this error was arguably that he was working by analogy: drawing analogies *from* culture *to* nature, and projecting an essentially cultural conception onto the natural world. A number of historians of science, as well as social scientists, have suggested that Darwin too was guilty of this same fault. Darwin drew inspiration, as we have seen, from Malthus's theory of population limits for his idea of the selection mechanism; and less consciously perhaps from the political economy of the Scottish school for his ideas on the positive benefits of competition. What has not been proposed, I believe, is that the essential role of *variations* in Darwin's theory, and the fact that they are random and undirected, have any counterpart or derivation in cultural or economic thinking.

With Lamarck it is exactly this *cause* of *variation* which is conceived in 'cultural' terms. Characters are acquired by the animal through its own efforts, in a way similar to that in which men acquire learning and material property through devoting themselves to study and to business. What is more, animals may in Lamarck's theory pass on their bodily acquisitions, in an organic equivalent of the inheritance of material property or of the transmission of cultural knowledge in education, from one generation to the next.

Thus Lamarckism has an intrinsic teleological and progressive aspect to it, since the evolutionary process in the Lamarckian view is actually propelled by the strivings of organisms to satisfy those new needs of theirs which are continually arising. Again we might relate this progressive quality of Lamarck's theory to the cultural and social ethos of the Enlightenment and the Revolution; much in the same way that Darwinism has been set by many commentators in its nineteenth-century context of industrial, technological and commercial progress, and has been connected to the Victorian work ethic, with its emphasis on self-improvement and competition both at the individual and the national levels. The fact is, however, that this analysis is much more appropriately applied to *social* Darwinism, or to Spencerism, than it is to Darwin himself. Darwin saw no necessary progression in the rise or succession of natural species; merely that those of greater fitness survived. The more fit might in other senses be either 'higher' or 'lower' species. Indeed it was precisely on the grounds that his conception of evolution *lacked* overall direction, and random variations were without purpose or meaning, that Darwin, as I have emphasised, was made the subject of fierce philosophical attack.

One of Darwin's leading critics on these grounds was Samuel Butler, who besides his activities as novelist and man of letters, was deeply interested in the theory of evolution, and wrote several books himself on the subject. Though it may take us down something of a sidetrack, it will be worth examining Butler's views, which make their appearance not only in his serious biological works, but also find their expression in satirical form in his novel *Erewhon*.[14] The reason for choosing Butler out of all of Darwin's opponents is that Butler was especially occupied with the analogy of evolution in machines; and it is arguable that his ideas on technology and tools were even directly influential on some architectural theorists of the modern movement, specifically Amadée Ozenfant and Le Corbusier. Butler played a great part in rehabilitating Lamarck's theory, and the evolutionary contributions of Erasmus Darwin and Buffon, by publication of his *Evolution Old and New*.[15] This book was intended to promote a Lamarckian position while at the same time seeking to diminish Darwin's prestige by suggesting that he was not as original as he first appeared; indeed Butler entered into a bitter feud with Darwin, based on the accusation that Darwin had not properly acknowledged his debts to these precursors.

When *The Origin of Species* first appeared, Butler read it and became immediately a convinced and enthusiastic Darwinist — partly because of the demolition of Christian mythology and the assault on traditional religious beliefs which the theory implied. Later he read a book called *The Genesis of Species* by St George Mivart, in which he found, to his amazement, an attack on Darwin — made by a Roman Catholic biologist — which was not an attack on evolution.[16] Mivart's book took a Lamarckian position. Butler discovered, as he did also slightly later still from the 'Historical Sketch' added to *The Origin of Species*, that Darwin had had several illustrious predecessors, including Lamarck; and Butler much preferred Lamarck's theory to that of Darwin. Butler took a special pleasure, with every topic, in adopting a stance exactly contrary to popular wisdom and to received ideas; and so it is perhaps not too cynical to attribute at least part of this shift in his position to the possibility that Darwin first appealed to him because of the scientific and theological iconoclasm of his theory, but that later when Darwinism became orthodoxy, Butler moved to defend another unpopular cause.

However this may be, Butler certainly became a staunch Lamarckist, and wrote a book *Life and Habit* (whose title itself refers to a conception very close to Lamarck's 'acquired characters') in defence of a teleological, directed explanation of the evolutionary process, arising out of the 'needs and experiences' of creatures.[17] *Life and Habit* was an attack on the mechanical, materialist philosophy which Butler saw underlying natural selection. (Later Bernard Shaw was to develop his own Lamarckian ideas of 'creative evolution', as expounded in *Man and Superman* and *Back to Methuselah*, out of a similar horror for the 'hideous fatalism' of Darwin's theory. Shaw acknowledges that in these plays, Butler's 'extremely fresh, free and future-piercing suggestions have an obvious share'.)[18]

The two successive stages of Butler's thought are reflected in the structure of a number of chapters in *Erewhon*, where the hero of the story visits the Colleges of Unreason, and hears the contrasting evolutionary arguments of two of the professors. The first of these professors represents a Darwinian point of view; the second a Lamarckian position. (We know this since, apart from anything else, Butler explains the intended significance of these *Erewhon* episodes in *Life and Habit*.)[19] The interest from the present point of view (and the paradox, as we shall see) is that Butler chooses to mount both sides of this biological discussion, somewhat whimsically, by means of the *analogy* with the evolution of technology.

The chapters in question are in fact reworkings of the substance of two essays which Butler had written some time earlier in New Zealand, entitled 'Darwin among the Machines'[20] and 'Lucubratio Ebria'[21] (the latter carrying the Lamarckian ideas). The two professors serve in effect to re-present the arguments of these two articles; while they also bolster their positions by swapping quotations from the great Erewhonian authority, *The Book of Machines*. The whole account thus lightly conceals its more serious purpose behind a *jeu d'esprit*, an extended improvisation on the amusing possibilities of transposing evolutionary theory into the mechanical field.

The first Erewhonian professor asks whether the conventional distinctions we make between machines and organisms have any reality, or whether any differences which remain are not disappearing very quickly. Machines depend on external sources of power; but then so do animals and plants. Animals are capable of regulating and controlling their own activity; but then is not the same function performed in the steam engine by the governor and the automatic mechanisms which control supplies of oil and fuel? Animals and plants are capable of reproduction of their own kind, which might not seem immediately to be true of machines. But then even flowers need the help of insects. There are some types of animal which do not reproduce, but depend on the agency of others always, such as the drones among bees.

The frightening thing about machines, the Erewhonian professor argues, is that their evolution — through 'descent with modification' — seems to be proceeding so fast. If they have achieved so much in a few thousand years of their evolution so far, who is to say what machines might not achieve in a few thousand years more? We are already the slaves of machines, he says; very soon they will overtake us and become superior in every way — not only in power but in intelligence. Men will become a mere parasitic species, spending their time in labouring to supply the wants of machines. His proposed remedy — which the Erewhonians had in fact adopted some time before the visit of the story's hero — was to destroy all machines completely before their influence and domination could grow too great to be overcome.

The effect of Butler's satire here is an attack on the mechanistic concept of organic evolution which, Butler came to believe, Darwin represented. By showing the self-evident absurdity of treating machines as though they possessed the capacities of organisms, Butler intends to show the inadequacy of treating organisms as though they were machines. For this purpose he develops a theme which in many ways parallels the Darwinian approach to the study of evolution in artefacts taken by the anthropologists. It is a short step from this to the proposition that their evolution is a process not directly controlled by man; and therefore one which could perhaps get out of his control entirely.

The identity of method between Pitt-Rivers and Balfour and the Erewhonian author is complete. Like the anthropologists, the latter

> attempted to support his theory by pointing out the similarities existing between many machines of a widely different character, which served to show descent from a common ancestor. He divided machines into their genera, subgenera, species, varieties, subvarieties, and so forth. He proved the existence of connecting links between machines that seemed to have very little in common, and showed that many more such links had existed, but had now perished. He pointed out tendencies to reversion, and the presence of rudimentary organs which existed in many machines feebly developed and perfectly useless, yet serving to mark descent from an ancestor to whom the function was actually useful.[22]

The second Erewhonian professor (whose opinions the Erewhonians had ignored) claimed that machines were not so potentially dangerous as the first writer had argued; and that machines, so far from evolving in their own right and threatening man by their superiority, were, on the contrary, evidence of a new and higher stage in the evolutionary development of man himself. 'In fact, machines are to be regarded as the mode of development by which the human organism is now especially advancing, every past invention being an addition to the resources of the human body.'[23] It is the second professor who refers to man as a 'machinate mammal', and to machines as man's 'extra-corporeal limbs' (partaking, no doubt, in Lotka's 'exosomatic' style of evolution). He develops the analogy of tools with limbs in this passage:

> The lower animals keep all their limbs at home in their own bodies, but many of man's are loose, and lie about detached, now here and there, in various parts of the world — some being kept always handy for contingent use, and others being occasionally hundreds of miles away. A machine is merely a supplementary limb; this is the be all and end all of machinery. We do not use our own limbs other than as machines; and a leg is only a much better wooden leg than any one can manufacture.

> 'Observe a man digging with a spade; his right fore-arm has become artificially lengthened, and his hand has become a joint. The handle of the spade is like a knob at the end of the humerus; the shaft is the additional bone, and the oblong iron plate is the new form of the hand which enables its possessor to disturb the earth in a way to which his original hand was unequal.'

The professor goes on:

> 'Having thus modified himself, not as other animals are modified, by circumstances over which they have not even the appearance of control, but having, as it were, taken forethought and added a cubit to his stature, civilisation began to dawn upon the race, the social good offices, the genial companionship of friends, the art of unreason, and all those habits of mind which most elevate men above the lower animals, in the course of time ensued.'[24]

The professor continues by expressing some misgivings about whether, with the replacement of the functions of man's physical body by mechanical substitutes, the forces of competition and natural selection would cease in the end to act on the body, and so a general physical degeneracy might result. Ultimately, he suggests, the body might become purely rudimentary and man would consist of nothing more than soul and intelligence. Even at the time of writing, man had already become dependent on his mechanical limbs to a great degree, especially in old age. '"His memory goes in his pocket-book. He becomes more and more complex as he grows older; he will then be seen with see-engines, or perhaps with artificial teeth and hair."'[25] On the other hand, the professor argues that wealth, more advanced methods of communication and travel, and more highly developed forms of social organisation, all increase man's adaptation in a still more powerful way than do those earlier achievements of civilisation, mechanical tools and spoken or written language.

Of the two Erewhonian professors, the second one's arguments are thus intended by Butler to illustrate how, just as the progress of machines makes improvements in the adaptation of man's artificial limbs, achieved through purposeful effort and not by blind Darwinian chance, so, he implies, the evolution of his natural limbs (and those of all lower animals, and plants) take place by similar, Lamarckian means.

The great paradox or irony of these chapters of *Erewhon* arises out of the way in which Butler chooses to present his debate about the nature of organic evolution, by means of the analogy with technology. At the time when he wrote 'Darwin among the Machines' and 'Lucubratio Ebria', Butler was a (biological) Darwinist. The first essay, as its title indicates, applies Darwinian theory directly to machines. The second elaborates a *Lamarckian* interpretation of the nature of *cultural* evolution, of tools as man's extra organs; but Butler is quite explicit on the point that nothing of this kind occurs in the evolution of other species. 'The limbs of the lower animals have never been modified by an act of deliberation and forethought on their own part.'[26] At this point Butler was, rightly in the hindsight of present-day biological and anthropological opinion, a Darwinist with respect to biological evolution, and a Lamarckist for cultural evolution.

Later, as has been described, Butler came to adopt a Lamarckian view of both processes. If the *Erewhon* episodes are read as a biological debate between Lamarck and Darwin — and in *Life and Habit* they are explicitly interpreted as such — then the fact that this is presented through the mechanical analogy introduces a fatal flaw. Because, as we now believe, the Lamarckian argument is quite right in the cultural case, but quite wrong — unluckily for Butler — in the biological.

The important point for the distinction is very clearly stated in the passage quoted from the second professor. Technological evolution *differs* from biological by virtue of the participation of the mind of man and his active intellectual intervention in the process. Man introduces that intention and purpose which is lacking from the uncontrollable chance nature and 'fatalism' of organic evolution. Where the animals have not 'even the appearance of control' over their own circumstances, man has 'taken forethought', he has the all-important capacity for anticipating circumstances, and has 'added a cubit to his stature'.

In the 1920s Le Corbusier and Amadée Ozenfant, in developing the artistic theory of Purism, advanced the concept of the *objet-type*. Certain stereotyped and mass-produced objects — the tobacco pipe, the guitar, the characteristic designs of bottle, carafe, cup and drinking glass common to every café in Paris and familiar from Cubist still-life — were all seen by the Purists as the end-products of processes of technological evolution, and conceived very much in the spirit of the Erewhonian theory. We shall examine this idea more fully in chapter 9. The feature of the Purist 'type-object' which is of especial interest here is the fact of its being imagined, like in *Erewhon*, as an extension of the human body or a substitute organ.

Le Corbusier and Ozenfant say that Purism has taken its *objets-types* 'for preference from among those that serve the most direct of human uses; those which are like extensions of man's limbs, and thus of an extreme intimacy'.[27] Indeed, in Ozenfant's later writings, the explicit term *objets-membres-humains* is introduced to refer to those artefacts which take on their characteristic forms through their proximity and hence their fit to the human body; as for example the violin, the chair, or any tool used in the hands.[28]

The question arises whether Ozenfant or Le Corbusier had read *Erewhon*. The correspondences are very close: in references by Ozenfant to machines as 'relays' created by man and comparable to the products of animals, such as the bee's honey;[29] in the obvious suggestion of the Purists' notion of 'mechanical selection', as we shall see, by Butler's 'Darwin among the Machines'; or in the small but not perhaps coincidental point that it is the tobacco pipe which Butler chooses to illustrate 'vestigial organs' in artefacts,* and the pipe too which is one of the Purists' classic and favourite *objets-types*.[30] The final illustration to Le Corbusier's *Vers Une Architecture*, indeed, depicts a briar pipe; and this comes at the conclusion of a chapter devoted largely to industrial evolution and the threat, or challenge, presented by technology to human values.[31]

The question of influence is a difficult one to answer with any finality; but there is what would seem to be some very strong evidence to be found in volume 18 of the Purists' journal *L'Esprit Nouveau*, on an unnumbered page facing the editorial. Each issue of the later volumes of the magazine carries a list of books whose significance is unexplained (they are not 'books received' nor are they newly published), but which appear to be books gaining the seal of approval of the editors as truly embodying 'l'esprit nouveau'. The list in volume 18 includes Butler's *Life and Habit* in French translation.[32]

Although the concepts of the type-object and technical evolution make their appearance in several articles in earlier issues of *L'Esprit Nouveau* (and these sorts of general ideas were widely current in architectural and design theory at this period), it is only in later issues — specifically in volumes 23 and 24, in articles devoted to the 1925 Exposition of Decorative Arts[33] — that the

---

* An amusing point to which Lionel March has drawn my attention is the distinctly contrasting role played by tobacco pipes in William Morris's Utopian novel *News from Nowhere* (London, 1891). Here the body of the pipe, in contradistinction from the severity of form of the *objet-type*, acts rather as the field for the most elaborate and fanciful decoration, through which each individual smoker expresses his particular personality. (See the episode in chapter 6, 'A Little Shopping'.)

recognisably Butlerian resonances become evident. It is here that *objets-membres-humains* are first introduced, with a discussion of how files and copying machines extend the capacities of our memories, how in our wardrobes are arranged our *membres auxiliaires* to protect us from heat and cold, and how 'decorative art' (which should properly concern the production of useful objects *without* decoration) becomes a kind of branch of orthopaedics or the manufacture of artificial limbs.[34] It seems highly probable that these 'paradoxical definitions' were inspired by Butler and *Erewhon*.

# 9

# How to speed up craft evolution?

The interest of archaeologists and anthropologists in technological evolution was, obviously, turned towards artefacts of the past, and to artefacts presently in use in various cultures. The parallel interest of designers and architects was, equally clearly, directed rather towards the future, to the production of new designs. For designers, the study of the history of the development of tools or of building types was valuable in so far as it could reveal principles or methods which might then be consciously applied in contemporary practice.

But there was an immediate and paradoxical difficulty here, since the evolutionary view of the design process in primitive cultures stressed, as we have seen, the very long periods of time over which such evolution was assumed to have occurred. Also there was the implication, in an extreme 'Darwinian' formulation of the analogy, that variations in the form of the artefact were introduced (accidentally) or at least without any very great measure of forethought. Assuming that it was desirable, was it even possible for the modern designer to emulate these supposed evolutionary processes of primitive and vernacular handicrafts? Would it mean allowing a similar extent of time for 'selection' to be applied; and would it involve a conscious and deliberate attempt to avoid anticipating, in imagination, the results of 'variations' in the form? It is these puzzles, and the various responses which were in effect made to them, which form the subject of this and succeeding chapters.

One possibility, with the merits of simplicity at least, was just to *accept* the necessity for a considerable length of time over which the evolutionary process had to be stretched; and to make a series of artefacts with slight variations, subject them to test in real use, select those with somewhat more satisfactory performance, copy them and test them again, and so on, over what might admittedly need to be tens or even hundreds of years. We have seen exactly such a proposal put by Fergusson, in his suggested method for the design of the 'Anglo-Protestant' church.

The objection which would, we might suspect, have been made to this idea by the twentieth-century exponents of evolutionary design ideas was that the industrial and social developments which had been accelerating through

the previous century simply did not provide the stability of context necessary
for evolutionary design methods to work. In the time that several 'generations' of selection would take to be made, the nature of the original design
problem, the functions of the artefact, the available materials and manufacturing methods, all would have changed; and this 'environmental' change
would be so fast as to prevent any evolutionary adaptation in the form of
the artefact from keeping pace. Indeed, according to many writers, it was
possible to attribute much of the failure of nineteenth-century architectural
and industrial design precisely to the collapse of the vernacular tradition and
the disappearance of handicraft methods — phenomena which themselves
had been brought about by the industrialisation of manufacture and by
rapid changes both in public taste and in the patterns and requirements
of domestic and social life.

I said that arguments along these lines would, 'we might suspect', have
been made; because the fact is that this paradox is one which is inherent, but
rather seldom faced explicitly, in the writings on this subject of such figures as
Herman Muthesius and Walter Gropius, as well as Ozenfant and Le Corbusier.
There is no real squaring up to the issue which their position creates of how
an appeal to the virtues of 'evolutionary' design in the production of traditional handicraft objects can be reconciled with an acknowledgement of the
rapidity of contemporary technological progress and social change. Let us
examine some of these writings briefly; after which we can turn to the various
openings which seemed to provide ways out of this dilemma.

In essays and speeches dating from the immediate pre-First-World-War
period, Hermann Muthesius presents a picture of the evolution of the products
of industrial manufacture which has a definitely discernible basis in biological analogy. He proposes the possibility of developing in modern architecture a number of building types of standardised design, which will be
produced through collective rather than individual effort, and which will
meet the emerging, general and communal requirements of the new society.

Thus in a speech to the Deutscher Werkbund made in 1914, Muthesius says
that 'Architecture essentially tends towards the typical. The type discards
the extraordinary, and establishes order.'[1] Elsewhere in the same speech he
makes reference to various engineering products — the turbine engine, the
telescope, the steamship and the camera — as representing stabilised types,
lying at the end of processes of technical evolution; with the definite implication that this corresponds in some way to organic evolution — 'the way from
individualism to the creation of types is the organic way of development'.
Muthesius certainly knew Semper's *Der Stil*, and it is possible to suppose that
he might have been thinking back to Semper's doctrine of *Urformen* in this
connection.

Muthesius was quoted in an earlier chapter, from an essay of 1913, on the

subject of survivals and 'vestigial organs' in artefacts. It is clear from the
passages cited that he conceives of any particular type of artefact, that is to say
an artefact for some specified function, as having a proper and 'definitive'
form. This type-form may not and probably will not be discovered right
away; but once it has been reached then, the implication is, the design will
be completely resolved and no further changes will be necessary or desirable.

Walter Gropius takes up a similar argument in his writings on art education and industrial design. This is particularly in evidence in his explanation
of the re-orientation of the teaching programme of the Bauhaus in the fields
of applied art and design for manufacture when, after 1923, this became
directed more towards promoting a unified, collective style of the sort called
for by Muthesius and the Werkbund supporters. The contribution of personal
individual expression to design — stressed in the earlier craft-oriented
Expressionist phase of the Bauhaus — was now to be minimised, or at least
brought into line with the demands of function and of machine production,
in the development of 'type' designs suitable for mass manufacture. Whereas
'expression' requires of a form the correspondence to certain individual
desires, says Gropius, and renders that form personal and particular to some
special time and place, the demands of 'intellect' direct the form towards
some universally standardised type in accordance with its given function. The
history of design — 'of the evolution of things into shapes' — is the history of
this struggle between the opposing forces of intellect and desire.[2]

Making this distinction in a late essay from 1937 contributed to the anthology *Circle*[3] (but which reiterates his ideas from the previous decade), Gropius
writes:

> The questions concerning the object or purpose of a thing [i.e. those susceptible
> to 'intellect'] are of a super-individualistic nature; they represent the organic
> evolution as we see it in nature. For example, the development of a technical
> apparatus, such as a locomotive, is the result of the intellectual work of
> numerous individuals who, like links in the chain of development, built up on
> the efforts of their predecessors.

In Gropius's plan for modern design education he would stress the importance of collective effort built on a shared basis of knowledge and theory.
Purely personal artistic inclinations and tastes would be subordinated to or
harmonised in a new cultural unity in design, which would be functionalist
in character. 'Today, we insist upon the form of a thing following the function
of that thing, upon the desire for expression of its creator following the same
direction as the organic building-up processes in nature, and not running
counter to that direction.' The result of such a scientific communal attitude
to design will be the emergence of archetypal or standard forms; 'no longer
must the isolated individual work continue to occupy pride of place, but

rather the creation of the generally valid type, the development towards a standard'.[4]

It was the programme of the Bauhaus in its middle period, one might say, to set out consciously to create *new* types, suitable to the new materials and to mechanical means of production. Many critics would allow that at the strictly stylistic level this was certainly achieved in several Bauhaus products; that the designs which were created for lamps, appliances, the tubular steel chair, did indeed in this aesthetic sense attain the status of 'types', and passed into the collective unconscious of the design world and into the anonymity of mass manufacture. It would be hard to mount an equivalent argument at the level of utilitarian function, however; to suggest that the Bauhaus actually instituted many practical engineering improvements in these items of household equipment.[5] And what is very apparent is that neither Gropius nor his colleagues were at all clear as to how such types — in the functional and engineering sense — could be synthesised immediately on the drawing board, and much more rapidly than had ever been possible in the long processes of evolution by trial-in-use.

The most fully elaborated theory of artefact types and mechanical evolution on a biological model, to be found amongst twentieth-century architects, is that embodied in the philosophy of Purism. At the end of a passage discussing some possible equivalences between the organs of the body and the parts of buildings, Le Corbusier cries out with characteristic enthusiasm: 'BIOLOGY! The great new word in architecture and planning.'[6] This exclamation is generally indicative of Le Corbusier's continuing excitement over biological analogy (although why he should say here that biology is the 'new word' is perplexing, since this quotation is from late in his career, and his own interest in the subject starts from the early twenties — not to mention of course the good hundred years of biological analogies in architecture before that) (figure 23).

One should not expect anything too explicit or straightforward from Le Corbusier's writings, however, and ideas about evolution in design in his early books are to be inferred as much from illustrations as they are to be read from the text. For example, in *Vers Une Architecture* there is presented a series of racing cars, historically arranged and showing the gradual application to their body design of aerodynamic principles, over the caption 'In search of a standard'.[7] In an accompanying diagram a series of shapes are compared for their air resistance. An ovoid body or cone 'which gives the best penetration is the result of experiment and calculation, and this is confirmed by natural creations such as fishes, birds etc. Experimental application: the dirigible, racing car.'[8] Le Corbusier is fond of illustrating the evolution of car designs. The series which shows the vestigial relics of carriage forms, in *La Ville Radieuse*, has been mentioned already. This set of pictures is accompanied by a parallel series which is very similar to that in *Vers Une Architecture*, depicting

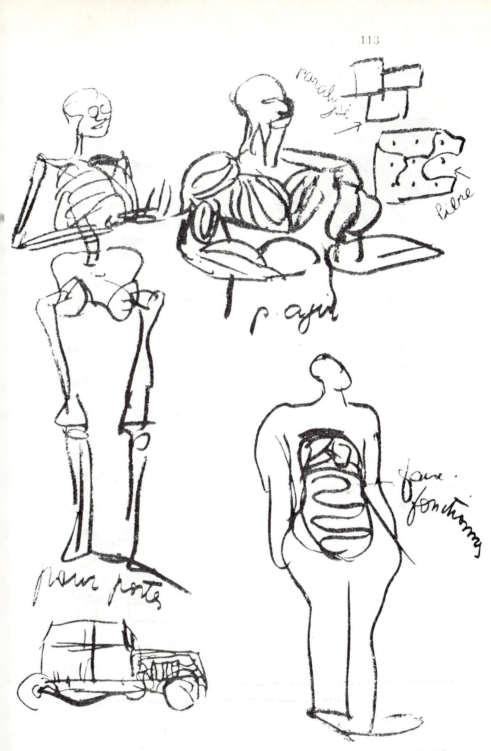

23 Le Corbusier, biological analogies with architectural plans and with car design.

# 1900

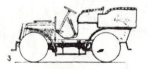

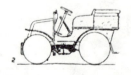

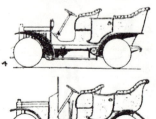

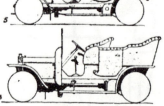

ÉVOLUTION

DES

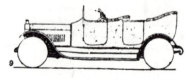

FORMES

DE

24   Evolution of motor cars.

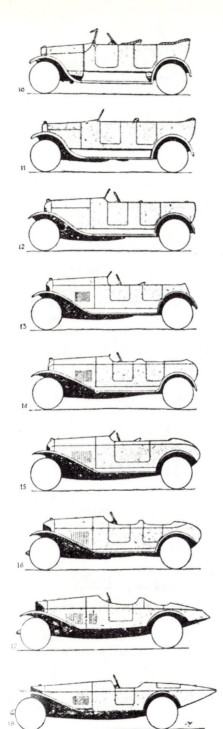

1921

cars with aerodynamically shaped bodies, and in which the first illustration is of an aeroplane next to a car.[9] In one issue of *L'Esprit Nouveau* there is a double page spread devoted to the 'Evolution des Formes de l'Automobile 1900—1921' (figure 24).[10]

One of the best-known sequences of plates in *Vers Une Architecture* shows the development of the Greek temple form from its relatively crude Doric beginnings to its apotheosis in the Parthenon.[11] The temples are set alongside illustrations of cars — Humber, Hispano-Suiza, Delage. We may suppose that this is intended by Le Corbusier in part to indicate some common factors between the evolution of temples and racing cars, and in part to contrast the differences; particularly when the illustration is put in the context of the debate over equivalent issues by Viollet-le-Duc, Semper and others to which Le Corbusier surely, if indirectly, is harking back.

In order to comprehend fully the evolutionary arguments of *Vers Une Architecture* it is necessary to go back to the principles of Purism in painting, of which Le Corbusier and Ozenfant were the originators and chief proponents. In point of fact the text to *Vers Une Architecture* itself is made up from revised versions of articles which had appeared previously in *L'Esprit Nouveau*, over the joint signatures (or rather joint pseudonyms) 'Le Corbusier—Saugnier' (Saugnier being Ozenfant's mother's name, adopted by him as a *nom de plume*).[12]

The principal idea behind Purist theory was that certain simple universal geometrical forms were capable of inducing in the spectator correspondingly universal primary sensations, which would be quite uncoloured by culture or by the individual's particular background; and that these forms could therefore provide the basis — the *mots fixes* — for a universal plastic language — a sort of visual Esperanto, to put it unflatteringly — which would transcend narrow cultural or historical limitations.[13] At the same time the Purists recognised that any form, however pure and simple, would inevitably come to have attached to it in any particular culture other secondary associations of an incidental or 'literary' character.

An art based exclusively on these secondary attributes, as for example Surrealism, would be closed to all but the initiated, to those who could decipher its significance because of their special knowledge, and who thus possessed the key to its language. An art based on the primary qualities alone would on the other hand be in danger of becoming solely decorative, and without power to excite the emotions. But an art based on both qualities simultaneously, which was the ambition of Purism, would be capable — so the argument ran — of engaging the emotional faculties of the spectator by means of the secondary associations; and *through these*, of leading him on to a contemplation of higher-order plastic relationships of a mathematical, abstract and universally valid nature, as conveyed by the standardised forms of the primary elements of composition.

The second important component of Purist theory concerned mechanical evolution, particularly the evolution of household utensils and tools. Purist painting developed from Cubism, and took as its subject matter everyday objects, the *objets-types*, chosen for the anonymity of their design, their universal and unchanging stability as forms, their simple geometry, and their lack — so it was supposed — of special literary or extraneous associations. The leading candidates for *objets-types*, according to Le Corbusier and Ozenfant, were objects of a 'banality that makes them barely exist as subjects of interest in themselves, and hardly lend themselves to anecdote'.[14]

The origin of each type-form the Purists saw as lying in a gradual process of technical evolution, at the end of which a perfect standard had been found. In a triumphant sequel to Darwin — and perhaps with an unacknowledged inspiration in Samuel Butler — the Purists announced the discovery of the 'Law of Mechanical Selection'.

> This establishes that objects tend towards a type that is determined by the evolution of forms between the ideal of maximum utility, and the satisfaction of the necessities of economical manufacture, which conform inevitably to the laws of nature. This double play of laws has resulted in the creation of a certain number of objects that may thus be called standardised.[15]

The Purists are very insistent that the operation of this law of selection is essentially a matter of economy; their argument being that the evolution of tools and machines is towards maximal performance for minimal cost or minimal expenditure of effort. Given particular functional requirements, and given this criterion of selection according to economy, then the forms of objects designed to fulfil that function will converge on some standard universal type.

What is more, the Purists claim that these standard type-forms, since they have evolved according to 'laws of nature', will embody precisely those primary geometrical elements which form the basis of their universal plastic language. The significance of the carafe, the guitar or the briar pipe for Purist painting is thus that, precisely because they are the end-products of this extended process of evolutionary selection, they will necessarily possess elementary geometric forms, they will be anonymous and association-free, and they can therefore serve to convey plastic values and relationships of the desired mathematical and general character.

There is one further aspect of the Purist evolutionary argument. Mechanical evolution and natural evolution are similar processes, so the Purists claim, and conform to identical natural laws. Thus the aesthetic qualities which we discern both in machines and in organisms have a common origin.[16] There is a special additional reason why we should find the forms of *objets-membres-humains* to be visually satisfactory; and that is because of their conformity to the shapes and scale of the human body (itself a product of selection). The aesthetic qualities of both organisms *and* machines are therefore incidentally produced in their evolution, and not consciously sought. The difference in the *fine* arts is that there the artist has deliberate aesthetic intentions to achieve the similar results.

   This idea of the 'naturalness' of machine evolution is one which is pursued by Ozenfant in his book *The Foundations of Modern Art*, under the heading 'The Engineers' Aesthetic(?)'.[17] We are wrong, he says, to speak of machinery and tools as 'artificial' rather than 'natural'; they are 'relays' used by nature, extensions of the limbs of man. The products of the machine obey natural laws, are subject to 'universal forces' which compel them, in time, to take on the most efficient possible forms. This according to Ozenfant is a quite automatic, inevitable process. 'A machine that turns out good work is a healthy machine: its organs rigorously satisfy mechanical, therefore natural, laws. Its products by degree become stereotyped because the play of forces is unchanging and their effect is to compel such products into certain shapes, their optimum.'[18] The forms of industrial products and machines in Ozenfant's view are determined by the properties of materials and the structural roles these materials play in the design of each object, as well as by their functions and the demands of economy. It is not quite correct to speak of the engineers' imagination as 'aesthetic', he says, since 'their products are predetermined; for the natural laws to which, with ever-increasing efficiency, we respond, by degrees bring out their definitive form'.

> Ten years ago every electric-light bulb had a point, through which the air was drawn to make the vacuum; a point which interrupted light. Someone thought of evacuating air through the base, and so the point vanished and the bulb became spherical. Thus we like it better and it serves us better: but was there any aesthetic impulse behind all this? No! it was solely due to the automatic functioning of evolution![19]

   Where there seems to be an arbitrary variety in engineering products, as for instance in the coachwork of automobiles, this is because the engineers have had aspirations towards becoming artists, and have not submitted to the logic of mechanical demands. 'Aesthetics, introduced into the sphere of mechanics, is always an indication of inadequacy somewhere.' Ozenfant admits that even the apparently functional motor cars of the period bear witness to an aesthetic sense on the part of their designers. (Bugatti, Voisin and the brothers Michelin were all former art students, as he remarks.) But in time the area in which this aesthetic taste can be exercised will be progressively reduced, as every feature in the end submits to demands of efficiency and engineering logic. 'The motor, starting from a certain principle, inevitably gets stereotyped, and the most efficient unit is the one that will inevitably be adopted everywhere. When that time comes there will be no

place for aesthetic invention, which serves to hide the absence of knowledge.'[20]

To come back to Le Corbusier's juxtapositions of cars with Greek temples
in *Vers Une Architecture*; the implication is that the automobile – or the
aeroplane, or the ship, in Le Corbusier's other illustrations – evolves
according to functional engineering criteria and moves towards an ever
more satisfactory organisation of the design and resolution of the mechanical
problem. Meanwhile the series of temples demonstrates a sculptural evolution towards an ideal standard of plastic beauty, without any necessary
reference to function, but judged according to mathematical and aesthetic
criteria of a universal nature. In both cases the result of the process is
the production of a perfect type, where the parts are all in a coherent
relationship to each other, and the design achieves unity; beyond which
no further progress is possible, and the 'type-form' is established.

Le Corbusier was saying that these two aspects, functional and plastic,
both arise in the majority of design problems and most especially in
architecture, and they must therefore be resolved simultaneously. This is
clear from a later essay in which he refers to the solution of functional
problems again in 'biological' terms:

> The biological aspect, this is the intended purpose, the problem which is
> posed, the utilitarian basis of the enterprise.
>
> The plastic aspect, this is a physiological sensation, an 'impression', a pres-
> sure on the senses, the forced card.
>
> The biological affects our common sense,
> The plastic affects our sensibility and our reason.[21]

The temple and the car therefore represent from the aesthetic point of view
two distinct levels of achievement. It is important to appreciate that both
Le Corbusier and Ozenfant quite definitely reject the idea, with which they
have been often incorrectly associated and which was very widespread
among their contemporaries, that the satisfaction of functional and utilitarian needs in design will by itself *necessarily* mean that the results must
be beautiful.[22]

There is certainly the strong likelihood in their view that the products of
machine evolution will possess visual qualities that will appeal to our
intellectual faculties –we will recognise and admire the rightness of the work.
But the satisfaction of these utilitarian requirements is only the *precondition*,
Le Corbusier says, for proceeding towards the higher aim of art, especially in
architecture, that is to touch the emotions[23] (the 'lyric' qualities of architecture, as Ozenfant calls them[24]). (There is a certain contradiction here, it
must be said, with the original Purist doctrines. In Purist painting the
'primary' forms were to appeal to the reason by virtue of their mathematical

and abstract character, while the secondary associative qualities engaged the emotions. In *Vers Une Architecture* and in Le Corbusier's later writings, he seems to see the 'plastic aspect' as appealing *both* to emotions and to the reason.) Machines are incapable of inspiring the depths of feeling and aesthetic emotion which works of art may, the Purists say. Has anyone seen a bicycle, says Ozenfant, that could move men to tears?[25]

At the level of practical function, however, the 'biological' level, there is no call for aesthetic intervention, and the functional form of the *objet-type* is produced quite automatically through evolution. To go back to the question posed at the beginning of this chapter, and to examine how it is addressed by the Purists: it is clear how the theory of the *objet-type* is applied to existing objects, to explain their standardised forms, but what bearing does it have on the task of designing new forms, new types?

One odd feature of Purist theory, to which Reyner Banham has drawn attention, is that the classic *objets-types* are represented (like Muthesius's types) as being the final points in completed processes of evolution. The double law of economy and function *'has resulted*, in the perfect tense' in the production of ideal forms, the implication being that no further improvement or change is possible. 'A remarkable attitude', says Banham, 'for two authors who had gone out of their way to indicate that the whole basis of life was undergoing a technical revolution.'[26] Banham remarks on the correspondence of the Purists' attitude with that put into the mouth of Socrates by Valéry in his *Eupalinos, ou l'Architecte*:

> *Phaedrus*:   There are some admirable tools, neat as bones.
> *Socrates*:   They are self-made, to some extent; centuries of use have necessarily discovered the best form, uncountable practice achieves the ideal, and there stops.
> The best efforts of thousands of men converge slowly towards the most economical and certain shape.[27]

The fact is that when one reflects on many of the examples adduced by the Purists as *objets-types*, one realises that they are hardly the characteristic products of the new industrial world, but on the contrary are handicraft objects whose function would indeed change very little over time – musical instruments, the tobacco pipe, cups and jugs. They might be affected by technological progress in their method of manufacture perhaps, but very little in their mode of use. It should be remembered that the central tenets of Purist painting were classical ones, and that the concern was for forms which were universal and unchanging, rather than those which were fashionable and transient.

Thus the Purist argument may have a certain plausibility when applied to simple hand tools or domestic utensils, even where these survive from stable agricultural societies into modern technological culture. There is a parallel from natural evolution here, where we find examples of stable forms of organisms which, once they are reached, undergo no further changes. Certain species seem to have stopped evolving millions of years ago, and to have altered very little since. Some examples are the crocodile, the tortoise and many insects. (Whether they represent 'optima' in relation to their particular environments, and whether these environments have themselves remained essentially unchanged, is another question.) P. B. Medawar takes the toothbrush as an analogous example of such a case of complete and finished evolutionary design in an industrially manufactured product: 'toothbrushes retained the same design and constitution for more than a hundred years'.[28] And in his book *Mind and Matter* Erwin Schrödinger instances the bicycle as another case.[29] It has reached 'the attainable perfection and has therefore pretty well ceased to undergo further changes'.* Ozenfant had made the same point, in a caption to a photograph of a lady cycling: 'A Cyclist Thirty Years Ago. Fashion has changed, but the bicycle-type is already established.'[30]

What *is* paradoxical about the Purists' position, as Banham indicates, is the implication that equivalent stable type-forms have been achieved in a similar manner for such novel technological inventions as the radio set, the motor car or the aeroplane; where the speed of change in their mechanical development, the introduction of new materials and new methods of manufacture, the evolution of their function in many respects, has been so rapid as not to have allowed the time, the stability of the 'functional environment', which was such a crucial component of the evolutionary process in artefacts, in primitive and craft-based methods of production.

One point of which Le Corbusier is quite sure is that in architecture such evolution has lagged behind engineering and industrial design; and the development of comparable type-forms for buildings is something on which modern architects should urgently be working. He is fully aware in fact — and this is the contradiction — of the problem of the speed of change in

*It is an amusing incidental irony, which does not really detract from Schrödinger's general point, that since he wrote, the bicycle has undergone a significant evolutionary change, for the very reason that in its basic structural design it was by no means perfect. The bicycle has been a popular example for illustrating technological evolution, and the classic 'diamond frame' design has been claimed to provide maximum strength with minimum weight. As L. B. Archer reports, however, structural engineers have on many occasions pointed out that a much stronger frame would be of X-shape. Some early X-frame bicycles were built as far back as 1886, and electronic tests have more recently confirmed this shape to be superior in strength for equivalent weight. But still, in the 1950s, Archer says, 'the industry . . . steadfastly refuses to depart from its 70-year-old tradition and falls back on the limp explanation that "the purchaser wants a bicycle that *looks* like a bicycle and will not buy anything which looks extraordinary"' ('Design Research', *Design*, 91 (July 1965), 35). Since then, in the last few years, a number of X-frame bicycles have been introduced and have had a wide sale among a public now perhaps more conditioned to change and more ready to accept strange innovations.

modern society, and the difficulties which this creates for an evolutionary process of design; indeed the last chapter of *Vers Une Architecture* discusses just this topic:

> the tools that man has made for himself, which automatically meet the needs of society, and which till now had undergone only slight modifications in a slow evolution, have been transformed all at once with an amazing rapidity. These tools in the past were always *in man's hands*; today they have been entirely and formidably refashioned and for the time being are out of our grasp.[31]

Le Corbusier has no coherently formulated answer to this dilemma — indeed he does not even state the problem itself with any clarity. But it is possible to infer hints of a solution in his continual invocation (as with Ozenfant) of the methods of the engineers. The engineers were able to produce new types successfully, because their procedures in design were based on mathematical and scientific *theory*. We shall come back to this argument later. Meanwhile there were at least two other possibilities for 'speeding up craft evolution'; neither of which was advanced by the Purists, but both of which were to be found quite widely advocated elsewhere.

## 10

# Design as a process of growth

The first of these ideas for 'speeding up craft evolution' depends on nothing more than a very loose metaphor. The notion is here that the designer might imitate not the evolution of the species collectively, but rather the process of growth of the individual. The animal or plant starts from a seed, which is supplied with nutriment, and which develops into the fully-grown organism. In so doing it interacts in various ways with its environment, and its form becomes progressively more complex. In what might poetically be seen as a roughly parallel process, the designer develops an originally ill-formed and undeveloped 'seminal' idea into a gradually elaborated and finished design. During this development there is a continual interaction between the 'growing' design and its 'environment' — that is, the critical assessments and evaluations made by the designer.

It might be possible to try to support this idea, if rather shakily — although I have not found the particular extension of the argument advanced anywhere by writers on design — by calling attention to the fact, as was widely known and discussed in nineteenth-century biology, that the development of the animal embryo goes through a series of stages which appear to correspond roughly to the evolutionary history of the species as a whole; that, as it was phrased, 'ontogeny recapitulates phylogeny'.[1] The suggestion, in the technological analogy, would thus be that the designer might somehow 'grow' forms on the drawing board in a way which could parallel their evolution by trial and error in practice, but which would take up only a fraction of the time.

On any close examination the whole notion collapses in inconsistencies. The growth of an organism follows a fixed developmental programme, which has a certain latitude or flexibility in response to environmental circumstances, to be sure, but for which the essential 'design' is carried from the beginning in the inherited genetic material. This 'design' of course has been produced over many generations, through evolution. If we wanted an analogy for the development of the organism in the design or architectural world, it would be much more reasonable to compare it to the process whereby a *finished* design — let us say, expressed in a set of drawings or in instructions of some other type — is realised in material form, through those instructions being carried into effect by the fabricator or the builder.

Still, the fact of these simple objections did not deter a number of architectural theorists of the last century and of the modern movement from making such a 'growth' analogy with design; although it is only fair to add that most of them were writing prior to the discoveries of modern genetics, and that the confusion of development with evolution was one that was very much encouraged by certain current biological and philosophical theories, to be traced principally to the work of Herbert Spencer.

Spencer describes in his *Autobiography* how his own interest in evolution was aroused originally when he found fossils exposed in the cuttings whose construction he worked on as a railway engineer; and how he was as a result inspired to read Lyell's *Principles of Geology*, and through Lyell's account came to learn about Lamarck's work.[2] Spencer was not convinced by Lyell's critical rejection of Lamarck, however. Later, reviewing a book on physiology, he first became aware of the principles enunciated by the embryologist von Baer, concerning the general course of development from fertilised egg to adult organism.[3] Von Baer's work showed that the development of the embryo seemed always to move from the general to the particular, and that the simple, undifferentiated and homogeneous form of the egg was progressively changed into the complex and heterogeneous form of the mature creature.

Von Baer was not an evolutionist; but it appeared to later workers, among them Haeckel, that the successive stages of the developmental process which von Baer had investigated followed in an approximate way the very long-term evolutionary phases through which the species as a whole had passed — the 'recapitulation' hypothesis. C. U. M. Smith paraphrases an example discussed by von Baer himself: 'The chick begins simply as a vertebrate, then becomes an air-breathing vertebrate, then a bird, then a terrestrial bird, then a gallinaceous bird and finally a domestic chicken.'[4]

We may notice by the way that these discoveries of mid-nineteenth-century embryology, together with the Darwinian theory, provided a physical basis of explanation for those phenomena which *Naturphilosophie* had tried to account for by recourse to the abstract and metaphysical concept of the archetype. The embryos of all vertebrates, for example, are much more alike (due to their common evolutionary origin) than are the adult vertebrates themselves. T. H. Huxley, for one, urged very strongly that the question of 'homology' be approached through embryology.[5]

The ideas of von Baer were important in the formulation of Spencer's own theory of biological evolution; but more than this, they shaped his much grander and broader conception of cosmic evolutionary development as a whole. For Spencer, evolution was a process manifested not just in organic nature, but in the material world too; and not only in plants and animals, but in man, society and culture. Spencer published an article declaring his

SPENCER

support for a belief in the evolution of natural species, entitled significantly 'The Development Hypothesis', in 1852;[6] and he stated his position more fully in the *Principles of Psychology* published in 1855.[7] There is thus some justice in the claim which has sometimes been made for the priority of Spencer over Darwin and Wallace, both of whom certainly had high regard for Spencer. (It has even been proposed that Darwinism might more properly be called 'biological Spencerism' than Spencer's social and political philosophy, 'social Darwinism'.)

Spencer, however, as he realised later to his mild regret, had originally missed the central Darwinian idea of selection – and it was only in the 1860s (in the *Principles of Biology*) that he began using the phrase 'the survival of the fittest' which Darwin himself later took over.[8] For his larger theory of cosmic evolution, Spencer developed a famous and much-repeated definition, which shows how closely he identified the two processes of the evolution of the species and the development of the individual. Spencer made various revisions to this definition throughout his life. One of the more succinct runs: 'Evolution is a change from a state of relatively indefinite, incoherent, homogeneity to a state of relatively definite, coherent, heterogeneity.'[9] I have referred above in rather loose terms to the concepts of 'growth' and 'development' as though they were interchangeable; but it should be said that Spencer was careful to distinguish the two, as he applied them both in biology and in sociology. By growth he referred to simple increase in bulk; by development, an increase in structure, or a progressive differentiation of form.[10] It is this latter process which, according to him, universally characterises evolution.

Spencer's ideas, particularly his social philosophy, met with huge popular interest; and his influence was especially strong in the United States. He made a widely reported visit to the country in 1882, and his books had a large American circulation. It is perhaps arguable in this light that evidence of the influence of Spencer is to be found in what Leopold Eidlitz has to say about evolution in relation to architecture and design – writing, as we recall, in the early 1880s.

For instance, Eidlitz links a discussion of the evolution of medieval archi- INFLUENCE tecture in terms of progress in construction technique with the idea that the architect in the process of design can 'evolve' 'single cells' to correspond to groups of persons who will inhabit the building; and that he will 'develop for the purpose an appropriate structural form'.[11] There is here, therefore, a rather loose metaphorical reference to growth and evolution which would apply without clear distinction as well to the evolution of architectural forms over some lengthy historical period as to the development of a single specific design in the mind or on the drawing board of the architect.

The same is true for Montgomery Schuyler when he declares: 'Architectural forms are not invented; they are developed, as natural forms are developed, by evolution.'[12] The context of the remark is the evolution of the pointed arch throughout the medieval period. But the clear implication, from what follows, is that modern engineering can much more quickly develop new forms — for a single given problem indeed, like the Forth Bridge — without the necessity of actually building a series of progressively improved versions.

Eidlitz

law of
evolution

There is some talk in Eidlitz's *The Nature and Function of Art* of a mysterious 'general law' which applies to the entire natural world, including physical material. For instance, Eidlitz declares that 'Nature never essays to compose forms, she acts upon a much broader and simpler law, which governs all matter.'[13] The operation of this law he describes in the following terms: 'Matter moves, accumulates, and distributes itself, and in doing so facilitates or retards relations of matter of all kinds. Every relation of matter has a certain stability, which, in highly organised matter, becomes perceptible in the shape of energy of function.'[14] I think there can be little doubt that Eidlitz here refers to the 'law' of evolution, on Spencer's definition.

Sullivan

When we move to Louis Sullivan, the influence of Spencer is not a matter for speculation, since Sullivan relates in *The Autobiography of an Idea* how his introduction to evolutionary thinking was principally through his reading of Spencer. 'Spencer's definition implying a progression from an unorganised simple through stages of growth and differentiation to a highly organised complex, seemed to fit his [Sullivan's] own case.'[15] Spencer was not the only biological author known to Sullivan; he also read Asa Gray, Huxley, Tyndall and Darwin.[16] But his reaction to Darwin, though highly enthusiastic, was apparently uncritical; and does not seem to have had the same effect as reading Spencer. 'In Darwin he [Sullivan] found much food. The Theory of Evolution seemed stupendous.'[17]

There are two reasons why Spencer should 'fit Sullivan's own case' better than Darwin. The first of these is to do with Spencer's identification of evolution with development. Like Eidlitz and Schuyler, Sullivan does not really differentiate, in his application of the growth/evolution metaphor, between the evolution of some structural principle such as the arch, or the column and lintel, through architectural history, and the development of a given design in the individual architect's mind from the 'seed' of an idea, which then grows and is shaped.

The seed is a recurrent image in Sullivan's writing; or sometimes it is a germ, or an acorn. Given nourishment and time to mature, the seed of an architectural design can grow quite naturally — unless it be trapped inside a husk of 'intellectual misconceptions' — and develop into the fully grown design. Sullivan mentions reading Beecher Wilson's *The Cell in Development and Inheritance* in order to study 'the power that ante-dates the seed-germ', and describes how he was in the habit of redrawing Wilson's diagrams of the stages of mitosis from memory.[18] Frank Lloyd Wright takes up the metaphor:

'An inner-life principle is a gift to every seed. An inner-life principle is also necessary for every idea of a good building.'[19]*

Sullivan first learned about both German philosophy and literature and the work of Spencer from a fellow draughtsman in the office of Le Baron Jenney, John Edelmann.[20] It was from Edelmann that Sullivan derived his 'theory of suppressed functions', which was the origin of 'Form follows function'. The nature of this theory is not made plain in *The Autobiography of an Idea*. From other evidence it seems, however, that the central notion was of a series of functions which lay 'suppressed' or dormant in the architectural problem, being 'released' through the architect's work as he developed a form.[21]

These ideas can be related directly to Spencer's evolutionism. Spencer saw the increase in heterogeneity and the differentiation of *form* which occurred in evolution to be associated with an emergence and progressive differentiation or specialisation of organic *function*. In simple organisms, the same functions are carried on homogeneously throughout the body — hence their viability is not threatened by the removal of some part, and the removed part may even itself be capable of independent survival. In higher organisms, the parts become more differentiated, particular functions are carried on in special localised organs, and so the operation of the body as a whole may be vulnerable to the failure or removal of some specialised part. As Spencer expresses it, in moving up the evolutionary scale there is to be found 'a gradual diminution in the number of like parts, and a multiplication of unlike ones. In the one extreme there are but few functions, and many similar agents to each function; in the other, there are many functions, and a few similar agents to each function.'[22] Spencer was introduced to this phenomenon of the 'physiological division of labour' by a study of the work of Milne-Edwards.

Thus an evolutionary development towards a more 'definite coherent heterogeneity', in Spencer's phrase, would be a result or expression of the performance of ever more specific and distinct functions by the various organs of the body. Spencer is indeed properly described not just as an evolutionist, but as a *functionalist*. He gives two causes for the adaptations of organs through evolution: one of these is natural selection, but the second and more important cause, for Spencer, is 'the increase or decrease of structure consequent on increase or decrease of function'[23] (i.e. a Lamarckian mechanism).

---

*The use of the rather surprising word 'gift' in this context is a reference by Wright, we may assume, to the geometric Froebel 'gifts' which he played with as a boy, and which, as R. MacCormac has shown, played such a significant part in the early development of Wright's formal vocabulary and his geometrical principles of organisation in buildings according to regular grids. The analogies with crystal structure and crystal growth are also very strong. 'Froebel's Kindergarten Gifts and the Early Work of Frank Lloyd Wright', *Environment and Planning B*, 1 (1974), 29–50.

In both the natural and the social worlds, the appearance of structure is to be explained in terms of function. 'To understand how an organization originated and developed, it is requisite to understand the need subserved at the outset and afterwards.'[24] It is not difficult to see the attraction of Spencer's views for someone with Sullivan's concern for the relation of form to function in architecture.

Furthermore, progressive differentiation and specialisation of function in the animal body necessitates an increase in the functional *interdependence*, in Spencer's word 'coherence', of the parts. This quality of functional coherence is central to Sullivan's idea of the 'organic' in architecture — as indeed we have seen already from his scornful remarks about architectural 'hybrids'. In *Kindergarten Chats* Sullivan speaks of the necessity, if a building is to be 'organic', for the function of every part to 'have the same *quality* as the function of the whole', and for the parts 'to have the quality of the mass', 'to partake of its identity' (his equivalents effectively for 'unity' and the 'correlation of parts').[25]

He makes a distinction between logical thinking, by which he means overly mechanical or exclusively analytic thinking, and organic thinking. Organic thinking involves seeking a 'regular and systematic subdivision of function within form' which can detect the overall similarity, the organic quality of the whole structure 'descending from the mass down to the minutest subdivision of detail'.[26] Such an organic philosophy in architectural design stands in direct opposition, as Sullivan sees it, to the mechanical and additive compositional procedures of the Beaux Arts, with their disregard for the coherence of functional interrelations between the different elements from which the whole building is made up.

I mentioned that there were two main reasons behind Spencer's particular appeal for Sullivan. Discussion of the second reason will divert us slightly from the main argument; but this is still the place for a brief account. Spencer's social philosophy, being permeated with biological analogy, saw social forms and structures as the product of different environmental circumstances. 'While spreading over the Earth mankind have found environments of various characters, and in each case the social life fallen into, partly determined by the social life previously led, has been partly determined by the influences of the new environment.'[27] Spencer conceived of society as an organism, and the institutions of society as organs. The 'physiological division of labour' in the animal body was paralleled by the specialisation of employment in society.[28] Social organisations represented adaptations of the collective 'organism', conferring fitness in the struggle for social survival in the face of natural conditions, and in competition with other social groups.

We will come in due course to a critique of this kind of biological social science, which was associated above all with the name of Spencer, and to an analysis of its consequences. Here we can simply notice how such a view of society provides strong encouragement to an 'ecological' or environmental theory of artistic style, along the lines indicated in an earlier chapter. Spencer saw social forms and social institutions —themselves evolved in response to natural environment — as shaping the thoughts and actions of men —and not the other way round. Such ideas, applied in art or design, would attribute stylistic or formal differences not to the imagination or inventive power of individual designers but to varying social conditions and utilitarian needs.

*[margin handwritten note: environment shaping man & not vice versa]*

That Sullivan thought that the development of an 'organic' architecture would depend on the creation of a truly democratic society has already been mentioned. Echoing Spencer, Sullivan talks of the people, all the people, whose thought is given visible form in building, as constituting a 'social organism'.[29] Only a democratic social organism can produce an organic architecture. In modern society the expression of the influence of machine methods of production in building is another consequence — although the machine is not to be allowed to dominate.

I should not want to leave the impression that I believe the whole of what Sullivan, and subsequently Wright, referred to as 'organic' in architecture can be attributed to the influence of Spencer. The word refers, for the two men, to a much more complex congeries of ideas, whose sources can be traced back in one direction to the functionalism of Greenough, Schuyler and Eidlitz, and in another to the tradition of Romantic naturalism and the picturesque in architecture.* These broader philosophic and aesthetic connotations of the term, going beyond narrow and specific biological analogies, have been well explored by Donald Egbert in his essay 'The Idea of Organic Expression and American Architecture'.[30] Against this background Egbert sets a variety of attitudes shared by Sullivan and Wright: their ideas about composition, their distaste for Renaissance architecture, and their preference — demonstrated particularly in Wright's later work —for asymmetric, natural, easy response in architectural form to the demands both of the site and of the building's functions. Organic architecture required the expression of the designer himself, besides just expression of functional needs and materials of construction; and in Sullivan's view, at least, the 'functions' of a building might be as much 'emotional' as practical ones.[31]

A certain flowing quality, a plasticity or *continuity* was also involved: in Sullivan's case, manifested in his use of stylised plant forms in decorative treatments carried out in his favourite terracotta; in Wright's case in the integration of the structural elements of a building into an interconnected

---

*The French periodical *Revue Générale de l'Architecture* has been credited with first launching an 'Organic Architecture' in 1863; named, so the editor writes, 'because it is, in relationship to the Historic and Eclectic Schools, what the organised life of animals and vegetables is in relationship to the unorganised existence of the rocks which form the sub-stratum of the world'. Quoted by P. Collins, *Changing Ideals in Modern Architecture, 1750–1950* (London, 1965), p. 156.

system, and in the moulding of its interior spaces into an interpenetrating and continuous spatial whole.

It is, however, the characteristically Spencerian ideas in Sullivan's writings about design as a growth process, or rather a developmental process, which are both based on a much more definite (if wrongly conceived) biological analogy than are these other meanings of 'organic', and which represent a distinctly new analogy between human and natural design, not previously developed by other writers (with the exception of the vague foreshadowing in the quoted remarks of Schuyler and Eidlitz). The fact remains nevertheless that Sullivan's formulation, though possibly a highly suggestive metaphor and helpful to Sullivan in his own work, did nothing to solve the *theoretical* problem which arguably it set out to meet: how evolution of 'organic' forms in architecture could be achieved by the designer at his drawing board, without the time available for protracted trial of real buildings in actual use.

# 11
# 'Biotechnics':
# plants and animals as inventors

We now come to a second way in which a biological or 'organic' method in design might seek to escape the problem of excessive time involved in mimicking the natural evolutionary process. This is to be found in the concept of 'biotechnique' or 'biotechnics', which attracted some interest amongst designers in the late 1920s and 1930s. In essence the proposal was this: that in the evolution of plants and animals, nature herself had already made a great variety of 'inventions', embodied in the designs of organs or in the adaptations of the limbs. These inventions solved in ingenious ways all kinds of functional and engineering problems — structural, mechanical, even chemical, and electrical. What was required was a diligent study of the engineering of nature, and man would find there the solution to all his technical needs; natural models requiring only to be copied in the design of machines or structures. In this way, instead of technological evolution needing to be highly time-consuming, it could 'borrow' the time already invested in the organic evolution of these natural counterparts to human artefacts.

The history of the 'biotechnical' idea is somewhat difficult to reconstruct; but it would appear to originate in part in a tradition of popular books on the subject of the analogies between nature and machines, published from the 1870s onwards. Among the best known of these authors is the Reverend J. G. Wood, who wrote a whole series of works on natural history for the general reader, including a study of animal architecture, *Homes without Hands*.[1] The particular book of Wood's which is relevant here is entitled *Nature's Teachings: Human Invention Anticipated by Nature*.[2] His express purpose is 'to show the close connection between Nature and human inventions, and that there is scarcely an invention of man that has not its prototype in Nature'.[3] *Nature's Teachings* is a long catalogue of 'parallels between nature and art', classified according to the human industry or activity in which each invention is used — 'nautical', 'war and hunting', 'architecture', 'tools', 'optics', and so on (figure 25). It is Wood's belief that since so many of man's existing tools and machines have been anticipated in organic adaptations, 'so it will be surely found that in Nature lie the prototypes of inventions not yet revealed to man'.[4] Among the natural models for man's architectural ideas which he lists,

25   Rev. J. G. Wood, 'The Home'.

besides the various types of building constructed by animals, Wood does not fail to mention the celebrated inspiration for Paxton's glass roofs at the Crystal Palace in the flanged undersurface of the leaves of the giant water lily *Victoria Regia*.

From the beginning of the nineteenth century the debate on teleology in biology had been carried on by reference to evidence of design in nature. Paley's *Natural Theology* is filled with examples, as in his descriptions of the structure of skeletons, and of how cunning is the mechanical contrivance with which the loads are taken and the one bone pivots on another. As perhaps the latest in date, and the most massive exposition of the argument from design, we can instance J. Bell Pettigrew's *Design in Nature*,[5] published in 1908, whose three huge volumes were intended no doubt to overwhelm the reader with their demonstrations of divine handiwork in the systems of the animal body. Clearly, it was a simple step to reverse such arguments: to move from the proposition that the organic body is as cleverly arranged as a mechanical device to the suggestion that the mechanic might do well to follow the ingenious design of organisms.

Several rather obscure and now forgotten books follow the general lines of Wood's *Nature's Teachings*, but with a curious special emphasis on the inventive capacities of plants. In 1907 the playwright and philosophical essayist Maurice Maeterlinck produced *L'Intelligence des Fleurs*,[6] on the theme of plant adaptations and how evolution has already traversed the route of mechanical discovery which man's intelligence is only now retracing.

> In a world which we believe to be without feeling and without intelligence, we imagine first of all that the least of our ideas creates new combinations and new relations. But if we look at things more closely, it seems more than likely that we really are not capable of creating anything at all. We are the last comers on this earth. All we do is rediscover what has always been in existence, and like children we follow in wonder the path which life has traversed before us.[7]

Maeterlinck refers in passing to a work by Henri Coupin, *Les Plantes Originales*, which sounds to be rather similar to his own book. I have been unable to examine a copy; however, several other titles in English by Coupin, including *The Romance of Animal Arts and Crafts* and *The Wonders of Animal Ingenuity*, are on closely related topics.[8]

The tradition is carried on by the German biological populariser Raoul Francé, whose little book *Die Pflänze als Erfinder* (*Plants as Inventors*),[9] first published in Stuttgart in 1920, is mentioned appreciatively by Moholy-Nagy in *The New Vision*.[10] A reference also appears in Karel Honzík's contribution to the *Circle* anthology, 'A Note on Biotechnics',[11] of which more shortly. Moholy-Nagy describes Francé as having 'devoted himself to an intensive study' of the analogy between biology and technology, and says that 'he calls his method of research and the results "biotechnique"'.[12]

*Plants as Inventors* is not a scholarly work, and Francé's botany is highly idiosyncratic. The biological emphasis is on discussion of the mechanical forces which govern the growth processes and structural forms of plants, with some additional account of their hydraulic and metabolic mechanisms, and of the reproductive systems of flowers. The greater part of the book, however, is devoted to a theoretical argument about design. *All* forms in organic nature, according to Francé, because they are the product of selection, are the *necessary* outcome of the functions served; and for any given biological problem there is a *unique*, optimal form which provides its solution.

It is the operation of the law of 'economy' or least expenditure of energy which governs the processes by which perfected forms have been selected and developed. All forms to be found in the technical sphere – in man's inventions – may be shown to have their counterparts in natural 'inventions'. 'We have in this one law', says Francé, 'the explanation in one formula of life – all life, mechanics – all mechanics, industry, architecture, all the ideas of the artists from the builders of the pyramids to the expressionists, the experiments of the present.'[13] In order to find a technical solution to some given need, the 'biotechnical student' must seek the solution of the identical need in some biological example, and then imitate that arrangement.

Francé goes even further in his claims about biotechnical forms. Not only is the identical range of forms to be found in nature and in technology, but this variety is in itself made up out of a strictly limited repertoire of only seven simple component parts, the 'biotechnical elements'. These elements are of a geometrical, Platonic character, and they comprise the 'crystalline' form, the sphere, the plane, the rod, the ribbon or strip, the screw and the cone. The whole argument of the book is effectively summarised by Francé himself in these words: *'The laws of the least resistance and economy of action force equal actions to lead to the same forms, and force all processes in the world to develop according to the law of the seven fundamental forms.'*[14]

There are a number of specific examples offered of inspiration for mechanical inventions of various sorts coming from the adaptations of animal and plant life. The principles of the swimming behaviour of unicellular creatures are applied to the design of the hulls of ships. Cooling mechanisms in plants might provide the model for new types of refrigerator. It is quite striking how many of Francé's illustrations and applications relate to architectural design. The detailed form of a house is analysed to demonstrate that it is composed wholly out of the seven biotechnical geometric units. The skeletons of silica algae and the cells of plants are both discussed, and shown to demonstrate engineering principles which might be copied in new types of bricks or the design of structural frameworks.

It will not have escaped the reader how extraordinarily close are the affinities between Francé's biotechnical programme and the principal elements

of the Purist theory of the *objet-type* and of mechanical evolution. The stress
in both cases is on the satisfaction of function within the strictest economy
of means, the resulting evolved forms being supposed to be made up out of a
limited vocabulary of elementary geometric components. (Whether there is
any direct influence to be traced from Francé to Le Corbusier and Ozenfant
is not, however, so clear; Francé is not acknowledged in, for example, *L'Esprit
Nouveau.*)

In the early 1930s Moholy-Nagy, as mentioned, was championing Francé's
ideas at the Bauhaus. Moholy-Nagy believed that while in the design of
machines men have often hit accidentally on solutions which have turned
out subsequently to have precedents in nature, it may still be possible to
devise 'organically functioning' works which have no such natural prototypes. What is important is to follow the general *principles* of nature's methods.
'In all fields of creation, workers are striving today to find purely functional
solutions of a technical-biological kind: that is, to build up each piece of work
solely from the elements which are required for its function.'[15]

Later in the thirties several authors take up the biotechnic theme,
although it is hard to trace the precise connections between different
appearances of similar ideas. The architect Frederick Kiesler pursues
some extensively developed biological analogies in an article 'On Correalism
and Biotechnique',[16] published in 1939 but which was apparently based on
an earlier manuscript 'From Architecture to Life'[17] completed in 1930.
'Correalism' is Kiesler's own coinage, to mean the study of the relationships between man and his natural and technological environments. The
term 'biotechnique' Kiesler also claims to have invented, and he says that
it appeared first in an article by him on town planning printed in an issue of
*De Stijl* in 1925.[18] (This claim appears to be invalidated by the fact that
Francé's book was published some five years previously.)

The argument of 'Correalism and Biotechnique' is complex, and much of it
is obscured by invented terminology, and overlaid with summaries of relevant and irrelevant issues in contemporary science. The basic ideas, however, are as follows.

(1) Tools, and architecture, are created to mediate between man and the
natural environment, and they thus form a second interposed 'technological environment'.
(2) Technology serves various basic needs of man; and of these the most
basic is his physical health.
(3) There is a place for a new science which would study the historical
development of technology and its effects on man; which would inves-
tigate the 'need-morphology of its growth'.

All tools go through a characteristic process of evolution, which according
to Kiesler can be divided into a number of stages. He illustrates this with
reference to the design of knives (figure 26). There is a *standard type* of artefact

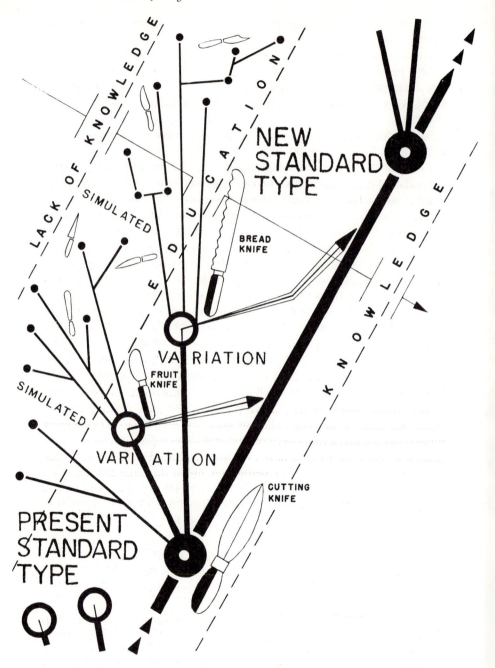

26   F. J. Kiesler, diagram to show the process of evolution of 'standard types' of artefacts (in this case knives).

(knife) which meets any given need (cutting in general); there are *variations* which evolve from the standard type for different purposes (bread knives, fruit knives etc.); and there are what Kiesler calls *simulated* artefacts — by far the largest category — which are characterised by their functional inefficiency and their 'insignificant' deviations from the standard. Needs may change over time, and when this happens the standard type evolves so as to meet the new need, and becomes in due course a new type. Meanwhile the variations and simulations radiate off the main route of evolution of the standard.

For Kiesler the simple copying of natural prototypes, however, is *not* the method of biotechnique. In fact this can in his view be a dangerous approach; and he (somewhat oddly) attributes the eventual destruction of the Crystal Palace by fire to the fact that its construction was based on too simple a biological analogy. For Kiesler biotechnique is a design method which involves turning, or as he says 'polarising', natural forces towards human purposes. In this context he makes a distinction between 'biotechnique' and 'biotechnics', attributing the latter term to Patrick Geddes and defining it as 'nature's method of building, not . . . man's'.

At the end of his article Kiesler presents an application of biotechnique to the design of a new form of bookcase or 'mobile-home-library'. Once again it is very difficult to see how Kiesler can reconcile his arguments about the slow evolution of standard types with this 'test of the validity' of biotechnical method. He says that six out of the twelve stages of the evolutionary cycle, from the appearance of a new need to the emergence of a new type, in themselves occupy 'approximately thirty years'. It seems an arbitrary and unsupported figure in any case; but that aside, the evident fact is that Kiesler himself has not taken thirty years on the same stages of his bookcase design — indeed he does not seem to have even gone through more than one stage ('invention'). We see then that despite his use of the term 'biotechnique', Kiesler has not escaped from the paradox inherent in urging an evolutionary design method on the modern designer; since his rejection of the idea of adopting ready-made solutions from nature blocks the way out which Francé and others offered.

Honzík's 'Note on Biotechnics' in *Circle* (1937)[19] takes the form of a more general discussion, and does not put forward any specific methods for design. Many familiar points are covered once more: evolution of the forms of artefacts towards 'perfected' standard types, 'vestigial organs' in artefacts, the proposal that nature employs basic geometric forms in construction. The *Victoria Regia* reappears, this time to be compared with the concrete floor construction of the Fiat factory in Turin (figure 27). Honzík is sceptical, however, of Francé's claim that all forms in nature are perfectly adapted, or that there is a necessary and unique relation between function and form. If so, why should there be 6,000 different species of the unicellular Dia-

27    Underside of the leaf of the *Victoria Regia* water lily (left) (which provided Paxton with the inspiration for the ridge-and-furrow roof construction of the Great Exhibition building), for comparison with the concrete car ramp in the Fiat factory, Turin (right).

tomaceae living under identical conditions? In technology and the applied arts the claim is even more doubtful: 'our technique is very imperfect compared to Nature's'. Perfect solutions to technical problems are generally found, if at all, only after generations of experiment by hundreds of workers (again, the problem of time). In technological evolution, according to Honzík, progress towards the ideal, although a general tendency, is by no means guaranteed:

> human products and structures develop through the will and intention of man and move towards their intrinsic perfection. They seek a final form that can only be spoiled deliberately by the emergence of new conditions. For instance, the best possible shape of chair can be superseded by a new form, arbitrarily invented for the purpose. But that new and arbitrary shape will soon disappear just because it is not the perfect one. Or if humanity were willing to start sitting in a new position the perfect shape of chair would have to be modified accordingly.[20]

The article which immediately follows Honzík's in *Circle* is Lewis Mumford's 'The Death of the Monument'.[21] In it, Mumford describes a future 'biotechnic' architecture and town planning, which would be characterised by flexibility and an openness to change, providing opportunities for growth. In Mumford's case the word 'biotechnic' comes from a different source: he owes it to Patrick Geddes, the biologist and pioneer town planner, whose ideas Mumford keenly followed and promoted.

Geddes's book on planning, *Cities in Evolution*,[22] of 1915, had introduced in print the terms 'palaeotechnic' and 'neotechnic' to categorise successive ages in technological history. 'Palaeotechnic' referred to the crude, primitive and wasteful phase of the Industrial Revolution, and 'neotechnic' to an emerging industrial order conducive to health, beauty and harmony with the natural environment.[23] Mumford uses Geddes's coinage 'biotechnic' in the architectural context to describe a design philosophy which would favour light, low structures over the massive and monumental; and which would suggest that mechanical services for buildings might be simplified and decentralised. The whole discussion is curiously prophetic of the 'alternative technology' movement of the 1970s, for instance in Mumford's mention of the possibility and advantages of local small-scale sewage treatment systems, and 'special sun-reflectors . . . as auxiliary heaters'.*

The 'so-called Machine Age', Mumford says, has made an unsubtle and thoughtless use of mechanical power and apparatus, which has largely served to encumber and complicate life — where a 'biological' technology, taking as its model the economy of means and ingenuity of anatomical structures and physiological mechanisms, would serve on the contrary to simplify urban living, and would liberate rather than enslave.

Mumford's description of this future biotechnical approach to design is, like Honzík's, very broad. He does not point to any possibilities for inspiration in specific biological phenomena, beyond general allusions to economy of material and effort, and the processes of growth; and it seems that for him the biotechnic philosophy has more to do with larger Utopian political and economic goals than it has with the everyday working procedures of designers.

At the detailed methodological level, nonetheless, technical history shows many examples of designers, especially engineering designers, who whether aware of the 'biotechnic' literature or not, have consciously sought constructional or operational principles in organisms which might be copied in mechanisms. The history of the development of aviation, for example, particularly in the early years, shows how much was learned by the pioneers through careful investigation of the flying techniques of birds, bats and

---

*It is fascinating to see the precise arguments of this article of Mumford's together with France"'s botanical examples from *Plants as Inventors*, combined in a very recent book in this tradition, Felix Paturi's *Geniale Ingenieure der Natur* (Düsseldorf and Vienna, 1974), translated as *Nature, Mother of Invention* (London, 1976), which turns 'biotechnic' ideas to the service of a proposed remedy for world crises of ecology, pollution and energy supply.

winged seeds. Other equivalent instances are to be found in civil engineering and in ship design. That branch of modern engineering, appearing during the 1960s, which has been named 'bionics' — by rough etymological analogy with electronics — has deliberately systematised the study of those biological mechanisms which promise to have practical applicability in man-made devices.[24] The special emphasis of bionics has been in the areas of cybernetics and information processing.

What happens fairly rapidly, of course, in a field such as aviation, is that the original principles discerned from the study of bird flight, say, become abstracted and codified into a generalised theory of the behaviour of flying bodies; they come to form part of the subject of aerodynamics, and this theoretical knowledge then applies equally and interchangeably to both birds and aeroplanes. The element of simple analogy is typical only of the historical beginnings of such subjects. It is more in the occasional peculiar technical innovation, in areas of engineering unsupported by such a theoretical base, that we would expect to find a specific biological model to be the conscious inspiration.

## 12

# Hierarchical structure and the adaptive process: biological analogy in Alexander's 'Notes on the Synthesis of Form'

One of the most influential books on architectural and design theory of the last few years has been Christopher Alexander's *Notes on the Synthesis of Form*, published in 1964.[1] The reasons for the initial impact of the book were various, but first among them was the fact that Alexander argued clearly, without slogans or polemics, for a rational, explicit design method to replace intuitive individualism. The general argument was followed with a specific proposal for a technique for analysing the complex structure of design problems, using set and graph theories — that is, the mathematics of classification and structural relationship. The method was applied by way of illustration to the design of an Indian village. The book seemed to present the case for a scientific, communally understandable design method with a particular mathematical means by which this might be achieved.

But the proposal was to prove subsequently disappointing to those who tried to put it into practice, and even to Alexander himself, who has now renounced altogether the approach advanced in his early work. The reasons for this disappointment have perhaps not been clearly articulated up to now.

I will argue that, although a superficial reading of *Notes on the Synthesis of Form* might suggest only hints — and even at one point a denial — of any analogy from biology, and although its theoretical discussion is couched in the language and framework of ideas of cybernetics, in fact its epistemological basis is essentially biological throughout. It refers back in effect, I will suggest, to the tradition of biological analogy in both anthropology and in the literature of the modern movement in architecture, whose history we have been following here. If the issues are recast in cybernetic terms, and with reference specifically to the work of W. Ross Ashby, then this is because the subject with which Ashby is dealing is the formal mechanism not only of learning, in the brain, but also, and more relevantly here, the accumulation of adaptations of behaviour and body in organic evolution.

Most important of all, it is Alexander, I will propose, who is not just the most recent but so far as I know the only theorist of design since the 1930s deliberately to take up the issue with which the last two chapters have dealt:

*distinction betw. self conscious and un self conscious*

how to achieve by a 'selfconscious' design method the results of the evolutionary design processes operating in primitive cultures or in the vernacular. Moreover Alexander's solution is quite different from those examined so far — indeed it depends on developments in biological thinking (and in cybernetics) which themselves only date from the 1940s and 1950s. Later I will argue that the failures of Alexander's method have some of the same root causes as fallacies arising from the biological analogy in its other applications.

Alexander introduces for the sake of his argument a broad distinction between two kinds of design process, one which he calls 'unselfconscious', the other 'selfconscious'. Roughly speaking, the unselfconscious process is that which goes on in primitive societies, or in the traditional handicraft or architectural vernacular contexts; while the selfconscious process is that which is typical of present-day, educated, specialised professional designers and architects.[2] The distinction is not an absolutely sharp one, as Alexander allows; and in the historical development of design one is to imagine a gradual transition from unselfconscious to selfconscious methods. But for the purposes of theoretical analysis, the two ends of this continuum are identified and contrasted as representing quite distinct methods of producing functional designs.

The real distinction between the two processes, in Alexander's view, may be discerned by looking at the way in which design, or the production of useful objects, is taught in either case. In the unselfconscious craft situation, the teaching of craft skills is through demonstration, and by having the novice imitate the skilled craftsman, until he gets the 'feel' of the various tools and techniques. Thus he learns by practising the actual skill itself. With the selfconscious process, on the other hand, the techniques are taught by being formulated explicitly and explained theoretically.

In the unselfconscious culture, says Alexander, the same form is repeated over and over again, and all that the individual craftsman must learn is how to copy the given prototypes. But in the selfconscious culture there are always new problems arising, for which traditional given solutions are inappropriate or inadequate; therefore it is necessary to bring to bear some degree of theoretical understanding, in order to be able to devise new forms to meet the new needs. Alexander says, 'I shall call a culture unselfconscious if its form-making is learned informally, through imitation and correction. And I shall call a culture selfconscious if its form-making is taught academically, according to explicit rules.'[3]

Up to this point, therefore, we have the essential elements of the same analysis of craft processes in primitive cultures and in vernacular design as was made in nineteenth-century archaeology and by several of Alexander's predecessors in architectural theory, as recounted here in earlier chapters.

Alexander goes on to state quite abruptly and categorically that the unself-conscious process produces good results, the selfconscious process bad ones; and asks the question why this should be.

This statement is very uncompromising, certainly contentious, and no doubt would be challenged by many. Yet Alexander could find wide support for his claim that traditional craft processes have created — and continue to create, where they survive — more fitting, better adapted and indeed more beautiful results than are achieved by certainly the majority of modern professional designers — even, possibly, by the most talented.

This theme is already prominent in much of the early functionalist literature; as for example in Greenough and Fergusson, who point to the superior aesthetic as well as technical achievements of the traditional boat-builders, say, or carriage-builders, over their contemporary 'selfconscious' architect counterparts. It is a recurrent leitmotif — like the mechanical analogy and the biological analogy — throughout modern architectural theory. We need only mention the example of the English Arts and Crafts movement, and its Continental influence, or point out such sentiments in the writings of such characteristically 'modern' figures as Marcel Breuer and Adolf Loos.[4] Perhaps the most famous and surely one of the most vigorously argued statements, one which might serve to stand for all the rest, is that to be found in Loos's essay of 1910 on 'Architecture',[5] where he describes the intrusion, into a tranquil landscape with peasant houses and farm buildings (not made by the peasants, but 'made by God'), of a villa designed by an architect. The villa strikes 'a false note'; like an 'unwelcome scream'. It is immaterial, says Loos, whether the architect be bad or good; in either case the former harmony and beauty are ruined.

More recently new attention has been directed towards both the visual and the functional qualities of vernacular architecture — especially in connection with energy and environmental questions — by such critics and theorists as Rudofsky, Fitch and Olgyay, among others.[6]

To this extensive debate, and to its aesthetic aspects in particular, I will not try to contribute anything here. It is clearly not an issue that may be resolved easily or decisively. It seems useful to make two simple points, however. The first is that, whatever qualitative judgements one might make about its products, the unselfconscious process did *work* at a functional level — if not universally, at least in many and widespread instances. It was capable of producing artefacts which are undoubtedly extremely ingenious in their design, which exploit physical effects or properties of materials which scientific analysis is only just coming to appreciate; and all this done without the unselfconscious designer having recourse to theoretical principle or understanding. Since the process worked, it seems important, as Alexander argues, to look rather closely to see precisely how it did work; and to determine whether there are lessons for the present-day designer.

The second point is that the products of unselfconscious design have been achieved within very severe limitations of material and manufacturing technique; much more restricted than those available to the selfconscious designer.* It is all very well to compare a modern house, say, with an Eskimo igloo and point to the former's unarguable superiority in terms of comfort, structural soundness, convenience and so on. But it is the comparative merits of the *processes of design and production*, not their actual historical achievements, which are at issue here.

One is not obliged to follow Alexander all the way in his opinion that the products of unselfconscious design processes are universally good, and those of the selfconscious process bad, in order to see the value of his concern to discover, through a closer inspection of the nature of 'adaptation' in the unselfconscious case, how its results are actually achieved. It is at this point that the extensive biological component of Alexander's argument enters in.

Alexander refers to the idea of gradual adaptation in craft or building evolution in the unselfconscious process, taking place slowly over long periods of time, as 'the myth of architectural Darwinism', and to the brief explanation 'that over many centuries such forms have gradually been fitted to their cultures by an intermittent though persistent series of corrections' as only 'vague handwaving'.[7] But this is rather disingenuous, since it is in effect precisely the explanation which he himself is putting forward. He emphasises elsewhere the importance of the lengths of time over which the process takes place, the forces of tradition, and the cumulative and gradual effects of correction of any recognised failures – or 'misfits' as he calls them – in the design as they occur.

It is true, perhaps, that architectural *Darwinism* is not the proper term; but it is nevertheless technological *evolution* by trial and error which he is talking about. What he is demanding is a much more detailed explanation, however, of the inner workings of the adaptation process than simply the mere incantation of the terms 'adaptation' and 'evolution'; and this understanding is to come principally, he proposes, from W. Ross Ashby's *Design for a Brain* – Ashby's cybernetic account of how adaptation is able to take place (either in learning or in evolution) in highly complex systems such as organisms (or in certain complicated artefacts), due to the particular nature of the interconnection between their various parts.

A number of other basic concepts in *Notes on the Synthesis of Form* can be related – and indeed are so to some extent by Alexander himself – to parallel ideas in biology. The first of these concepts is the relationship between the

---

*It is also worth reflecting on the fact that such primitive (as distinct from vernacular) architecture as survives today is to be found in those parts of the globe which are most extreme and inhospitable climatically – deserts, tropical regions, the far north – and thus has to cope with much more severe problems of environmental control than those which in general face 'modern' architecture in temperate climates.

*form* of a designed object and its *context*; or put the other way round, between the terms or requirements of the design problem and its solution. The activity of design is concerned with achieving a *fit* between the one and the other: 'every design problem begins with an effort to achieve fitness between two entities: the form in question and its context. The form is the solution to the problem; the context defines the problem.'[8]

Together the form and context may be considered as an *ensemble*; and the parallel in biology is of course the ensemble comprised by the organism and its environment. 'In this case we are used to describing the fit between the two as well-adaptedness.'[9] Alexander cites the biologist Albert M. Dalcq and also L. J. Henderson, author of *The Fitness of the Environment*, on the subject of the mutual relationship between environment and organism and its resulting effect on organic form.[10] It is clear that the term 'fit' or 'good fit', as Alexander uses it, corresponds to a technological equivalent of biological fitness.

In passing we may note that a similar parallel is made by Herbert Simon in *The Sciences of the Artificial* when he speaks of the 'Environment as Mold' in connection with the design of man-made objects. 'Fulfillment of purpose or adaptation to a goal involves a relation among three terms: the purpose or goal, the character of the artifact, and the environment in which the artifact performs.'[11] (The introduction by Simon of the *third* term, the purpose or goal, is of crucial importance and it is Alexander's omission of this factor that runs him into trouble.) Suggestions of the environment/organism analogy, put in terms of form and context, or problem and solution, also occur in the work of such recent design theorists as Jones, Archer and several others.[12]

For a discussion of how this well-adaptedness in the relationship of form to context in artefacts is achieved, Alexander goes then to cybernetics and to Ashby. In fact the argument which Alexander makes (in a chapter on 'The Source of Good Fit')[13] about the way in which adaptation can occur, and about the speed at which it takes place, in either organic or in special kinds of mechanical systems, is based closely on Ashby's account of an 'adaptive machine' of his own invention, described in *Design for a Brain*, and called by him the Homeostat.[14]

Cybernetics was defined originally by Norbert Wiener (who gave the subject its name) as 'the science of control and communication in the animal and the machine'. For Ashby the subject covers the abstract study of the behaviour of all kinds of complex systems, whether to be found in the real world or not — as Pask puts it, systems so constructed as to 'exhibit interaction between the parts, whereby one controls another, unclouded by the physical character of the parts themselves'.[15]

Cybernetics has become almost synonymous in the popular view with the subject of computers and computing science. And indeed Ashby equates the term with the 'theoretical study of machines — electronic, mechanical, neural or economic — much as geometry stands to a real object in our terrestrial space'.[16] Nevertheless, included in the scope of cybernetics, in Ashby's view, would be the kind of complex 'machine' or system with which biology deals — that is, the organism and more especially the brain. Ashby sees the greatest promise for applications of cybernetics in the biological field, in fact; and sees its techniques as being particularly suited to dealing with the special problems of complexity which the biologist faces.

The name of Ashby's machine, the Homeostat, refers to the concept of 'homeostasis' first developed by Walter B. Cannon in his important book *The Wisdom of the Body.*[17] 'Homeostasis' expresses the capacity of the body for regulating its internal state, for maintaining its physiological stability, in the face of disturbances coming from the external environment. Every organism is subjected in the short term (on a daily, hourly or minute to minute basis) to a series of such disturbances; and these provoke reactions by the organism through which it alters either itself or the environment in such a way as to minimise their disruptive effect.

A typical example of stability in the face of short-term fluctuations of this kind is the constant body temperature maintained by warm-blooded creatures through very large changes of the surrounding air temperature. Any rise in the external temperature is typically and automatically met by various bodily changes: slowing takes place in the metabolism rate so that less body heat is produced, the body starts to sweat and so loses heat by evaporation of water from the skin, and so on. Equally a temperature drop will induce another set of reactions: shivering, which produces heat by muscular activity, an increase in the metabolic rate, a slight erection of the hair or feathers so as to trap a thicker insulating layer of air in the interstices, and so on.

Any number of features of the body's chemical and physical mechanisms can be shown to work on similar self-regulating principles. It was the achievement of cybernetics to draw attention to the fundamental operating principles by which a similar regulating effect to that achieved in the body can be produced by many modern (and not so modern) automatic mechanical or electronic control systems. The tail-vane which keeps a windmill facing into the wind is an ancient example; James Watt's steam engine governor, with its pivoted weights flung centrifugally to work the steam throttle and thus control the engine's speed, is another. A familiar modern instance from the architectural context, one which performs a function precisely equivalent to the body's constant temperature mechanism, is the thermostatic control of central heating plant.

Cannon confined the use of the word homeostasis to refer to such physiological regulating mechanisms of the body which serve to insulate the various internal organs from environmental disruption. Wiener and Ashby, however, extend their meaning for the term, even within the biological sphere, to give it a much wider sense. As Wiener puts it, 'The process by which we living beings resist the general stream of corruption and decay is known as homeostasis.'[18] Similarly, in Ashby's argument, all adaptations of the body, as well as all adapted forms of *behaviour* in animals, should be regarded as homeostatic, in so far as they serve regulating functions which act to ensure the continued survival of the individual or of the species.

Bodily adaptations, and instinctive forms of behaviour, being acquired through evolution, are essentially the product of trial and error. Certain simple forms of conditioned *learning* process may also be based, at least in part, on trial and error in another form. The animal experiments tentatively with various modes of behaviour, and discovers through pain and failure what are unsuccessful strategies, until in the end it finds, with pleasure, what actions lead to success. One example which Ashby gives is that of a kitten in front of a fire, discovering by moving first too close, and then too far away, what is the distance at which it can keep comfortably warm.[19]

It follows that there is an important formal parallel in this sense, to which J. W. S. Pringle and Ashby have drawn attention, between the cybernetic mechanisms of simple learning and those of adaptation in evolution.[20] Both are error-correction processes in which feedback from the environment — either through recognition of failed behaviours and reinforcement of successful ones, or in the form of natural selection, respectively — serves to maintain the stability of the organism, to confer on it homeostasis, and to further its survival.

Whether an animal will survive or not in particular circumstances depends on a series of what Ashby calls 'essential variables'.[21] These variables might be, for example, the amount of oxygen in the blood, levels of pressure or heat on the skin, amounts of infection in different parts of the body. Exactly which variables are the essential ones in any given case might be discovered by observation, by making large experimental changes in a whole number of variables and observing whether these result in only transient changes in the system, after which the initial stable state is attained once more, or whether, when the variables are taken beyond some limits, the organism is caused to change to 'something very different from what it was originally',[22] i.e. it either adapts, or perishes. Having defined the 'essential variables' in these operational terms, it follows that 'survival' can have an equally objective definition: 'it occurs when a line of behaviour takes no essential variable outside given limits'.[23]

We are now ready to look more closely at Ashby's Homeostat. It is a machine whose purpose is to simulate, in highly simplified form, the kinds of stability or homeostasis which are to be found in the organism — both Cannon's physiological regulators *and* the stability conferred by adaptations of body or behaviour, acquired either through evolution or through learning.

We need not be concerned here with the technical workings of the machine. All we need to know is that it contains several pivoted magnets; and if these magnets are displaced from their equilibrium positions, for instance through their being moved forcibly by hand, then the device reacts in such a way as to return them to their stable state once more. At this level the machine shows homeostasis of the first kind, on a par with the thermostat, or with the body's automatic means of regulation.

But the Homeostat is capable of demonstrating stability at a higher level than this. It is in Ashby's word, not simply stable, but 'ultra-stable'.[24] The 'essential variable' of the device is represented by an electrical relay, through which currents flow only when the movements of the magnets go beyond some critical position. The interpretation of this situation in the biological context is that the 'physiological limits' of the machine have been exceeded; that it is faced with circumstances with which the normal 'bodily' regulating mechanisms cannot cope, and it must react through some more radical response if stability is to be maintained.

*stability*

What happens in these circumstances is that the machine moves a series of switches, essentially at random, which in effect re-wire the circuitry of the Homeostat in a whole series of successive, differing arrangements. This goes on until the machine hits upon an arrangement which causes the current to cease in the 'essential variable' relay. The whole process, it may be seen, amounts to a search, via a series of trials and errors, until some new configuration is hit upon such that the magnet system is once again stable.

The Homeostat is now 'ultra-stable', since it can by this means counteract the effect of much more serious disturbances than just a slight forced movement of the magnets. For example, it is possible for the operator to move one of the *switches* arbitrarily; and still the machine can respond, using the remaining switches, so as to regain equilibrium. It should be pointed out that the Homeostat can be taken to represent either an organism on its own (and the operator its 'environment'), or else, more interestingly, the system comprised by both organism and environment interacting together (since the dividing line or distinction between the two is in this situation only arbitrary). The forced change in the switch in this latter context might be regarded as some sudden large change in the environment, to which a (biological) organism then adapts.[25]

Ashby summarises his arguments about the two levels of biological stability, demonstrated via the Homeostat, in the following passage:

> the disturbances which come to the organism are of two widely different types (the distribution is bi-modal). One type is small, frequent, impulsive, and acts on the main variables. The other is large, infrequent, and induces a change of step-function form on the parameters to the reacting part. Included in the latter type is the major disturbance of embryogenesis, which first sends the organism into the world with a brain sufficiently disorganised to require correction (in this respect, learning and adaptation are related, *for the same solution is valid for both*) [my italics]. To such a distribution of disturbances

the appropriate regulator (to keep the essential variables within physiological limits) is one whose total feedbacks fall into a correspondingly bi-modal form. There will be feedbacks to give stability against the frequent impulsive disturbances to the main variables, and there will be a slower-acting feedback giving changes of step-function form to give stability against the infrequent disturbances of step-function form.[26]

The adaptive behaviour shown by the Homeostat, Ashby argues, is therefore in cybernetic terms directly analogous — though at a highly simplified level — to that shown by the organism. He maintains that ultra-stability can plausibly be argued to have been developed through natural selection; and he discusses the question of the role which the gene pattern plays in adaptation, seen from the cybernetic view.[27]

We can now return to Alexander, and examine how these cybernetic ideas of Ashby's are interpreted in the context of artificial design. In the 'unselfconscious' design process — that is in technical evolution through trial in practice — the main function of the user or maker of artefacts (often the same person) is to recognise 'misfits' — evident functional failures — of these objects in use. The primitive craftsman 'reacts to misfits by changing them; but is unlikely to impose any "designed" conception on the form'[28] (i.e. the changes he makes, the 'variations', are error-correcting only and do not anticipate the results of selection).

What is the parallel between this interacting system of the artefact, human agent and 'environment' or context on the one hand, and the self-regulating, 'ultra-stable' behaviour of the Homeostat — or the organism with its environment, which it models — on the other? 'Disturbances' come to the artefact from the changing environment; these are the cause of the 'misfits' or failures in the design which the user recognises. He acts to correct them, by making some alteration in the form. He could, in principle, make alterations at random, until he found some one change which produced the required effect.

Note that the Homeostat in effect goes through a random search for some new permutation of its component parts which will re-establish stability of the system. This models in the schematic way the random search which is constituted by genetic mutation and variation in the organism, or alternatively, the simplest trial and error in the processes of learning in the brain. In the case even of the process of unselfconscious, craft evolution, it would be more plausible to imagine, rather than a completely random process, the craftsman being able to anticipate at least in some degree what kind of change will produce the required correction. It is perhaps possible to argue, though, that given sufficient time it is not critical to the process that the right change be made always, since the same fault will persist and eventually the appropriate solution will be found.

The whole system — of artefact, human agent and environment — is in this situation self-regulating, self-correcting. It displays the property of homeostasis. The disturbances from the environment against which the system is stable may be of various kinds occurring over various time scales. One of the examples which Alexander gives is the way in which changes in air temperature provoke a reaction from the Eskimo in his igloo, who either opens holes or closes them with lumps of snow so as to return the temperature to the required level.[29] Here again, this is a direct equivalent of Cannon's homeostatic physiological mechanisms acting to control temperature in the animal body. The Eskimo's actions are those of a kind of primitive man-driven thermostat.

We might not think of these kinds of alterations to architectural form as constituting the real business of design. Remember, however, that Ashby described the 'ultra-stability' of the organism, and of the Homeostat, as resisting *two* kinds of environmental disturbance; the one 'small, frequent, impulsive', the other large and infrequent, requiring a change in the 'parameters to the reacting part' of the organism — that is to say a process of learning, in the brain, or a process of adaptation of bodily form, in evolution.

The reorganisation of the igloo form — an effective if small 're-design' — over the short term, from hour to hour, is an example of the former; as is, in a more elaborate way, the automatic response of modern air-conditioning and heating machinery. Over the longer time scale more extensive, and, what is of greater importance, permanent and non-reversible reorganisations of the actual forms of artefacts are effected either by modification — by rebuilding or altering part of a house, or making changes to some feature of a tool — or else by altering not the physical object itself, but the *design*, when a new copy is made.

To summarise then, the reaction of the user/maker of an artefact to correct 'misfits' arising as a result of environmental changes can be to make either of two types of change to the object in response: firstly, a short-term one like, with a building, opening a window or lighting a fire to control the temperature — not what we would usually call design, but which does nevertheless alter the building's effective form or behaviour. (These correspond to the physiological regulatory mechanisms controlling the 'small, frequent, impulsive' disturbances.) Or, secondly, a structural change over the longer term (corresponding to an adaptation of bodily form), usually by building a new, copied version to a slightly modified design; that is, through technical evolution.* In our window example we would have the opening and shutting of the window at the shorter time scale (this being an easily and rapidly revers-

---

*This evolutionary re-design over the longer term might of course be intended to secure a more effective reaction to the short-term types of environmental change; as with improvements to the design of an air-conditioning installation and its thermostatic control.

ible operation); and the incorporation of some re-designed window into a new building which otherwise copies the form of previous buildings, over the longer time scale.

So far, I have tried to show how Alexander in effect transposes an elaborated version of the theory of craft evolution, as it was formulated by Pitt-Rivers and followers, or by the Purists, into the language and conceptual framework of cybernetics. We now reach the crux of his argument: his diagnosis of the breakdown of the 'unselfconscious' process, and his prescription for a new type of mathematical or systematic design method which will produce results equivalent to craft evolution by simulating its mechanism.

There were essentially two features of the unselfconscious process, Alexander argues, which allowed evolved 'adaptive' change in the form of the designed object to be achieved successfully. The first feature we are very familiar with from previous discussion: it was the great length of time available during which the environment or the context of the design problem was relatively unchanging (i.e. not undergoing permanent irreversible change); or at least was only changing slowly. It was in these circumstances that selection, by prolonged testing of the artefacts in actual use, could be effective. The second feature, which follows from the fact of objects being copied with only small variations in form, was that just one or just a few aspects of the form were altered at each step.

It is Alexander's assumption that the 'misfits', the observed failures in the design, will some of them be causally interdependent, others of them independent of each other. If an alteration of form is made to correct one 'misfit', then it is possible, if they are causally interrelated, for that correction to result in the appearance or reappearance of some other 'misfit'.[30] That is to say, in solving one sub-problem, either a new sub-problem arises, or else the already previously achieved solution to some other connected sub-problem is thereby disrupted.

In the worst circumstances this process might ramify and continue indefinitely, without stability, without successful adaptation being ever produced. As Alexander points out, whether a certain level of adaptation *can* in fact be achieved under these circumstances is crucially dependent on the degree of interconnection between the factors — that is, on the overall structure of the system in question. Where the factors, the 'misfits', are all entirely independent of each other, there is no interconnection, and the problem is trivial; but this clearly is not characteristic of design problems of any interest or complexity. Where all the factors are completely interdependent, then the difficulty is wholly insoluble.

It is reasonable to assume, however, that in complex systems which *are* capable of adaptation — either in organic or in artefact evolution — the degree of interconnection must be somewhere between these extremes. Indeed, the assumption is capable of formal cybernetic proof: as Ashby says, 'For the accumulation of adaptations to be possible, the system must not be fully joined.'[31] In fact the system must consist of a number of relatively independent sub-systems, each of which can adapt in partial isolation from other sub-systems, and hence without disturbing such adaptations as have been previously accumulated in those sub-systems.

Herbert Simon makes the same point, through a memorable parable about two watchmakers, Tempus and Hora.[32] Tempus makes watches by a method which involves fitting all the many pieces simultaneously; so that if he is interrupted, the uncompleted mechanism falls apart, and he must start from the beginning again. Naturally, as a result, he rarely finishes a watch. Hora makes watches which have as many pieces and are equally complex; but he works by building the parts into small sub-assemblies which are stable in themselves, and then putting these assemblies together. If Hora is interrupted he only loses a part of his work, and the time he takes to complete a watch is only a minute fraction of the time taken by Tempus — depending how frequently both are disturbed in their work.

Alexander has a more or less equivalent illustrative example concerning a system of interconnected light bulbs, which is taken directly from Ashby.[33] A light illuminated is taken to represent a 'misfit' (an environmental disturbance) and a light turned off represents 'good fit' or adaptation. Lit bulbs have a certain probability of turning off again in a fixed length of time; but there is also a probability of one lit bulb having the effect of turning other unlit ones on again. In these circumstances the time taken for all lights to go off and a stable state re-established depends once again on the nature of the interconnections between the bulbs. Adaptation is achieved quickest where there are few or no interconnections at all; but in connected systems, it is those which are connected in relatively isolated groups or sub-systems which adapt fastest.

The purpose (or at least, one purpose) of both illustrations, Simon's and Ashby's, is to teach a lesson about biological evolution: that because organisms are such very complex (i.e. richly interconnected) systems, it is only possible for them to evolve at all, even slowly, if their structure is organised hierarchically; that is, in Simon's words, they are 'composed of interrelated subsystems, each of the latter being, in turn, hierarchic in structure until we reach some lowest level of elementary subsystem'.[34]

To go back to Alexander and his analysis of the supposed failure of the selfconscious process of design amongst formally educated professionals in modern societies: Alexander's argument centres on the point that in this selfconscious process, in order to overcome the time problem, the designer is obliged to work, not by trying out the real object in practice, but by testing a *representation* or *model*. The alternating phases of 'variation' and 'selection' which went on in craft evolution are so to speak transferred into the mind and onto the drawing board. The designer makes what Alexander calls a 'mental picture' of the form (and, he might have added, also makes physical pictures); and he makes a mental picture of the context. Then he *imagines* or simulates the interaction between the two, the critical testing of the form against its environment, rather than carrying this out in the real world, as would be done in the unselfconscious case.[35]

Alexander indicates the structure of the selfconscious process, in his terms, by means of a diagram (figure 28, centre). To quote his description:

> Here the design process is remote from the ensemble [form plus context] itself; form is shaped not by interaction between the actual context's demands and the actual inadequacies of the form, but by a conceptual inter- action between the conceptual picture of the context which the designer has learned and invented, on the one hand, and ideas and diagrams and drawings which stand for forms, on the other.[36]

A picture of the modern design process as a cyclic (or perhaps helical)[37] one, moving between alternate phases of 'hypothesis' and 'critical evalua- tion', has become commonplace in the recent literature of design theory (though significantly, as we shall see, there is no cyclical character to Alexander's proposed new design method).[38] Several writers have also made the connection between such models of modern design procedure and Popper's generalised trial-and-error scheme for creative processes in science and in art.

Some preliminary design hypothesis is made, perhaps of a rather simpli- fied nature; is tested (in theory or in imagination) against the stated require- ments or functional context; in the light of those tests is modified; and so on repeatedly. Simon refers to this as the 'generate-test cycle'. In Simon's view the (selfconscious) design process is seen 'as involving first the generation of alternatives and then testing of these alternatives against a whole array of requirements and constraints. There need not be merely a single generate-test cycle, but there can be a whole nested series of such cycles.'[39]

Selfconscious design is thus characterised, Alexander suggests, by the testing of artefacts, both in the mind and by means of externalised models — though Alexander puts less emphasis on these — as for example drawings, solid models, or perhaps symbolic mathematical or computer models. (Of course there are circumstances even in modern industrial production where a novel artefact may be tested by building an actual prototype and subjecting it to real trial in use. This is often the case with the design of utensils for mass manufacture; and may even, given sufficient resources and long enough pro- duction runs, be practicable with such large items as cars. But it is the fact that many identical objects are manufactured, and that their individual cost is relatively low, which make this possible. Alexander's analysis, by contrast, is mainly directed towards architecture — and could also be applied to several areas of large-scale engineering — where the requirement is for a single, uni-

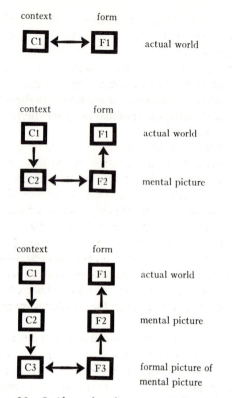

28   C. Alexander, diagram to indicate the structure of three types of design process: the 'unselfconscious' process (top), the 'selfconscious' process (centre), and Alexander's proposed new process (bottom).

que and extremely expensive building, structure or machine which will never be exactly repeated. Here testing in practice would not only take too long, it would obviously be too cumbersome and too costly.)

It is Alexander's contention that the mental images with which self-conscious designers represent the contexts of design problems are incomplete and incorrect, that *they fail to correspond properly in their structure to the real situation*, and that this is a major cause of trouble and failure in modern design practice.

> Though design is by nature imaginative and intuitive, and we could easily trust it if the designer's intuition were reliable, as it is it inspires very little confidence. In the unselfconscious process there is no possibility of misconstruing the situation: nobody makes a picture of the context, so the picture cannot be wrong. But the selfconscious designer works entirely from the picture in his mind, and this picture is almost always wrong.[40]

Alexander's idea is that the designer makes an assessment of the structure of the problem in hand, by reference to a set of preconceived — and as Alexander would argue, generally misconceived — mental categories or pigeonholes.[41] In order to make the complexities of the problem more manageable, the designer analyses or tries to analyse its structure into a number of component parts which he can then tackle separately. In the architectural context these might be defined by such familiar categories perhaps as 'circulation', 'acoustics', 'economics' and so on.

Alexander's argument is that this kind of mental analysis fails to represent correctly the true hierarchical structure of the problem as it really is; it fails to isolate the separate and independent sub-systems, but instead lumps together factors from what are in reality different sub-systems. The result of this is that the accumulation of adaptations in relatively independent sub-systems now becomes impossible — because the sub-systems are not treated independently. Each factor that the designer attempts to get right in one part of the problem sets off a series of ramifying effects in other areas, which upset whatever progress he may have already made there. The system has become too highly interconnected; and so the time taken to reach a stable equilibrium — to achieve 'good fit' — is excessively long. In these circumstances, the designer fails.

We might say that, in Alexander's diagnosis, the selfconscious designer is unable to achieve that 'coherence' which for many of the nineteenth-century critics constituted the special quality of 'organic' works. Recall how Cuvier saw the correlation — the coherence — of the parts of the body in terms of a series of organic sub-systems which might be arranged in a hierarchy of ranked functional importance. Cybernetics provides for Alexander an idea which, though obviously historically very remote from Cuvier, can be seen to be related. The hierarchical organisation of complex systems such as organisms is a necessary condition of the adaptive processes which go on in their evolution.

The remedy which Alexander offers for the failure of selfconscious design involves an attempt to correct the fuzzy, intuitive and mistaken images in the designer's mind, and to give them a more explicit and organised structure, as what he calls 'formal pictures of mental pictures' (see figure 28, bottom).[42] A great part of the remainder of his book is devoted to describing a method whereby the true structure of the design problem, the context, may be determined by means of a process of hierarchical decomposition using a set-theoretic approach; and how from out of this analysis an appropriate form may be derived.

The implication is, clearly, that if the designer *can* understand the real hierarchical organisation of his problem, he will be able to make changes to his design, to correct 'misfits', in a way that is cumulative and does not undo his previous work. Thus he can in effect simulate a speeded up kind of technical evolution in his head, and on the drawing board; and he can beat the problem of the excessive time required by the unselfconscious or craft design process.

What one would immediately expect Alexander to mean by these 'formal pictures of mental pictures', and what seems to follow as the logical conclusion to his argument, is a plea for greater precision to be given by designers to their mental 'models'; this to be achieved, presumably, by the same sorts of ways that increased precision is given to our mental pictures of other aspects of the physical world, through scientific research and the development of ever better explanatory theoretical models — models whose structure might in some cases be mathematical.

The problem with a set of architectural drawings, for example, as a symbolic picture or model of a building is that they present an inadequate means for the rigorous testing of the form against the requirements of the programme or context; they are a model of what the proposed building will look like, how it will be disposed three-dimensionally in space, but not of how it will behave. A building's anticipated performance can only be predicted indirectly from them, by powerful exercise of the imagination or a great deal of prolonged and laborious calculation, depending on the characteristics of the design under consideration. What is more, the drawings provide very little representation, in effect, of the building's context or functional environment. One complete half of the 'ensemble' is almost completely missing. The physical or climatic environment is imagined probably in most cases only in the most general way, as is the anticipated behaviour of the building's occupants. Since the process of design involves an imagined interaction between form and context, the fact of having neither any very well-formulated mental images, nor any physical representations of the different aspects of the functional context, would clearly be a considerable disadvantage.

Curiously, however, Alexander does not see his call for 'formal pictures of mental pictures' in this light. He does not see it as a question of attempting to model particular forms or designs, and their functional environments or contexts, with greater rigour and flexibility, for instance mathematically — although he certainly admits that 'given a new design, there is often no mechanical way of telling, purely from the drawings which describe it, whether or not it meets its requirements'.[43] The subject of the 'formal picture' which he proposes is in fact something very odd.

Here I propose to leave Alexander for the time being, and to return in due course to try to account for the strange turn which his argument takes at this point. I will attempt to demonstrate how Alexander's design method manifests some peculiar inconsistencies, which can be in part attributed to the element of fallacy which permeates the whole of biological analogy as applied to culture and technology. Meanwhile, having reached the end of this presentation of the development of the analogy in theoretical and to some extent historical sequence, I now propose to examine at some length in what ways it is based on false reasoning, and is therefore misleading and dangerous. In time this will bring us back to Alexander and beyond.

## 13

# The consequences of the biological fallacy: functional determinism

The title of this chapter alludes to a phrase used by Geoffrey Scott in *The Architecture of Humanism*.[1] Scott's 'Biological Fallacy', however, refers to a rather particular failing of the evolutionary parallel as it was applied to architectural history. This is only one, I would suggest, out of many and various consequences which follow from the mistaken proposition that the evolution of human culture as a whole, and technical evolution in particular, are processes that are directly analogous to the evolution of organisms through variation and natural selection. (Perhaps even to talk of cultural 'evolution' implies an element of biological analogy. Possibly, however, we can accept the word in this context as a shorthand term, to convey the meaning which it had before its annexation into biology, of a process of change, development or unfolding of any kind.)

I have already touched briefly on the distinctions between cultural and organic evolution in chapter 8, where the principal differences were indicated between the respective theories of Lamarck and Darwin. I suggested there — relying largely on Medawar's presentation of the argument — that the evolution of culture has 'Lamarckian' properties which, according to modern biological opinion, serve to differentiate its working from that of organic evolution in certain fundamental respects.

To recapitulate these points: the first difference is that, in the Darwinian and neo-Darwinian theory, the occurrence of variations is either treated as perfectly random, or else is attributed to causes which have no connection with the animal's environment and habits. The way in which organisms seem to be perfectly fitted to their ways of life — all the evidence which supported the 'argument from design' — is attributable wholly to the effects of selection. So teleology in biological evolution is a kind of optical illusion: the process *appears* to be a directed and purposive one, because only those variations are preserved which *turn out* to be adaptive when subjected to selection.[2] No changes in the body of the individual which are produced during its lifetime as a result of environmental changes, be these advantageous or disadvantageous, are transmitted to that individual's offspring ('acquired characters' are not heritable).

*Darwins 'elective' evolution - vs- Lamarcks teleological view*

According to Lamarck's theory, on the other hand, variations were supposed to be directly caused by the organism's own attempts to become better adapted to a changing environment. A habit acquired by an animal during its life, or an adaptive bodily change, *could* be passed on to the next generation. Thus in Lamarck's view biological evolution was driven by the deliberate efforts of creatures, and the whole movement of the evolutionary process was conceived in teleological and progressive terms. Darwin's theory implied — though Darwin himself was hardly happy or willing to accept the consequence, and it was not a point always appreciated by those who sought to apply Darwinism to social affairs and to human history — that evolution was without direction, without any over-riding purpose or plan.

The theory of Darwin, using Lederberg's terms, is an 'elective' theory of evolution, where the environment chooses appropriate changes in organisms from the range offered by variation. Lamarckism is an 'instructive' theory, where the environment is imagined to be able to exercise a direct effect on organisms, and to 'teach' them to change themselves in appropriate ways.

It is the fact that cultural evolution is an 'instructive' process in an analogous sense which gives it its 'Lamarckian' characteristics. The information which passes from one generation to the next, in culture, and which may thus be said to be inherited, is transmitted in the first place via the oral tradition. Language, unique to the human species, provides the channel by which the accumulated experience of each generation in coping with the problems of life can be passed on to the next. For many animal species, each generation meets the world no better prepared than its predecessors (or only marginally so, through genetic evolution). But human beings can, through language, develop a collective historical sense and memory, build up a body of traditional wisdom, and pass on their hard-won skills and knowledge through the instruction and education of their children, through religious customs and taboos, through art and artefacts, through social organisation — in short through culture.

Not that teaching in itself is a uniquely human trait, by any means, since many animals are able to instruct their young by a process of demonstration. Through the means of language, however, it is clearly possible for parents to teach their children by 'telling' as well as 'showing'. What is more, language introduces the possibility for an individual — and through him any number of other persons — to acquire 'vicarious experience'. The individual is able, by hearing others relay the details of actions or events where he was not present, to acquire the benefit of experiences not undergone or witnessed by himself. It is in this sense that language is a much more powerful agent for teaching than is mere demonstration. For private experiences, those of people quite remote, or even dead, become the property of many through being retailed by word of mouth.

When cultural information is passed on orally, there are limits placed on this process by the capacity of one man's memory to store information and of the next man's to learn. But with the introduction of written records, and subsequently their copying in large numbers through printing, these limits can be transcended, and the possibility arises of a cumulative growth and storage of knowledge and experience in books and libraries. (The same is true, to a limited extent — and was so even before the invention of printing — of tools and artworks.) Where before there had to be a continuous unbroken linking chain of information between the generations, or else something would be lost, now information can jump wide gaps in time. Thus Aristotle can convey his findings and opinions as directly to the present-day biologist as he did to Cuvier or to his own contemporaries. The most outstanding and characteristic feature of this last phase of cultural evolution is, of course, the rise of organised science.

Cultural evolution has the two typically Lamarckian properties: that 'acquired characters' *are* heritable; and that the deliberate efforts of individuals *do* contribute something, so that while one might not attribute purpose to the evolutionary process in itself, there is still a genuinely teleological character to the changes effected by the sum of these individual actions.

Furthermore, cultural evolution or change differs entirely from organic evolution — whether pictured according to the Lamarckian or the Darwinian theory — in the way in which the hereditary information is transmitted 'exosomatically', outside the body; and by the fact that the storage of such information is *cumulative*. Hence the cultural process is in a certain sense a directional one, since men retain a historical record of what is past, and practical or scientific knowledge builds always on the discoveries, observations and theoretical ideas of previous generations. (Whether or not one is prepared to call such a movement in science or in technological ability progressive is another issue.)

Let us now examine what theoretical consequences follow if cultural evolution *is* equated with organic evolution, or is assumed to possess Darwinian characteristics. The fallaciousness of these consequences is evident enough, once the arguments are made plain; but of course the trouble with much of the analogy as expounded in the design or archaeological literature is that the chain of reasoning is not laid open for inspection, and so we are left with general tendencies or predispositions towards certain views, which are broadly encouraged by the fallacies involved.

The first result, curiously, is that the individual designer or craftsman tends to fade away, and even disappears altogether. Certainly his conscious and deliberate contribution to the creation of designs is seriously underestimated and undervalued. In natural evolution the production of fitness (i.e. 'design') is achieved entirely through selection, working on variations in the animal body which are generated randomly or fortuitously.* If the same is imagined to be true of technical evolution, then the only role for the manufacturer of artefacts is that of copying and of making small accidental or 'blind' changes as he does so. Such assumptions are made quite explicitly in the theory of craft evolution of Pitt-Rivers and Balfour.

The craftsman, in the evolutionary analogy, becomes merely a kind of midwife, his purpose to assist at the rebirth of the inherited design. The real, effective 'designer', in this view, is the 'selective' process which is constituted by the testing of the object in practical terms when it is put into use. The craftsman has only an error-correcting function; he spots failures in certain versions of the design of some artefact, and copies those other versions in which the failure does not occur — like the horticulturalist picking out specimens of flowers with the desired qualities for further breeding. Alternatively, he may detect a shortcoming in a design, and make changes randomly in that particular feature, in the hope of hitting by chance upon some appropriate alteration. What is not imagined is that he anticipates in any conscious way the results of such changes, or that he intentionally makes alterations to the design which are meant to produce specific effects.

Just as Darwin inverted the argument from design, and 'stole away' God as designer, to replace Him with natural selection, so the Darwinian analogy in technical evolution removes the human designer and replaces him with the 'selective forces' in the 'functional environment' of the designed object.

We have seen the tendency of the nineteenth-century critics, for example,

---

* I am aware of making a vast simplification here, and of passing over the whole of a prolonged and extensive debate in biology about the 'randomness' or otherwise of variations, or what 'random' really means in this context. Perhaps it may serve here to notice that a strictly neo-Darwinian position, and an insistence on the absolutely blind and haphazard nature of the ultimate source of variations, can still be reconciled, according to some authorities, with many features of organic adaptation which to others have appeared to demand a directed or teleological explanation. Thus Baldwin, Schrödinger, Waddington and Simpson have shown how Lamarckian effects may be feigned or simulated through natural selection. Others such as Whyte, and recently Campbell, have argued that the selectors acting in the evolutionary process may be internal as well as external. For instance, they may be 'structural' (i.e. only certain organic forms or structures are allowable by the laws of physics, chemistry or geometry), or else they may be 'vicarious' (i.e. some internal mechanism 'represents' the selective features of the external environment, as for example the way in which taste sensations of bitterness or sweetness may stand, imperfectly, for the nutritional qualities of various foods). Campbell argues indeed for models of perception and of creative thought which are also based on a trial-and-error or 'variation and selective retention' mechanism. Thus he would argue that *at the limits of the unknown*, thought, and the senses, proceed on a quite 'nonprescient' and aleatory basis. Such a view does not of course deny the human capacities for foresight, anticipation and intentional action at an everyday level. See D. T. Campbell, 'Unjustified Variation and Selective Retention in Scientific Discovery', *Studies in the Philosophy of Biology*, ed. F. J. Ayala and T. Dobzhansky (London, 1974), pp. 139–61.

to attribute the design of the Gothic cathedrals – their prime example of evolution in architecture – to an anonymous collective of monks and masons responding to the social and material conditions of twelfth- and thirteenth-century France. Modern scholarship would present a rather different view of the imaginative contribution of a few particular historical figures, and would also point to the abruptness rather than smooth continuity of stylistic change. (It was perhaps the paucity and relative obscurity of historical documentation for the medieval period which previously allowed the evolutionary and collective interpretation.)

Again, the Purists in their choice of *objets-types* favoured the anonymous, the banal; they concentrated typically on small utensils of mass manufacture. It was, possibly, less contentious to claim such objects as the products of 'natural law' – to deny in effect the human contribution to their design – than it would have been with such larger artefacts as buildings, with their wider stylistic variations and the more obvious evidences of personal authorship in their appearance. Walter Gropius too, in his new plan for the Bauhaus, called for the abandonment of individual prejudices and personal tastes (the forces of 'desire'), and for their replacement by a collaborative, 'scientific' or 'organic' method of working (according to the dictates of 'intellect').

If the designer disappears, then any element of individual choice or purpose which he might exercise when designing disappears with him. The forms of designed objects are conceived as being wholly the product of their 'environment', the functional context in which testing or 'selection' acts. This process is perfectly automatic, deterministic. The phrase 'Form follows function', from being an aesthetic prescription that form *should* follow (i.e. express and not conceal) function, becomes a scientific assertion of causality: that form emerges as a necessary and unique consequence of function. As Choisy said of the flying buttress, 'il ne fut point inventé, il s'imposa'.[3] Not only is there no human contribution to the designed object itself, but it is further implied that somehow the functions of artefacts – i.e. their environment, in the analogy – are in turn capable of definition without reference to human purposes and choices, and that by extension the measures of 'fitness' according to which selection of designs is made are also somehow amenable to objective and absolute definition.

The position is wholly paradoxical, of course, since 'fitness' in relation to 'environment' in the analogy corresponds to the appropriateness of an artefact for its intended purpose. The assessment of this appropriateness is something which, of its very nature, must be a matter of human judgement and taste; while the concept of an intended purpose without a human agent having the intentions or the purposes is perfectly absurd.

Nonetheless, these are the consequences of following an extreme 'functional determinist' position through to its logical (or rather, illogical) conclusion.

Those architectural theorists who adopted such a stance imagined that the functions (environments) of artefacts or buildings might in some sense be defined *prior* to the derivation of their forms; indeed the forms would come automatically out of that definition of function. We will come to examine shortly the way in which this conception is in truth incompatible even with a strict interpretation of the biological analogy. Even in the biological case, neither 'environment' nor 'fitness' are defined in any absolute or objective sense, but always in relative terms -- relative to the organism; and the idea that they might be defined in the absolute is based, I will suggest, on semantic confusions and on a misunderstanding of the biological theory.

But let us for a moment see what kinds of emphases in theoretical analysis were arguably the product or concomitant of such ideas; and what strategies were, perhaps unconsciously, adopted to conceal their shortcomings. Suppose the 'environment' of an artefact is to be imagined as having an independent existence in its own right, and that the criteria for selection of designs possessing greater 'fitness' are to be as well-defined and as independent of personal preference as possible; then the tendency will be to concentrate on those more utilitarian functions about which there is a great measure of consensus, and where there is little disagreement on criteria for satisfactory performance.

*(biased) emphasis on aspect of designs performance which does not therefore question/reflect on other criteria*

Everyone (or nearly everyone) will agree that a cup should hold water, or that a building should stand upright and keep out the rain. Because such functional requirements are so generally accepted, the impression might be sustained that they are objectively determinable, that they meet certain supposedly universal or 'biological' human needs, and are not the subject of culturally and individually variable choices. Certainly it will be progressively more difficult to preserve this impression the further the 'functions' or aspects of the 'functional environment' considered move away from the strictly practical, and towards the decorative, expressive or symbolic.

The accusation of materialism — an excessive concern with the constructional and practical aspects of architecture — was one that was levelled frequently at both Semper and Viollet-le-Duc; and my argument here would explain how this materialism — in so far as the charge is a fair one — would go along with their penchant for biological analogy. Semper attempted to fend off the criticism by arguing that the 'variables' in his equation of style included cultural, social and spiritual factors, as well as material constraints. In fact in the introduction to *Der Stil*, Semper is himself critical of what he names specifically as the materialist philosophy in design, which would have it that materials and utilitarian functions alone give rise to form.[4]

*Semper's limited material reference*

Again it is impossible to deny Semper's awareness of the expressive and symbolic nature of architectural forms, or his belief that, through the expression of higher values, and through the historically inherited language of decorative motifs and elements, mere building is raised to the status of architecture. Earlier we saw how Semper, while attracted by the idea of applying Darwinian principles to architectural history, drew attention to the precise difference between organic and technical evolution which I have been labouring here: that the latter is, in his words, the free product of man's 'intelligence . . . genius, will, knowledge and power'. It is thus very debatable whether Semper himself can be finally accused of perpetrating any biological fallacy in this respect. What *can* be argued is that the evolutionary analogy is certainly conducive to the kind of materialist bias which is undeniably to be found in Semper's system, whatever Semper's own reservations and qualifications might have been.

For someone taking up a harder line materialist stance than Semper — prepared as he was to separate consideration of practical function from that of ornament — the phenomenon of *decoration* could clearly be embarrassing, and would have to be somehow explained away. Viollet-le-Duc's tactic here was to try to deny altogether the existence of architectural decoration — other than attached sculpture, wall painting etc. — and to provide functional explanations for what he would have argued were only apparently decorative features, but which in fact served necessary structural and practical uses. This is especially the case with his treatment of Gothic, as Sir John Summerson has brought out so well in his essay on Viollet-le-Duc in *Heavenly Mansions*.[5]

Summerson distinguishes between a materialist philosophy of architecture, in which the function is held to determine absolutely the resultant form, and what he calls a 'rationalist' philosophy, by which he means the same as functionalism in its aesthetic sense — that is, the belief that architecture should have a functional *rationale*, and should display its purpose to the observer in a rational manner. As Summerson puts it, the difference is between 'an architecture which aims at fulfilling certain specifiable functions with the nearest approximation to absolute efficiency and economy' on the one hand, and 'an architecture which seeks to express its function dialectically — to offer a visible argument to the spectator' on the other.[6]

In his enthusiasm for Gothic, springing from an original emotional response to the poetic qualities of the great French medieval buildings, Viollet-le-Duc was led to an effort to interpret this personal response in explicit, communicable, rational terms; and was inclined to go too far in the process. Given the basic Gothic structural problem, then the mechanical means by which a solution had been found was certainly capable of rational analysis, up to a point. But, it goes without saying, the initial overall problem was not itself set in any comparably 'rational' manner. And even Viollet-le-Duc's insistence on the necessary structural role and perfect economy of the separate features of the Gothic vault, for example, have been shown to be exaggerated in the light of subsequent experimental and theoretical analysis, such as the well-known critique of the engineer Pol Abraham.[7] The danger in Viollet-le-Duc's method, which carried over into the philosophy of the modern movement in this century, was the confusion of means with ends, and the confusion of materialism or functional determinism with the functionalist aesthetic or with 'rationalism' in Summerson's sense.

Neither Viollet-le-Duc nor Semper can be accused in the end of any thorough-going functional determinism. True style, for Semper, is 'a certain degree of perfection' achieved only through artistic response to the 'environmental' demands of the problem in hand. And for Viollet-le-Duc, as we have seen, there is nothing guaranteed or automatic about the relation of style to material means and social conditions; and it was only for certain very particular periods in history that he was prepared to allow that true style had been achieved.

In point of fact it is rather difficult to find any one figure, even in the modern movement, who is prepared openly to declare allegiance to the most extreme determinism or materialism. The likeliest candidate is the Socialist architect Hannes Meyer, Gropius's successor at the Bauhaus, for whom the process of design consisted wholly in scientific and systematic analysis of the programme of requirements for a building, out of which the form, materials and even the textures and colours to be used would 'come about automatically'.[8]

The Purists, Le Corbusier and Ozenfant, argued by contrast from a distinctly qualified position. They acknowledged the role of human creativity and aesthetic impulse in architecture and even in the design of tools; but they removed this to a higher plane of activity, the realm of pure form and plastic relationship, in which the artist could operate only when the 'utilitarian basis of the enterprise' had been properly established and the 'biological' requirements of function had been satisfied. (Meyer simply denied the existence of any such higher formal and aesthetic realm altogether.) Within the restricted functional and utilitarian realm, according to the Purists, there was no room for the personal, the intuitive, the speculative. It was necessary simply to determine and then submit to the logic of the problem as posed.

We have seen this argument well illustrated in the quotations from Ozenfant's *Foundations of Modern Art*, where he expresses quite clearly the view that the evolution of artefacts in their mechanical and functional aspects is governed by (rather than constrained within or guided by) physical and natural laws which are quite rigid and unbreakable. Interference by human aesthetic or creative impulse can only serve to confuse and retard what must be recognised as an ineluctable progress towards mechanical efficiency. The products of the machine are 'compelled' into 'certain shapes, their optimum'.

The imagination of the engineers is not aesthetic, since their creations are 'predetermined'. 'Aesthetic invention' is an indication of 'inadequacy' in the sphere of mechanics, and 'serves to hide the absence of knowledge' (although Ozenfant rather spoils his argument in the example of the 'automatic functioning of evolution' in the case of the light-bulb, when he says that '*someone thought* of evacuating air through the base').

Even the Purists' *objets-types* hardly bear out their claim for this supposed automatic nature of the evolutionary process — let alone their strange suggestion that this evolution would necessarily produce standardised designs which would turn out to be made up from those elementary Platonic solids which were to constitute the 'words' of the new formal language of Purism.*
For it is very obvious that they have quite deliberately chosen only those objects which conform to certain pre-established formal criteria, of simplicity, geometrical purity and so on. There has been a great deal of judicious aesthetic selection exercised by Le Corbusier and Ozenfant over and above any 'mechanical selection' which might have gone on in the objects' technical evolution. Many contemporary mass-produced articles, though no doubt cheaply produced and probably functionally quite serviceable, were, not surprisingly, over-ornate, ill-proportioned and certainly not of simple geometric form; as Le Corbusier well illustrates with selected pages from mail-order catalogues reproduced in *La Ville Radieuse* and elsewhere.[9]

It is clearly possible to find artefacts with widely differing forms answering to essentially equivalent functional purposes — perhaps decorated in a variety of styles, or even without decoration. Despite this, discussion has continued among design theorists of a materialist persuasion as to whether there might not be at least *some* types of artefact, particularly mechanical or engineering structures, whose forms would be largely or even wholly determined by functional requirements and the constraints of material and technique. The search for supposed examples of uniquely determined forms appears only to have turned up the crane hook;[10] and the general claim is obviously highly dubious.

As David Pye has so wittily and persuasively argued, the notion of any manufactured object being 'purely functional' or 'purely utilitarian' is on

---

*Is there really such a thing as functional determinism? examples?*

---

* It is perhaps possible to sustain the argument that in certain limited areas of manufacture in the nineteenth century, particularly in artefacts constructed from metal components worked by machine tools, there was some tendency towards geometric design of this ideal Purist character. Herwin Schaefer in his book *The Roots of Modern Design* (London, 1970) shows some pictures of scientific instruments and other metal tools from the early 1800s which have an uncannily 'modern' and Purist appearance for exactly this reason (for instance figure 3, p. 11). But the argument applies obviously only to a very narrow range of materials and processes. Any casting, die-stamping or moulding process would have none of these limitations, for example — a fact to which the output of much nineteenth-century mass production bears eloquent witness. As a matter of fact later on Ozenfant comes to acknowledge this point — with a tinge, one senses, of regret — when he says that the use of such materials as rubber leads away from 'geometric' form in design. 'The tendency towards electrification' also, he says, 'is creating machines that are practically formless.' 'Our mechanism is primitive, and that is why it still looks gratifyingly geometric.' *Foundations of Modern Art* (London, 1931; revised edn., New York, 1952), p. 154.

closer examination an unreal one; and what are often regarded as 'unavoidable' requirements of function, or limitations of material, are in fact matters of intentional choice on the part of the maker.[11] Many 'functional' requirements may be resolved ultimately into requirements for economy — in the broadest sense of economy in the manufacture, economy in material used, and so on. With the expenditure of more resources, more money or more effort, it will generally be possible to produce objects which will all serve the same intended purpose equally well, but for which the range of possible forms is correspondingly widened. The Purists' dual 'laws of nature' are in fact deliberately imposed by man.

This is not to say that function and materials do *not* constrain the designer in any way; indeed I shall argue later that the geometrical and topological constraints, for example, which limit the possibilities of architectural arrangement are in many cases rather severe ones. The point is, rather, that design problems are not 'objectively' determined in the first place, but are created by cultural values and human purposes. The designer or client may change these purposes at will. And the decision to meet any problem with a solution that is maximally 'efficient' according to some engineering or economic criterion is itself also a matter of cultural choice —not imposed by any absolute external or inevitable necessity.

It certainly seems reasonable to suggest that, once *given* certain functional specifications, and once *given* fairly stringent requirements of economy (imposed by choice), then there might be *parts* or features of certain artefacts where the form would be able to vary only within rather strict limits, while in other parts the opportunity for morphological variety would be so much greater. We have seen how Greenough suggested this in relation to the hulls of sailing ships (by comparison with the forms of buildings); and the equivalent example of the general aerodynamic form of high-speed aeroplanes has been proposed more recently as a case where there is claimed to be a convergence onto a narrow range of possible shapes.[12] (Similar hydrodynamic and aerodynamic constraints act of course on the external forms of fishes and birds.)

But even in these instances, there is considerable possibility for alternative arrangements (and decorative schemes even) *inside* the fixed hull or envelope. It is precisely at those points in the design, one might argue, where the functional specification is rather weak, that an efflorescence of ornament would be expected — as in the figure-heads of sailing ships, well clear of the clean lines of the hull and away from the 'ship-shape' layout of decks and rigging.

We will come back to the conception that decoration is something which flourishes in those parts of an artefact where the limitations imposed by function are not so severe. Here, we may notice a tendency amongst certain modern movement designers and theorists to seek out deliberately those seeking out objects ē extreme specifications or environments imposing extreme specifications so that 'minimalism' (the aesthetic) can be executed un[der] guise of inevitability/necessity

196   *The evolution of designs*

kinds of artefact where the functional specifications could perhaps (improperly) be represented as being *so* restrictive as to prevent *any* incorporation of ornament whatsoever. As previous chapters have shown, their favourite examples were vehicles of all kinds, or the larger civil engineering works such as bridges or aircraft hangers. By a selective focussing on these types of machines or structures, they could thus avoid confronting the embarrassing difficulties posed to functional determinism by objects or buildings which traditionally carried decorative or functionally 'unnecessary' features.

As Pye says, besides 'cheap', the expression 'purely functional' in design parlance can often be shown to mean either 'stream-lined' or else, more rarely, 'light'.[13] It is clear that requirements for all three of these attributes would tend to be in conflict with the addition of ornament. In the design of vehicles, the properties of minimal weight and minimal air or water resistance are obviously at a premium (as Henry Ford was anxious to impress on his designers, with his injunction to 'simplicate, and add lightness!'). No doubt the modern movement's admiration of bicycles, and the characteristic enthusiasm for streamlining amongst such American industrial designers of the thirties as Raymond Loewy and Norman Bel Geddes, are related to this fact. We see that the requirements for lightness in artefacts which must be portable, or must move under their own power, is again reducible to a requirement for economy. With the reduction of weight and the consequent reduction of the amount of material used one would expect that the available field for decoration would be correspondingly narrowed.

In more recent years, some visionary and avant-garde architectural groups have found inspiration for building design in the forms of rockets, space capsules, underwater vehicles, or shelters built for polar exploration. This phenomenon is no doubt attributable in large part to a futurist preoccupation with technological imagery for its own sake. But there is also, I believe, an element of this same trend to seek out 'functional environments' of such extreme severity that the form is imagined to be wholly determined by engineering considerations. (There is the additional attraction to the futurist sensibility that such machines or dwellings are without cultural precedent, and thus freed from unwanted historical or traditional associations.)

Since buildings do not need to be carried or to move, it might be supposed that lightness is not an important requirement in architecture. Buckminster Fuller thought otherwise, and had a phase at one time of confounding architects by asking them how much their buildings weighed[14] – of course they did not know. There is, however, the matter of the transport of building materials to the site, and it was this question that particularly concerned Fuller. (His own 'Dymaxion' house was entirely prefabricated, packed in a (surprisingly small) container, and delivered to the site by rail or road.) Even more significantly, there is the consideration that the upper parts of buildings must be supported on the lower parts; and in large span or very tall constructions the requirement for reduction of weight in the superstructure assumes considerable importance — hence the 'functional' character of bridges, of the roofs of large enclosures, and in particular of the vaults of Gothic architecture.

The other side of this occupation with functional constraints and engineering limitations was that the modern movement tried to ignore or to suppress such traditional applications of the architect's skill as the design of gardens, or monuments, where formal composition and symbolism are of the essence. The attempt was even made to determine the design of churches by exclusive reference to a 'functional' analysis of liturgical patterns.

We left Christopher Alexander in the last chapter at a point where his discussion in *Notes on the Synthesis of Form* was about to take a rather peculiar direction. We should now go back to pick up Alexander's line of argument — which I will try to show is explicable in terms of the functional determinist position just described.

Remember that Alexander was making the case for better 'formal pictures' to replace or supplement the hazy and misconceived mental images which 'selfconscious' designers carry in their heads. In order to derive such formal pictures, he proposed that the designer list all the anticipated possible failures of the design to meet its functional requirements, that is, anticipated 'misfits', in his terms. These are to be chosen '(1) to be of equal scope, (2) to be as independent of one another as is reasonably possible, and (3) to be as small in scope and hence as specific and detailed and numerous as possible.'[15] The purpose is that by stating the areas of possible misfit at this very detailed level, it will be possible to avoid wrong-headed preconceptions about the structure of the problem in hand. The 'misfit variables' are to be equal in scope so that some requirements are not subsumed partly or entirely within the broader frame of reference of others, and for the same reason they are to be independent of one another. They are to be small in scope also because in this way the prejudice of ready-made semantic categories — 'acoustics', or whatever it might be — is avoided.

The next step, after having listed as many 'misfit variables' as possible, is to determine systematically whether or not in each case they are at all interrelated; that is to say, taking the misfits two by two, whether the designer can find some reason (or conceptual model) why there should be a causal relationship between each pair. What is produced therefore is an abstract structure of relationships (interactions) between unit elements (misfits). This is then amenable, as Alexander illustrates, to mathematical treatment using the methods of automatic classification, so that the structure is decomposed in a hierarchical manner into a series of levels of groupings of the 'misfit variables'.[16] The theory is that in this way, as described, the real causal structure of the problem is revealed, and the groups of variables at each level correspond to relatively independent parts of the problem, to which it is possible to find separate solutions one at a time.

The 'formal picture' which Alexander himself is referring to is a formal picture *not* of the structure of the designed object itself (since it has not been designed yet), nor indeed of the structure of its environment or context as such. It is a model solely of the imagined interrelationships between those points or aspects where the one fails to fit the other ('misfit variables'). This is surely, from a logical point of view, a most paradoxical sort of thing to be proposing. In order to imagine and set down these misfits in the first place, it must be that the designer has at least some image or mental picture both of context *and of form* − even if this be only the crudest and vaguest 'design hypothesis' −in order that he can imagine such a misfit at all. Furthermore, he can only be in any degree precise about the nature of this misfit and in what ways it might be causally interrelated with other misfits, to the extent to which he is prepared to be precise about exactly what form, what detailed design, he is proposing to fit to the given functional context.

But Alexander has been loath to admit, throughout, that the selfconscious designer must bring some *specific* proposed form, some design hypothesis, into conjunction with its context before he may embark on any testing and evaluation. Indeed, quite the opposite, the implication of his whole argument is that preconceptions about form are to be avoided, and that the form will emerge out of a precise definition of the context. Although his diagram of the unselfconscious process shows a 'mental picture of the context' *and* a 'mental picture of the form', he then goes on to argue that it is the designer's mental picture of the context which is wrong, with no further mention made of the mental picture of the form.[17]

Alexander is concerned to make a specific denial, in a footnote, that there is any sense in which the context or function defines form *uniquely*. In general, he says, there will be several forms capable of meeting the given functional programme.[18] The fact is, however, that the whole structure of his argument has two large and decidedly determinist implications. First, the context (the problem) is capable of exact specification in the absence of consideration of particular forms, particular designs (and further, that 'good fit' is also capable of definition in the abstract). Second, given this precise definition of the context (the problem environment), then in some way the form will follow by a kind of mapping or natural extension of one into the other.

What is strange, as already mentioned, is that a stricter adherence to the terms of the original biological analogy ought in itself to have kept Alexander from falling into these particular errors. Ashby in *Design for a Brain*, for instance, is careful to specify a definition of environment in the biological context which is made in strictly operational terms. 'Given an organism, its *environment* is defined as those variables whose changes affect the organism, and those variables which are changed by the organism's behaviour. It is thus defined in a purely functional, not a material, sense.'[19] Notice that Ashby's formulation has the consequence that a change in the organism may very well effect a corresponding change in (that particular) organism's environment — if its result is that new environmental variables not previously impinging on that organism are now brought into play. To put it in characteristically cybernetic terms, the relationship is a *feedback* one: 'The organism affects the environment, and the environment affects the organism.'[20]

If we follow the consequences of these observations for the strict analogy in design, then we find that since biological environment is defined only in relation to the organism, so by analogy the 'functional environment' of an artefact would be defined only together with and by reference to that artefact itself. There is an *interaction* between form and function. A change in the environment, i.e. in the required functions of a designed object, will elicit an appropriate change in the form; but conversely a change in the form of the object will have an effect on the functional environment.

I have already remarked in an earlier chapter on the relative nature of biological 'fitness' which, it is clear, would follow from the relative nature of environment. Different creatures must by virtue of their differences have different environments; and thus the modes of behaviour and qualities of bodily form which are conducive to survival in each case, i.e. the factors determining fitness, will also differ correspondingly. How is it then that 'environment' and 'fitness' can be imagined, either in biology itself or in the analogy with design, as being respectively an objective entity and an absolute measure?

I offer the tentative suggestion that one cause is semantic, arising from the everyday usage of the two words. We are accustomed to taking 'the environment' to signify natural landscape or urban surroundings — which perhaps encourages the idea of a separate entity existing in its own right. With 'fitness' the problem is more serious, since two rather distinct shades of meaning which the verb 'fit' can carry in English are easily confused. 'To fit' can mean 'to touch at all points', to be geometrically matched with, in the sense in which the clothes fit the man, or the tenon fits the mortice. Alternatively the word has a much more general meaning: 'to be appropriate' or well-adapted for some given purpose. It is of course the latter meaning which the term 'fitness' carries in biology.

In general the designer will be concerned, obviously, with producing 'good fit' between the form and its context in the larger interpretation of being appropriate to, as measured with reference to some given goal or intention. It is quite clear from Alexander's discussion of the subject of fit and misfit that it is this appropriateness or rightness against a variety of criteria which he refers to when he first introduces the terms.[21] And yet it is fair to say that most of the concrete examples which he goes on to give, to convey the idea of 'good fit', emphasise the geometrical 'close fit' aspect; and that this is a consequent source of error.

One illustration he uses is the method by which a metal surface is ground level in engineering, by first placing it in contact with another standard block whose surface is already known to be flat.[22] The standard block is inked, and when the metal surface to be levelled is placed in contact, only those parts in slightly higher relief take the ink. The engineer then grinds away at the inked parts, and fits the surface again, until it is perfectly matched to the standard. The example is a peculiarly deceptive one, because 'fitness' here, i.e. appropriateness, is achieved precisely by making the blocks 'fit' in the 'close fit' sense. The goal or purpose is *flatness*; and it is against some measure or scale of flatness, i.e. the standard surface, that the degree of geometrical fit and so fitness is measured. The engineer wants to make the block flat because he has some practical purpose in mind for which a level surface is needed. But in other logically entirely equivalent instances he might require the production, very exactly, of metal surfaces to specified *non-flat* shapes; such as the moulds for pressing sheet steel panels for car bodies.

To contrast this with another situation to make the point clear: imagine instead a slowly accumulating layer of dust settling on the standard block. This layer of dust will also take up a perfectly flat surface on its underside, it will thus 'fit' the block. And yet there is no purpose in this, no adaptation of form to context. Again, we might say that a footprint in the sand is precisely fitted — in a geometric sense of touching at all points — the shape of the foot which makes it. And yet the footprint has no function for which it is designed. This is not like the fit between foot and shoe, for example. If 'fit' *is* conceived in the 'close fit' sense, however, this leads on naturally to the erroneous suggestion that 'fitness' is capable of measurement in quantitative and absolute terms, without reference to wider purposes or values.

Other examples given by Alexander emphasise the notion of a direct correspondence or one-to-one mapping between form and context. He speaks of a 'diagram of forces', a 'constructive diagram' which defines or suggests the form. Thus a diagram of traffic flows at an intersection can suggest the widths and directions of the required roads.[23] Alexander speaks of the designer understanding 'what the context demands of the form', and of the form being 'defined by the programme'.[24] Other illustrations he gives to convey this idea include the pattern formed by iron filings in a magnetic field, or the shape taken up by a soap film in response to internal and external air pressures.[25] The metaphor thus represents the requirements or specifications for a designed object as a set of *mechanical* forces; indeed Alexander quotes D'Arcy Thompson's remark in this connection that a form is 'a diagram of forces'. The soap bubble too is the subject of a section in *Growth and Form* on the role of surface tension and problems of space partitioning and close-packing in the forms of cells.

form as
diagram
of forces
↓
truss as
materialized
force field

Now I do not wish to suggest that problems to do with the resolution of mechanical forces, or for that matter questions of geometric 'fit', are unimportant in design; they are clearly of the first importance. It is as crucial that the shape of a building should fit its immediate surroundings in a geometric sense, and that the rooms inside and the constructional elements fit with each other and with the overall shape, as that the design of a glove fit the hand. Equally it is true in structural engineering design that, in a way that can be immediately appreciated visually, the shapes of girders, bridges or vaults are 'diagrams' of (strictly mechanical) forces.

But the danger in thinking of the overall functional (as opposed to specific structural or mechanical) requirements which a designed object is to fulfil in terms of a set of physical forces acting on the form of that object, is that this encourages the idea that such forces are all amenable to precise scientific specification, and that the form will be produced directly by the action of those forces. Alexander wrote an article in 1966 with the significant title – echoing D'Arcy Thompson's dictum – 'From a Set of Forces to a Form'.[26] Here the notion of fit or fitness is not discussed explicitly, but instead Alexander gives a rather general definition for the term 'force'; which might in this context be either a physical force, like the force of gravity, or else it might be a social 'force', of convention or taste, or it might correspond to some supposed universal psychological or behavioural tendency, or it might be an economic or technological force. These forces would operate in what one might imagine as a variety of (spatial and non-spatial) 'environments' surrounding the natural or the designed object. It is these forces which, in Alexander's contention, the form must yield to and acknowledge; it must reconcile them all.

As his example to illustrate this idea, however, Alexander takes the shape of a sandy surface, a dune or a beach, worked into a regular pattern of ripples by the action of the wind. The forces in this case (gravity, friction, wind pressure) are, as Alexander acknowledges, solely mechanical ones; and in the particular stable form which results these several forces are in equilibrium. In speaking of natural forms, Alexander does not make any reference in the essay in question to organic form, only to inorganic; nor does he resort to any explanation along similar lines to his account of the ripple pattern for the adapted forms of creatures or plants.

What he does do, however, is to compare the origins of the form of the sand dune or similar natural patterns with the origins of man-made objects and their shapes, and he points to a 'basic difference' between the two. This is that

> A natural object is formed directly by the forces which act upon it and arise within it. A man-made object is also formed by certain forces; but there are many other latent forces which have no opportunity to influence the form

directly, with the result that the system in which the object plays a part may be unstable. The form can be made stable with respect to all these forces only by artificial means.[27]

By 'artificial means' he refers to the process of design. Since it is up to the (selfconscious) designer to anticipate all the relevant forces and to imagine them acting on his proposed design ('they have no opportunity to influence the form directly') he may fail to consider some of the forces at all, or wrongly interpret their interactions, so the design will be unsatisfactory ('the system . . . may be unstable') in certain ways. This is the problem of the inadequacy of mental pictures.

*wind/ dunes*

But Alexander misses the much more important difference which separates any inorganic form, like the sand ripples or the bubble, both from organic forms and from the forms of those man-made objects such as tools, machines or buildings which are designed for well-defined practical purposes. This is that adaptations of form in both latter cases serve to *resist* those forces in the environment which threaten stability and survival; they serve to further the goals of the organism or the user respectively, in the face of those aspects of the environment which are hostile to those goals. It is *not* as though the form were a kind of plastic amorphous mass which simply receives the impress of external forces to give it its shape. There are conditions in the environment which are related to the purposes of the organism or artefact, certainly, and in a sense these 'forces' constrain or partly determine their form. But each organism or artefact has its own internal structure and organisation, its own integrity; and is not indefinitely deformable or malleable.

*casting/ mould*

Herbert Simon speaks of the environment as a 'mould', and this suggests something like a jelly-mould, into which the liquid material of the organism or artefact is poured and sets solid. This is quite the wrong image.* Although organism and environment are certainly all the time in constant interaction, this is *not* like the interaction of the wind and the sand dune; the organism does not yield and give to every moulding force from its environment – as the sand is pushed this way and that by the wind – for if it did so it would very soon be dead. It would be truer to say that the organism survives despite, indeed in defiance of, the destructive forces in its environment (this is the precise purpose of the 'regulating mechanisms', to protect the organism from environmental disturbance). On the other hand there will be beneficial aspects or forces in the environment which the organism will depend on and will turn to its advantage. Similar observations would apply to designed objects in relation to their functional environments.

---

*Bergson makes this point with the same image in *Creative Evolution*. The relation of the organism to its environment is not that of casting to mould. Adaptation is an active response (although Bergson attributed this response to the impetus of the *élan vital*). See A. Ruhe and N. M. Paul, *Henri Bergson: An Account of his Life and Philosophy* (London, 1914), p. 194.

If Alexander had stuck more closely to the terms of his own biological, or rather cybernetic, analogy, then he would have avoided some (if not all) of these difficulties. He would have been obliged to regard the designed object and its 'functional environment' as logically inseparable and mutually defining — truly as an 'ensemble' in his own terms. And he would have been obliged to treat their (simulated) interaction as a proper feedback process, in which the (mental or 'formal') representation of some artefact would be brought into contact with the representation of its environment; its (theoretical) performance tested; both form and context altered as a result; more tests made; and so on round in a continuing cycle. His argument should, one might suppose, have led him to propose a kind of simulated, and hence speeded up, version of technical evolution, carried on in the drawing office or in the 'design laboratory', and using mathematical or computer models to represent form, context and their interaction.

There could be no way, in such a scheme, in which the form would come out of the context; in which the design problem would, so to speak, produce its own solution. It would be necessary to bring some preconceived, pre-established design (even if this be only a very sketchy or ill-defined proposal) to the problem in hand in order that any process of testing and evaluating its anticipated performance could begin in the first place. In the biological analogy this would correspond to the way in which selection is at any point always acting on the inherited 'design' which has been passed down from the whole of the species' evolutionary history.

But instead, Alexander's proposed design method is, as we have seen, a kind of 'one-pass' procedure. He allows that the original definition of a design problem is a matter of personal choice and intention; and that even the list of 'misfits' which the designer compiles will have a 'personal flavour' and reflect his particular view of the problem.[28] But having listed these misfits, then the way in which this method is described from that point on involves a single phase of hierarchical decomposition of the problem's structure, followed by a single phase of translation of the 'constructive diagrams' so provided into the resulting form.

There is one last paradox involved here. 'Fitness' or 'good fit' in the technological analogy means appropriateness to purpose. Alexander uses the term to express the adaptation of the overall form to the overall context. In the biological case we have little difficulty in drawing the outer boundary between organism and environment, and imagining fitness as a measure of the adaptation of the one to the other. However, in cybernetic terms, as Alexander himself points out, the distinction is a relatively arbitrarily determined one. It is quite legitimate cybernetically to treat the adaptation of a particular organ in relative isolation, for instance; in which case, the remainder of the body of the organism forms part of the 'environment' of the organ. The organs are adapted to each other as the whole organism is to the environment outside.

The same applies with perhaps even greater force in the design world. Here the form/context boundary is only fixed in relation to what the designer and his client *have decided is being designed.* (Indeed it is a prevalent disease among designers to be continually enlarging the terms of reference of the problems they have been set — to keep moving the form/context boundary further out.) In Alexander's words: 'The form is part of the world over which we have control, and which we decide to shape while leaving the rest of the world as it is.'[29] The design of a nut must fit an 'environment' which is very largely constituted by some given size of bolt, while the two together may be designed for a larger 'environment' still, such as an engine or a car. This is to say nothing more than that larger artefacts are made up generally from numbers of smaller discrete and identifiable component parts, all fitted or adapted to each other.

There is thus no distinction in principle between the form/context boundary of a design problem taken as a whole and the boundaries of the various subsidiary problems of design subsumed within the whole. It is possible that within the course of the design process the overall boundary and problem environment may be relatively unchanging, fixed by the terms of the exercise, the designer's brief. But even this is unusual, and it is very common for both designer and client to revise their original goals and intentions in the light of information which the process of design itself produces. What is very certain is that, within the problem considered as a whole, the separate 'environments' of each sub-problem will be continually altering, and the boundaries between problems moved, as the various aspects of the design are worked on.

> We ought always really to design with a number of nested overlapped form—context boundaries in mind. Indeed the form itself relies on its own inner organisation and on the internal fitness between the pieces it is made of to control its fit as a whole to the context outside.[30]

The implication, of course, is that the question of defining and measuring 'fitness', the question of evaluation according to stated purposes, is involved right down to the lowest levels of detail of the design problem. And what is more, the purposes at lower levels will be *only determined* by virtue of prior decisions about form made at a higher level, that is to say these purposes will only emerge in the course of the design process as particular forms are proposed and evaluated.

The point is very well made by Herbert Simon. Simon shows how some overall purpose for an artefact is decided at the boundary, or 'interface' as he terms it, between object and environment.[31] It is at this boundary that the degree of fitness or adaptation to the general purpose is measured. When we think of a clock in relation to its purpose, for example, 'we may use the child's definition: "a clock is to tell time"'. So far as fulfilment of this main purpose is concerned, it is quite irrelevant how the internal mechanism of the clock is constructed, just so long as it works — tells time — in the environment chosen. There may well be several different but equally effective mechanical means for constructing clocks *for the same environment*: they might be clock-work or electric-driven, they might have pendulums or escape wheels, and so on. In Simon's words:

> we often find quite different inner environments [Simon refers to the inter-face as a division between an outer and an 'inner environment' — by which he means the internal organisation of the object or organism] accomplishing identical or similar goals in identical or similar outer environments — airplanes and birds, dolphins and tunafish, weight-driven clocks and spring-driven clocks, electrical relays and transistors.[32]

*Once the decision is made* to drive a clock by means of a spring or to regulate it with an escapement, then this decision establishes a series of goals or purposes for the several internal parts of the mechanism. Each given wheel or lever now has a special function, a purpose in the 'environment' created by the other parts which it engages or to which it is connected. The purposes at each level of internal organisation are thus set in relation to the decided way of fulfilling a more general purpose at a higher level. Only when it is decided to drive the clock by electricity must the internal mechanism comprise some sort of electric motor; and the particular decided arrange-ment of this motor will determine the subsidiary functions of the motor's parts, such as the coils or magnets. In a spring-driven mechanism, quite clearly, these types of components have no place, no function at all.

By the way in which Alexander presents his design method he seems to imply that the definitions of all the 'misfits', hence all the judgements of value, are to be made at the outset; and then a wholly logical and value-free series of operations may be performed so as to produce the form more or less automatically from there on. He thus completely overlooks the dif-ficulty that at lower levels in the hierarchy of components or sub-problems within the design of the object, the functions of these components may very well only be decided as the process of design goes forward. At every level hypothetical proposals may be advanced as to suitable details or components, the 'environment' of each detail, and criteria for the evaluation of its 'fitness', being determined by the very nature of those proposals themselves.

I have suggested in this chapter that the biological analogy was conducive to a belief in functional determinism in design; it removed the designer, it encouraged an exclusive attention to utilitarian functions, and it sug-gested that designed objects were the product of selection exercised by their 'functional environments'. I do not want to imply that this was the sole factor behind such a belief, however. There was another fallacy involved which was perhaps equally significant, and though this had little to do directly with the consequences of applying biological concepts to design, it is very relevant to my argument in the chapters which follow, and so a short account is in order.

Because the theorists of the modern movement admired the engineers, they wished to emulate their methods; and these methods they believed to be *scientific* ones. The engineers, it was thought, had the secure authority of science behind their work, and it was this scientific basis which gave their designs their originality and power. In the view of science which the architectural and design theorists took, however, it seems fairly plain that they were victims of a misconception which has been widely held within the philosophy of science itself, and which Karl Popper has been very actively concerned to expose: the so-called 'inductive fallacy'.[33]

The inductive view of scientific procedure suggests that, from a simple accumulation and patient observation of the facts of nature, a pattern or law will emerge of its own accord and will impose itself on the scientific observer. What in fact happens — as Popper has most forcefully urged — is that the scientist, so far from being a passive observer, himself imposes some hypothetical explanation *onto* the phenomena in question (his observation is 'theory-laden'), and then tests, by means of experiment, to see whether this hypothesis fits. The process is cyclical, so that a hypothesis creates demands for more observations, according to which the hypothesis may be modified. The origin of the hypothesis is in the whole body of relevant knowledge which constitutes that part of the science in question which has been developed so far. Hypotheses are framed, that is to say, in relation to what Popper would refer to as the 'World Three' of 'objective knowledge'[34] (of which more in the next chapter).

It will be very clear how the inductive conception of scientific method would serve as a model for the sort of proposed systematic design method which Alexander puts forward. A series of discrete requirements, or 'forces', or 'misfits', is analysed, and out of this analysis comes, so it is argued, the resulting form of the object or building in question. Alexander talks about the problems which arise 'in trying to construct scientific hypotheses from a given body of data' as being comparable with the task of producing architectural form out of the set of given requirements.[35] It should be said that Alexander's point in this connection is that both processes, the creation of scientific hypotheses and of architectural form, demand invention and are *not* logically deductive ones, nor are they capable of being mechanised. But although he admits that 'the data alone are not enough to define the hypothesis', he suggests that what are required besides are only some organising principles of clarity and simplicity. What he does not pursue in any way is the key psychological question of where hypothesis and where invention, be they in the scientific or in the design field, ultimately come from.

The typical approach to design which characterised much of the work of the 'design methods movement', and which was taught in many architectural schools during the 1960s, implied a similar methodology to Alexander's, although of a more informal nature. First 'data' were collected and assembled into the 'programme'; meanwhile all premature urges to define the form and shape of the building were suppressed. And then, through an analysis of this programme, the designer was encouraged to determine what form the logic of his analysis must produce; he had to find out 'what the building wanted to be'.

We have seen how Hannes Meyer, as a design methodologist ahead of his time, described his own approach in more or less the same terms. One of the principal intentions of the first-year course at the Bauhaus was deliberately to destroy any preconceptions the incoming students might have about design, and to wean them away from traditional ideas. Symptomatic of this mood are Meyer's remarks: 'our knowledge of the past is a burden that weighs upon us, and inherent in our advanced education are impediments tragically barring our new paths'.[36] 'I try to approach the design entirely without any prepossessions or preconceived ideas.'[37] (What an extraordinary — indeed tragic — distortion of the whole purpose and nature of education these statements of Meyer's betray!) As Hillier and Leaman put it, '"Rationality" in design was virtually equated with purging the mind of preconceptions, to make way for a problem solving method which linked a procedure to a field of information.'[38] In this climate the notion of the value of an inherited body of understanding about buildings, and of the absolute necessity for design hypotheses to be based precisely on 'preconceptions' of some kind, were obviously not ones likely to find much support.

As I have tried to show here, and as others have pointed out before, this 'rational' view of design is in fact quite irrational. The designer always imposes some 'design hypothesis' onto the particular problem with which he is faced — a hypothesis which, like the scientific hypothesis, must again have its origins largely in the body of collective knowledge which designers possess about existing and past artefacts and their behaviour and properties. Hillier and Leaman's paper, from which the quotation above comes, is called 'How is Design Possible?'; and it is their argument, as here, that the designer's preconceptions — as they term them, his 'prestructures' — are exactly what makes design possible at all, and indeed what makes possible the identification of a design problem in the first place.[39]

The origins of the design methods movement's concept of 'rational design' have been traced epistemologically in an earlier essay by Hillier, Musgrove and O'Sullivan, 'Knowledge and Design'; which again emphasises, in criticism of this conception, that 'prestructures' and a knowledge base are crucial to the designer's capacity for action in the production and evaluation of design hypotheses.[40] The relationship of 'rational' design methods to the inductive fallacy in the philosophy of science is also pointed out in this same paper.

## 14

# The consequences of the biological fallacy: historical determinism and the denial of tradition

In the previous chapter I described two ways in which proponents of the biological analogy dealt with the question of ornament on buildings or on useful objects: either by ignoring or denying its existence, or else by separating two spheres of interest in design, the 'utilitarian' and the 'plastic' in Purist terms. Our review of the work of the evolutionary ethnologists has illustrated a third possibility: that decoration on utilitarian artefacts might be interpreted as a vestigial survival of some previously functional feature, and could thus be accounted for in wholly historical and 'genetic' terms. If the view is taken that functional constraints control the shapes of artefacts in part but not in whole, and that decoration is to be found in those parts where the constraints allow a measure of free play to the design, then the tendency is to treat ornament as the mere complement or antithesis of function, a kind of fortuitous and purposeless elaboration of form on which the pressures of selection fail to act. Objects on which the functional demands have become less rigorous — like Balfour's ceremonial axe — will show a compensating increase in the extent and complication of their decoration. The idea is encouraged that the forms of artefacts consist of an irreducible functional body or kernel, with a shell or loose-fitting decorative garment around it —what Leroi-Gourhan called the 'non-functional envelope . . . made up of survivals'.

I do not believe that such a conception is entirely wrong in itself, but it has dangers in that it treats ornamental or formal qualities of man-made artefacts as meaningless, or regards them as significant only inasmuch as they serve to connect one object to others through an evolutionary chain of successive copyings. It is a rather similar point, though more generally made, and not exclusively concerned with ornament, which I take to be at the centre of Geoffrey Scott's attack on the 'Biological Fallacy' in *The Architecture of Humanism*.

Scott's book was published in 1914, in a period of revulsion from biological analogies in many fields (including anthropology). Scott is full of passion in his denunciation of their baleful effects on the study of architectural history:

> Of all the currents that have lapped the feet of architecture, since architecture

fell to its present ruin, the philosophy of evolution must be held to have been
the most powerful in its impulse, the most penetrating in its reach. The tide
of that philosophy, white with distant promises, is darkened, no less, by the
wreckage of nearer things destroyed.[1]

Scott's argument is that an evolutionary approach to architectural criticism
encourages the search for precedents and influences — 'The most odious
characteristics of an art become convenient evidences of heredity and environment'[2] — at the expense of any account of the intrinsic qualities of the
building, any assessment of the personal contribution of the designer, and any
real judgement about the relative worth of designs.

The principle of evolutionary art history, says Scott, is 'that things are
intelligible through a knowledge of their antecedents'.[3] Exclusive attention
is therefore directed towards *sequence*; and the result is a *levelling* tendency,
where minor works which serve largely to establish connections, or which
provide the germ of something developed more fully at a later stage, are
all accorded equal attention along with the highest and most mature
achievements of the art. Scott's main concern was to communicate the
sensuous aesthetic delight in pure formal relationships which he saw in Renaissance architecture. So he was particularly upset by the evolutionists'
antipathy to the Renaissance, which they dismissed, he says, as 'capricious',
on account of its formal inventiveness and discontinuity in stylistic development.*

*defense
of Renaissance*

There is another aspect of the biological metaphor to which Scott directs
his attack, which he parcels together as all part of the same evolutionary
fallacy, but which ought to be conceptually separated. This is the idea that the
progression of styles as a whole, in art and architecture — not just the chain
of influences linking individual works — conforms to some general historical
pattern or law. The example of the application of this idea which he holds
out for special obloquy is the depiction of the Renaissance as divisible into
phases of childhood, manhood, decline and senility.[4] The consequence, as
he points out, is that Mannerism and Baroque are then treated as periods
of decadence and weakness, where these are in fact styles of great intellectual
and artistic vigour. At the same time a spurious value becomes attached
to what is characterised as 'strong' and 'healthy' in styles, by contrast with
what is perhaps fragile and transient, but no less valuable for that.

What Scott is offering as an 'evolutionary' analogy in the second case
is clearly in fact a developmental or growth metaphor — of the birth, maturity
and death of styles. If it is to be interpreted as an evolutionary metaphor, then
this can only be in a roughly Spencerian sense. Even that would be not

* One target of Scott's critique here was probably Lethaby's little history book
  *Architecture* published just three years earlier (London, 1911), which is permeated by
  evolutionary interpretations, and which passes over the whole of the Renaissance
  (the 'style of boredom') in a mere six pages.

quite right, though. Spencer certainly equated the characteristics of bio-logical development and biological evolution. But he did *not* imagine evolu-tion, organic or cultural, as a repetitive and cyclic process — like the suc-cessive development and demise of many individuals, so to speak — with alternating phases of rise and decline. Spencer allowed on occasion that there might be retrogressive phases in evolution (back towards homogeneity and simplicity), and that it was not always smooth or uninterrupted.[5] But the broad picture of the process painted by his theory was of a generally one-directional continuous trend towards greater complexity and hetero-geneity.

It would be fairer to associate this 'life-cycle' theory of the progress of styles in art with that larger tradition of systematic history which has at-tempted to identify empires or civilisations whose rise and fall might be argued to follow some few universal types of pattern. Popper says that this 'ancient doctrine' can be found in the works of such various political and historical thinkers as Plato, Vico and Machiavelli.[6] The idea seems to have been first given a consciously statistical treatment, and applied to more than one 'empire', by Quételet, the Belgian author of *Social System and its Laws* (published in 1848).[7] Later came an effort by the Russian political writer Nikolai Danilevsky to identify 'culture-historical types', of which he lists twelve, according to a classificatory method adopted from Cuvierian bio-logy[8] (Danilevsky's original training was in botany). The general approach is one which has been taken up in this century by Spengler, Toynbee and by the sociologist Sorokin.[9]

Our attention has lately been drawn, by Gombrich and others, to the pernicious influence of this 'historicism' in the study of art and architecture.[10] Historicism is the name given by Popper to the belief that regularities or trends in human history are discernible, so that predictions can be made of its future course — if not in detail, at least in general terms.[11] Nineteenth-century historicism in German art history is related back by Gombrich to the influence of Hegel and his *Philosophy of History*.[12] I have already touched in an earlier chapter on the 'ecological analogy' which might be said to be implied in the concept of artistic style as a product or necessary concomitant of the social, technological and religious conditions of the time. If, as Hegel saw it, style in the arts is an expression of the collective spirit of a society, and if that spirit is imagined to be undergoing a progressive evolution, then the proposition follows that stylistic changes will themselves succeed each other in some definite and in principle predictable sequence.

Popper's definition of historicism includes beliefs in either of the two kinds of imagined historical trend or pattern: a repeated cycle, showing characteristics supposedly similar in many civilisations, or a continuous progressive 'evolutionary' movement throughout the history of the whole race.[13] Both types of theory imagine a determinism and inevitability in the movement of history; but in the latter case especially there is the implication that what is newer is by that token better. Thus a premium is placed on novelty and legitimacy seems to be given to the idea of the artistic avant-garde, continually in revolution, continually in advance of public taste. Popper himself, indeed, in *The Poverty of Historicism*, links 'moral modernism' or 'moral futurism' — the idea that the morally good is what is ahead of its time — with 'its counterpart in an aesthetic modernism or futurism'.[14]

Meanwhile the theory of the *Zeitgeist* is also debilitating for historical explanation and detailed criticism, as Gombrich points out.[15] The assumption is made *a priori* that a unity of style exists between all the arts of a period, and the critic simply seeks to confirm this belief by the selection of appropriate correspondences. To the more objective and uncommitted observer these claims for stylistic unity seem often to be *post hoc* rationalisations, and there are many phases in Western art where the prominent stylistic characteristics of the music of the period, say, are distinctly at odds with those of the visual arts, and again with those of literature. Gombrich himself is only prepared to envisage the possibility of some very broad correspondences across the arts, which might arise from a general atmosphere of conservatism or of experiment.

I do not propose to dwell at any length on this subject of historicism in art criticism and theory, for one reason because as mentioned it has recently been well aired elsewhere. It certainly seems more than plausible to connect a political and philosophical historicism with the tenets of architectural futurism: the extraordinary symbolic importance attached by the modern movement in architecture to the new science and technology and the new industrial materials of steel and glass;* its repeatedly announced ambition

---

* One figure from the design world in whose writings the idea of the relentless upward dynamic of technological progress is particularly strong is Buckminster Fuller. For Fuller the trend is always towards higher speeds for vehicles, greater efficiencies for machines, better performance achieved at lower cost and with less material and energy input — the 'Dymaxion' principle. He has a chart which is very symptomatic of his philosophy, showing the number of chemical elements discovered up to a given date, represented as a curve which climbs ever more steeply towards the twentieth century. (See R. W. Marks, *The Dymaxion World of Buckminster Fuller* (New York, 1960), p. 152.) Fuller argues that these discoveries give a rough indication of the pace of scientific progress generally, and beyond that, of cultural and technical evolution as a whole; since, as he argues, social and political life follow economics, economics follow industry, industry follows technology and technology follows pure science. (The chart is actually entitled 'Profile of the Industrial Revolution'.) The designer contributes to but at the same time must fall in with the necessary direction of this trend. In characteristic Fuller argot: 'The visibly quickening chronologicality has therefore valid significance ... [The] consistent acceleration takes place without man's consciousness of its shaping.' (Of course the basis of Fuller's graph is in itself quite spurious. After the discovery of all the naturally occurring elements, the extrapolated curve — not shown by him — would continue perfectly flat.) It is revealing to see how embarrassed Fuller has become in recent years — as shown by his answers to questions asked at his public lectures — by recent calculations of the finiteness of the earth's resources, and by the general mood of disenchantment with technology.

to create an architecture which would be instrumental in bringing about a new social order; and the way in which any hint of the revival of traditional forms was castigated by historicist critics as 'immoral' and retrogressive.

What is of interest here is the extent to which historicism in design theory can be legitimately linked with the strictly biological analogy embodied in the idea of cultural change as a process of evolution. (Thus Gombrich associates the rise of futurism in art with both the 'emergence of Hegelian historicism and Darwinian evolutionism'.)[16] There is no doubt that the 'evolutionary' social theories of Spencer, Morgan, Tylor and others, as applied to the general movement of cultural history, were imbued with a strongly progressive spirit, in both the technological and moral senses. The passage through Morgan's stages of savagery and barbarism – or their equivalents – towards civilisation marked at the same time a development in the complexity and sophistication of man's tools, an increase in his control over the natural environment, and a move towards greater justice and higher standards of social behaviour as expressed in legal codes, religious beliefs and social institutions. The high point of the whole process was that reached by the Anglo-Saxon race in the nineteenth century. Spencer's view of history was also a confessedly deterministic one: he rejected free will as an illusion, and considered the impact of 'great men' on the course of events to be minimal – the chain of causation being the other way round, ideas and feelings being shaped by society.[17]

The strange thing to realise in retrospect, despite all the talk of 'social Darwinism', is how little the *Darwinian* theory really justified any such analogy. In the first place there was no *necessary* suggestion of progress in the 'survival of the fittest' – because fitness was always relative, and because the only *ultimate* criterion of overall fitness (as distinct from those qualities conferring relative fitness on competitors) was the fact of survival. It is through fitness being imagined to be measurable in absolute terms that the apparently progressive quality is introduced, so allowing the idea that one species, or more sinisterly one race within the human species, is 'fitter' than another – and that human evolution is headed towards the production of intellectual or physical supermen (with 'fitness' carrying a certain gymnastic overtone).

In the second place, Darwin did not propose – as Spencer did – any *law of evolution* as such, any goal or state towards which it was directed; he offered only a mechanism for the operation of selection, dependent on certain assumed laws of heredity and variation. On the contrary, Darwin effectively accepted the evolution of natural species on earth as a singular historical occurrence. The 'evolutionary' metaphor in deterministic theories of history owes much more to the earlier teleological and vitalist approaches to natural evolution, to Lamarck and to Lamarckists, than it does to Darwin.[18]

T. H. Huxley, Darwin's apologist, curiously *did* believe in a 'law of evolution of organic forms'. He believed not that Darwin had formulated such, but that this law was bound to be discovered 'sooner or later'.[19] What is odd, as Popper points out, is that Huxley most definitely did *not* subscribe to the idea of a law of social progress, and he made a clear separation between the two ideas.[20] His imagined law of natural evolution would not presumably have pictured the process as one of improvement in any sense.

Much later, in the 1940s, Julian Huxley propounded a theory of evolutionary progress, defined as a continuing improvement in all-round biological efficiency through 'increased control over and independence of the environment'.[21] (Huxley mentions how a similar criterion of independence was used by Spencer to describe evolutionary advance.) But even this was more by way of a generally observed *trend*, which was by no means universal in evolution – there are many instances where such efficiency appears to have declined – and with no guarantee of its continuation in the future. (Also it may be questioned whether 'progress' as so defined represents any amelioration from the point of view of human values.)

Where Darwin's theory *did* form the basis of analogy in the social sciences was in the ideas of competition, selection and survival.[22] If Darwin himself had been influenced originally by the market theories of the political economists and by Malthus's arguments about population and the food supply, then the reapplication of 'natural selection' to the political and economic fields was all the more rapid. The fact was that Darwinism, applied improperly to social affairs, appeared to condone or acquiesce in, as 'natural' and healthy necessities in society, gross differences of wealth and social position, a corresponding neglect of welfare or charity towards the poor and sick, and cut-throat business competition of the most vicious and acquisitive sort. The support of Darwin's thinking was further invoked, as is well known, in attempts to lend scientific respectability to *a priori* assumptions and simple prejudices about supposed innate genetic differences in the intelligence and capacities of different races; and to dignify the virtues, as they were seen, of aggressive militarism and imperial conquest.

This side of social Darwinism is a large subject and not one to be entered very deeply here. Its relevance to the design and art-historical analogies is rather small. There are two points, nevertheless, to be made in this context. The first is that, besides any other fallacies involved, the belief that one race is *superior* to another and the notion that there is *virtue* in competition, hence that it should not be interfered with by legislative controls or by moral restraint, turn on the combination of the selection mechanism with the quite un-Darwinian and historicist belief that evolution is progressive, and will 'naturally' and inevitably lead to improvements – in the health, wealth and general moral condition of society.

The second perhaps more important point here is that there was understandably and quite rightly a severe general reaction which took place in the early years of this century in many academic subjects (though not admittedly in some more disreputable areas of political thought) against the excesses, and the sinister political implications, of such 'biological' theories of society. And in this reaction, the relatively innocuous technological analogies with biology seem to have suffered by association and — at least in archaeology and anthropology — to have been swept away along with the rest.

## The denial of tradition

As we saw at the beginning of chapter 13, the property which distinguishes cultural from organic evolution in a quite fundamental respect is that 'inherited' cultural information is passed on outside the body, via language and teaching. Material culture can be cumulative in a very obvious way: artefacts, tools, books, survive and are collected in museums and libraries. And cultural or scientific *knowledge* can be cumulative in a rather more interesting sense; not simply that historical records or scientific 'facts' pile up, but that our whole understanding of some phenomenon or event is built up out of this mass of data and in relation to a larger structure of existing ideas. These ideas and data can be transformed, reinterpreted, 'revolutionised' even, while still based on the same inherited material which history and tradition provides.

Popper has introduced a most useful set of descriptive terms to mark off this body of 'objective knowledge' from the contents of the individual mind, and to indicate the degree of relative autonomy from the thoughts of individual men which it comes to assume.[23] He distinguishes three 'worlds'. The first world, World One, is the objective world of material things. World Two is the subjective world of minds. What is new in the evolution of human culture is the appearance of a third world, distinct from the previous two although entirely parasitic upon them. This World Three is a world of 'objective structures which are the products, not necessarily intentional, of minds ... but which, once produced, exist independently of them'.[24] It is, in Popper's own words, 'the world of intelligibles, or of *ideas in the objective sense*; it is the world of possible objects of thought: the world of theories in themselves, and their logical relations; of arguments in themselves; and of problem situations in themselves.'[25] World Three is embodied, physically, in World One artefacts of many kinds such as books and tools. It has an existence which is relatively independent of the World Two thoughts and opinions of particular men — though it has its ultimate origins in and is accessible through these thoughts alone. It comprises knowledge that is in many cases not even *known* by individuals.

One of Popper's favourite examples for demonstrating this last point is a book of logarithm tables, which no man, it is safe to say, carries in his head, or ever has done — not even Napier. It is possible indeed for modern tables of logarithms to be prepared by computer. And yet the knowledge comprised in such tables is of enormous practical importance and is in daily use by engineers for all kinds of real world projects. Even with less mechanical and repetitious subjects than logarithms, it is still quite possible for authors — let alone their readers — not to know in detail the contents of their own work. And when these authors die, their works may sit on library shelves for years, centuries even, before they are re-read and their significance appreciated.

To those who argue that conjectures, theories, books, journals, are only linguistic or symbolic expressions of subjective mental states, or means of communicating mental states between individuals, Popper offers the following demonstration of the (more or less) independent existence of the world of objective knowledge, in the form of two 'thought experiments':

> Experiment (1).   All our machines and tools are destroyed, and all our subjective learning, including our subjective knowledge of machines and tools, and how to use them. *But libraries and our capcity to learn from them survive.*
> Clearly, after much suffering, our world may get going again.
> Experiment (2).   As before, machines and tools are destroyed, and our subjective learning, including our subjective knowledge of machines and tools, and how to use them. But this time *all libraries are destroyed also*, so that our capacity to learn from books becomes useless.[26]

It is obvious in this second case that it would take an enormously longer time for civilisation to recover and reach again the same level of knowledge. Notice, by the way, Popper's mention of tools and machines here — he might well have included buildings — as well as libraries; and how both thought experiments require their destruction.

We might imagine on first thoughts that a theory of culture which emphasised evolution would be concerned precisely with the nature of tradition, and if it had any political flavour at all, that flavour would be conservative. (Nature does not, hence culture should not, make any jumps.) Nevertheless, as we have seen, an evolutionary theory of architectural history held a particular appeal for those nineteenth century writers and those modern movement architects whose aims were essentially revolutionary: to create a new style, free from historical precedent, free from the load of cultural baggage which was weighing the designer down.

The paradox is understood by appreciating how, if cultural evolution is compared directly with organic evolution, the whole World Three body of traditional knowledge and the historical accumulation of man-made products — precisely what constitutes culture, we might say — tend, like the human designer himself, to disappear. Cultural 'evolutionism' involves a strange denial of the very fact of culture.

Let me try to show how this phenomenon manifests itself in various aspects of modern design theory. (I am not suggesting here that the biological analogy is the *cause* or whole explanation of these other ideas; simply that it coincides or fits together with them into an (apparently) coherent larger theoretical structure.) The first of these aspects is a certain view of artistic language and artistic communication, as found for example in the writings of the Purists Ozenfant and Le Corbusier.

While allowing the inevitability of 'secondary' associations or significance attaching to geometric forms of any sort, the Purists were interested in the 'primary' qualities of pure geometry which could serve, as they believed, to provide the *mots fixes* of a visual language that would transcend particular cultures and would require no prior knowledge for its comprehension. The similar idea is to be found elsewhere in the theory of early-twentieth-century painting, in Expressionism, most notably in Kandinsky's writings, where the proposal is made, as Alan Colquoun puts it, that 'shapes have physiognomic or expressive interest which communicates itself to us directly'.[27] Such Expressionist theory no doubt had considerable impact on modern architectural philosophy, especially because of the abstract and non-representational nature of architectural forms and their composition.

For example, the functionalism of the modern movement taught that the meaning of a building and the meaning of its component elements could be made perfectly transparent and directly accessible. The meanings signified would be no more, and no less, than a communication and a demonstration of the social and utilitarian functions served. The building, it was thought, could 'mean' simply *what it was*; it would convey an explanation of its nature and purpose through its open legibility and lack of guile, even though its forms be completely unfamiliar and without precedent.

The Expressionist theory of artistic communication presupposes some direct sympathy or resonance (even 'vibrations') between artist and audience. It is a theory diametrically opposed to that of the greater part of modern linguistics, or of the formal mathematical theory of communication, which study the ways in which information or meaning is conveyed by the operation of conventionalised codes. Here forms acquire significance only by virtue of their relationships to the larger structures of meaning in which they are situated, and in the context of prior *expectations* established in the observer or recipient of a message by virtue of his acquaintance with the given code. The opposition of these theories has been most profoundly, as well as entertainingly, illuminated in relation to aesthetic philosophy by Gombrich.[28]

Because of the anxiety of the modern movement to sever its connections with 'the styles' and in particular to escape from the language of the Classical orders, it was anxious equally to escape from an acknowledgement that the communication of meaning in architecture might be dependent on evolved structures or codes which were the product of convention, of time, and of the general public experience of buildings of the past. (It is not without significance, I think, that Hannes Meyer, the arch-functionalist, was an enthusiast

Expressionist communication theory — objects
purely 'transparent' / self-evident / self reflexive

physiognomic, visceral/unmediated contact

for Esperanto, for a 'supranational language' (as too was Herbert Spencer). Meyer was also in favour of the use of shorthand, because it was 'a script with no tradition'.)[29] Thus an Expressionist view of 'direct' communication of meaning through forms with supposed universal significance, outside history and culture, would be a most attractive one.

Popper has not developed, in any very extensive way, the application of his theory of three worlds to the phenomenon of language, but he is perfectly clear that natural language is one of the most characteristic and important of World Three products. And it will be equally clear that whereas the whole view of language as a social product, dependent on convention and developed historically, is a quintessentially World Three conception — the subjective World Two of minds interacting with and via the relatively autonomous language structures of World Three — the Expressionist theory of communication, on the other hand, is one which excludes World Three, substituting some imagined direct interaction of one individual mind with another individual mind.

There is a second and closely related way in which culture, and Popper's World Three, tend to vanish from view in modern movement functionalism. This is in the picture (of a kind which we find well represented in Alexander's work) which it offers of the relationship of man to the natural environment. With the rejection of historical styles and traditional forms in architecture, the attention of designers was directed towards new consideration of the basic utilitarian functions of building: control of climate, the way in which the various 'biological' needs of the occupants — for light, fresh air, hygienic conditions and so on — are satisfied, the material and engineering problems of construction. It was from the basis of a fundamental analysis of these material and practical functions of building that, for someone like Hannes Meyer for example, the forms of the new architecture were to be derived. Thus architecture was seen in many respects in the role which the Erewhonian author saw for all material artefacts, constituting a kind of skin or outer layer interposed between man and nature, shielding him from environmental forces or disturbances.

health

Tools and buildings were conceived solely as instruments for achieving utilitarian goals which might all be ultimately referred to the principal goal of ensuring survival of the human species and reproduction of the social order (social organisation and human institutions being themselves thought of as 'adaptive' devices in the struggle against nature or in the competition with other human groups). We have seen Frederick Kiesler putting such a view quite explicitly: that tools and architecture form a 'technological environment' between man and his natural surroundings, and that this technology serves basic human needs, of which the most important, according to Kiesler, is physical health.

There is a tradition in anthropological theory, associated above all with the name of Bronislaw Malinowski, which has seen culture in precisely this light. Thus Malinowski writes, in *A Scientific Theory of Culture*:

> The problems set by man's nutritive, reproductive, and hygienic needs must be solved. They are solved by the construction of a new, secondary, or artificial environment. This environment, which is neither more nor less than culture itself, has to be permanently reproduced, maintained, and managed.[30]

*applying 'scientific theory' to culture*

The theory of culture, Malinowski says, must 'take its stand on biological fact'. The essential needs of man's physical body are first met by arrangements for 'feeding, heating, housing and clothing'; while at the same time provision must be made for protection against animal and human enemies, and against physical dangers. 'All these primary problems of human beings are solved for the individual by artifacts, organization into coöperative groups, and also by the development of knowledge, a sense of value and ethics.'[31]

The creation of tools, the building up of social structures and the acquisition of knowledge in order to meet the basic bodily requirements, set up a 'secondary type of determinism': institutions of education and tradition are required, to pass on the knowledge and to provide stability and continuity in the social order; other features of culture, for example political and judicial, are needed to ensure the integration of the social group so that it may function harmoniously as a productive and life-preserving system; even artistic and recreational activities can be related back directly, says Malinowski, 'to certain physiological characteristics of the human organism'.[32]

More recent work in anthropology which borrows an 'ecological' methodology from the study of animal behaviour continues in this kind of functionalist tradition which Malinowski represents.[33] Meanwhile an 'adaptive' theory of material culture and social organisation along similar lines has been developed in the last few years in archaeology, where efforts have been made to apply quantitative methods and modelling techniques to archaeological phenomena; as for example most comprehensively by David Clarke in his *Analytical Archaeology*.

*to anthropology*

Clarke draws extensively on cybernetics and turns particularly to Ashby for his formulation of a 'general model for archaeological processes'. This model envisages the culture of some particular people as a complex whole, which is in a state of continuous dynamic interaction with its environment. The term culture, in this context, is taken to mean the entire combination of social organisation, religious tradition, economic system and material culture, grouped together and regarded as a single grand system. In a phrase quoted by Clarke from Binford, it is 'the total extrasomatic means of adaptation'.[34]

*defn. of culture*

Culture acts, for Clarke, as a regulator, protecting itself and the individuals within it from the extreme effects of environmental change. That part of the

*[handwritten margin note: defining culture as sort of 'maintenance jacket' for Society for purposes of ensuring phys. survival]*

cultural system which serves this regulating function forms a kind of 'insulating' medium, as he terms it, between the members of the culture and the environment or context.

*[handwritten margin note: culture →]*

> The regulator blocks and filters the extreme range of external fluctuations by constraining their variety and maintaining the essential system parameters within certain limits. From the point of view of survival, systems integrating good regulating subsystems are better able to survive unchanged than similar systems with less efficient 'insulation'. Regulation controls the flow of variety from the environment to the system coupled to it. Much of social and material culture can be seen as in part exercising a regulating control over the effect of external and internal variations upon the system outcomes.[35]

This description relates quite clearly to the regulating or homeostatic function – identified by Cannon and modelled by Ashby – performed by the physiological mechanisms and by adaptations of behaviour in the individual; and it marks the extension of the same formal concept to cover culture generally.

We see that what Clarke has done is to represent the whole of some given culture as an adaptive system, which responds to the forces impinging on it from the environment ('environment' to include other, neighbouring cultures, as well as nature) by appropriate changes and reorganisations – these changes serving to maintain the stability and continuity of the culture (its 'homeostasis') and to increase its adaptedness for the particular circumstances. It is Clarke's argument that the information which is stored in and which passes through the cultural system serves the ultimate purposes of survival; that the total sum of cultural information, much greater than that which any one man could carry, confers 'fitness' on the group. The more efficiently and effectively a cultural system can convey this 'survival information' to the new individuals who carry it on, so the better fitted it will be, not only for continued existence, but for growth in numbers, diversification, and for exploiting progressively more difficult and unpromising environments. In Clarke's words: 'Cultural systems are therefore information systems of cumulatively acquired knowledge partly replacing instinctive behaviour in man and selectively advantageous in his struggle for survival.'[36]

The idea can be, and has been, criticised on two grounds. The first kind of criticism questions the extent to which a deterministic chain of causality can be claimed to reach from the necessities of biological survival to the varieties of cultural phenomena, particularly those such as the fine arts, religion or the more abstract sciences which are the remotest from utilitarian or economic activities. Marshall Sahlins, in a critique of anthropological functionalism, has argued that a 'law of diminishing returns' applies to functionalist explanations, so that

> the further removed the cultural fact from the sphere of utility to which it

is referred — the organic, the economic, the social — the fewer and more mediated must be the relations between this fact and the phenomena of that sphere; and consequently the fewer and less specific are the functional constraints on the nature of the custom under consideration. So the less determinate will be the explanation by functional virtues; or, conversely, the greater will be the range of alternative cultural practices that could equally (or even better) serve the same purpose.[37]

As Sahlins points out, the attempt at a utilitarian explanation of the nature of *language* on Malinowski's part led to a serious impoverishment, whereby words were conceived simply as tools with which to get a 'grip' on things, or as instruments with which to act upon other people.[38] Amongst modern 'sociobiologists' such as E. O. Wilson, language is similarly explained as serving an adaptive communication function, rather than as the means for constructing an autonomous world of signification with its own internal structure and relationships.[39] The effort to provide a biologically adaptive purpose for the arts led even further in the direction of trivialisation (as in Herbert Spencer's idea of art as a kind of recreation or pastime).

Our interest in the present study is in material artefacts serving largely practical functions, and clearly these would lie, along Sahlins's notional spectrum, at the end closest to the 'sphere of utility'. Even the most highly developed works of architecture still serve, amongst other purposes, the basic functions of enclosure and protection from the elements. And in primitive societies no doubt the primary use of many artefacts was directly in helping man cope in his struggle against natural forces, and in modifying the natural environment. What this view fails to represent, however, is the way in which, as society becomes more advanced technically, becomes materially more highly developed, so the greater part of the 'environment' with which the individual is in contact even indirectly is not a natural environment any more, by a man-made one. As Herbert Simon says, 'The very species upon which man depends for his food — his corn and his cattle — are artifacts of his ingenuity. A ploughed field is no more part of nature than an asphalted street — and no less.'[40]

Indeed, many of the artefacts produced in modern society are not artefacts which protect man immediately from the forces of nature (like raincoats, or even houses); but are artefacts which enable him to deal with other artefacts (like tin-openers, or pencil sharpeners), or, more importantly, artefacts which help him deal with other men (such as books and telephones, or money). Instead of imagining man and his natural environment as interacting and this interaction being mediated or buffered by material artefacts, it would be more reasonable to present a picture of civilised man as living in an environment largely of his own creation, constituted by artefacts, with the natural environment existing alongside or else outside and beyond this manmade world.

Thus, although many artefacts may have originally had functions which were very largely concerned with immediate matters of economic necessity — and it is arguable that this was true of primitive language — as time goes by and material culture develops, so this world of material objects progressively acquires for itself a degree of autonomy and independence; it creates its own internal 'problems' and its own dynamic. The similar point is made specifically by Popper in relation to 'objective knowledge': that while the first functions served by the social communication of knowledge might have been in coping with the contingent practical difficulties of daily life, at a later stage and certainly within the framework of organised science the pursuit of knowledge is regulated, as Popper says, rather 'by the idea of truth, or of getting nearer to the truth . . . than the idea of helping us to survive'.[41]

Though Popper promotes an image of the growth of scientific knowledge which is loosely analogous to organic evolution — in that 'competing' hypotheses are subjected to critical test, and those which are best able to withstand that criticism (the 'fittest') will be retained, will survive — he is quick to point out that this has no necessary or simple relationship to human survival in general. 'I did not state that the fittest hypothesis is always the one which helps our own survival. I said, rather, that the fittest hypothesis is the one which best solves the *problem* it was designed to solve.'[42] Popper makes this argument in relation to scientific knowledge; and he draws a sharp distinction in this context between the nature of the growth of 'pure knowledge' on the one hand, and the growth of applied knowledge together with the evolution of tools and material artefacts (in whose design the knowledge is applied) on the other. This distinction is to do with the fact that pure knowledge evolves, or is evolved, in the direction of greater generalisation and ever increasing integration of previously disparate areas of understanding.

The evolution of applied knowledge and of artefacts, meanwhile, is in an opposite direction, always differentiating into increasing numbers of ever more specialised applications (in the case of knowledge) or into specialised instruments for ever more particular purposes (in the case of tools and machines). As Popper says, the overall trends of these two contrasting types of 'evolutionary' change — in science and in technology — had both been remarked on by Herbert Spencer[43] (although Spencer's universal law of evolution does not in itself acknowledge such a distinction, suggesting on the contrary that evolution in all fields was in the same general direction).

By drawing attention to the differences between 'the evolutionary tree of instruments and that of pure knowledge', Popper says that he hopes to offer 'something like a refutation of the now so fashionable view that human knowledge can only be understood as an instrument in our struggle for survival'.[44] I am not quite sure whether Popper intends to imply by this opposition that the purposes of material artefacts *are* by contrast exclusively to aid human survival; but I am inclined to think that he must not. Elsewhere, for example, he talks of the 'autonomy' of the work of art, and the idea that the art of painting, regarded as a whole, creates its own internal relationships and problems.[45] Artistic aims in general, he says, are 'independent of the aim to survive'.

It appears possible to envisage an equivalent 'Popperian' view of the evolution of useful artefacts along the lines of his conception of both artistic and scientific development, which is by no means *wholly* or even largely directed towards or constrained by matters of simple physical survival. Even organic evolution, Popper believes, does not necessarily and universally lead to 'what may be called "utilitarian" results',[46] and this is all the more true of the evolution of culture. In the history of art the production of previous artists, and the previous output of the individual himself, will give rise to problems. The artist will pursue solutions to these problems, which are subject to a selective process, are subject to criticism, in the light of artistic aims and standards. In Popper's words, 'our aims can change and . . . *the choice of an aim may become a problem*; different aims may compete, and new aims may be invented and controlled by the method of trial and error-elimination.'[47]

In the equivalent picture of technology, we would have an evolving world of useful artefacts which acquires its own internal problems and aims and its own internal criteria for choices made between those aims. Its direction and development would not be controlled by 'selective forces' to do with human survival, but would be constrained by other factors arising from the previous course of technological history and its problems. Clarke's archaeological theory does not deny tradition in one sense; it acknowledges the existence of an inherited body of cultural information — indeed it assigns this a crucial role. But it does deny to material culture this autonomy, this 'life of its own'; and it sees all artefacts in a wholly utilitarian light, as forming nothing more than an elaborate 'life-support system'.

The second ground for criticising the biologically 'adaptive' and functionalist theory of culture is if anything a more fundamental one. It turns on the argument that the central feature of culture is language, and that through language man imposes onto the natural world a structure of cultural and symbolic *meaning* by which the 'utilitarian' or the 'economic' is defined in the first place. It is not some universal and unavoidable problems of practical necessity, imposed by man's biology and by the natural environment, which are responded to and solved with the use of cultural instruments, in this view. It is the conceptual categories of culture itself which originally create the ostensibly 'practical' problems — this practicality being largely a matter of cultural choice, and only in a minor way constrained by real material or biological necessity.

As Sahlins expresses the opposition of these two alternatives, it is a matter of

whether the cultural order is to be conceived as the codification of man's actual purposeful and pragmatic action; or whether, conversely, human action in the world is to be understood as mediated by the cultural design, which gives order at once to practical experience, customary practice, and the relationship between the two.[48]

*determinism*

This kind of criticism of the 'biological' position does not deny that certain material conditions are ultimately necessary for the continuation of human life: adequate food supplies, bodily warmth, a certain freedom from disease and so on. What it does claim is that the limitations placed by the fulfilment of these conditions on the *possibilities* for social organisation, for systems of economic production, for the apparatus of technology, are very loose ones. Man must eat to live: but he can (in most parts of the world) choose to eat any of a great variety of animal or plant species; he can prepare these foods in any of an almost infinite number of combinations, by a great range of cooking methods; and he can serve them according to social conventions governing the timing of meals, their setting, their polite forms and ceremonials and so on, which have very little or nothing to do with the biological function of nutrition, but which have a great deal to do with the cultural meanings with which the whole process is invested and according to which it is organised. It follows that all the 'economic' activities, of agriculture, the manufacture of agricultural tools and cooking utensils, the trading of foodstuffs, and so on, which are created to supply the alimentary 'needs' of society, all stem from what are at bottom a set of *cultural* choices. Instead of there being a deterministic relation between the biological necessity and the cultural form, biology serves only to set extreme limits on the cultural; it provides a 'negative determination', as Sahlins puts it, of the realm of cultural possibilities.[49]

## 15

# What remains of the analogy? The history and science of the artificial

What remains then, that is useful and true, out of the variety of analogies made between biology and the applied arts? It will help to clarify matters if the answer to this question is divided into two parts, the one concerned with history, the other with science. Indeed the confusion as to whether a theory of the design of artefacts should or could be a scientific as opposed to a historical theory is something which has bedevilled biological analogies since they were first formulated — as this account has, I hope, shown. In making this division I propose to differentiate between history and science in terms of the *actual*, as against the *possible*. As W. C. Kneale has said,

> it seems possible to maintain that science should be distinguished from history (in the largest sense of that word), not as the study of universal truths from the study of singular truths, but rather as the study of what is possible or impossible from the study of what has been or actually is the case. Speaking metaphorically, we may say that science is about the frame of nature, while history is about the content.[1]

The biological analogy, despite its association with functionalist and historicist fallacies, leaves us with an overall picture of the history of technology — particularly in its earlier phases — which can, I believe, still be extremely helpful in guiding theory and research.

The starting point from which the 'evolutionary' aspects of the analogy began was the simple fact that in the production of many artefacts, especially in the craft or vernacular traditions, one object is very often *copied* in its design (perhaps with minor differences) from another. The truth of this observation is not altered by any of the criticisms of the last two chapters. The fact of copying gives rise to a *continuity* in form and appearance, when the 'genetic' links are followed between a series of artefacts successively copied, each from the last. The characteristic form of the artefact may undergo a gradual *transformation* as a result of the small alterations introduced at each stage. The fact of many similar artefacts being thus produced with related but not identical forms (and functions) results in the appearance of what may be termed 'populations' of objects, amongst which it may be possible to identify 'types' according either to functional or to morphological criteria.

There may be geographical 'diffusion' of these populations, as a result of the objects (or the knowledge of how to make them) being carried by migrating artisans, or being transported through trade, capture in war and so on. It is perhaps possible for the series formed by repeated copyings to diverge into two or more branches, such that later members along the divided branches are functionally and formally quite distinct. (It may also be possible for branches to converge; this is a point we will come back to.) Thus far, to the extent to which a biological metaphor fits the case, it is not seriously misleading.

A programme something along these lines was proposed for the study of man-made objects by the critic George Kubler, in his *The Shape of Time: Remarks on the History of Things*.[2] Kubler in turn drew inspiration both from the work of the anthropologist Kroeber,[3] and from Henri Focillon's *Vie des Formes*,[4] which Kubler calls 'the boldest and most poetic affirmation of a biological conception of the nature of the history of art'.[5] Focillon's concern was exclusively with the fine arts; with the 'internal' laws by which the forms employed in art are governed and organised, and how they develop in time. But Kubler defines his area of interest to include tools and other useful objects, and the purpose of his book is 'to draw attention to some of the morphological problems of duration in series and sequence'.[6] A further purpose is to offer some corrective or counter-balance to the amount of attention given in twentieth-century art history to iconographical study, to the relative neglect of formal or morphological questions.

This emphasis throughout is on continuity in the history of the forms of artefacts, as they are replicated and their designs transmitted so as to produce sequences which may extend in some instances over extremely long periods. 'Everything made now', Kubler says, 'is either a replica or a variant of something made a little time ago and so on back without break to the first morning of human time.'[7] He introduces the notion of a 'prime' object, which possesses a degree of novelty and original invention in its form (it is a 'mutant'); to be distinguished from the mass of replicas in which the same form is reproduced and perhaps degraded.[8] Certain sets of objects or works may be grouped into 'form-classes'. Complex objects may be made up from assemblies of separate parts or 'traits', each with its own sequential development.

> The closest definition of a formal sequence that we can now venture is to affirm it as a historical network of gradually altered repetitions of the same trait. The sequence might therefore be described as having an armature. In cross section let us say that it shows a network, a mesh, or a cluster of subordinate traits; and in long section that it has a fiber-like structure of temporal stages, all recognisably similar, yet altering in their mesh from beginning to end.[9]

like a 3-D Escher dwg.

David Clarke in *Analytical Archaeology* has lately offered a theoretical approach to the treatment of archaeological material which has many affinities with Kubler's proposals, but is set within a more precisely quantitative and statistical framework and supported by some applications to real data. The validity of this part of Clarke's work is not in my view affected by the criticisms made of his 'general model' in the last chapter; although this method, as we shall see, is essentially descriptive only, and provides no real explanation of the phenomena involved.

The central image in Clarke's work in this respect is of a population of artefacts (or perhaps of larger aggregations of artefacts) distributed in space (both in physical space and in abstract 'classificatory space'), and undergoing gradual transformation in time, through growth or decline in numbers, through change in possession of different attributes, and thus through a gradual transition from one artefact type to another.[10]

In making such an analysis, the need for independent means of dating, other than the criteria of typological similarity or morphological relationship themselves, is paramount if the danger of circularity in the argument is to be avoided. This point is made strongly by Childe[11] — perhaps in reaction to the progressive evolutionism of the nineteenth century — when he emphasises how chronological evidence will be decisive in determining the evolutionary relationship in each instance, whether it represents a transformation towards more efficient or more complex and elaborated forms, perhaps, or whether it is alternatively a degenerating or 'devolutionary' series (as with the Celtic coins studied by Evans, for example).

Taking a single type of artefact, the known occurring examples may be tabulated by their typological characteristics and by their occurrence in time to yield a description of the changes occurring in that type. Clarke describes the kind of pattern of change which might be expected in some highly idealised hypothetical case.[12] At each period of time, or 'phase', there is a population of artefacts distributed normally around a dominant category and for each particular category or characteristic combination of attributes possessed by the artefact, there is a process of gradual increase in numbers over time, from rather few to a point where the category is dominant and most numerous, and then dwindling away again to disappearance.

Thus at each stage there is, in this very simplified and regular idealisation, a dominant category for the artefact type, and there are most examples to be found of this dominant form. But at the same time there are some rather fewer numbers of residual representatives of now 'archaic' and disappearing categories, and there are correspondingly a few representatives of emerging, new and 'prototypical' forms. Clarke has produced detailed empirical evidence, from finds of pottery and flint tools, to show the application of this theoretical model to actual data.[13] And he has other examples of a comparable process, in which the individual attributes of more complex artefacts, such as the decorative motifs on pottery and gravestones, are shown to lie in a similar 'lenticular' distribution about a moving modal form.[14]

What Kubler and Clarke provide us with is a descriptive account of historical sequence in the development of artefact types, and means for describing their morphological change. We have learned from the argument of previous chapters to reject the idea that there is any simple or single *necessary* direction to such changes, or any deterministic character to the process of change in itself. Why then is it that directional changes *are* to be observed in certain sequences of objects – as is undoubtedly the case?

A number of possibilities present themselves. The first is a rather speculative suggestion: that there is some feature of the actual *process* of copying, as applied to particular forms, which results in similar distortions – the same *kind* of miscopying, in effect – being introduced at every stage. This explanation is essentially a psychological one. There is something in the way in which certain forms are perceived and reproduced by copyists which gives rise to (unconscious yet systematic) transformations, conforming to some regular trend. My own copying experiments with drawings (see chapter 7) have demonstrated this effect at a perhaps rather trivial level. In a different field, that of linguistics, it is well established that highly regular types of change occur historically in pronunciation, for example, in the same direction in separate languages and in a way which is unrelated to changes in meaning.

A second possible cause of such systematic trends is to do with the play of fashion. This is an area which has been brilliantly illuminated from a theoretical point of view by Gombrich; as in his essay 'The Logic of Vanity Fair'.[15] The arts as much as economic life may be the scene of competition, in which each artist or craftsman strives to outdo his predecessors in the production of certain results or impressions. One example familiar from the evolutionary histories of architecture might, as Gombrich points out, be very plausibly interpreted in this light:[16] the sequence of French Gothic cathedrals, specifically the progressive increase in the heights of their naves, from 114 feet at Notre Dame, to 119 at Chartres, to 124 feet at Rheims, to 138 feet at Amiens. The sequence culminates in the spectacular attempt to vault the choir at Beauvais at a height of 157 feet; a project ending in disaster. The towers built by rival families in some Tuscan towns such as San Gimignano offer another precisely comparable case.

From the sublime to the (often) ridiculous, a field notoriously liable to competitive trends of this kind is the design of women's clothing – the subject of a celebrated quantitative study made by Kroeber in collaboration with Jane Richardson.[17] It might be expected that sequences here would be extremely fickle; however, by measuring the positions of hemlines, waistlines and necklines over a period of three centuries, Kroeber and Richardson were able to show a regular fluctuation in the dimensions of dresses, moving back and forth between limits set by the constraints of decency at one extreme, and complete coverage of the body at the other. Clarke has a sequence illustrating the elaboration of decoration on English grandfather clocks between the seventeenth and nineteenth centuries which might be interpreted in similar terms; from a simple and austere treatment, to baroque elaboration, and back to simplicity.[18]

Gombrich shows how these competitive trends are subject to a kind of artistic 'inflation', by which the attempts to achieve ever more pronounced and emphatic effects in themselves devalue the currency in which they are bought. 'Competition for attention can lead to the unintended consequence of simply lowering the value of what you have been doing before.'[19] For this reason, as well as owing to technical limitations, the competitive spiral may lead to a crisis, at which the sequence abruptly ends. Alternatively, the excesses provoked in the one-upmanship of fashion may themselves create the circumstance in which a striking impression may be produced by moving in the exact opposite direction. Where a flamboyant luxuriance of decoration is the norm, then an unadorned purity of form will seem all the more dramatic. So the pendulum swings back once more.

There is a third possible cause of directional sequence in changes of artefact design, which for our subject here is by far the most important. It is to do with actual technical improvements, increases in the efficiency or performance of utilitarian objects or machines. We do not have to attribute any automatism to the process, nor do we have to deny the imaginative contributions of individual designers, to allow that repeated attempts to design some specific type of tool or apparatus may be progressively more successful in achieving the desired practical ends. Thus the first steam engines might have been ramshackle, inefficient and unreliable, whereas later models incorporated many improvements, to increase speed, power, strength or economy.

Such sequences of technical progress might in principle arise in two ways. The end-point of the series might be consciously envisaged by the craftsman or engineer from the beginning, with each successive try reaching nearer and nearer towards that goal. Gombrich offers two examples of this: the aeroplane, where the general ambition to make a powered flying machine long preceded the development of the requisite material and engineering means; and an example drawn from his own special area of interest, the evolution of technical means in painting for the achievement of a realistic illusion of the third dimension.[20] These processes of technical change, as Gombrich says, are thus genuinely 'Lamarckian' in the way in which their direction is the result of deliberate efforts to meet some perceived 'need' or to achieve some practical intention.

Alternatively, a series of unanticipated discoveries might occur along the course of the development of the object, which might be recognised to offer improvements and would thus be incorporated. 'Once bronze was shown to cut better than stones, iron better than bronze and steel better than iron, these alternatives had only to be invented and presented for rational men to use them for their cutting tools.'[21]

Instead of attributing increases in efficiency (or 'fitness') in artefacts to selection exercised by some abstract 'functional environment', this view brings attention back to the designer himself, and the rational choices which he makes amongst available technical means so as to achieve definite practical ends. The designer finds himself in a specific historical situation, facing some particular *problem*. He responds to the logic of that situation with some design solution, and this in itself produces a change in the problem: it creates a new problem. Meanwhile parallel developments in other technologies change the repertoire of possible materials, manufacturing methods, mechanical devices, components, and so on, available to the designer; and social or cultural changes perhaps alter the functional demands which the artefact is designed to meet. Both Popper and Gombrich have argued in favour of an 'analysis of situations' in some such terms as a methodological alternative to historicist theories and an answer to their 'poverty' — Popper for the social sciences, Gombrich for the history of art and by extension for technological and design history.[22]

Henri Focillon has given an account of our favourite evolutionary topic, Gothic architecture and its engineering, according to essentially this method.[23] He treats developments in cathedral construction as a series of *experiments*, the results of each one informing the next. 'By experiment', he says, 'I mean an investigation that is supported by prior knowledge, based upon a hypothesis, conducted with intelligent reason, and carried out in the realm of technique.' Some experiments may have been inconclusive, wasted. Others showed the feasibility of various structural expedients, such as the flying buttress or certain variants of the ribbed vault. It should not be assumed that the logic according to which the results were judged was wholly an engineering logic; it might be the 'logic of the eye', or the 'logic of the intellect', all of which might either coincide, or be in conflict.

> But it is, nevertheless, admissible to suppose that the experiments of Gothic art, bound powerfully one to the other, and in their royal progress discarding all solutions that were either hazardous or unpromising, constitute by their very sequence and concatenation a kind of logic — an irresistible logic that eventually expresses itself in stone with a classic decisiveness.[24]

Another period in the history of architecture of which we might imagine an account being profitably made through an analysis of its 'situational logic' is the development of the skyscraper office building in the Chicago of the 1880s and 1890s. Such an analysis would treat the basic problem set by restricted sites, the constraints of the requirement for daylight, the economic demand for a maximum of floor space; the mechanical inventions required to make buildings of such a height possible — principally the elevator and new designs of foundation; the limits of masonry construction, and their transcendence with the introduction of the steel frame; the contribution of electric light, fireproofing, improvements in plumbing; the competitive element in the drive towards even greater heights.

In general we can see that an approach to 'artificial history' through the logic of situations can provide an understanding of progressive development in the technical aspects, without resort to any deterministic theory of the necessity of one step following upon another. There is a *logic of priorities*, by which it is necessary for certain inventions or discoveries to be made before others are possible (thus the construction of the high-speed computer, though its principles were worked out a century earlier, had to wait on certain developments in electronics; or, another example, the pneumatic tyre exploited prior progress in the technology of vulcanising rubber). Again the logic of the matter clearly demands, in the kind of sequence represented by the substitution of stone by iron by bronze by steel in cutting instruments, that the historical order follow the relative merits of the materials in question. But this logic only defines the *preconditions* under which opportunities for various new technological 'moves' are created, and it does not determine their nature or future direction.

To sum up: the explanations of artefact sequences made according to a situational logic will be related to the cultural and social circumstances in which the demand for the artefact is created and given meaning; to the constraints imposed on design by technological and material means available at each historical juncture; and to the body of knowledge, scientific or otherwise, by which the designer is informed and on the basis of which his design 'hypotheses' are made and tested. Changes in form, and the emergence of 'types', will be the result of processes which represent responses to *problems*, and which must be referred to *purposes*. The study of typology and morphology *by themselves* (which is in effect what Clarke proposes) provide no such explanation, and, as Kubler says, avoid 'the principal aim of history, which ... has been to identify and reconstruct the particular problems to which any action or thing must correspond as a solution'.[25]

If the craft tradition provides many examples of nicely graduated series in which the changes in the forms of artefacts are small and slow, it is nevertheless easy, and increasingly so with the advance of technology, to point to abrupt transitions, radical innovations, large jumps which serve to break these sequences and which leave the analogy with biological evolution rather hard to sustain. It is quite beyond the scope of this study to try to give any theoretical account of the processes of technical invention or the nature of creativity in design — which are large enough subjects for books in their own right. Perhaps at the most general level, however, without going very far into the psychology of the question, it is possible to attribute radical novelty in the design of artefacts to two kinds of mental operation.

The first is through existing parts or components of a designed object, themselves perhaps produced by slow processes of technical evolution, being put together into new arrangements: a principle of *fusion* and/or *recombination*. Included within this category would be the kinds of inventive process alluded to briefly in chapter 6, by which new types of object are created by the amalgamation of two or more old ones: the convergence of several lines in the family tree of artefact evolution. Where the designer has access to a substantial body of information about artefacts from cultures remote both geographically and historically from his own, then even if he replicates such designs in their entirety (like the facsimile of the Parthenon in Nashville, Tennessee), the chain of copying is by this fact enabled to cross large gaps in time and space; and if he recombines elements or parts of designs drawn from many eclectic sources, the sequences become correspondingly more complex.

The second operation depends in a different way on the accumulation of historical cultural and scientific knowledge. Empirical experience of a range of related designs provides a body of knowledge and understanding on the basis of which it is possible to build a generalised *theory* of that class of artefacts, and so use the theory to extrapolate, beyond the tried cases, to hypothetical but related designs as yet not constructed.

An imaginary example drawn from the history of cookery may serve to illustrate these ideas. We might suppose that in primitive, stable or isolated cultures, culinary recipes are transmitted from one generation to the next with changes occurring only gradually (perhaps occasioned by the changing availability of different foodstuffs, changes in cooking technology, the vagaries of fashion in eating habits, etc.); so that the 'artefact sequence' represented by the succession of many versions of the same meal would show a genuinely evolutionary character. (Notice, incidentally, the very clear illustration which this example offers of the distinction between the inherited 'design', the recipe — in biological terms the 'genotype' — and the particular individual artefacts, the meals — or 'phenotypes' — in which the recipe is realised. Also the description of the dish which the recipe constitutes comprises no representation of what it tastes like, or even necessarily any picture of what it looks like, but only a set of instructions by which to make it.) Each generation of cooks makes the dish 'like mother used to make it', in the sure knowledge that by following the same procedure it will come out just as before.

When cooks become aware of recipes from other countries or other historical periods than their own — perhaps through the circulation of printed cookery books — then they are freed from the limitations of their particular traditional culinary culture, and they can experiment with an eclectic cuisine, perhaps combining separate elements of dishes from different regions and traditions. These combinations may be more or less successful, to the degree to which the cook can achieve a coherence, a 'correlation of the parts'. The creation of wholly new dishes, and not just minor rearrangements of existing ones, will be dependent on the cook having a general understanding of the *principles* of different cooking processes, of the chemical and biological reactions, perhaps, which various ingredients undergo, and of the general kinds of effect and taste which novel combinations and treatments will produce. As the prophet of scientific gastronomy, Brillat-Savarin, put it:

> The sciences are not like Minerva, who sprang fully armed from the brain of Jupiter; they are daughters of time, and take shape imperceptibly, first, by the combination of methods learned from experience, and later by the discovery of principles derived from the combination of these methods.[26]

We might say in general of the transition from craft procedures to 'selfconscious' methods that empirical knowledge, gradually codified perhaps into scientific knowledge, about the performance of actual past designs begins to allow predictions to be made about the engineering performance of new, hypothetical designs which differ substantially from tested precedent — so much so as to make a simple slight extrapolation unreliable. In the craft tradition, since there are no radical departures from the repeated type, it is possible for artefacts to be made which are technically very sophisticated, which exploit physical principles, chemical processes or the properties of materials in very subtle ways — but without any of their makers having any *theoretical* understanding of how these effects are achieved. The principles have been discovered empirically, and *are embodied in the inherited design*. We might speak, in a sense, of information being conveyed within the forms of the artefacts themselves. The craftsman knows how to make the object, he follows the traditional procedure (the recipe); but in many respects he literally *does not know what he is doing*.

It is rather in the nature of the problem that evidence for these observations is somewhat hard to come across, since we have little recorded documentary evidence from craftsmen of their actual methods of working; and, of course, they will in any case not have set down what they themselves do not know. Here and there it is possible, nevertheless, to pick up scraps of information which are sufficient to demonstrate beyond much doubt that these assertions are broadly true. These instances are mostly cases where the change is actually being made from a craft-based design process to a more consciously theory-based approach; and the actual individuals who have made this transition in their own lifetime are able to articulate what has happened.

Possibly the most striking illustration of this kind is provided by George

Sturt's remarkable and fascinating book *The Wheelwright's Shop*, to which new attention has been drawn by the design theorist Christopher Jones, among others.[27] Sturt worked building farm wagons in the nineteenth century, and the book is his collected reminiscences, written at a time (the 1920s) when the old craft was finally disappearing. It provides a detailed testimony to the role of traditional technique – the knowledge of how, but without the knowledge of why – passed on from craftsman to craftsman, in preserving the continuity of tried and tested forms.

From what Sturt says it appears that the detailed information required for the construction of this extremely complex and subtly designed object, the wagon – no one timber of which was straight or square, but all precisely curved and tapered – was not stored in written records or in drawings at all, except for a few templates for particular components. Instead the information was stored in the heads of the wheelwrights, in their almost instinctive skills in cutting and shaping each piece; stored as an accumulated body of lore and tradition, shared between many men; learnt, through apprenticeship, either by verbal rules, or as physical actions and through the sequences of steps required to make each different part of the work; and stored above all in the shapes of existing wagons themselves, which were there to copy and to follow.

With certain features of the designs, it is quite clear from Sturt's account that no one, no one at all, knew their explanation, not even Sturt himself, although he was an educated man in charge of the shop and had many years of learning from the example of master craftsmen. It took him years of reasoning and reflection to appreciate exactly why it was that a wheel must be 'dished' to a certain degree, what it was that fixed the diameter of wheels or the particular curve or taper of each plank. The experienced craftsman knew that these features were necessary, but did not question them or understand their meaning analytically.

> There was nothing for it but practice and experience of every difficulty. Reasoned science for us did not exist. 'Theirs is not to reason why.' What we had to do was to live and work to the measurements, which had been tested and corrected long before our time in every village shop across the country.[28]

An equivalent example to that of Sturt, in the field of ship-building, is provided by J. S. Russell, who acted as naval architect to Brunel on the Great Eastern (an unhappy collaboration), and who was the author of the first systematic treatise on his subject in English, a magnificent book entitled *The Modern System of Naval Architecture*.[29] Russell had seen a revolution in the building of large ships during his own career, the change from timber construction to iron, and from sailing ships to steam propulsion. He had also been instrumental in the creation of the new profession of naval architecture, distinct from the craft of ship-building; and he makes the – not unexpected –

analogy with the equivalent professional and craft distinction in the design of buildings.* The new naval architect will work by science, calculation, 'headwork', where the craftsman worked by imitation, by copying and by inherited, manual skills.[30]

The need for theoretical texts such as his own, Russell says, is occasioned by the enormous changes in scale, techniques and materials of ship construction, to which the traditional methods and craft knowledge have become inapplicable. Only by means of a theoretical, scientific understanding can the performance of new unbuilt designs of ships be predicted with accuracy. In fact, as Russell recounts, a great number of the early experiments during the 1820s with large iron ships had been disasters — ships which overturned on launching, ships calamitously underpowered, ships whose stability could be ensured only by adding extra floats or masses of cement ballast. The design of these vessels had been based on erroneous rules of thumb, and on principles supposedly drawn from traditional boat-building experience but which were as it turned out 'misknown, and misbelieved, and mistaught'.[31] The true but only tacitly known principles of the old craft techniques had been lost or ignored and were only to be rediscovered through scientific experiment and calculation (for example, by Russell's own work in hydrodynamics, and that of such contemporaries as Froude, Griffiths and others). As Russell says:

> The forms and proportions of ships, prescribed by traditional knowledge, and universally employed in the early parts of this century, have either ceased to exist, or are preserved as relics. Some even of the principles, which prescribed these forms, and were called Science, have lost their hold on the minds of men, and are abandoned.[32]

Our earlier example from cookery provides another case in point. It is quite possible to bake bread, to brew beer or to make an omelette without the slightest chemical knowledge of the (extremely complex) reactions and biological processes which go on in each case. The same is true of those 'recipes' which are used in the building trade. Vitruvius gives a detailed account of the chemical reactions of lime and of pozzolana when they are mixed with water for making mortar and concrete — an account which is, as one might imagine from the general state of Roman chemical theory, completely erroneous.[33] This was unimportant so long as the means of manufacture and the structural characteristics of these building materials were known by empirical experience.

* The car designer Raymond Dietrich has described how he and his colleague T. L. Hibbard, who together set up LeBaron Carrossiers in the early 1920s, wanted to make the break from the carriage-building tradition which had continued to dominate car body design technique up to that date; and how they turned for their model to the design process in architecture. 'We wanted to be to cars what architects are to buildings.' 'The Dietrich Story — Part 1', *Veteran and Vintage* (February, 1974), 156–62.

It is an implication of this general point — that in craft production a degree of knowledge relating to effective or well-adapted designs is embodied in the craft products themselves and in traditional methods of manufacture, without that knowledge being appreciated or recorded consciously — that if the craft techniques and forms are abruptly abandoned, then that knowledge, acquired through many generations of trial and error, is altogether and unwittingly lost. (The effect is the same as in Popper's 'thought experiments', where tools and machines were destroyed along with libraries.) It is not *necessarily* assimilated, in its entirety, into the consciously held analytical, scientific body of knowledge, set down in writing, which informs the self-conscious designer or engineer who replaces the craftsman and who works from principle rather than precedent. Russell's account of nineteenth-century ship-building illustrates this point.

When new designs are made which represent substantial departures from precedent, and where there is no opportunity for the testing of these designs in the real world through constructing prototypes — as in the case of buildings, civil engineering works, large and costly 'one-off' machines and vehicles, and so on — then it becomes necessary to make certain theoretical *predictions* during the course of the design process about their anticipated performance. These predictions may be of a more or less specific or precise nature. They will have to do with the appearance of the artefact; with its physical behaviour in certain respects (perhaps strengths of structural members, weather-resisting properties of materials, the physics of the heating or lighting of buildings, whatever it may be); with the way in which people will use the object or building or behave in relation to it, how they will perceive it, even what their aesthetic judgements about it may be.

It would be reasonable to expect that such predictions would be more difficult to make, and less trustworthy (though no less important, for that) towards the psychological and aesthetic end of this range, and more reliable towards the geometrical, material and physical end. Indeed the predictions in these latter respects may be based in time on scientific knowledge of the properties of materials and structures, and the principles governing the behaviour of classes of related designs, of which the artefact in question represents one instance. This scientific knowledge is of course a formalisation, a generalisation and an extension of the empirical knowledge gained originally through the trial-and-error processes of the craft tradition — developed and tested perhaps in programmes of deliberate controlled experiment. We can see how an increase in generalised or scientific knowledge about the performance of artefacts in these physical and material aspects may be the cause of a departure from craft methods, since it opens up opportunities for radical innovation. At the same time, looked at in another way, such knowledge may be called for precisely because of the breakdown or abandonment of craft procedures (as in the case of hydrodynamics and ship design in the nineteenth century).

I offered the suggestion, in a previous chapter, that the architects and design theorists of the modern movement were guilty, in the view which they took of scientific method, of falling into the 'inductive fallacy'. A second related misunderstanding about science and about its possible applications in design has been that somehow design method could be made scientific, and that there was some possibility of an equation of *design method* with *scientific method*. Whatever parallels might be made between design and scientific procedures in terms of Popper's scheme of alternating hypothesis and test, of 'conjecture and refutation', the fact is that the nature and purpose of the two enterprises are fundamentally distinct. Design is concerned with making unique material objects to answer to specific purposes; while science is concerned with making statements about the characteristic behaviour of general classes of objects or phenomena under given conditions, and defining the limits on these classes and this behaviour. The relationship of the two has been made very clear by Lionel March in his essay 'The Logic of Design'.[34]

If the modern movement theorists had actually gone to the engineers whom they admired and asked them how they went about the business of design, the engineers would have told them that, in all but the simplest and most highly constrained problems, their methods involved essentially the same element of intuition and speculation as did architecture or the applied arts. The key difference between the design processes of engineers and architects was not in the logic of their respective design methods, which was largely the same, but in the body of scientific knowledge which informed and constrained design in either case. The engineers were, and are, the possessors of a body of scientific theory about structures and machines; and it is this body of understanding which provides them with their design hypotheses, with their first preliminary sketch proposals or germinal ideas for designs. Furthermore, once an initial sketch is somewhat developed and begins to be filled out with detail, then the body of scientific understanding is brought to bear again, because it is in the light of this knowledge and the predictions of performance which it allows that the proposed design can be reliably and rigorously criticised and tested and accordingly modified.

The architects were unable to make use of science in architecture, because there was no science *of* architecture – or at least only a rather undeveloped science. That is to say, there did not exist, nor does there exist, a corpus of knowledge of a scientific kind at an abstract level about classes of existing and hypothetical buildings and their behaviour which can be compared with the mechanical and structural theory of the engineers.

This is not to say that *no* body of general or collective knowledge ('World Three' knowledge) exists in architecture. It quite evidently does, in what is transmitted in architectural education, in architectural literature and, not least, embodied in the designs of existing and historical buildings themselves. But such knowledge is not, with certain areas of exception, of an organised, explicit, communally available and, most important, *scientific* nature. The exceptions are provided by the findings of what has traditionally been distinguished as 'building science': studies of building performance in relation to physical and meteorological environment, the properties of building materials, and the engineering behaviour of architectural structures. If we are to talk about an architectural science in more general terms, then certainly such a science must start from, and incorporate, this existing building science.

We are brought back to the questions which I posed in chapter 1: how far can and should the project of a building or architectural science extend? More generally, what are the features or properties of artefacts of all kinds to which scientific study should be directed, and about which scientific predictions might be made?

My answers will necessarily have to be abbreviated and tentative ones. First, I suggest that, if we are to interpret the history of artefacts through a 'logic of situations', then we must accept as a corollary that certain features of artefacts, of their perception and mode of use by those who experience and employ them, are *in principle* beyond the reach of scientific predictions. The particular meanings which attach to artefacts, the aims which they serve, the exact ways in which they are seen and evaluated aesthetically, hence to some extent people's behaviour in relation to them, are all products of the specific historical situations in which the objects or buildings are made and from which the observers or users come, and they are changed at every step by the new problems which those situations throw up and by the new and individual responses which those problems evoke.

The relation between the observer and the work of art or man-made object is mediated by the cultural structures of World Three; and these structures, and the meanings which they generate, are continually being transformed. We do not have to espouse a complete aesthetic relativism – as Gombrich shows – to accept that, because of our education and our awareness of history, every 'move', the appearance of every new work, alters the context in which we understand and appreciate not only that work itself, but in principle all other works as well.[35] Kubler calls this the 'T. S. Eliot effect', after Eliot's observation of how 'every major work of art forces upon us a reassessment of all previous works'.[36]

For these sorts of reason I am extremely sceptical of a great deal of the work which has been done in the last few years in architectural and environmental psychology and sociology. This seems to hold as a working assumption the belief that regularities of a reproducible and universal, presumably biologically-based, kind may be determined in the behavioural or aesthetic responses which people make to certain architectural forms, spatial arrangements, uses of colour and so on. As Hillier and Leaman suggest, such research is carried on within a biologically conceived 'man–environment paradigm' which actually removes the middle term, removes the structures of World Three, through which the man-made world acquires significance and is understood at all.[37]

The most that could be expected in this direction, in my view, is that certain very general perceptual constancies or behavioural dispositions might be attributable to the human physiological makeup; and that physiology would set the 'outer limits' — to speak very vaguely — on the broad *ways*, or would establish the general *logic*, according to which objects might be seen and given meaning. But this is obviously a long way from making detailed predictions about aesthetic or behavioural responses to particular works on particular historical occasions.

Incidentally, this criticism is not intended to deny the value of certain types of sociological research whose purpose is to canvass the users' assessment of some building *after* it has been put up and occupied, or perhaps to seek consumers' opinions of a given commercial product. It is only to argue that the findings of such studies — a kind of dignified 'market research' if you will — are essentially retrospective; and that if any predictions or response to future objects or buildings are made on their basis, then these are by way of short-term extrapolations only and lack any wide or long-range application.

Meanwhile the laws of physics, the laws of chemistry, the geometrical laws of three-dimensional space — on which rest, ultimately, the applied sciences of the engineering disciplines, including traditional building science — are clearly not altered by the course of technological or cultural history. (Only our *knowledge* of them may change.) Thus the predictions which may be made with their support about future buildings or other artefacts must be accorded a quite different status.

I offer this argument in support of the proposition that 'sciences of the artificial' must confine themselves, in so far as they aim to have long-term or reliable predictive powers, to the physical and material behaviour and attributes of artefacts. Whether the argument be accepted or not, there is a second and much more pragmatic reason for starting from this engineering end of the subject, and that is to do with what Medawar would refer to as the 'agenda of research'.[38] It makes sense to begin in research with problems which there is actually some hope of solving in the short run rather than those which may possibly be of the most pressing political or immediate practical concern (which fact does not guarantee that they are readily soluble, since science works always at the frontiers which it has presently reached and cannot jump far beyond these). What is more there is a 'logic of priorities' in science, by which the investigation of certain sorts of question is absolutely dependent on having answers to other questions which are logically prior.

To take an illustration from architecture: supposing we wish to predict something about the way in which people will perceive or experience an architectural interior which is not yet built, it is obviously essential at the very least to be able to make accurate physical predictions first about that interior itself — about its dimensions; about its colours, which will depend on the materials of the surfaces and on the ways in which light enters the room and is reflected; about the temperature of the air, which will depend on a host of meteorological, material, mechanical and thermodynamic factors, and so on. Such predictions are by no means trivial, and some rather sophisticated physical and geometrical models are required in order to make them.

What then are the directions in which building science should now move? It is fair to say that most work in the subject in the past has concentrated on the behaviour of isolated building elements and the physical, chemical and structural properties of different building materials. More recently, and particularly with the development of computer models, efforts have been made to take a more holistic view, and to study the complex behaviour of the various *systems* from which the building is made up: the structural system, the ventilating and heating systems, the lighting system. This work has created needs for the description and classification of the geometric forms of building, since in order to generalise the results of experiments about the relation of physical performance of buildings to their shapes it is clearly necessary to have some way of characterising their designs in geometrical terms.

These results would be applied in the design process in the evaluation of schemes, as for instance when a hypothetical proposal for a building is put forward and the knowledge gained from the scientific activity is applied to making calculations of its particular anticipated performance in the various respects. But at the same time this knowledge informs the making of the 'hypotheses' in the first place, since these are not produced blindly but on the basis of a general understanding of the *sorts* of structures which may be appropriate for the building in question, the *sorts* of lighting which will be achieved by certain kinds of geometric arrangements of windows and walls, or whatever.

Thus the contribution of building science to architectural design is at two levels: it provides the means for predicting the behaviour of *particular* proposed designs in the physical and engineering aspects; but beyond this, and more broadly, it defines (in principle) the limits on *possible* designs which the given constraints impose. The design problem as a whole is only determined, as we have seen, by the purposes which the artefact is to serve, and in relation to some cultural framework which gives the object meaning. This is even true of artefacts as utilitarian-seeming as the beams or columns of an architectural structure. The need for the structural element is referrable to the purposes which the building as a whole is meant to serve, and these purposes are in turn created culturally.

Nevertheless, once a requirement for buildings, and hence beams, is decided upon, then it is the role of structural engineering to determine the possibilities for their design — which will be a function of the materials used, the patterns of loading, their profile in cross-section and so on. Tests of the strengths of beams can show the limits on their lengths or slenderness — beyond which the members fail or are unsafe — given certain values for these constraining factors.

It is not just limitations on the material possibilities in design which may be susceptible to systematic investigation. Design is concerned above all with the *arrangement* of elements or components — material or spatial — in different two- or three-dimensional configurations. Here the laws of geometry or topology also place restrictions, possibly quite severe ones, on the range and number of spatial arrangements which are possible for certain classes of design. We can thus distinguish, in structural design for example, between the selection of an appropriate configuration (the study of possible configurations from which the designer's choice is made being essentially a matter for combinatorial analysis) and the assignment of appropriate sizes to the elements of that configuration — what Spillers has termed 'parametric design'.[39] (The distinction is exemplified in any handbook of structural steel tables, where the configuration of each available steel member is given as a schematic cross-section and the possible sizes are listed separately in tabular form.)

Some nineteenth-century work on mechanisms, such as that of Reuleaux, had the purpose of enumerating possible arrangements of such mechanical elements as gears and linkages by means of a formal 'algebra of machines'.[40] Developments in combinatorial mathematics over the last few decades, together with the introduction of computer techniques, have provided the tools with which to carry forward Reuleaux's programme. For instance, the representation of mechanisms in mathematical form as graphs separates out the structural relationships between the components (i.e. how the drive or movement is transmitted from one part to another) from the incidental details of their specific sizes, shapes or materials of construction. As Freudenstein and Woo have argued, this opens up the very interesting possibility of an abstract classification of machines according to their structure, and independent of the particular functional uses — hoists, baby carriages, typewriters — to which they might be put.[41] Furthermore in certain limited areas it offers the prospect of being able to list *all* possible machines of a given class.

Some equivalent exercises in the enumeration of combinatorial possibilities of arrangement in design have been carried out in other areas of engineering, as for instance in cataloguing possible configurations for electrical circuits or possible ways of bracing framed structures for buildings. In the architectural context, I myself have made some studies of the possibilities for the topological arrangement of rectangular rooms in small rectangular plan layouts, these possibilities being regarded as distinct where the relationships of adjacency between the rooms are different, and no account being taken of dimensions.[42] These investigations have been taken further by various colleagues, and we have been able to enumerate all such plan arrangements with up to nine rooms and to classify these possibilities according to different properties of architectural interest. Meanwhile it has been shown, by March and Earl, how in principle a similar enumeration may be made of all topologically distinct sub-divisions of the plane into regions — i.e. all 'plans' in a very general sense — without restriction to any particular geometric discipline, rectangular or otherwise.[43]

The implications of this sort of work are that, if for example it is decided to design a house layout in which there are to be a given number of rectangular rooms adjacent to each other in certain specified ways and arranged all within a surrounding rectangular boundary, then the number of topologically distinct possibilities for that layout is finite, and they may be exhaustively tabulated. Limitations on the areas, proportions or dimensions of the rooms will set further bounds on the 'solution space' within which all admissible arrangements are contained. Of course the designer may not wish to restrict himself in this way to a rectangular geometry, or he may change his mind about the adjacencies or sizes of rooms — in which case the number and character of the possible solutions, and the boundaries of the solution space, will alter correspondingly.

The fact that houses in Western industrial societies consist very frequently of sub-divisions of an enclosed volume into rectangular spaces is a cultural peculiarity. Indeed the way in which the artefact 'house' may be identified at all in any society is by reference only to some cultural definition. Houses are obviously not limited in any obligatory or absolute way to consisting of rectangular rooms arranged together in various ways; but *where they are so made up* the limitations set by the geometry of the situation, as revealed by an investigation of the sort described, must necessarily apply. Topological and dimensional constraints set bounds, one might say, on what is allowable or feasible in the design of such plans, but within these bounds they do not by any means define what is desirable, let alone what particular choices the architect might actually make in any given scheme.

Whether such intrinsic material or spatial constraints are of real practical consequence for design will depend very much on how severe or restrictive they turn out to be. At this stage the question is one of open debate. In a rather different, anthropological context (and in the course of an anti-functionalist polemic) Sahlins expresses doubt on whether the 'negative determinations' set by physics, chemistry and biology on culture are of very great interest, since, as he argues, they are generally so loose and permissive.[44] But he is talking of institutions, forms of behaviour and language, not of material artefacts, which we might well imagine would be much more narrowly constrained by the laws of physics or geometry. Certainly, the limitations on architectural arrangement of the kind outlined above are much more constraining than most architects would intuitively — and without seeing the mathematical demonstration — allow.

Where might all this involve any biological analogy? There is a shared body of mechanical and structural theory which would apply equally to the study of artefacts and to the anatomy or 'engineering' of animals and plants. Indeed in biology there is currently something of a revival of interest in the kind of engineering analysis of organic structures and mechanisms which D'Arcy Thompson pioneered, and through which, as we saw in the account of the 'principle of similitude', it is possible to determine limitations on the possible forms and structures of organisms — their sizes, weights, strengths, speeds of locomotion and the like. Some attention has also been given, for instance by Rosen, to the question of whether the designs of organic systems approach 'optimality' in an engineering sense.[45] (The difficulty in a mathematical treatment of such problems, as Rosen says, is in the definition of appropriate cost functions according to which the success of the structures or organic processes in question can be measured.)

It is perhaps not quite right to speak of an *analogy* here any more, rather of two separate fields of study in which the same theoretical and analytical tools might be brought to bear. Still, there are certain broad similarities between artefacts and organisms to do with the coordination and purposiveness of their designs, the integration of their functioning parts and systems, which would possibly require the same kinds of analytic approach for their understanding in mechanical or engineering terms. And certainly there would seem to be potential application of some ideas from the theory of systems, coming from biology, to the sciences of the artificial.[46]

Where the two subjects have the most in common, in my view, as the foregoing has perhaps indicated, is in the study of *morphology*; not morphology in the purely descriptive sense in which Goethe originally conceived it, but morphology in the sense of the study of possible forms, of which the actual historical forms of organisms and of artefacts represent particular cases. After an explanation of homology — similarity of form due to common descent — was provided by *The Origin of Species*, the question of analogy in biology, as the zoologist C. F. A. Pantin has observed, was rather brushed aside. But, as Pantin says, 'within the animal kingdom functionally analogous organs may achieve a remarkable similarity in quite unrelated creatures. The analogy is closest where the imposed functional specification is the most detailed.'[47]

It is Pantin's argument that, for example, the functional specification for an eye must be very precise and cannot vary much between animals (assuming an equivalent standard of vision is to be provided), since the nature of the incoming light stimuli and the optics of the situation remain exactly similar, and the different ways the stimuli can be satisfactorily received are rather few. On the other hand there are very many different ways in which the problem of locomotion can be solved, and the specification here is much looser. It is the motor organs, though, which give any creature its characteristic general appearance, and this accounts for a great deal of the variety in animal form. Meanwhile the brains and eyes are always much the same. 'An octopus is obviously staring at you − it is its arms that make it so inhuman and uncouth.' Analogies are 'far from trivial', Pantin says, and the physiologist does not hesitate to argue 'by analogy' from the details of the octopus nerve or brain to the same organs in man, despite the great evolutionary gulf between the two species.

In a paper on 'Organic Design' Pantin comes to some very interesting conclusions provoked by the subject of analogy.[48] He suggests that some nineteenth-century views of evolutionary change were of a process through which the forms of organisms could be almost indefinitely and continuously deformed in any direction. As he puts it, 'The older conceptions of evolutionary morphology stressed the graded adaptation of which the organism is capable, just as putty can be moulded to any desired shape'[49] (Darwin used the term 'plastic').

Pantin's reflections on the matter suggest, as we have seen, that on the contrary there are only certain ways of meeting given functional specifications, that the materials available are of a restricted variety, and that there are strict constructional limitations set by 'engineering' considerations. His chosen metaphor for the morphological possibilities of organic structure would not be modelling clay, but rather a child's constructional toy such as 'Meccano': 'a set consisting of standard parts with unique properties, of strips, plates and wheels, which can be utilised for various objectives such as cranes and locomotives'.[50]

We see that Pantin puts a new kind of interpretation on the 'conditions of existence' of Aristotle and Cuvier. For them the conditions of existence were a theoretical teleological device, an appeal to final causes, whose only explanation could be metaphysical. What Pantin suggests is that there are 'conditions of existence' embodied in the material basis of life and in the physical laws which govern organic structure and process (indeed inorganic structure too). These conditions account for that distinctness of animal (or vegetable) species which Cuvier had insisted on, and for similar reasons. While Cuvier had argued that certain combinations of parts or organs were impossible functionally, Pantin is widening this argument to assert that in fact only certain structures or parts in themselves are possible.

What emerges is some sort of synthesis of, or compromise between, two views: at the one extreme the complete unalterable functional integrity of each separate species and the impossibility of any transformation of one into another, which had been the Cuvierian position; and at the other extreme, a complete evolutionary plasticity allowing transformation in any direction and with any result. Transformation clearly is possible, and has taken place through what appears to be a slow moulding, pushing and pulling, pinching and squeezing of organic forms into new shapes. But this process is channelled, Pantin says, along certain given routes, whose direction is constrained by the permutational possibilities of the 'component parts' and by the limited engineering possibilities available for the solution of any given functional problem.

Transferring all this back to the discussion of the design of man-made artefacts, we see that an evolutionary view of their history, in the craft tradition, would have to take account of the material, geometrical and mechanical limitations within which this evolutionary process must be constrained — the 'conditions of existence' of each artefact type. The same would apply where artefacts of novel form are created by recombination, amalgamation or on the basis of generalised engineering principle. This fact would provide a logical explanation of 'analogies' in the designs of man-made objects — similarities of form not attributable to any connection through common cultural influence.

As Hermann Weyl has said, evolution is a historical process, and an account of its evolution alone does not offer scientific explanation of any phenomenon. 'Explanation . . . is to be sought not in its origin but in its immanent law. Knowledge of the laws and of the inner constitution of things must be far advanced before one may hope to understand or hypothetically to reconstruct their genesis.'[51] In architecture this needs what W. R. Lethaby was calling for over sixty years ago, 'a systematic research into the possibilities of walls and vaults, and of the relations between the walls and the cell, and between one cell and another'.[52] 'Some day we shall get a morphology of the art by some architectural Linnaeus or Darwin, who will start from the simple cell and relate it to the most complex structure.'[53]

# NOTES

## 1. INTRODUCTION

1. J. T. Bonner, 'Analogies in Biology', *Form and Strategy in Science*, ed. J. R. Gregg and F. T. C. Harris (Dordrecht, 1964), pp. 251–5. See p. 251.
2. A. Colquoun, 'Typology and Design Method', *Perspecta*, 12 (1969), 71–4. See p. 72.
3. H. Simon, *The Sciences of the Artificial* (Cambridge, Mass., 1969).
4. P. Collins, 'Biological Analogy', *Architectural Review*, 126 (1959), 303–6.
5. P. Collins, *Changing Ideals in Modern Architecture 1750–1950* (London, 1965).

## 2. THE ORGANIC ANALOGY

1. J. A. Stewart, *Notes on the Nichomachaean Ethics of Aristotle* (2 vols., Oxford, 1892), vol. 1, pp. 194–5, commenting on Aristotle, *Nichomachaean Ethics*, book 2, chapter 6, section 9.
2. For an account of the origins of the concept of organic form — applied both to work of art and to organism — in Greek philosophy, with particular reference to Plato as well as to Aristotle, see G. N. Orsini, 'The Ancient Roots of a Modern Idea', *Organic Form: the Life of an Idea*, ed. G. S. Rousseau (London, 1972), pp. 7–23. Quoting the critic Rudolf Eucken, Orsini draws attention to the connotation, rather different from its modern biological sense, which the word 'organic' kept right up to the eighteenth century, of 'instrumental' or 'used as a tool'. This is a point which is very relevant to my own argument here. The implication is, as Coleridge remarked, that the terms 'mechanical' and 'organic', now representative of an almost polar opposition, had meanings which were originally close, with a common reference to purpose and teleology. The ideas of the German Romantics, and of Coleridge, about organic form, are further discussed in P. C. Ritterbush's essay in the same volume, 'Organic Form: Aesthetics and Objectivity in the Study of Form in the Life Sciences' (*ibid.*, pp. 26–59). For Coleridge's idea of the organic in his Shakespearian criticism, see *Coleridge's Essays and Lectures on Shakespeare*, ed. E. Rhys (London and New York, 1907), pp. 46–7.
3. Aristotle, *On the Parts of Animals*, book 1, part 5, section 645. See translation by W. Ogle (Oxford, 1911).
4. For a full history of functionalist aesthetics, see E. de Zurko, *Origins of Functionalist Theory* (New York, 1957).

5. F. Hutcheson, *An Inquiry into the Original of our Ideas of Beauty and Virtue* (Glasgow, 1725). Lord Kames, *Elements of Criticism* (2 vols., Edinburgh, 1761). See E. de Zurko, *Origins of Functionalist Theory*, pp. 78—82.

6. P. Collins, *Changing Ideals in Modern Architecture 1750—1950*, chapters 14 and 15.

7. G. Scott, *The Architecture of Humanism* (London, 1914), chapters 4 and 6.

8. See C. U. M. Smith, *The Problem of Life* (London, 1976), chapter 15, 'Descartes'. Also C. C. Gillispie, *The Edge of Objectivity* (Princeton, 1960), p. 92.

9. See C. U. M. Smith, *The Problem of Life*, pp. 177, 180—3.

10. J. O. de la Mettrie, *L'Homme Machine* (Leyden, 1748), trans. G. C. Bussey and M. W. Calkins as *Man a Machine* (Chicago, 1912).

11. See A. Vartanian, *La Mettrie's 'L'Homme Machine'* (Princeton, 1960), pp. 14—16.

12. *Ibid.*, p. 34; and C. U. M. Smith, *The Problem of Life*, pp. 175, 183, 220.

13. C. C. Gillispie, *The Edge of Objectivity*, p. 285.

14. Quoted by P. Collins, *Changing Ideals in Modern Architecture 1750—1950*, p. 152.

15. L. von Bertalanffy, *Problems of Life* (London, 1952; references are to New York, 1960 edn). See pp. 16—19.

16. *Ibid.*, p. 16.

17. See A. Vartanian, *La Mettrie's 'L'Homme Machine'*, p. 134.

18. D'Arcy W. Thompson, *On Growth and Form* (Cambridge, 1917; references are to abridged edn, ed. J. T. Bonner, Cambridge, 1961).

19. *Ibid.*, pp. 230—8.

20. *Ibid.*, p. 230.

21. *Ibid.*, pp. 251—8.

22. E. de Zurko, *Origins of Functionalist Theory*, pp. 40—1.

23. R. Wittkower, *Architectural Principles in the Age of Humanism* (London, 1962).

24. *Vasari on Technique*, trans. L. S. Maclehose, ed. G. Baldwin Brown (London and New York, 1907), pp. 96—7.

25. R. Wittkower, *Architectural Principles in the Age of Humanism*, p. 11 and plate 1a, drawing by Francesco di Giorgio.

26. See P. H. Scholfield, *The Theory of Proportion in Architecture* (Cambridge, 1958), 'Criticisms of Renaissance Theory', pp. 72—81.

27. D. R. Hay, *The Science of Beauty, as Developed in Nature and Applied in Art* (Edinburgh, 1856). See also Hay's *The Natural Principles and Analogy of the Harmony of Form* (Edinburgh, 1842).

28. *Anatomical Memoirs of John Goodsir, FRS*, ed. W. Turner (2 vols., Edinburgh, 1968), vol. 1, pp. 142—5. See also 'Mathematical Modes of Investigating Organic Forms', vol. 2, pp. 213—9.

29. See P. H. Scholfield, *The Theory of Proportion in Architecture*, 'The Golden Section in the Nineteenth Century', pp. 98—9.

30. Sir H. Read, *The Meaning of Art* (London, 1931; references are to 3rd edn, 1951). See p. 27.

31. See P. H. Scholfield, *The Theory of Proportion in Architecture*, chapter 6, 'The Return to the Incommensurable (2)', pp. 98—116.

32. For some beautifully illustrated scientific expositions see A. H. Church, *Types of Floral Mechanism* (Oxford, 1908); and A. H. Church, *On the Interpretation of Phenomena of Phyllotaxis*, Botanical Memoirs no. 6 (Oxford, 1920).

33. For a discussion see L. March and P. Steadman, *The Geometry of Environment* (London, 1971), pp. 229–32.

34. D'Arcy W. Thompson, *On Growth and Form*, for example chapter 6 on spirals and chapter 7 on the shapes of horns.

35. Sir T. Cook, *Spirals in Nature and Art* (London, 1903).

36. Sir T. Cook, *The Curves of Life* (London, 1914).

37. *Ibid.*, plate 8.

38. E. Haeckel, *Kunst-Formen der Natur* (Leipzig and Vienna, 1904).

39. S. Colman, *Nature's Harmonic Unity: A Treatise on its Relation to Proportional Form*, ed. C. A. Coan (New York, 1912).

40. For example J. Hambidge, *Dynamic Symmetry: The Greek Vase* (Yale, 1920), and J. Hambidge, *The Elements of Dynamic Symmetry* (Yale, 1926); M. Ghyka, *Geometrical Composition and Design* (London, 1958).

41. J. Hambidge, *Dynamic Symmetry: The Greek Vase*, p. 7.

42. O. Jones, *The Grammar of Ornament* (London, 1856).

43. C. Dresser, *The Art of Decorative Design* (London, 1862); and C. Dresser, *Principles of Decorative Design* (London, Paris and New York, 1873).

44. C. Dresser, *Principles of Decorative Design*, p. 96.

45. L. Day, *Nature in Ornament* (London, 1892). See M. Binney, 'The Mystery of the Style Jules Verne', *Country Life Annual* (London, 1970), pp. 130–3.

46. L. Sullivan, *A System of Architectural Ornament* (Washington, 1924).

## 3. THE CLASSIFICATORY ANALOGY

1. A. O. Lovejoy, *The Great Chain of Being* (Harvard, 1936).

2. See G. S. Carter, *A Hundred Years of Evolution* (London, 1957), p. 16.

3. P. C. Ritterbush, *The Art of Organic Forms* (Washington, 1968), p. 6.

4. Linnaeus, *Philosophia Botanica* (Stockholm and Amsterdam, 1751; references are to 4th edn, Halae ad Salam, 1809). See section 156, p. 172. Quoted by M. Foucault in *Les Mots et les Choses* (Paris, 1966), trans. as *The Order of Things* (London, 1970). See p. 146.

5. Aristotle, *Politics*, book 4, part 4, section 1290. See translation by B. Jowett (Oxford, 1885).

6. See M. Foucault, *The Order of Things*, p. 154. Maupertuis's discussion of monsters is to be found in his 'Essai sur la Formation des Corps Organisés', *Oeuvres* (4 vols., Lyon, 1756), vol. 2, pp. 139–68, in particular section 42, p. 147.

7. J. W. von Goethe, *Italienische Reise 1786–8*, diary entry for 17 April 1787. Trans. W. H. Auden and E. Mayer as *Italian Journey* (London, 1962; references are to 1970 edn). See pp. 258–9.

8. J. W. von Goethe, letter to Charlotte Stein, 8 June 1787. See *Letters from Goethe*, trans. M. von Herzfeld and C. Melvil Sym (Edinburgh, 1957), p. 192. The theory of the *Urpflanze* is developed more fully in Goethe's pamphlet *Versuch die Metamorphose der Pflanzen zu Erklären* (Gotha, 1790), trans. with commentary by A. Arber, *Chronica Botanica*, 10:2 (1946), 63–126.

9. R. Owen, *The Archetype and Homologies of the Vertebrate Skeleton* (London, 1848).

10. G. S. Carter, *A Hundred Years of Evolution*, p. 17.

11. For a general discussion of nineteenth-century morphological work and ideas, see the entry by Patrick Geddes, the biologist and town planner, under 'Morphology' in *Encyclopaedia Britannica*, 9th edn (24 vols., Edinburgh, 1875–89), vol. 16, pp. 837–46.

12. R. J. Haüy, *Traité de Mineralogie* (4 vols. and atlas, Paris, 1801).

13. P. C. Ritterbush, *The Art of Organic Forms*, p. 14. An early example is provided by Nehemiah Grew, *The Anatomy of Plants Begun* (London, 1682).

14. J. D. Le Roy, *Ruines des Plus Beaux Monuments de la Grèce* (Paris, 1758); J.-F. Blondel, *Cours d'Architecture* (12 vols., Paris, 1771–7); J. N. L. Durand, *Recueil et Parallèle des Edifices* (Paris, 1801).

15. J.-F. Blondel, *Cours d'Architecture*. See R. D. Middleton, 'Jacques-François Blondel and the *Cours d'Architecture*', *Journal of the Society of Architectural Historians*, 18 (1959), 140–8.

16. J. N. L. Durand, *Précis des Leçons d'Architecture* (2 vols., Paris, 1823–5).

17. J. N. L. Durand, *Recueil et Parallèle des Edifices*.

18. J. N. L. Durand, *Précis des Leçons d'Architecture*, vol. 1, p. 27.

19. P. C. Ritterbush, *The Art of Organic Forms*, p. 9.

20. *Ibid.*, pp. 9–10.

21. L. H. Sullivan, 'Kindergarten Chats', serialised in *Interstate Architect and Builder* (Feb. 1901–Feb. 1902); republished in book form as *Kindergarten Chats* (New York, 1947). See p. 160.

## 4. THE ANATOMICAL ANALOGY

1. See C. C. Gillispie, *The Edge of Objectivity*, p. 268.

2. R. Lee, *Memoirs of Baron Cuvier* (London, 1833), p. 99.

3. *Ibid.*, pp. 79–83.

4. C. C. Gillispie, *The Edge of Objectivity*, pp. 277, 279.

5. W. Coleman, *Georges Cuvier, Zoologist* (Harvard, 1964), p. 68.

6. G. Cuvier, *Rapport Historique sur le Progrès des Sciences Naturelles depuis 1789 et sur leur Etat Actuel* (Paris, 1808), p. 330; quoted in M. Foucault, *The Order of Things*, p. 265.

7. F. Vicq d'Azyr, *Système Anatomique des Quadrupèdes* (Paris, 1792), 'Discours préliminaire', p. lxxxvii; quoted in M. Foucault, *The Order of Things*, p. 228.

8. See M. Foucault, *The Order of Things*, p. 266.

9. *Ibid.*, in particular pp. 218, 226–32.

10. *Ibid.*, p. 267.

11. G. Cuvier, *Leçons d'Anatomie Comparée* (5 vols., Paris, 1800–5); quoted in W. Coleman, *Georges Cuvier, Zoologist*, p. 143.

12. W. Coleman, *Georges Cuvier, Zoologist*, p. 172.

13. G. Cuvier, *Leçons d'Anatomie Comparée*, vol. 1, p. 47; quoted in R. Lee, *Memoirs of Baron Cuvier*, p. 71.

14. G. Cuvier, *Leçons d'Anatomie Comparée*, vol. 1, p. 46; quoted in W. Coleman, *Georges Cuvier, Zoologist*, p. 68.

15. W. Coleman, *Georges Cuvier, Zoologist*, p. 120.

16. G. Cuvier, *Recherches sur les Ossemens Fossiles* (4 vols., Paris, 1812), 'Discours préliminaire', vol. 1, p. 1; quoted by R. Lee, *Memoirs of Baron Cuvier*, p. 85.

17. G. Cuvier, *Recherches sur les Ossemens Fossiles*, 'Discours préliminaire', pp. 60—1. The 'Discours préliminaire' to this book was trans. R. Kerr as *Essay on the Theory of the Earth* (Edinburgh and London, 1813), where this passage appears on pp. 94—5. It was republished also in separate book form in French as *Discours sur les Révolutions de la Surface du Globe* (Paris, 1825).

18. W. Coleman, *Georges Cuvier, Zoologist*, p. 123.

19. H. Greenough, *Form and Function. Remarks on Art, Design and Architecture*, ed. H. A. Small (Berkeley and Los Angeles, 1947), p. 57. This book is an edited version of the *Memorial of Horatio Greenough*, ed. H. T. Tuckerman (New York, 1853), which in turn was based on 'Horace Bender' [pseud. H. Greenough], *The Travels, Observations, and Experience of a Yankee Stonecutter* (New York, 1852).

20. Le Corbusier, *Précisions sur un Etat Present de l'Architecture et de l'Urbanisme*, Collection de L'Esprit Nouveau (Paris, 1960), 'Le Plan de la Maison Moderne', p. 24.

21. From a letter by Perronet to the *Mercure de France*, April 1770; quoted in R. D. Middleton, 'Viollet-le-Duc and the Rational Gothic Tradition' (6 vols., unpublished Ph.D. thesis, Cambridge University, 1958), vol. 2 (no pagination).

22. From a letter by Patte to Marigny; quoted in *ibid.*, vol. 2.

23. R. D. Middleton, 'Viollet-le-Duc and the Rational Gothic Tradition'.

24. *Ibid.*, vol. 3.

25. See Sir J. Summerson, *Heavenly Mansions, and other Essays on Architecture* (London, 1949), chapter 6, 'Viollet-le-Duc and the Rational Point of View', pp. 135—58.

26. E. E. Viollet-le-Duc, *Dictionnaire Raisonné de l'Architecture Francaise du XIe au XVIe Siècle* (10 vols., Paris, 1854—68), 'Style', vol. 8, p. 482. Cf. also 'Trait', vol. 9, pp. 197—214, in particular figures 1 and 3.

27. *Catalogue des Livres composant la Bibliotèque de Feu M. E. Viollet-le-Duc Architecte* (Paris, 1880), p. 147, entry no. 1129.

28. E. E. Viollet-le-Duc, *Dictionnaire Raisonné de l'Architecture Francaise*, 'Restauration', vol. 8, pp. 14—34. See specifically p. 15.

29. J. Fergusson, *An Historical Enquiry into the True Principles of Beauty in Art, more especially with reference to Architecture* (London, 1849), p. 181.

30. E. E. Viollet-le-Duc, *Entretiens sur l'Architecture* (2 vols., Paris, 1863—72); trans. H. van Brunt as *Discourses on Architecture* (New York, 1875); trans. under same title by B. Bucknall (Boston, 1889; references are to edn. republished in 2 vols., London and New York, 1959).

31. L. Eidlitz, *The Nature and Function of Art, More Especially of Architecture* (London, 1881).

32. *Ibid.*, pp. 361—2.

33. M. Schuyler, 'Modern Architecture', *Architectural Record*, 4 (1894), 1—13; republished in *American Architecture and Other Writings*, ed. W. H. Jordy and R. Coe (Harvard, 1961; references are to abridged edn, New York, 1964).

34. *Ibid.*, p. 76.

35. *Ibid.*, p. 77.

36. *Ibid.*, pp. 77—78.

37. Galileo Galilei, *Discorsi e Dimostrazioni Matematiche Intorno a Due Nuove Scienze*

(Leiden, 1638); trans. H. Crew and A. de Salvio as *Dialogues Concerning Two New Sciences* (New York, 1914). See p. 2.

38. See Herbert Spencer, *The Evolution of Society* [Selections from *The Principles of Sociology*], ed. R. L. Carneiro (Chicago, 1967), editorial introduction, pp. xiii—xiv.

39. Galileo Galilei, *Dialogues Concerning Two New Sciences*, p. 131.

40. E. E. Viollet-le-Duc, *Dictionnaire Raisonné de l'Architecture Francaise*, 'Style', vol. 8, p. 483.

41. L. Eidlitz, *The Nature and Function of Art, More Especially of Architecture*, pp. 299—300.

42. A. T. Edwards, *Architectural Style* (London, 1926); republished as *Style and Composition in Architecture* (London, 1944).

43. P. E. Nobbs, *Design: A Treatise on the Discovery of Form* (Oxford, 1937).

44. D'Arcy W. Thompson, *On Growth and Form*, chapter 2, pp. 15—48. A brief up-to-date treatment is given by R. McN. Alexander, *Size and Shape* (London, 1971). For an attractive popular discussion see J. B. S. Haldane, *Possible Worlds* (London, 1927), 'On Being the Right Size', pp. 18—26.

45. See J. T. Bonner, *Morphogenesis: An Essay on Development* (Princeton, 1952), p. 12.

46. D'Arcy W. Thompson, *On Growth and Form*, chapter 2 pp. 15—48.

47. P. E. Nobbs, *Design: A Treatise on the Discovery of Form*, p. 269.

48. Le Corbusier, *La Ville Radieuse* (Paris, 1933); trans. as *The Radiant City* (London, 1964). See p. 206 and elsewhere.

49. D'Arcy W. Thompson, *On Growth and Form*, p. 35.

50. R. B. Fuller, *Ideas and Integrities* (Englewood Cliffs, N. J., 1963), 'Preview of Building'; reprinted in *The Buckminster Fuller Reader*, ed. J. Meller (London, 1970). See p. 294.

51. See R. B. Fuller, *Synergetics* (New York, 1975).

52. See for example D'Arcy W. Thompson, *On Growth and Form*, pp. 154—69; and E. Haeckel, *Die Radiolarien* (2 vols., Berlin, 1862).

53. See A. Klug and J. T. Finch, 'Structure of Viruses of the Papilloma-Polyoma Type: 1. Human Warts', *Journal of Molecular Biology*, 2 (1965), 403—23.

54. L. Martin, L. March and others, 'Speculations', *Urban Space and Structures*, ed. L. Martin and L. March (Cambridge, 1972), pp. 28—54; L. March, 'Elementary Models of Built Forms', *Urban Space and Structures*, pp. 55—96; L. March and M. Trace, *The Land Use Performances of Selected Arrays of Built Forms*, Land Use and Built Form Studies Working Paper no. 2, Cambridge University Department of Architecture (Cambridge, 1968).

55. J. S. Huxley, *Problems of Relative Growth* (London, 1932). See also *Essays on Growth and Form, presented to D'Arcy Wentworth Thompson*, ed. W. E. le Gros Clark and P. B. Medawar (Oxford, 1945).

56. For a review, see *Ekistics* 36: 215 (1973), special number on 'Size and Shape in the Growth of Human Communities', which covers applications of allometric techniques in the social sciences generally, and in organisation theory, as well as to geographical, urban and architectural systems.

57. R. Bon, 'Allometry in the Topologic Structure of Architectural Spatial Systems', *Ekistics*, 36: 215 (1973), 270—6. Also R. Bon, 'Allometry in Micro-

Environmental Morphology', Special Papers Series, Paper E, *Harvard Papers in Theoretical Geography*, Laboratory for Computer Graphics and Spatial Analysis, Department of City and Regional Planning (Harvard, 1972).

58. This point is made by R. J. Mainstone, *Developments in Structural Form* (London, 1975), in a discussion of 'Natural and Man-Made Forms', pp. 19—20.

59. Recent experiments in the design of cellular automata are suggestive in this connection (see *Essays on Cellular Automata*, ed. A. W. Burks (Urbana, 1970)); and there is a growing mathematical literature on the cell-growth problem (see for example F. Harary, E. M. Palmer and R. C. Read, 'On the Cell-Growth Problem for Arbitrary Polygons', *Discrete Mathematics* 11 (1975), 371—89). W. J. Mitchell at the University of California, Los Angeles, has made some experiments with computer simulation of stochastic processes of urban growth by the accretion of cells. From a rather different perspective, B. Hillier and A. Leaman's ideas about spatial syntax and spatial language involve the concept of urban growth processes operating by the aggregation of cellular units (B. Hillier, A. Leaman, P. Stansall and M. Bedford, 'Space Syntax', *Environment and Planning B*, 3 (1976), 147—85).

## 5. THE ECOLOGICAL ANALOGY

1. H. Greenough, *Form and Function: Remarks on Art, Design and Architecture*, 'American Architecture', pp. 57—8.
2. *Ibid.*, p. 58.
3. H. Greenough, *Form and Function: Remarks on Art, Design and Architecture*, 'Structure and Organisation', p. 117.
4. *Ibid.*, p. 118.
5. L. Eidlitz, *The Nature and Function of Art, More Especially of Architecture*, p. 358.
6. *Ibid.*, p. 358.
7. L. H. Sullivan, *Kindergarten Chats*, sections 12 and 13, pp. 42— 8.
8. *Ibid.*, p. 43.
9. *Ibid.*, p. 46.
10. E. E. Viollet-le-Duc, *Dictionnaire Raisonné de l'Architecture Francaise*, 'Style', vol. 8, pp. 474—97 and 'Unité', vol. 9, pp. 339—46.
11. *Ibid.*, 'Style', vol. 8, p. 481.
12. *Ibid.*, 'Style', vol. 8, p. 495.
13. *Ibid.*, 'Unité', vol. 9, p. 341.
14. *Ibid.*, 'Unité', vol. 9, p. 341.
15. L. Eidlitz, *The Nature and Function of Art, More Especially of Architecture*, p. 371.
16. H. Greenough, *Form and Function: Remarks on Art, Design and Architecture*, 'American Architecture', p. 49.
17. L. H. Sullivan, *Kindergarten Chats*, p. 219. (From an essay, 'The Young Man in Architecture', read before the Architectural League of America, Chicago, June 1900.)
18. E. E. Viollet-le-Duc, *Dictionnaire Raisonné de l'Architecture Francaise*, 'Unité', vol. 9, pp. 339—46.
19. E. E. Viollet-le-Duc, *Discourses on Architecture*, lectures 17 and 18 on 'Domestic Architecture', vol. 2, pp. 246—344. See in particular pp. 267—8.

20. E. L. Garbett, *Rudimentary Treatise on the Principles of Design as Deducible from Nature and Exemplified in the Works of the Greek and Gothic Architects* (London, 1850). See N. Pevsner, *Some Architectural Writers of the Nineteenth Century* (Oxford, 1972), chapter 19, 'Greenough and Garbett', pp. 188—93. Also R. W. Winter, 'Fergusson and Garbett in American Architectural Theory', *Journal of the Society of Architectural Historians*, 17 (1958), 25—30.

21. G. Semper, *Der Stil in den Technischen und Tektonischen Künsten oder Praktische Aesthetik: Ein Handbuch für Techniker, Künstler und Kunstfreunde* (2 vols., Munich 1878—9). That Viollet-le-Duc owned a copy is shown by the *Catalogue des Livres composant la Bibliotèque de Feu M. E. Viollet-le-Duc Architecte*, p. 133, entry no. 1009. Connections between Viollet-le-Duc and Semper are discussed by R. Middleton in 'Viollet-le-Duc's Academic Ventures and the *Entretiens sur l'Architecture*', *Gottfried Semper und die Mitte des 19 Jahrhunderts* (Basle and Stuttgart, 1976), pp. 239—54. See p. 242.

22. G. Semper, *Wissenschaft, Industrie und Kunst* (Braunschweig, 1852). For discussion of this pamphlet, which contains thoughts provoked by the Great Exhibition of 1851, see N. Pevsner, *Some Architectural Writers of the Nineteenth Century*, chapter 24, in particular p. 259; and L. D. Ettlinger, 'On Science, Industry and Art: Some Theories of Gottfried Semper', *Architectural Review*, 136 (1964), 57—60.

23. G. Semper, *Kleine Schriften*, ed. M. and H. Semper (Berlin and Stuttgart, 1884), p. 351. See N. Pevsner, *Some Architectural Writers of the Nineteenth Century*, p. 261.

24. G. Semper, *Kleine Schriften*, 'Ueber Baustile', pp. 395—426. See p. 402. This essay was translated by the Chicago architect John Root, together with F. Wagner, and published as 'Development of Architectural Style', *The Inland Architect and News Record*, 14 (1889), 76—8 and 92—4; and 15 (1890), 5—6 and 32—3.

25. G. Semper, *Kleine Schriften*, pp. 267—8.

26. For example G. Semper, *Der Stil*, vol. 2, pp. 1—8, 77—9.

27. L. D. Ettlinger, 'On Science, Industry and Art: Some Theories of Gottfried Semper', p. 58.

28. G. Semper, *Kleine Schriften*, pp. 351—68. See L. D. Ettlinger, 'On Science, Industry and Art: Some Theories of Gottfried Semper', p. 58.

29. A. Choisy, *Histoire de l'Architecture* (2 vols., Paris, 1899), vol. 1, p. 14. Quoted in R. Banham, *Theory and Design in the First Machine Age* (London, 1960), p. 26.

30. L. H. Sullivan, *Kindergarten Chats*, p. 229.

31. For a recent somewhat dyspeptic account, see D. Watkin, *Morality and Architecture* (Oxford, 1977).

32. G. Semper, *Der Stil*, vol. 2, pp. 262—3. Also *Die Vier Elemente der Baukunst* (Braunschweig, 1851); and *Kleine Schriften*, pp. 283—6.

33. G. Semper, *Der Stil*, vol. 1, pp. 8—9.

34. G. Semper, 'Practical Art in Metal and Hard Materials: its Technology, History and Styles', manuscript dated 1854 in Victoria and Albert Museum, London, classmark 86 FF 64, pp. 15, 18. (It appears that the true date of the manuscript is 1852. See R. D. Middleton, 'Viollet-le-Duc's Academic Ventures and the *Entretiens sur l'Architecture*', p. 252, n. 29.)

35. See L. Harvey, 'Semper's Theory of Evolution in Architectural Ornament', *Transactions of the Royal Institute of British Architects*, N.S. 1 (1885), 29—54, with nine plates. See p. 29.
36. Quoted (in English) in H. Semper, *Gottfried Semper: Ein Bild seines Lebens und Wirkens* (Berlin, 1880), and reproduced in L. D. Ettlinger, 'On Science, Industry and Art', p. 58. The whole lecture is printed in German in *Kleine Schriften*, pp. 259—91.
37. G. Semper, *Kleine Schriften*, p. 262.
38. E. E. Viollet-le-Duc, *Dictionnaire Raisonné de l'Architecture Francaise*, vol. 9, p. 324, plate 18.
39. I am indebted to Dr R. D. Middleton for this information.
40. H. Damisch, introduction to E. E. Viollet-le-Duc, *L'Architecture Raisonnée* (Paris, 1964).
41. *Ibid.*, p. 19.
42. E. E. Viollet-le-Duc, *Dictionnaire Raisonné de l'Architecture Francaise*, 'Style', vol. 8, p. 495.
43. E. E. Viollet-le-Duc, *Discourses on Architecture*, vol. 1, p. 426.
44. L. Harvey, 'Semper's Theory of Evolution in Architectural Ornament', p. 29.
45. G. Semper, *Der Stil*, vol. 1, p. xv. See N. Pevsner, *Some Architectural Writers of the Nineteenth Century*, p. 263.
46. G. Semper, *Die Vier Elemente der Baukunst*. Cf. also L. D. Ettlinger, 'On Science, Industry and Art: Some Theories of Gottfried Semper', p. 59.
47. See N. Pevsner, *Some Architectural Writers of the Nineteenth Century*, p. 261, n. 33.
48. L. D. Ettlinger, 'On Science, Industry and Art: Some Theories of Gottfried Semper', p. 58.
49. G. Semper, 'Development of Architectural Style' *The Inland Architect and News Record*, 14 (1889), 76.
50. *Ibid.*, p. 76.
51. *Ibid.*, p. 77.

## 6. THE DARWINIAN ANALOGY

1. C. Darwin, *On the Origin of Species by Means of Natural Selection, or the Preservation of Favoured Races in the Struggle for Life* (London, 1859). References here are to the Penguin edition (Harmondsworth, 1968). This reproduces the original text of the first edition, which was subsequently changed and the argument weakened by Darwin as he yielded to some of his opponents. The 'Historical Sketch' which was included from the third edition onwards is, however, printed in the Penguin edition.
2. *Ibid.*, p. 117.
3. *Ibid.*, chapter 1, 'Variation under Domestication', pp. 71—100.
4. Sir C. Lyell, *Principles of Geology* (3 vols., London, 1830—3).
5. Quoted by C. C. Gillispie, *The Edge of Objectivity*, p. 299.
6. See R. Lee, *Memoirs of Baron Cuvier*, p. 99.
7. See J. Maynard Smith, *The Theory of Evolution* (Harmondsworth, 1958; references are to 2nd edn, 1966). See p. 35.
8. See D. Bohm, 'Further Remarks on Order', *Towards a Theoretical Biology*, ed.

C. H. Waddington, vol. 2, *Sketches* (Edinburgh, 1969), pp. 44—5; and C. H. Waddington, *The Strategy of the Genes* (London, 1957), p. 65.

9. W. Paley, *Natural Theology* (London, 1802).

10. Sir C. Bell, *The Hand: Its Mechanism and Vital Endowments as Evincing Design* (London, 1833). W. Buckland, *Geology and Mineralogy Considered with Reference to Natural Theology* (2 vols., London, 1836).

11. C. C. Gillispie, *The Edge of Objectivity*, p. 317.

12. W. F. Cannon, 'The Bases of Darwin's Achievement: A Revaluation', *Victorian Studies*, 5 (1961), 109—34; reprinted in abridged form in *Darwin*, ed. P. Appleman (New York, 1970), pp. 40—5. See p. 44.

13. T. R. Malthus, *An Essay on the Principle of Population* (London, 1798). Darwin read Malthus in 1838. See *The Autobiography of Charles Darwin*, ed. N. Barlow (London, 1958), p. 120. A. R. Wallace was also inspired by reading Malthus.

14. B. Hillier and A. Leaman, 'How is Design Possible?', *Architectural Research and Teaching*, 3 (1974), pp. 4—11.

15. J. Fergusson, *An Historical Enquiry into the True Principles of Beauty in Art*, section 4, pp. 155—63.

16. *Ibid.*, p. 156.

17. *Ibid.*, p. 156.

18. *Ibid.*, p. 158.

19. *Ibid.*, p. 160.

20. *Ibid.*, p. 160.

21. H. Greenough, *Form and Function: Remarks on Art, Design and Architecture*, 'American Architecture', p. 59.

22. H. Greenough, *Form and Function: Remarks on Art, Design and Architecture*, 'Structure and Organisation', p. 121.

23. L. H. Sullivan, *Kindergarten Chats*, p. 123.

24. C. Darwin, *The Descent of Man* (2 vols., London, 1871).

25. Sir J. Lubbock, *Prehistoric Times* (London, 1865); and *The Origin of Civilisation, and the Primitive Condition of Man: Mental and Social Conditions of Savages* (London, 1870).

26. L. H. Morgan, *Ancient Society: Researches in the Lines of Human Progress through Barbarism in Civilisation* (New York, 1877).

27. E. B. Tylor, *Primitive Culture* (2 vols., London, 1871).

28. H. Balfour, introduction to Lt.-Gen. A. Lane-Fox Pitt-Rivers, *The Evolution of Culture and other Essays*, ed. J. L. Myres (Oxford, 1906), p. xviii.

29. See A. H. Quiggin, *Haddon the Head-Hunter: a Short Sketch of the Life of A. C. Haddon* (Cambridge, 1942).

30. For a brief historical account of the Pitt-Rivers collection, and a description of its classification, see B. Blackwood, *The Classification of Artefacts in the Pitt Rivers Museum Oxford*, Pitt Rivers Museum, University of Oxford, Occasional Papers on Technology 11 (Oxford, 1970).

31. H. Balfour, introduction to *The Evolution of Culture*, p. v.

32. A. Lane-Fox Pitt-Rivers, *The Evolution of Culture*, 'Primitive Warfare' (three lectures given to the Royal United Service Institution, 1867, 1868, 1869), pp. 45—185.

33. H. Balfour, introduction to *The Evolution of Culture*, p.v.

34. E. B. Tylor, *Primitive Culture*, vol. 1, p. 156.
35. H. Balfour, *The Natural History of the Musical Bow* (Oxford, 1899). The argument is also summarised in the introduction to *The Evolution of Culture*, pp. viii—xi.
36. C. Darwin, *On the Origin of Species*, chapter 9, 'On the Imperfection of the Geological Record', pp. 291—316.
37. *Ibid.*, p. 223.
38. With the discovery of the origin of variations in genetic mutations it was argued in some quarters that evolution was therefore characterised by radical and sudden changes rather than by transformation through gradual stages. This ignored the fact that individual mutations take place within a very much larger genetic *system*, which is highly stable, and with which the mutation in order to be selected for must be compatible (cf. L. L. Whyte, *Internal Factors in Evolution* (London, 1965) ). What is more important, any mutation which did produce a very extreme bodily change would probably tend — it might reasonably be argued — to disrupt the delicate adaptive balance of the organism so seriously as to ensure its elimination in the selective process. Such appears to be the fate of most monsters. The subject, however, has remained one of debate within biology; for instance R. B. Goldschmidt argued in favour of a theory of evolution which would involve some big occasional mutations, mostly fatal, but a few surviving: his theory of 'hopeful monsters' (*The Material Basis of Evolution* (Yale, 1940) ). Recently Karl Popper has proposed a variant of Goldschmidt's theory involving mutations which would produce large changes in behaviour, rather than in bodily form (*Objective Knowledge* (Oxford, 1972) pp. 281—4). In the much broader view, there are certainly periods of relatively fast and relatively slow evolution in organic species; but this is another matter.
39. H. Balfour, introduction to *The Evolution of Culture*, pp. vii—viii.
40. C. Darwin, *On the Origin of Species*, p. 220.
41. A. Lane-Fox Pitt-Rivers, *The Evolution of Culture*, 'Principles of Classification' (1874), pp. 1—19.
42. H. Balfour, introduction to *The Evolution of Culture*, p. v.
43. See B. Blackwood, *The Classification of Artefacts in the Pitt Rivers Museum Oxford*, p. 7. Also Col. A. Lane Fox, *Catalogue of the Anthropological Collection lent by Colonel Lane Fox for Exhibition in the Bethnal Green Branch of the South Kensington Museum* (London, 1874).
44. G. Semper, 'Practical Art in Metal and Hard Materials; its Technology, History and Styles', p. 15.
45. *Ibid.*, p. 18.
46. G. Klemm, *Allgemeine Kultur-Geschichte der Menschheit* (10 vols., Leipzig, 1843—52).
47. See L. D. Ettlinger, 'On Science, Industry and Art: Some Theories of Gottfried Semper', p. 59.
48. E. B. Tylor, *Primitive Culture*, vol. 1, p. 58.
49. Sir N. Pevsner, *Some Architectural Writers of the Nineteenth Century*, p. 259. See also L. Harvey, 'Style and Styles in Building', lectures given at the City and Guilds of London Institute, published in *The Building Budget* (Chicago),

3—5 (Sept. 1887—Sept 1889). These lectures include biographical details about Semper, and a résumé of his theory of style (Harvey was a pupil of Semper). For the connection with Prince Albert, see 5 (1889), 101.

50. *The Science Museum: The First Hundred Years* (London, 1957).

51. L. D. Ettlinger, 'On Science, Industry and Art: Some Theories of Gottfried Semper', p. 57.

52. G. Semper, *Kleine Schriften*, pp. 76—83.

53. O. Jones, *The Grammar of Ornament*, plates 2 and 3.

54. Society membership list in *Memoirs Read before the Anthropological Society of London*, 2 (1865—6).

55. H. Balfour, introduction to *The Evolution of Culture*, p. xviii.

56. M. Harris, *The Rise of Anthropological Theory* (London, 1969), pp. 151—4.

57. *Ibid.*, pp. 171—6.

58. *Ibid.*, p. 174.

59. R. Owen, *Lectures on Invertebrate Animals* (London, 1843), pp. 374, 379.

60. *Ibid.* Also quoted in R. Owen, *The Archetype and Homologies of the Vertebrate Skeleton* (London, 1848), p. 7.

61. H. Balfour, introduction to *The Evolution of Culture*, p. xviii.

62. *Ibid*, p. xix.

63. A. Koestler, *The Art of Creation* (London, 1964; references are to 1970 edn). See pp. 121—3.

64. D. A. Schon, *Displacement of Concepts* (London, 1963); republished as *Invention and the Evolution of Ideas* (London, 1967).

65. A. L. Kroeber, *Anthropology* (London, 1923; references are to 1948 edn). See p. 280.

## 7. THE EVOLUTION OF DECORATION

1. H. Balfour, *The Evolution of Decorative Art* (London, 1893).

2. A. C. Haddon, *Evolution in Art, as illustrated by the Life-Histories of Designs* (London, 1895).

3. H. Balfour, *The Evolution of Decorative Art*, p. 17—31 (also summarised on pp. 76—7).

4. *Ibid.*, p. 18.

5. *Ibid.*, pp. 19, 101—4 and plate 3.

6. *Ibid.*, p. 21.

7. *Ibid.*, p. 22.

8. *Ibid.*, p. 23

9. A. C. Haddon, *Evolution in Art*, p. 311. Some experiments of a similar kind to Pitt-Rivers's were used by Bartlett in his psychological studies of memory: F. C. Bartlett, *Remembering: A Study of Experimental and Social Psychology*, (Cambridge, 1932).

10. H. Balfour, *The Evolution of Decorative Art*, p. 28 and plate 2.

11. *Ibid.*, p. 27 and plate 1.

12. J. Evans, 'On the Coinage of the Ancient Britons and Natural Selection', *Proceedings of the Royal Institution*, 7 (1875), 476—87. Also 'On the Dates of British Coins', *Numismatic Chronicle*, 12 (1850), 127—36.

13. A. Lane-Fox Pitt-Rivers, *The Evolution of Culture*, 'The Evolution of Culture', p. 41.

14. C. Alexander, *Notes on the Synthesis of Form* (Harvard, 1964), pp. 53—4.

15. See E. H. Gombrich, *Meditations on a Hobby Horse* (London, 1963). p. 10. Also *Art and Illusion* (London, 1960), where the spectator's *interpretation* of the work is conceived in trial-and-error terms. See pp. 221—32. Also K. R. Popper, *Objective Knowledge: An Evolutionary Approach* (Oxford, 1972), 'Of Clouds and Clocks', pp. 206—55. See pp. 253—4.

16. A. Lane-Fox Pitt-Rivers, *The Evolution of Culture*, 'The Evolution of Culture' pp. 41—2 and plate 4, 'Ornamentation of New Ireland paddles, showing the transition of form'.

17. A simile suggested by a description in H. Balfour, *The Evolution of Decorative Art*, pp. 60—1, of a comparable series of Hawaiian grotesque figures; in which it is properly the mouth, rather than the nose, which spreads over the whole face, and swallows the remainder of the design.

18. *Ibid.*, pp. 32—4 and figure 10.

19. *Ibid.*, pp. 40—8 and figures 13—17; also H. Schliemann, *Troy and its Remains* (London, 1875), in particular figures 132, 133, 155, 183, 185, 207 and 219.

20. H. Balfour, *The Evolution of Decorative Art*, p. 110.

21. R. H. Lang, 'Archaic Survivals in Cyprus', *Journal of the Anthropological Institute*, 16 (1887), 186—8. See p. 187.

22. See examples given in H. Colley March, 'The Meaning of Ornament, or its Archaeology and its Psychology', *Transactions of the Lancashire and Cheshire Antiquarian Society*, 7 (1889), 160—92, with eight plates.

23. *Ibid.*, p. 166. V. Gordon Childe, however, says that the word was invented by Sir John Myres.

24. See A. C. Haddon, *Evolution in Art*, pp. 91—3; H. Balfour, *The Evolution of Decorative Art*, pp. 107—10; F. H. Cushing, 'A Study of Pueblo Pottery as Illustrative of Zuni Culture-Growth', *Fourth Report of the Bureau of Ethnology 1882—3* (Washington, 1886), pp. 473—521.

25. H. Balfour, *The Evolution of Decorative Art*, p. 110.

26. F. H. Cushing, 'A Study of Pueblo Pottery', pp. 519—20.

27. H. Balfour, *The Evolution of Decorative Art*, pp. 114—15 and figure 43.

28. *Ibid.*, p. 115.

29. P. B. Medawar, *The Future of Man*, BBC Reith Lectures 1959 (London, 1960), p. 96.

30. Le Corbusier, *The Radiant City*, p. 33.

31. H. Muthesius, 'The Problem of Form in Engineering', originally published in *Jahrbuch des Deutschen Werkbundes* (Jena, 1913), pp. 28—32. References are to translation in *Form and Function*, ed. T. Benton, C. Benton, D. Sharp (London, 1975), pp. 115—17.

32. S. Butler, *Erewhon* (London, 1872; references are to Harmondsworth, 1970 edn).

33. *Ibid.*, pp. 214—15.

34. See for example H. Colley March, 'The Meaning of Ornament, or its Archaeology and its Psychology', plates 1 and 5; and A. C. Haddon, *Evolution in Art*, pp. 84—9.

35. See W. H. Goodyear, 'Origin of the Acanthus Motive and Egg-and-Dart Moulding', *Architectural Record*, 4 (1894), 88—116.

36. A. C. Haddon, *Evolution in Art*, pp. 157—8.

37. B. F. Fletcher, *The Influence of Material on Architecture* (London, 1897).

38. *Ibid.*, p. 5.

39. *Ibid.*, chapter 3.

40. Vitruvius, *The Ten Books on Architecture*, book 4, chapter 2. See translation by M. H. Morgan (Harvard, 1914; republished New York, 1960), pp. 107—8.

41. H. Colley March, 'The Meaning of Ornament, or its Archaeology and Psychology', plate 5; reproduced in A. C. Haddon, *Evolution in Art*, p. 349. See also *ibid.*, p. 116. The discovery of these tombs was reported by C. Fellows in *A Journal written during an Excursion in Asia Minor 1838* (London, 1839), chapter 8, 'Lycia'.

42. A. C. Haddon, *Evolution in Art*, p. 115.

43. H. Colley March, 'The Meaning of Ornament, or its Archaeology and Psychology', p. 171.

44. *Ibid.*, plate 5, tomb labelled '3'.

45. For a discussion see N. Pevsner, *Some Architectural Writers of the Nineteenth Century*, pp. 264—5.

46. E. E. Viollet-le-Duc, *Discourses on Architecture*, vol. 1, p. 52.

47. E. E. Viollet-le-Duc, *The Habitations of Man in all Ages*, trans. B. Bucknall (London, 1876), pp. 174—5, 208—15.

48. E. E. Viollet-le-Duc, *Discourses on Architecture*, vol. 1, lecture 2, plate 1.

49. B. F. Fletcher, *The Influence of Material on Architecture* (London, 1897), p. 9.

50. H. Muthesius, 'The Problem of Form in Engineering', p. 115.

51. *Ibid.*, p. 115.

52. Le Corbusier, *The Radiant City*, p. 33.

53. *Ibid.*, p. 33.

54. K. Honzík, 'A Note on Biotechnics', *Circle: International Survey of Constructive Art*, ed. J. L. Martin, B. Nicholson, N. Gabo (London, 1937), pp. 256—62. See p. 259.

55. See E. Schrödinger, *Mind and Matter*, 1956 Tarner Lectures (Cambridge, 1958); published with *What is Life?* (Cambridge, 1967; references are to this edn). See p. 111.

56. J. Maynard Smith, 'Sexual Selection', *A Century of Darwin*, ed. S. A. Barnett (London, 1958), p. 237, figure 47.

57. A. Leroi-Gourhan, *Le Geste et la Parole* (2 vols., Paris, 1964—5). vol. 2, *Memoire et Technique*, p. 122.

58. H. Balfour, *The Evolution of Decorative Art*, p. 75.

59. *Ibid.*, p. 74.

60. V. Gordon Childe, *Piecing Together the Past: The Interpretation of Archaeological Data* (London, 1956), p. 36.

## 8. TOOLS AS ORGANS

1. A. J. Lotka, 'The Law of Evolution as a Maximal Principle', *Human Biology*, 17 (1945), 167—94. See p. 188. See also discussion in P. B. Medawar, *The Future of Man*, lecture 6, pp. 88—103, in particular p. 96.

2. P. B. Medawar, *The Future of Man*, p. 97.

3. See C. C. Gillispie, *The Edge of Objectivity*, pp. 182—3, 262—3.

4. *Ibid.*, p. 263.

5. *Ibid.*, p. 272.

6. J. B. de Lamarck, *Histoire Naturelle des Animaux sans Vertèbres* (7 vols., Paris, 1815–22), vol. 1, p. 181. Translation in E. S. Russell, *Form and Function: a Contribution to the History of Animal Morphology* (London, 1916), p. 221.

7. J. B. de Lamarck, *Recherches sur l'Organisation des Corps Vivants* (Paris, 1802).

8. P. B. Medawar, *The Uniqueness of the Individual* (London, 1957), p. 13.

9. B. Willey, *Darwin and Butler: Two Versions of Evolution* (London 1960), p. 46.

10. H. G. Cannon, 'What Lamarck Really Said', *Proceedings of the Linnaean Society*, 168 (1957), 70–85.

11. C. C. Gillispie, *The Edge of Objectivity*, p. 276.

12. P. B. Medawar, *The Future of Man*, p. 89. The Lederberg distinction is from J. Lederberg, 'Genetic Approaches to Somatic Cell Variation: Summary Comment', *Journal of Cellular and Comparative Physiology*, supplement 1, 52 (1958), 383–401.

13. P. B. Medawar, *The Future of Man*, p. 91.

14. S. Butler, *Erewhon* (London, 1872; references are to Harmondsworth, 1970 edn).

15. S. Butler, *Evolution Old and New* (London, 1882).

16. St George Mivart, *On the Genesis of Species* (London, 1871). See B. Willey, *Darwin and Butler*, p. 72.

17. S. Butler, *Life and Habit* (London, 1877; references are to 2nd edn, London, 1910).

18. G. B. Shaw, Preface to 'Major Barbara', *Collected Plays with their Prefaces* (7 vols., London, Sydney, Toronto, 1971), vol. 3, p. 32. See *G.B.S. 90: Aspects of Bernard Shaw's Life and Work*, ed. S. Winsten (London, 1946), in particular the contributions by C. E. M. Joad, J. D. Bernal and W. R. Inge.

19. S. Butler, *Life and Habit*, pp. 230, 243–4.

20. 'Cellarius' [pseud. S. Butler], 'Darwin among the Machines', *The Press* (Christchurch, New Zealand), 13 June 1863. This essay was rewritten and enlarged by Butler, and republished as 'The Mechanical Creation', *The Reasoner* (London), July 1865.

21. S. Butler, 'Lucubratio Ebria', *The Press*, 29 July 1865. Both this article and 'Darwin among the Machines' were reprinted in *The Notebooks of Samuel Butler*, ed. H. F. Jones (London, 1912; references are to 1926 edn).

22. S. Butler, *Erewhon*, p. 214.

23. *Ibid.*, p. 223.

24. *Ibid.*, p. 223.

25. *Ibid.*, p. 224.

26. S. Butler, *The Notebooks of Samuel Butler*, 'Lucubratio Ebria', p. 48.

27. A. Ozenfant and Ch.-E. Jeanneret [Le Corbusier], *La Peinture Moderne* (Paris, 1925), p. 167. Quoted in R. Banham, *Theory and Design in the First Machine*

28. For example, '1925 Expo. Arts Déco. Besoins Types, Meubles Types', unsigned editorial contribution to *L'Esprit Nouveau*, 23 (1925) (no pagination). See also discussion in A. Vidler, 'The Idea of Unity and Le Corbusier's Urban Form', *Urban Structure, Architects' Year Book XII* (London, 1968), p. 228.

29. A. Ozenfant, *Art* (Paris, 1928) trans. J. Rodker as *Foundations of Modern Art* (London, 1931; references are to revised edn, New York, 1952). See p. 151.

30. Le Corbusier, *Vers Une Architecture* (Paris, 1923) trans. F. Etchells as *Towards a New Architecture* (London, 1927). See p. 269.

31. Le Corbusier, *Towards a New Architecture*, 'Architecture or Revolution', pp. 249—69.

32. 'L'Esprit Nouveau: Les Livres', *L'Esprit Nouveau*, 18 (1925), unnumbered page facing editorial. *Life and Habit* appears as 'S. Butler, *La Vie et l'Habitude* (Trad. Valéry Larbaud), N.R.F.'.

33. '1925 Expo. Arts Déco. Besoins Types, Meubles Types'. Also '1925 Expo. Arts Déco. L'Art Décoratif d'Aujourd'hui' (unsigned), *L'Esprit Nouveau*, 24 (1925) (no pagination).

34. '1925 Expo. Arts Déco. Besoins Types, Meubles Types', fourth page of article.

## 9. HOW TO SPEED UP CRAFT EVOLUTION?

1. H. Muthesius, speech given to Deutscher Werkbund in 1914; quoted in part in translation in J. Posener, 'Hermann Muthesius', *Architects' Year Book X* (London, 1962), pp. 45—51. See in particular p. 51.

2. W. Gropius, 'Art Education and State', *Circle: International Survey of Constructive Art*, pp. 238—42.

3. *Ibid.*, p. 238.

4. *Ibid.*, p. 239.

5. See for example R. Banham's citation of Buckminster Fuller's opinion on this point in *Theory and Design in the First Machine Age*, pp. 325—6.

6. Le Corbusier, *My Work*, trans. J. Palmes (London, 1960), p. 155.

7. Le Corbusier, *Towards a New Architecture*, p. 136.

8. *Ibid.*, p. 136.

9. Le Corbusier, *The Radiant City*, p. 33.

10. 'Evolution des Formes de l'Automobile 1900—1921', *L'Esprit Nouveau*, 13 (1921), 1570—1.

11. Le Corbusier, *Towards a New Architecture*, pp. 124—5.

12. See A. Ozenfant, *Foundations of Modern Art*, p. 328.

13. A. Ozenfant and Ch.-E. Jeanneret [Le Corbusier], 'Le Purisme', *L'Esprit Nouveau*, 4 (1921), 369—86. See p. 372.

14. A. Ozenfant and Ch.-E. Jeanneret [Le Corbusier], *La Peinture Moderne* (Paris, 1925), p. 167. Quoted in R. Banham, *Theory and Design in the First Machine Age*, p. 211.

15. *Ibid.*, p. 167. Quoted in R. Banham, *Theory and Design in the First Machine Age*, p. 211.

16. A. Ozenfant and Ch.-E. Jeanneret [Le Corbusier], 'Le Purisme', p. 375. Also 'O. et J.' [Ozenfant and Jeanneret], 'Les Idées d'Esprit Nouveau dans les Livres et la Presse', *L'Esprit Nouveau*, 14 (1922), 1575—6.

17. A. Ozenfant, *Foundations of Modern Art*, p. 151.

18. *Ibid.*, p. 151.

19. *Ibid.*, p. 151.

20. *Ibid.*, p. 152.
21. Le Corbusier, *Précisions sur un Etat Présent de l'Architecture et de l'Urbanisme,* p. 126.
22. See Le Corbusier, *Towards a New Architecture*, p. 102; or A. Ozenfant, *Foundations of Modern Art*, chapter 5, 'Architecture', pp. 136–8.
23. Le Corbusier, *Towards a New Architecture*, pp. 102–3, 133, 187–207.
24. A. Ozenfant, *Foundations of Modern Art*, p. 137.
25. *Ibid.*, p. 155.
26. R. Banham, *Theory and Design in the First Machine Age*, p. 212.
27. P. Valéry, *Eupalinos, ou l'Architecte*, published with *L'Ame et la Dance* (Paris, 1924), pp. 186–7.
28. P. B. Medawar, *The Future of Man*, p. 97.
29. E. Schrödinger, *Mind and Matter*, p. 122.
30. A. Ozenfant, *Foundations of Modern Art*, p. 156.
31. Le Corbusier, *Towards a New Architecture*, p. 251.

## 10.  DESIGN AS A PROCESS OF GROWTH

1. The phenomenon was first described by F. Muller, and its treatment developed by E. Haeckel under the name of 'the fundamental biogenetic law'. See A. Weismann, *The Evolution Theory*, trans. J. A. and M. R. Thomson (2 vols., London, 1904), vol. 2, pp. 160, 172.
2. H. Spencer, *An Autobiography* (2 vols., London, 1904), vol. 1, pp. 175–6.
3. *Ibid.*, vol. 1, p. 384.
4. C. U. M. Smith, *The Problem of Life*, p. 271.
5. T. H. Huxley, 'On the Theory of the Vertebrate Skull', *Proceedings of the Royal Society*, 9 (1858), 381–457.
6. H. Spencer, 'The Development Hypothesis', *The Leader*, 20 March, 1852.
7. H. Spencer, *The Principles of Psychology* (London, 1855).
8. H. Spencer, *The Principles of Biology* (2 vols., London, 1864–7). Wallace urged Darwin to take up the phrase in preference to 'natural selection'. Darwin adopted it in the 5th edition of the *Origin* (1873). See R. L. Carneiro, introduction to *The Evolution of Society*, p. xx.
9. H. Spencer, 'What is Social Evolution?', *Nineteenth Century*, 44 (1898), 348–58. See p. 353.
10. See R. L. Carneiro, introduction to *The Evolution of Society*, p. xxxiv.
11. L. Eidlitz, *The Nature and Function of Art, More Especially of Architecture*, pp. 366, 380.
12. M. Schuyler, 'Modern Architecture', *American Architecture and Other Writings*, ed. W. H. Jordy and R. Coe, p. 78.
13. L. Eidlitz, *The Nature and Function of Art, More Especially of Architecture*, p. 358.
14. *Ibid.*, p. 358.
15. L. H. Sullivan, *The Autobiography of an Idea* (New York, 1934), p. 255.
16. See D. D. Egbert, 'The Idea of Organic Expression and American Architecture', *Evolutionary Thought in America*, ed. S. Persons (Yale, 1950), pp. 336–96. Also W. Connely, *Louis Sullivan as he Lived: The Shaping of American Architecture* (New York, 1960), p. 152.

17. L. H. Sullivan, *The Autobiography of an Idea*, pp. 254—5.
18. W. Connely, *Louis Sullivan as he Lived*, p. 214.
19. F. L. Wright, 'Modern Architecture', Kahn lecture, Princeton University, 1930. Quoted by D. D. Egbert, 'The Idea of Organic Expression and American Architecture', p. 352.
20. D. D. Egbert, 'The Idea of Organic Expression and American Architecture', p. 368. See also W. Connely, *Louis Sullivan as he Lived*, pp. 78, 91.
21. W. Connely, *Louis Sullivan as he Lived*, p. 90.
22. H. Spencer, *Social Statics* (London, 1851); quoted in *An Autobiography*, vol. 2, p. 9.
23. H. Spencer, *An Autobiography*, vol. 2, p. 7, where Spencer discusses ideas advanced in *Social Statics*.
24. H. Spencer, *The Principles of Sociology* (3 vols., London, 1876—96), vol. 3, p. 3.
25. L. H. Sullivan, *Kindergarten Chats*, p. 47.
26. *Ibid.*, p. 47.
27. H. Spencer, *The Principles of Sociology*, vol. 3, p. 325.
28. *Ibid.*, vol. 3, pp. 349—50, 352.
29. L. H. Sullivan, 'What is Architecture: A Study in the American People of Today', revised version of essay first published in *American Contractor* (January 1906), included in *Kindergarten Chats*, p. 299.
30. D. D. Egbert, 'The Idea of Organic Expression and American Architecture'.
31. L. H. Sullivan, *Kindergarten Chats*, p. 170.

## 11. PLANTS AND ANIMALS AS INVENTORS

1. Rev. J. G. Wood, *Homes Without Hands, Being a Description of the Habitations of Animals, Classed According to Their Principles of Construction* (London, 1875).
2. Rev. J. G. Wood, *Nature's Teachings: Human Invention Anticipated by Nature* (London, 1877).
3. *Ibid.*, p. v.
4. *Ibid.*, p. v.
5. J. B. Pettigrew, *Design in Nature* (3 vols., London, 1908).
6. M. Maeterlinck, *L'Intelligence des Fleurs* (Paris, 1907).
7. *Ibid.*, p. 21.
8. H. Coupin and J. Lea, *The Romance of Animal Arts and Crafts* (London, 1907); H. Coupin and J. Lea, *The Wonders of Animal Ingenuity* (London, 1910).
9. R. H. Francé, *Die Pflänze als Erfinder* (Stuttgart, 1920); trans. as *Plants as Inventors* (London, 1926).
10. L. Moholy-Nagy, *Von Material zu Architektur* (Munich, 1929); trans. D. M. Hoffmann as *The New Vision: From Material to Architecture* (New York, 1932). See pp. 53, 120.
11. K. Honzík, 'A Note on Biotechnics', *Circle: International Survey of Constructive Art*, pp. 256—62.
12. L. Moholy-Nagy, *The New Vision*, p. 54.
13. R. H. Francé, *Plants as Inventors*, p. 18.
14. *Ibid.*, p. 23.
15. L. Moholy-Nagy, *The New Vision*, p. 54.

16. F. J. Kiesler, 'On Correalism and Biotechnique: a Definition and Test of a New Approach to Building Design', *Architectural Record* (September 1939), 60—9.
17. *Ibid.*, p. 60, where the manuscript 'From Architecture to Life' is described as having been prepared for Brewer, Warren and Putnam in 1930.
18. F. J. Kiesler, 'Manifest: Vitalbau-Raumstadt-Funktionelle-Architektur', *De Stijl*, 6: 10/11 (1924—5), 141—7.
19. K. Honzík, 'A Note on Biotechnics', *Circle: International Survey of Constructive Art*, pp. 256—62.
20. *Ibid.*, p. 258.
21. L. Mumford, 'The Death of the Monument', *Circle: International Survey of Constructive Art*, pp. 263—70.
22. P. Geddes, *Cities in Evolution* (London, 1915; references are to revised edn, London, 1949). See also note 11 to chapter 3 above.
23. *Ibid.*, chapter 4, 'Palaeotechnic and Neotechnic', in particular pp. 33—8. See also P. Boardman, *Patrick Geddes, Maker of the Future* (Chapel Hill, N.C., 1944), p. 364, where the terms 'neotechnic' and 'biotechnic' are paired together. Mumford uses the word 'biotechnic' extensively in *The Culture of Cities* (London, 1938).
24. For a broad survey see L. Gérardin, *Bionics* (London, 1969). For more technical treatments of cybernetic and information processing applications, see *Cybernetic Problems in Bionics*, ed. H. L. Oestreicher and D. E. Moore (New York, 1968) and R. Gawroński, *Bionics: The Nervous System as a Control System* (Warsaw, 1971).

## 12. HIERARCHICAL STRUCTURE AND THE ADAPTIVE PROCESS

1. C. Alexander, *Notes on the Synthesis of Form* (Harvard, 1964).
2. *Ibid.*, p. 32.
3. *Ibid.*, p. 36.
4. E.g. M. Breuer, 'Where do we Stand?', lecture given in Zurich, 1933, printed in translation in *Form and Function*, ed. T. Benton, C. Benton and D. Sharp, pp. 178—83; A. Loos, 'Architecture', written in 1910 and published in *Trotzdem 1900—1930* (Vienna, 1931); references are to reprint in translation in *Form and Function*, pp. 41—5.
5. A. Loos, 'Architecture', p. 41.
6. B. Rudofsky, *Architecture without Architects* (New York, 1964); A. Rapoport, *House Form and Culture* (Englewood Cliffs, N.J., 1969), which includes an extensive bibliography of the subject of vernacular and primitive building; J. M. Fitch and D. P. Branch, 'Primitive Architecture and Climate', *Scientific American*, 207 (December 1960), 134—44; V. Olgyay, *Design with Climate* (Princeton, 1963).
7. C. Alexander, *Notes on the Synthesis of Form*, p. 37.
8. *Ibid.*, p. 15.
9. *Ibid.*, p. 16.
10. *Ibid.*, p. 15, n. 4, which refers to L. J. Henderson, *The Fitness of the Environment* (New York, 1913), and A. M. Dalcq, 'Form in Modern Embryology', *Aspects of Form*, ed. L. L. Whyte (London, 1951).

11. H. A. Simon, *The Sciences of the Artificial* (Cambridge, Mass., 1969), p. 6.
12. As for example in J. C. Jones, *Design Methods: Seeds of Human Futures* (London, New York, Sydney, Toronto, 1970), in particular pp. 15—20; L. B. Archer, 'An Overview of the Structure of the Design Process', *Emerging Methods in Environmental Design and Planning*, ed. G. T. Moore (Cambridge, Mass., 1970), pp. 285—307.
13. C. Alexander, *Notes on the Synthesis of Form*, chapter 3, pp. 28—45.
14. W. R. Ashby, *Design for a Brain* (London, 1952; references are to revised edn, 1960). See chapter 8, pp. 100—21.
15. G. Pask, *An Approach to Cybernetics* (London, 1961), p. 15.
16. W. R. Ashby, *An Introduction to Cybernetics* (London, 1956), p. 2.
17. W. B. Cannon, *The Wisdom of the Body* (London, 1932).
18. N. Wiener, *The Human Use of Human Beings* (New York, 1950), p. 85.
19. W. R. Ashby, *Design for a Brain*, pp. 12, 38.
20. *Ibid.*, in particular chapter 9, 'Ultrastability in the Organism'; J. W. S. Pringle, 'On the Parallel between Learning and Evolution', *Behaviour*, 3 (1951), 175—215.
21. W. R. Ashby, *Design for a Brain*, pp. 41—3.
22. *Ibid.*, p. 43.
23. *Ibid.*, p. 43.
24. *Ibid.*, chapter 7. 'The Ultrastable System', pp. 80—99. See also p. 108, and chapter 9, 'Ultrastability in the Organism', pp. 122—37.
25. *Ibid.*, pp. 104—6.
26. *Ibid.*, p. 136.
27. *Ibid.*, pp. 134—6.
28. C. Alexander, *Notes on the Synthesis of Form*, p. 77.
29. *Ibid.*, p. 49.
30. *Ibid.*, pp. 39—40, 116—17.
31. W. R. Ashby, *Design for a Brain*, p. 155. See the whole of chapter 11, 'The Fully-Joined System'.
32. H. A. Simon, *The Sciences of the Artificial*, pp. 90—2.
33. C. Alexander, *Notes on the Synthesis of Form*, pp. 39—41.
34. H. A. Simon, *The Sciences of the Artificial*, p. 87.
35. C. Alexander, *Notes on the Synthesis of Form*, chapter 5, pp. 55—70, and p. 77.
36. *Ibid.*, p. 77.
37. See *Views on General Systems Theory*, ed. M. D. Mesarovic (New York, 1964). The literature on design methods is quite extensive. For general reviews, see *Conference on Design Methods 1962*, ed. J. C. Jones and D. G. Thornley (Oxford, 1963); J. C. Jones, *Design Methods*; and *Emerging Methods in Environmental Design and Planning*, ed. G. T. Moore. For a historical review of the development of design methods and the 'design methods movement', see G. Broadbent, *Design in Architecture* (London, New York, Sydney, Toronto, 1973), pp. 252—71.
38. C. Alexander, *Notes on the Synthesis of Form*, pp. 91—2. Alexander mentions designers regarding their designs as 'hypotheses', but gives little emphasis to the idea that these hypotheses would be progressively refined in a series of tests, in cyclic or alternating fashion.
39. H. A. Simon, *The Sciences of the Artificial*, p. 74.

40. C. Alexander, *Notes on the Synthesis of Form*, p. 77.
41. *Ibid.*, pp. 61—70.
42. *Ibid.*, figure on p. 76, and p. 78.
43. *Ibid.*, p. 115.


13. FUNCTIONAL DETERMINISM

1. G. Scott, *The Architecture of Humanism* (London, 1914), chapter 6.
2. Cf. K. R. Popper, *Objective Knowledge: An Evolutionary Approach*, pp. 267—8. See also D. T. Campbell, 'Evolutionary Epistemology', *The Philosophy of Karl Popper*, ed. P. A. Schilpp (2 vols., La Salle, Ill., 1974), pp. 413—63.
3. A. Choisy, *Histoire de l'Architecture*, vol. 2, p. 237.
4. G. Semper, *Der Stil*, vol. 1, pp. xv—xvi.
5. Sir J. Summerson, *Heavenly Mansions, and other Essays on Architecture*, chapter 6, 'Viollet-le-Duc and the Rational Point of View', pp. 135—58.
6. *Ibid.*, p. 149.
7. P. Abraham, *Viollet-le-Duc et le Rationalisme Médiéval* (Paris, 1934); summarised in *Bulletin Monumental*, 93 (1934), 69—88.
8. Quoted in C. Schnaidt, *Hannes Meyer: Buildings, Projects and Writings* (London, 1965), p. 23.
9. For example, Le Corbusier, *The Radiant City*, p. 94.
10. L. B. Archer, 'Intuition versus Mathematics', *Design*, 90 (June 1965), 12—19. See p. 16. A second example offered by Archer is the ship's propeller. To be fair to Archer, though, the burden of his article is that intuition plays a much greater part in engineering design than has been acknowledged by some functionalists; and in relation to aeroplane design he remarks, for instance, that 'It is necessary that a hypothetical design shall first be laid down before analysis can begin.' Analytic aerodynamic calculation on its own can never produce an optimal — or indeed any — solution, but must always be applied to such a 'design hypothesis'.
11. D. Pye, *The Nature of Design* (London, 1964), pp. 8—11 and chapter 3.
12. See L. B. Archer, 'Intuition versus Mathematics', p. 14; and also discussion in A. Colquoun, 'Typology and Design Method', p. 73.
13. D. Pye, *The Nature of Design*, p. 9.
14. R. B. Fuller, *The Buckminster Fuller Reader*, 'Later Development of My Work', p. 83.
15. C. Alexander, *Notes on the Synthesis of Form*, p. 115.
16. *Ibid.*, chapter 9, pp. 116—31, and appendix 2, pp. 174—91.
17. *Ibid.*, p. 77.
18. *Ibid.*, p. 210, n. 11.
19. W. R. Ashby, *Design for a Brain*, p. 36.
20. *Ibid.*, p. 37.
21. C. Alexander, *Notes on the Synthesis of Form*, p. 16.
22. *Ibid.*, p. 19.
23. *Ibid.*, p. 88.
24. *Ibid.*, pp. 90, 92.
25. *Ibid.*, pp. 20, 89—90.

26. C. Alexander, 'From a Set of Forces to a Form', *The Man-Made Object*, ed. G. Kepes (New York, 1966), pp. 96–107.
27. *Ibid.*, p. 98.
28. C. Alexander, *Notes on the Synthesis of Form*, p. 102.
29. *Ibid.*, p. 18.
30. *Ibid.*, p. 18.
31. H. A. Simon, *The Sciences of the Artificial*, p. 6.
32. *Ibid.*, p. 8.
33. See for example K. R. Popper, *Objective Knowledge: An Evolutionary Approach*, 'Conjectural Knowledge: My Solution of the Problem of Induction', pp. 1–31; also 'The Bucket and the Searchlight: Two Theories of Knowledge', pp. 341–61.
34. See K. R. Popper, *Objective Knowledge: An Evolutionary Approach*, 'On the Theory of the Objective Mind', pp. 153–90.
35. C. Alexander, *Notes on the Synthesis of Form*, p. 75.
36. H. Meyer, 'Die Neue Welt', quoted in C. Schnaidt, *Hannes Meyer*, p. 93.
37. *Ibid.*, in C. Schnaidt, *Hannes Meyer*, p. 27.
38. B. Hillier and A. Leaman, 'How is Design Possible?', p. 4.
39. *Ibid.*
40. B. Hillier, J. Musgrove and P. O'Sullivan, 'Knowledge and Design', *Proceedings of the Third Environmental Design Research Association Conference*, ed. W. Mitchell (2 vols., Los Angeles, 1972), paper no. 29-3 [14 pp.].

## 14. HISTORICAL DETERMINISM AND THE DENIAL OF TRADITION

1. G. Scott, *The Architecture of Humanism*, p. 165.
2. *Ibid.*, p. 169.
3. *Ibid.*, p. 168.
4. *Ibid.*, pp. 172–4.
5. See R. L. Carneiro, introduction to *The Evolution of Society*, p. xli.
6. K. R. Popper, *The Poverty of Historicism* (London, 1957; references are to 1961 edn). See pp. 109–10.
7. L. A. J. Quételet, *Du Systeme Social et des Lois qui le Régissent* (Brussels, 1848).
8. N. I. Danilevsky, *Russland und Europa* (Stuttgart, 1920). See discussion in A. L. Kroeber, *Style and Civilizations* (Ithaca, N. Y., 1957), pp. 112–17.
9. O. Spengler, *The Decline of the West* (2 vols., New York, 1926–8); A. J. Toynbee, *A Study of History* (12 vols., Oxford, 1934–61). See discussions in A. L. Kroeber, *Style and Civilizations*, pp. 118–35 and elsewhere; in S. Pollard, *The Idea of Progress* (London, 1968), chapter 4; and in K. R. Popper, *The Poverty of Historicism*.
10. E. H. Gombrich, entry under 'Style' in *International Encyclopaedia of the Social Sciences*, ed. D. L. Sills (17 vols., New York, 1968), vol. 15, pp. 352–61; and 'The Logic of Vanity Fair: Alternatives to Historicism in the Study of Fashions, Style and Taste', in *The Philosophy of Karl Popper*, ed. P. A. Schilpp, pp. 925–57. Also D. Watkin, *Morality and Architecture*.
11. K. R. Popper, *The Poverty of Historicism*, p. 3.

12. E. H. Gombrich, 'Style' in *International Encyclopaedia of the Social Sciences*, pp. 357–8.
13. K. R. Popper, *The Poverty of Historicism*, p. 109.
14. *Ibid.*, p. 54.
15. E. H. Gombrich, 'Style' in *International Encyclopaedia of the Social Sciences*, pp. 358–9.
16. E. H. Gombrich, 'Evolution in the Arts [review of T. Munro, *Evolution in the Arts and Other Theories of Culture History*], *British Journal of Aesthetics*, 4 (1964), 263–70. See p. 269.
17. See R. L. Carneiro, introduction to *The Evolution of Society*, pp. xxv, xxxvi.
18. Cf. J. S. Ackerman and R. Carpenter, *Art and Archaeology* (Englewood Cliffs, N.J., 1963), p. 170, n. 2.
19. T. H. Huxley, *Lay Sermons* (London, 1880); references are to 2nd edn, 1881). See p. 214.
20. K. R. Popper, *The Poverty of Historicism*, p. 108.
21. J. Huxley, *Evolution: The Modern Synthesis* (London, 1942), pp. 564–5.
22. See for example R. Hofstadter, *Social Darwinism in American Thought 1860–1915* (Philadelphia, 1945); and W. Stark, 'Natural and Social Selection', *Darwinism and the Study of Society*, ed. M. Banton (London, 1961), pp. 49–61. For a critique of the genetical fallacies of social Darwinism, see P. B. Medawar, *The Hope of Progress* (London, 1972), pp. 69–76.
23. K. R. Popper, *Objective Knowledge: An Evolutionary Approach*, 'On the Theory of the Objective Mind', pp. 153–90.
24. B. Magee, *Popper* (London, 1973), p. 60.
25. K. R. Popper, *Objective Knowledge: An Evolutionary Approach*, 'On the Theory of the Objective Mind', p. 154.
26. *Ibid.*, pp. 107–8.
27. A. Colquoun, 'Typology and Design Method', p. 73, where he cites W. Kandinsky, *Punkt und Linie zu Fläche* (Point and Line to Plane) (Munich, 1926).
28. E. H. Gombrich, *Meditations on a Hobby Horse*, in particular 'Expression and Communication', pp. 56–69.
29. H. Meyer, 'Die Neue Welt', *Das Werk* (Zurich), 7 (1926). English translation in C. Schnaidt, *Hannes Meyer*, pp. 91–5. See p. 93.
30. B. Malinowski, *A Scientific Theory of Culture and Other Essays* (Chapel Hill, N.C., 1944; references are to New York, 1960 edn). See p. 37. For a discussion of 'Malinowski and "Neofunctionalism"', see M. Sahlins, *Culture and Practical Reason* (Chicago and London, 1976), pp. 73–91.
31. B. Malinowski, *A Scientific Theory of Culture*, pp. 37–8.
32. *Ibid.*, p. 38.
33. See M. Sahlins, *Culture and Practical Reason*, pp. 77, 87.
34. D. L. Clarke, *Analytical Archaeology* (London, 1968), p. 43.
35. *Ibid.*, p. 54.
36. *Ibid.*, p. 86.
37. M. Sahlins, *Culture and Practical Reason*, p. 77.
38. *Ibid.*, pp. 80–1.
39. E. O. Wilson, *Sociobiology: The New Synthesis* (Cambridge, Mass., 1975). Cf. M. Sahlins, *The Use and Abuse of Biology* (London, 1977), p. 62.
40. H. A. Simon, *The Sciences of the Artificial*, p. 3.

41. K. R. Popper, *Objective Knowledge: An Evolutionary Approach*, p. 264.
42. *Ibid.*, p. 264.
43. *Ibid.*, p. 262.
44. *Ibid.*, p. 264.
45. *Ibid.*, p. 253.
46. *Ibid.*, p. 253.
47. *Ibid.*, p. 253.
48. M. Sahlins, *Culture and Practical Reason*, p. 55.
49. *Ibid.*, p. 209.

## 15. WHAT REMAINS OF THE ANALOGY?

1. W. C. Kneale, 'The Demarcation of Science', *The Philosophy of Karl Popper*, ed. P. A. Schilpp, vol. 1, pp. 205–17. See p. 208.
2. G. Kubler, *The Shape of Time: Remarks on the History of Things* (New Haven and London, 1962).
3. Especially A. L. Kroeber, *Style and Civilizations*. See G. Kubler, *The Shape of Time*, p. 2, n. 1.
4. H. Focillon, *Vie des Formes* (Paris, 1934), trans. C. B. Hogan and G. Kubler as *The Life of Forms in Art* (New Haven, 1942; references are to revised edn, New York, 1948).
5. G. Kubler, *The Shape of Time*, p. 32.
6. *Ibid.*, p. viii.
7. *Ibid.*, p. 2.
8. *Ibid.*, pp. 39–40.
9. *Ibid.* pp. 37–8.
10. D. L. Clarke, *Analytical Archaeology*. See chapter 4, 'Material culture systems — attribute and artefact', and chapter 5, 'Artefact and type'.
11. V. Gordon Childe, *Piecing Together the Past: The Interpretation of Archaeological Data*, p. 164.
12. D. L. Clarke, *Analytical Archaeology*, p. 172 and Figure 34.
13. *Ibid.*, Figures 45–8, pp. 202–9.
14. *Ibid.*, Figure 30, p. 168; Figure 37, p. 176; Figure 38, p. 177.
15. E. H. Gombrich, 'The Logic of Vanity Fair'.
16. *Ibid.*, p. 929. The data are quoted from J. Gimpel, *The Cathedral Builders* (New York, 1961), p. 44.
17. A. L. Kroeber and J. Richardson, 'Three Centuries of Women's Dress Fashions, a Quantitative Analysis', *Anthropological Records*, 5 :2 (1940), 111–53.
18. D. L. Clarke, *Analytical Archaeology*, Figure 29, p. 164.
19. E. H. Gombrich, 'The Logic of Vanity Fair', p. 929.
20. E. H. Gombrich, 'Evolution in the Arts', p. 267.
21. E. H. Gombrich, 'The Logic of Vanity Fair', p. 941.
22. *Ibid.*, and E. H. Gombrich, entry under 'Style' in *International Encyclopaedia of the Social Sciences*. K. R. Popper, *The Poverty of Historicism*, in particular p. 149.
23. H. Focillon, *The Life of Forms in Art*, p. 9.
24. *Ibid.*, p. 9.
25. G. Kubler, *The Shape of Time*, p. 8.

26. J.-A. Brillat-Savarin, *La Physiologie du Goût* (2 vols., Paris, 1826), trans. A. Drayton as *The Philosopher in the Kitchen* (Harmondsworth, 1970). See p. 50.

27. G. Sturt, *The Wheelwright's Shop* (Cambridge, 1923). For J. C. Jones's comments, see his *Design Methods: Seeds of Human Futures*, pp. 17–19. Sturt wrote another book, under the pseudonym of George Bourne, on the subject of evolution in art, entitled *The Ascending Effort* (London, 1910); but in it, curiously, he makes little reference to craft evolution – even though he makes use of biological metaphor in *The Wheelwright's Shop*, referring to the wagon as an 'organism', to its 'adaptation' and so on.

28. G. Sturt, *The Wheelwright's Shop*, p. 19.

29. J. S. Russell, *The Modern System of Naval Architecture* (3 vols., London, 1865).

30. *Ibid.*, p. 301.

31. *Ibid.*, p. xxiv.

32. *Ibid.*, p. xxix.

33. Vitruvius, *The Ten Books on Architecture*, book 2, chapters 5 and 6.

34. L. March, 'The Logic of Design and the Question of Value', *The Architecture of Form*, ed. L. March (Cambridge, 1976), pp. 1–40.

35. E. H. Gombrich, 'The Logic of Vanity Fair', pp. 945–7. See also Popper's comments in the same volume, pp. 1174–80.

36. G. Kubler, *The Shape of Time*, p. 35 and n. 4.

37. B. Hillier and A. Leaman, 'The Man-Environment Paradigm and its Paradoxes', *Architectural Design*, 8 (1973), 507–11.

38. P. B. Medawar, *The Art of the Soluble* (London, 1967). See pp. 7, 87.

39. W. R. Spillers, 'Some Problems of Structural Design', *Basic Questions of Design Theory*, ed. W. R. Spillers (Amsterdam and New York, 1974), pp. 103–17.

40. F. Reuleaux, *The Kinematics of Machinery: Outlines of a Theory of Machines* (London, 1876).

41. F. Freudenstein and L. S. Woo, 'Kinematic Structure of Mechanisms', *Basic Questions of Design Theory*, ed. W. R. Spillers, pp. 241–64.

42. P. Steadman, 'Graph-Theoretic Representation of Architectural Arrangement', *Architectural Research and Teaching*, 2/3 (1973), 161–72. Also W. Mitchell, P. Steadman and R. S. Liggett, 'Synthesis and Optimisation of Small Rectangular Floor Plans', *Environment and Planning B*, 3 (1976), 37–70.

43. L. March and C. F. Earl, 'On Counting Architectural Plans', *Environment and Planning B*, 4 (1977), 57–80.

44. M. Sahlins, *The Use and Abuse of Biology* (London, 1977), pp. 63–6.

45. R. Rosen, *Optimality Principles in Biology* (London, 1967), pp. 6–7.

46. For a discussion see H. A. Simon, *The Sciences of the Artificial*, 'The Architecture of Complexity', pp. 84–118.

47. C. F. A. Pantin, *The Relations Between the Sciences* (Cambridge, 1968), p. 93.

48. C. F. A. Pantin, 'Organic Design', *The Advancement of Science*, 8 (1951), 138–50.

49. C. F. A. Pantin, *The Relations Between the Sciences*, p. 93.

50. *Ibid.*, pp. 93–4.

51. H. Weyl, *Philosophy of Mathematics and Natural Science* (Princeton, 1949), p. 286.

52. W. R. Lethaby, *Form in Civilization* (Oxford, 1922), p. 90.

53. W. R. Lethaby, *Architecture* (London, 1911; 3rd edn, Oxford, 1955), p. 2.

# INDEX

*Numbers in italics indicate pages on which illustrations appear.*